ROMAN WOMEN

THEIR HISTORY AND HABITS

ROMAN WOMEN

THEIR HISTORY AND HABITS

J. P. V. D. BALSDON

Illustrated

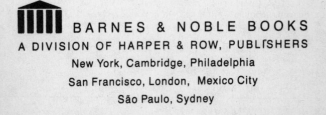

BARNES & NOBLE BOOKS

A DIVISION OF HARPER & ROW, PUBLISHERS

New York, Cambridge, Philadelphia

San Francisco, London, Mexico City

São Paulo, Sydney

A hardcover edition of this book was published by The John Day Company. It is here reprinted by arrangement.

First BARNES & NOBLE BOOKS edition published 1983.

Library of Congress Cataloging in Publication Data

Balsdon, J. P. V. D. (John Percy Vyvian Dacre), 1901–
  Roman women.

  Reprint. Originally published: New York: J. Day Co., 1963.
  Bibliography: p.
  Includes index.
  1. Women—Rome.   I. Title
HQ1136.B34 1983   305.4'0937   82-48825
  ISBN 0-06-464062-0 (pbk.)

83 84 85 86 10 9 8 7 6 5 4 3 2 1

CONTENTS

ILLUSTRATIONS

Following page 160.

1. The She-Wolf (*Lupa*) and the Twins.
   (a) In bronze on the Campidoglio at Rome (wolf, 5th century B.C.; twins of Renaissance date).
   (b) In mosaic from Aldbrough, Britain (probably 4th century A.D.), Leeds City Museum. *Photograph, Warburg Institute.*

2. A Vestal Virgin and a Roman Matron. Museo delle Terme, Rome. *Photographs, Mansell-Alinari.*

3. A young woman and an old woman. Museo delle Terme, Rome. *Photographs, Mansell-Alinari.*

4. Jewellery from the House of the Menander, Pompeii. Museo Nazionale, Naples. *Photograph, Sopraintendenza alle Antichità della Campania.*

5. Coin-portraits of Antony and Octavia (39 B.C.; type *BMC, Rep.* ii, 503, 135–7).
   Livia (*dupondius*; type *BMC, Emp.* i, 131, 79 f.).
   Agrippina i (*sestertius*; type *BMC, Emp.* i, 159, 81 ff.).
   Agrippina ii (*aureus*; type *BMC, Emp.* i, 174, 72–175, 76).
   112 Ashmolean Museum, Oxford.
   Cameo: Messalina and her Children. Cabinet des Médailles, Paris.

6. Head thought to be a portrait of Octavia.
   Private collection of Princess Kathleen Schwarzenberg.

7. Coin-portraits of Plotina (*sestertius*; type *BMC, Emp.* iii, 229, 1080).
   Sabina (*denarius*; type *BMC, Emp.* iii, 355, 911–13). 128
   Faustina i, with reverse (*aureus*; type *BMC, Emp.* iv, 56, 382).
   Faustina ii, with reverse (*aureus*; type *BMC, Emp.* iv, 164, 1084).
   Ashmolean Museum, Oxford.

8. Septimius Severus, Julia Domna, Caracalla (Geta defaced), painting on circular wooden panel from Egypt. Ehem. Staatliche Museen, Berlin.
   Coin-portraits of Julia Maesa (*sestertius*; *RIC* iv, ii, 61, 417).

Mamaea (*sestertius; RIC* iv, ii, 125, 676).

Soaemias (*dupondius; RIC* iv, ii, 60, 407).

Helena (type Cohen, *Monnaies de l'empire romain* v, 589, 1; pl. xv). Ashmolean Museum, Oxford.

9. Bride's toilet, from wall painting at Pompeii. Museo Nazionale, Naples. *Photograph, Mansell-Anderson.*

    Wedding scene, from stone relief at Mantua. Palazzo Ducale, Mantua. *Photograph, Mansell-Alinari.*

10. Husband and wife.

    (a) Etruscan, from Cerveteri (6th century B.C.). Museo Nazionale di Villa Giulia, Rome.

    (b) Roman (Republican period). Museo Vaticano. *Photograph, Mansell-Alinari.*

11. Portrait of a mother with her son and daughter (3rd century A.D.). Museo Civico Cristiano, Brescia. *Photograph, Mansell-Alinari.*

    Portrait of a baker (or perhaps a student of law) with his wife, from Pompeii. Museo Nazionale, Naples. *Photograph Mansell-Alinari.*

12. Dancing girls, mosaics of 4th/5th century A.D. from Piazza Armerina, Sicily. *Photograph, Fototeca Unione.*

13. Various coiffures. *Photographs, Mansell-Alinari.*

    (a) Five heads (imperial period). Museo delle Terme, Rome.

    (b) Julia, daughter of Titus. Museo Capitolino, Rome.

    (c) Flavian woman. Museo Nazionale, Naples.

    (d) Woman from Herculaneum. Museo Nazionale, Naples.

14. *Cultus.*

    (a) Stone relief from Neumagen (3rd century A.D.). Provincialmuseum, Trier.

    (b) Wall painting from grave at Cumae (4th/3rd century B.C.). Museo Nazionale, Naples.

15. A Gallic soap factory (or a pharmacy). Musée Départemental des Vosges. *Photograph, Vilair Scherr.*

    Shopping: buying belts and pillows. Galleria degli Uffizi, Florence. *Photograph, Mansell-Alinari.*

16. Girl decanting perfumes, from the Farnesina house in Rome (late Augustan period). Museo delle Terme, Rome.

PREFACE

‘History tells me nothing that does not either vex or weary me;
the men all so good for nothing, and hardly any women at all.’
Miss Morland in *Northanger Abbey*

INTRIGUING as ancient Roman women may have been, they are the
subject of no single work of deep and learned scholarship in English
or in any other language; and I regret the fact that, though by profession a scholar, I have not the time or the knowledge to write such a
book.

Nor is there any book about Roman women which covers as large
a field as I have tried to do. A number of books have been written
which give biographies of the most notable, or the most notorious,
ladies of the imperial court; but nobody, I think, has combined a
historical account of Roman women, notable and notorious alike with a
general description of woman's life in ancient Rome, particularly of her
married and family life.

I was not sure at the start what shape the book would take, and I had
hoped to be able to put the material together in such a way as to avoid a
split right down the middle, a division into two clearly marked parts,
History and Habits. But I was not clever enough to contrive such a
way of treating my subject.

While the second part of the book contains information which is not
easily discovered, the first—historical—part describes much that will
be familiar to those who have even a small knowledge of the Roman
world. The book is written in the belief that the subject is interesting,
and it is written for what the French call ‘le grand public cultivé.’ At
the same time—since my Publisher has generously allowed me considerable space for notes—I conceive that it may not be without its use
for the serious student.

Its history is this. I have been trying for thirty years to write a book
on the late Roman Republic, and I am only deterred by the knowledge
that the period is one which I still do not fully understand. A few
years ago I tried a new attack on the period; I tried to approach it

through its women, who·are the more worth attention because, as Miss Morland thought of history in general, they are usually taken for granted, and are hardly mentioned at all. The result was a paper on 'Roman Women in the late Republic', which I read to so many branches of the Classical Association that the reading of it became not merely a habit but a disease. Cauterization was the only cure; it had to be published. The Editors of *History Today* were good enough to translate it into their own kind of impeccable English and to publish it; they even persuaded me to write a further article on 'Women in the Roman Empire.' After that, Mr Colin Haycraft of *The Bodley Head* bullied me into taking these women and turning them into a book.

The work has had to be done very quickly, partly in intervals of a heavily committed life at Oxford, partly at greater leisure in that haven of generous hospitality and stimulating scholarship, the British School at Rome.

In several respects I plead guilty to deliberate inconsistency. In general I prefer to use the modern Italian name rather than the ancient Roman name for well-known places in Italy, but for one reason or another I have not done this in every case. Nor is the indexing consistent. I have indexed sometimes by *nomen*, sometimes by *cognomen*, using always the name which I thought that the reader was likely to look up first.

The list of my obligations is no small one. In Italy my first and greatest debt is to the Director and staff of the British School at Rome, particularly to Signorina Anna Fazzari and to Signorina Luciana Valentini. The Sopraintendenza alle Antichità di Napoli was generous and prompt in providing me with superb photographs of jewellery in the Museo Nazionale at Naples; and on a singularly hot day at Pompeii Professore M. della Corte and Signore Giacomo Turner, Segretario degli Scavi, generously allowed me to waste much of their time when I was engaged on what turned out in the end to be a wild goose chase.

In Oxford I received great help from a number of my friends. I learned a great deal at the start from conversation with J. P. Sullivan. Frank and Elizabeth Lepper and Stefan Weinstock read much of the book and criticized it most valuably at a fairly late stage. I enjoyed the skilled advice of Dr C. M. Kraay, Assistant Keeper of Coins in the Department of Antiquities in the Ashmolean Museum, in the selection of coins for illustrations; and on more than one scientific question I was helped in my own College by my colleague Dr R. F. Barrow and by John Ashworth, now Lecturer in the Department of Biochemistry in the University of Leicester. Sara Emery typed the book with speed and with skill; and Charles Hignett generously averted more than one disaster by his skilful reading of the proofs.

In London I am indebted to the editors of *History Today*, Mr Peter Quennell and Mr Alan Hodge, who published the articles out of which the book has grown, and who showed how splendidly the subject could be illustrated. From that moment Mr Colin Haycraft took control. Not every author of a book on ancient history has the advantage of dealing, in his publisher's office, with a first class classical scholar and few authors on any subject can have dealt with anybody more imaginative in suggestion or more generous in encouragement.

I wish in every one of these cases that I was capable of expressing adequately the very deep gratitude which I feel.

The origin of the illustrations is shown on pages 7 and 8. I am deeply obliged to those who have permitted their reproduction, in particular to Princess Kathleen Schwarzenberg for permission to use the charming photograph of the head thought to be a portrait of Octavia.

Exeter College, Oxford   J. P. V. D. Balsdon

INTRODUCTION

THE PERIOD which this book covers is a period of more than a thousand years, from the 'Foundation of Rome' by Romulus and Remus in 753 B.C. to the death of Constantine in A.D. 337. Indeed, since it cannot fail to mention Aeneas, who fled from Troy at its fall, in a year which Alexandrian scholarship fixed as what we call 1184 B.C., its scope is wider still. It covers the rule of the Kings (753–510 B.C.), the Republic (509–27 B.C.) and the first three and a half centuries of the Empire—the period in which Rome first set her own house in order and mastered the Italian peninsula, then acquired an Empire which ultimately extended from Solway Firth to the Sahara, from the Atlantic coast to the Euphrates.

Rome was never ruled by a woman. In the early days of the Kings and in the later centuries of the Empire the equivalent of a Salic law operated. Early Rome had no Queen (unless she was the King's consort) and later no woman was Empress of Rome in her own right. Always it was a male succession. But this does not mean that—not always behind the scenes—women were not from time to time immensely powerful, in the politics of the Republic and later in the administration of the Empire and in the formulation of imperial policy.

History is not exclusively the history of government. There is the whole social history of the Roman people, and the history of Roman women is the history of woman through the centuries in all the different strata of Roman society. And here we are fortunate in the fact that from as early as the fifth century B.C. a continuous succession of foreigners—Greeks in the main—wrote about Rome; so that we know what appeared to a foreigner to be the idiosyncrasies of Roman women. Plutarch's *Roman Questions,* for instance, are largely concerned with Roman women and their habits. Why, in the remote past if a Roman was returning from the country, did he always send a messenger ahead, to warn his wife that he was coming? Why did Roman women always kiss their close male relations and, after marriage, also the close male relations of their husbands? How explain the innumerable complications of the Roman marriage rites? Most extraordinary of all to a Greek was the fact that in Rome you were liable to meet respectable women at dinner parties.

The importance of women in public and social life in Rome derived, as it derives in all early societies, from two causes.

First they had, as women, their own peculiar magic. At a high level, therefore, their correct performance of, in particular, their sacerdotal duties was something on which the good health of the community depended. The wives of certain priests were priestesses in their own right. The Vestal Virgins were the emblem of the State's morality and the guarantee of its economic well-being. Moral delinquency on the part of a Vestal Virgin was, therefore, a kind of high treason and, when it suited the politicians, an irresponsible prank (a man entering a house during the celebration of a cult which was reserved for women) could be treated as a public crime.★

Secondly women bear children and are necessary for the survival of particular families and for the survival of society itself. Hence the political importance of arranged marriages among the Roman aristocracy; and, in a wider field, the Romans were obsessed from the second century B.C. onwards with the problem of a falling birth-rate, a problem all the more serious on account of the high rate of infant mortality and, indeed, of deaths in childbirth. Well-intentioned statesmen in the second century B.C. led the way and in due course the Emperors followed their lead. When exhortations were unavailing, substantial rewards were offered under the Empire to married couples who gave Rome the children which the State—in particular its hungry legions—needed.

In a developing society, the history of women is the history of their increasing emancipation. A hundred years and more before the end of the Republic women were in rebellion against a marriage system under which they were fettered to their husbands, unable to throw off the chains. They rebelled, too, against a senseless austerity. The practice of divorce, rare at first, grew common and eventually tedious. Novel diversions spread from Greece to Rome; young women—and young men too—started to take singing and dancing lessons.† History records the protests of the old men, the puritans and the prigs. But such change could not be arrested. Women emancipated themselves.

★ See pages 244 f.
† See pages 274 f.

They acquired liberty; then, with the late Republic and the Empire, they enjoyed unrestrained licence.

There were prostitutes; there were, in the late Republic and afterwards, expensive kept women; there was that perfectly respectable character, the concubine (*concubina*); and there was the *casta puella* the good wife, the *materfamilias* supervising the education of her sons and, together with her daughters, busy in making her husband's household clothes. The sensational women of the late Republic were the women who tired of being *castae puellae* and kicked over the traces. They became courtesans, sometimes notorious courtesans; or alternatively they interested themselves in their husbands' or in their sons' political careers, and won a different kind of notoriety. With the Empire, the stature of such women, for good and bad, increased. Few of the imperial families were without their startling women. Opportunities for pleasure and excitement were unlimited; so, given a weak husband or a young son for Emperor, were the opportunities of power.

Long as is the period from the Foundation of the City to the death of Constantine, it is only in the last four hundred years of this period, in the last days of the Republic and in the Empire, that we are on speakings terms with Roman women.

Before this, the earliest Roman world in which—on the stage admittedly—real characters of flesh and blood are to be encountered is not Roman at all, but Greek. For the numerous surviving plays of Plautus and Terence, acted in Rome at the very end of the third century B.C. and in the early years of the second, were adaptations of plays by Menander and other dramatists, which had been written and acted in Athens more than a hundred years earlier. The world of these comedies was as stereotyped as the modern world of pantomime. It was a world of elderly men with suspicious wives, of attractive, full-blooded and unprincipled young sons, of courtesans and pimps and procurers; and the happy ending, as often as not, lay in the discovery that the courtesan (a slave-girl, whose freedom had been purchased by her lover) had no right at all to her status. She was found to have been born free, exposed in infancy perhaps, and to have been victim of a wildly improbable chapter of accidents. The way was therefore open for her lover to marry and make an honest woman of her.

But these were Greek plays translated into Latin; and it is hard to know sometimes whether they have any relevance to Roman life at all.

After that there were the poets who sent poems to young women, and who wrote poems about them. The four greatest are enclosed, within little more than half a century, the last days of the Republic, the civil wars and the principate of Augustus. Catullus and Propertius were passionate, even romantic, lovers; Horace and Ovid were philanderers of the most cultivated kind.

From the Roman Empire we have the satirist's—in particular Juvenal's—vivid, venomous and vulgar picture of Roman women. To call Juvenal and Martial—even to call Tacitus—misogynists is stupid. In the language of hate and scorn, women cannot expect better treatment than is accorded to the rest of the society which, in the satirist's clever distortion, both shared and encouraged their degradation.

But how much of what the satirist wrote is true? That there were women in Rome of the types which Juvenal and Martial described is certain enough. But to reconstruct a whole society in their image would be as fatal as to reconstruct a picture of English society at the end of the last century from the plays of Oscar Wilde, or of English society in the twenties and thirties of the present century from the novels of Aldous Huxley and Evelyn Waugh. Lady Bracknell, Mrs Wimbush and Lady Metroland between them hardly provide the material for an historical picture of the English womanhood of half a century. For that you would have to go to a novelist of a less satirical kind, to Galsworthy; and though even Galsworthy's society has its lunatic fringe, its central interests have an affinity with the interests of the sober characters to whom, at the end of the first century A.D., the younger Pliny introduces us in his letters.

The women who are known to us from literature, in the main from the historians and the poets, were those who belonged to, or who interested, the upper class of society in the city of Rome itself. But the artist and the stone-cutter between them have left a different record, and a record which covers a far wider social range. All over Italy and in much of Europe, even of America today the museums are full of their portrait busts. And, for the women of the Caesars, there are coins— coins which, by convention, dispensed in portraiture with the flattering idealism which was expected of a sculptor. Women were depicted on the wall-paintings of since-resurrected houses and villas, at Pompeii and elsewhere. These, in as far as they show the great and the affluent, represent only a tiny and unrepresentative fraction of Roman womanhood. The lives of ordinary women—of the slave-girl, the freedwoman, the women of the lower and middle classes—we can reconstruct but vaguely, and only in as far as archaeology and epigraphy make reconstruction possible at all. Gravestones and monuments survive with inscriptions which can be read, appreciative inscriptions which record their domestic virtues, sometimes with carved reliefs which, however inaccurately and unskilfully, perpetuate their physical appearance. There are innumerable portrait heads and portrait busts to show us how they dressed and, most interestingly, how they did their hair. And, thanks to the archaeologist's spade, we can see and handle their possessions—the jewels they wore, the objects on their dressing-tables, their pots and pans.

The historians, the poets, the satirists—all were men; and it is a thousand pities that there survives no woman's record of her own outlook, whether on the prim days of the early Roman state, the kaleidoscopic days of the late Republic and the civil wars, or the extravagant and dangerous world of the Caesars. Few women wrote books and, of the books written, none has survived. One would give a lot for the chance of looking over Tacitus' shoulder as he read the record of her own tragic history and her family's which Nero's mother, the younger Agrippina, wrote and published.[1]

While, to the surprise of the Greeks and other foreigners, the men in every Roman family had two names and in some families they had three (the second in every case being the family name), women—under the Republic—had, almost universally,* to content themselves with a single name, the name of the family. If there were a number of sisters, their names were the same,† though it was necessary for convenience to distinguish them as 'the elder' and 'the younger', or as 'the first', 'the second' and 'the third', as boys with the same surname have to be distinguished at schools today. A woman retained her name after marriage,‡ but then the addition of her husband's name (in the genitive) made identification easier.

Under the Empire this strict economy in women's names broke down. Two names for a woman were common, the first her family name, the second taken from her father's third name or even from her mother; and it was often this second name which was commonly used. As a result, in many cases, one confusion replaced another. For the wife of Germanicus (really Vipsania Agrippina) and her daughter, the

* Exceptionally, in a family as distinguished as the Caecilii Metelli, a daughter had two names—Caecilia Metella.

† Each of the three sisters of the tribune P. Clodius at the end of the Republic was called Clodia.

‡ The name of the woman whom Juvenal declared to have been married eight times remained to the end the name which her parents had given her when she was born.

mother of Nero (whose name in full was Julia Agrippina) were both known as Agrippina. Both the wife of M. Aurelius and her mother, the wife of Antoninus Pius, were commonly called Faustina. As the Empire advanced, an inflationary process set in. The eldest daughter of M. Aurelius and the younger Faustina was Annia Aurelia Galeria Lucilla. The wife of Alexander Severus was, in this respect, something of a prodigy; she was called Gnaea Seia Herennia Sallustia Barbia Orbiana.

Since its subject is 'Roman Women', this book must deny itself the pleasure of describing the barbarous women on one side or the other of the imperial frontiers: those formidable women of Britain who, when they opposed a Roman landing in Anglesey in A.D. 60, 'brandished torches and looked like Furies, clad in black, their hair in disorder,'[2] or the chaste women of Germany, such women as Caracalla's captives who, asked if they preferred death or slavery, replied, 'Death', and when they were sold into slavery, cheated their purchasers by killing themselves and killing their children too.[3] And it must turn its back on splendid individuals: on Dido in legend[4] and, in history, on the Carthaginian Sophonisba,[5] on Cleopatra,[6] and on the leader of those defenders of Anglesey, Boudicca, 'a huge woman, as burly as a man, with fierce eyes and rasping voice, her abundant fair hair hanging loose to her waist'.[7] But there will be room, in the later Empire, for Zenobia; and many women will be described whose origin was provincial, but who were a Roman part of the history of Rome—the imperial ladies from Gaul, Spain and Africa and the startling Syrians, Septimius Severus' wife, Julia Domna and her sister Julia Maesa, the masterful grandmother of Elagabalus and of Alexander Severus. There will be room, even, at a lower social level, for a descendant of woad-stained Britons whom Martial praised for being a very perfect Roman wife.* For Romanization was Rome's genius, and the key to her abiding triumph.

* See page 202.

PART ONE

+++++++++++++++++++++++++++++++

HISTORY

I

EARLY REPUBLICAN ROME

++

1. The Foundation of the City:
the She-Wolf, and other Women involved

THERE WAS a story, based on the reputable authority of Aristotle, that—in the twelfth century before Christ, presumably—Aeneas and his companions, tired fugitives from vanquished Troy, ended their journey in Italy because, when the men were out hunting, their exhausted womenfolk, persuaded by a certain Romê, had set fire to the ships; so further journeying was impossible. There was an embellishment to the story—that, once the deed was done, the women panicked and fell on the necks of their male relations begging them to appease the anger of their husbands. Indeed there were those who declared this to be the remote origin of the practice by which in historical times Roman women always kissed their male relations when they met them; though scholars of a coarser vein explained the habit as a precaution to ensure that the women had not been drinking.[1]

Apart from burning their boats, women played no glorious part in the legendary foundation of Rome. A goddess, however, was not uninterested. Aeneas was the son of Venus; so Venus was the divine ancestress of the Roman people in general and, by a piece of subsequent smart practice—was not Aeneas' grandson called Iulus?—she became the divine ancestress of the family of Julius Caesar in particular. But there was no splendid human ancestress; it was from a female wolf (*lupa*) that Romulus and Remus were to derive their earliest taste of mother-love.

For, if legend was to be believed, Romulus and Remus, unwanted infant twins, had been set afloat in a basket at the remotest edge of the flooded Tiber, which soon receded, leaving them on dry land at the foot of the south-west corner of the Palatine hill. Here, descending from his hut on the hillside, the startled shepherd Faustulus found them refreshing themselves from the dugs of a she-wolf, as she placidly

21

licked their muddy bodies clean. The spot was to be for ever sacred; a fig tree marked it, the *ficus Ruminalis*; there was a cave (the *Lupercal*); and, up the hill, was the hut of the shepherd (the *casa Romuli*), to whose wife Acca Larentia the she-wolf transferred its responsibility for the twins' upbringing.[2]

The bronze group on the Capitol (the Campidoglio) in Rome today is a composite work for, while the wolf herself is Etruscan and belongs to the fifth century B.C., the babies are no older than the Renaissance. But a monument showing the children suckled by the wolf was erected on the very spot as early as 296 B.C.; and the miraculous event was portrayed on Roman coins from the third century B.C. onwards. Posterity has never been allowed to forget it. Today a caged wolf, prowling unhappily about behind bars at the foot of the Tarpeian rock in Rome, looks out on the tourists and the traffic, reminder of the city's simple start.[3]

But—for only in the most primitive version of the legend was it the she-wolf herself—who was the mother of the twins? There was an infinite confusion of conflicting stories, ascribable in part to the fact that *lupa*, which was Latin for a she-wolf, was Latin for a prostitute as well.

There were, for a start, the legends about Acca Larentia, in whose honour a festival was held in Rome each year on December 23rd. According to one of these she was the first great benefactress of the city of Rome, to whom she bequeathed her extensive wealth; and there were two different accounts of the manner in which her wealth had been acquired. The coarser version made her a prostitute (*lupa*) and a singularly successful prostitute at that. According to a more picturesque account the sacristan of the temple of Mars, bored as such people often are, once played dice against the god for two prizes, a meal and a woman. He lost, placed a splendid meal on the altar (it disappeared in a sudden flash), and left the charming Acca Larentia to spend the night in the temple. The god told her in a dream that her reward would come from the first man whom she met on the following morning. The man, whether young and handsome or old and unattractive—for both stories were told—married her, died and left her his wealth, which she in turn bequeathed to the city. According to a third version she was Faustulus' wife and became foster-mother to the twins. A later version still made her mother of twelve sons; in place of one who died she adopted Romulus, and the twelve were the original members of a priesthood which survived through the Republic and long into the Roman Empire, the Arval Brothers.[4]

Greek historians, concerned to connect Romulus and Remus with Aeneas who, after all, was Founder of the Roman people, gave them no such spectacular start in life. They variously described them as Aeneas' sons, as the sons of the Trojan woman Romê, or as Aeneas' grandsons, born of his daughter Ilia. But there was a certain chronological implausibility about such stories; for between Aeneas (contemporary with the fall of Troy in the twelfth century) and Romulus' foundation of the city of Rome in the eighth a gap of more than four hundred years had to be bridged.[5] The method was obvious. Aeneas must establish a dynasty and the gap be filled by his successors, Alban Kings. Rationalists in the second century B.C. performed the necessary bridging operation. Between Aeneas and Romulus they placed the succession of Alban kings; first Ascanius, the son whom he had brought from Troy, then Silvius, son of Aeneas and Lavinia, whom he had married in Italy, and after that generation after generation of Silvius' successors.[6] Ilia's name was turned into Rhea (the name of the mother of Jupiter) Silvia (the gentile name of the Alban kings).

The way was now open for simple melodrama, with villain and heroine. In the course of time a certain Amulius dispossessed his brother Numitor, rightful King of Alba, and to forestall vengeance on the part of Numitor's descendants, he disposed of Numitor's son out hunting and made his daughter Rhea Silvia a Vestal Virgin, there being no simpler way of ensuring that she should not be the mother of children. But she was debauched—whether by a stranger, or by Amulius, or, in the dutiful discharge of a Vestal Virgin's duties, as she fetched water, by Mars himself.

The twins were born and by Amulius' orders they were exposed—with no unhappy consequences.[7] They grew up and killed Amulius, restoring Numitor to the throne which was his by right; then they were sent from Alba to build a colony, the city which was to be Rome. And the time taken by all this was exactly 431 years from the fall of Troy. The gap from 1184 to 753 was nicely bridged.

But what of Rhea Silvia herself? Was she put in prison and did she die there? Was she imprisoned by Amulius and, in the course of time, released by her sons? Or was she thrown into the river (the Anio or the Tiber), and did the river-god marry her? All these stories were told.

II. The Rape of the Sabine Women

According to legend, then, Rome was a settlement of keen young men from Alba. Once the first walls were up, there was a need to draft rules for the new society, rules that were in the event to inaugurate some of the distinctive traditions of Roman civilization. First things first: the relationship of men and women. So, it was believed, Romulus devised that rigid and indissoluble form of marriage, *confarreatio*—'a sharing of spelt'—which for some centuries women accepted without question, and emancipated feminine thought rejected only when the very foundations of social life had begun to crack. So a moralist like the elder Cato would have told you.

By such marriage a wife was in the absolute power of her husband, and divorce was all but impossible. That is to say, she could not in any circumstances rid herself of her husband. He, on the other hand, in certain circumstances might rid himself of her. If she was unfaithful or if she took to drinking—drunkenness, it was argued, was the commonest cause of unchastity—she was punished summarily; her husband and her own relations were her pitiless judges. But if all went well, she was mistress of the house in her husband's lifetime; and if he died before her, she shared his property with the children or, if there were no children, and he had not made other dispositions, as he was entitled to do, she inherited the whole of his estate. The wealthy widow, pilloried by the satirists in the later, degenerate days of Rome, had, it seems, a very long history.

The most admirable of marriage rules are of little practical value without wives; and if legend was to be believed, the strapping young settlers were in this dilemma, that there were no women for them to marry. They had not brought women from Alba with them, for founding a city was not a woman's job; and their new neighbours were reluctant to give their daughters in marriage to youths who had already acquired the reputation of being young barbarians. The young men proceeded to show how well this reputation was deserved. They advertised a *festa*, a magnet to attract the neighbourhood as powerful in ancient Rome as in modern Italy. This was the festival which was to survive as the Consualia. Crowds attended and, at a signal from Romulus, every young man seized the most attractive young woman that he could find, and hurried her away. While the rest of the visitors fled in terror, the young women who had been seized, Sabines mostly, were treated with great delicacy. Untouched and unharmed that night, they listened on the following morning to a lecture by Romulus on the superiority of his new marriage institutions and, it is to be hoped, appreciated the privilege of being married in accordance with these regulations, as at once they were.[8]

This colourful story was part of the Roman historical tradition as early as the second century B.C. It may well have been invented in order to explain features of the Roman marriage service of historical times:* the forcible seizure of the bride, for instance, and the word 'Talasio', which was shouted by the marriage procession. For, so the story goes, the most attractive of all the Sabine women was seized by dutiful clients on behalf of a powerful and attractive Roman called Talasius, and as they hurried through the crowd, they ensured that she should not be taken from them by explaining that it was to the greatly respected Talasius that they were taking her. 'Talasio,' they cried, 'for Talasius.'

The sequel of 'the rape' did credit to all parties. The Sabines went to war with the Romans and—admittedly by exploiting the avarice of a Roman girl, a Vestal Virgin called Tarpeia[9]—one may well ask how, at this stage, there could be any Roman girls—they secured the Capitol. The Romans attacked them from their stronghold on the Palatine. There was fighting enough for honour to be satisfied; then the women themselves, by this time pregnant, intervened to separate the combatants. Peace was made, Sabines and Romans joining to form a single community. Indeed, if one of the many legends was to be believed, the Romans made an *amende honorable* to their wives' relations, promising never to call upon their wives to grind corn for a Roman man or to cook for them.[10] The undertaking, if it was ever made, was very soon forgotten.

III. Innocent Women, Lustful Men and a
Better Government to follow

The history of early Rome was written by men, not by women, and by profoundly conservative and self-consciously moral men at that. Obsessed by thoughts of the moral degeneracy of the times in which they lived, the last two centuries before Christ, they appreciated the fact that women as a sex were obviously of no great historical importance, but they were interested in individual women as exemplars: women of spectacular virtue, whose example should be an inspiration

* See page 184.

to a later degenerate age, or women who lapsed from virtue and were summarily punished in accordance with a stern moral convention which was never called in question.

Not that, except in its broad outlines, the history of Rome from its foundation by Romulus in 753 B.C. (or thereabouts) down to its capture by the Gauls in 390 is history at all.[11] But it is full of colourful legends, often with women—for good or bad—at their centre.

There was, for a start, supposedly in the middle of the seventh century, the story of a pathetic victim of innocent love. There were, improbable as it might seem, two sets of male triplets who were first cousins (their mothers being sisters)—the Horatii in Rome and the Curiatii in Alba. Once they had grown to splendid manhood, no better use was found for them than that they should fight a battle to resolve the question whether Rome should be incorporated in the community of Alba or Alba in that of Rome. Pathetically one of the Alban Curiatii carried a pledge of the Roman Horatia, sister of the Horatii, to whom he was engaged; it was a cloak which she had woven for him to wear at their wedding.

Drenched in his blood, it was the only object that Horatia had eyes for when, victor and sole survivor of the six, one of her brothers brandished it on his triumphant return from the battlefield to Rome. Distraught with grief, she had no word of congratulation for him; so he unsheathed his sword, and ran her through: 'Go with your untimely love and join the man you were to marry, you who have no thought for your brothers, dead or alive, or for your country. So perish every Roman woman who shall shed tears over Rome's enemies.'

Justice, it is true, took notice of his act; but in the event Justice approved it. Were these people men, or were they wild animals? So the polite Greek Dionysius of Halicarnassus reasonably asked, when he wrote his prosy account of this more than six hundred years later.[12]

The story of the end of the Etruscan monarchy and the foundation of the Republic at Rome in 510 B.C. is largely the story of two women, one bad, one good.

Women at the end of the monarchical period were the king-makers; first the noble Tanaquil, steeped in religious lore who engineered the succession first of L. Tarquinius Priscus, her husband, then of Servius Tullius, her son-in-law; next Tullia, who was Servius Tullius' daughter.

Tullia was a Lady Macbeth and a Goneril rolled into one. She contrived the deaths of her husband and of her sister, so that she might marry L. Tarquinius Superbus, her brother-in-law, and encourage him to usurp the throne of her father, King Servius Tullius. This was achieved, and as her carriage was driven back from the Senate House to the Esquiline, the driver drew up sharply, for in front of him lay the dead body of the late King. Tullia was moved by no such scruples; she took the reins and drove straight over her father's corpse.[13]

This is the beginning of Tarquinius Superbus' reign. Its conclusion was as sensational.[14] The army was in the field, besieging Ardea, capital of the wealthy Rutuli, twenty-three miles south of Rome, and one day, when they were drinking in the mess, there was a wager between Tarquin's sons, one of them called Sextus Tarquinius, and their cousin L. Tarquinius Collatinus as to the propriety with which their wives were likely to be behaving in their husbands' absence. At once the men mounted their horses and rode off to Rome, arriving as darkness fell, to find the princes' wives enjoying themselves at dinner parties. There was another nine miles to ride to Collatia (on the road to Tivoli) and it was late at night when they arrived. But Collatinus' attractive wife Lucretia was not in bed; she was hard at work, weaving with her slave-women. Collatinus had won his wager and, though he was not to know it, condemned his wife to death. Sextus had seen her.

A few days later Sextus called at the house alone—he was, after all, a cousin—and asked for a bed for the night. When everybody in the house was asleep, he went to Lucretia's bedroom, and entered her bed. He achieved his triumph by the simple trick of telling her that, if she refused him, he would kill her, kill a slave and leave his body naked in her bedroom, and tell the world that he had discovered them in the act and punished them summarily, as they deserved. Next morning, having won his night-battle, he rode back to camp victorious; the unhappy Lucretia summoned her husband, her father (who had been placed in charge of Rome by the King, when he went to the war) and her male relations—the very tribunal which would have judged her, had she been arraigned—and, once she had told them the hateful story, she stabbed herself to death. Her body was taken and exposed in the forum at Rome; L. Junius Brutus inflamed the populace to expel its King and subsequently, in proceedings which were a model of constitutional decorum, to elect two consuls and inaugurate government of a republican kind. Sextus Tarquinius was murdered by men—and there must have been many—who had a long-standing grudge against him; Queen Tullia made her escape from Rome 'pursued, wherever she went, by the abuse of men and women, who called down on her head the furies of her father'.[15]

Yet, even with the Republic established, history—if one may use the word—was to repeat itself, and for the second time an innocent woman was to be exposed to a tyrant's lust.[16] This was Verginia, in 449 B.C. Two years earlier the constitution had been suspended and a Commission of Ten (the Decemviri) had been set up to publish the laws. Having tasted power, they were reluctant to relinquish it and, after re-election for 450, they remained in office without authorization for 449. In this last year, while most of his colleagues were in the field, facing the attack and invasion of Rome's enemies, Appius Claudius, the Commission's sinister chairman, remained in Rome. 'Here there occurred another scandal, the outcome of sexual lust, no less disastrous in its outcome than that which, in the debauch and death of Lucretia, had caused the expulsion of the Tarquins from Rome and from the throne. The Decemvirs came to the same end as the Kings and lost their power for the same reason. Appius Claudius set his mind on debauching a plebeian virgin.'

She was fifteen years old, more than old enough for marriage, though she still went to school. It was when she was on her way to her school, which was near the Forum, accompanied by her governess (*nutrix*), that she was arrested by a certain M. Claudius, the client to whom Appius Claudius had entrusted the operation of his villainous plot. This M. Claudius claimed her, asserting that she was the daughter of one of his own female slaves, and that she had been taken as a baby by Verginius' wife and falsely represented as her own daughter. He dragged the girl to the tribunal of Appius Claudius, to substantiate his fantastic claim. Thanks to the spirited intervention of the ex-tribune L. Icelius, to whom she was engaged, and of P. Numitorius, her grandfather (or her uncle), the hearing was adjourned for a day and her father, L. Verginius, was fetched home from the army. On the next day Appius Claudius heard the case and, disregarding the evidence, adjudged Verginia as a slave-girl to his client. 'He was not by nature sound of mind, and now was spoiled by the greatness of his power, his soul turgid and his bowels inflamed because of his love for the girl.'[17] Verginius knew only one way of saving his daughter's honour. He stabbed her dead. There was a butcher's shop handy, with a knife on the table.

Her corpse was exposed, like Lucretia's, in the forum; 'The Matrons and maidens ran out of their houses lamenting her fate, some throwing flowers and garlands upon the bier, some their girdles or fillets, others their childhood toys, and others perhaps even locks of their hair that they had cut off.'[18]

Consternation followed; the army mutinied; the plebs seceded (for the second time in Roman history) to the *mons Sacer*; the Decemvirs were deposed and the republican constitution was restored; Appius Claudius was arrested; he appealed to the newly-created tribunes against being imprisoned 'in the company of a lot of burglars and thieves',[19] but he appealed in vain. Before the case was heard, he killed himself. His infamous client was banished. 'The ghost of Verginia, happier in death than in life, had wandered through many a home to ensure that the crime should not go unpunished; but now that not a single one of the criminals was left, it was at rest.'[20]

IV. The Mother of Coriolanus

At the fourth milestone from Rome to the south on the *via Latina* you would at the end of the Republic have seen a temple dedicated to the Fortune of Women (*Fortuna muliebris*), where celebrations were held twice a year, on December 1st, and on July 6th, attended by women who had been once, and only once, married (*univirae*). It had a famous cult statue, to whose expense women had subscribed, which after its dedication had miraculously spoken. Twice it had said, ' *Rite me matronae dedistis riteque dedicastis*'—'With propriety have you given me, and with propriety have you dedicated me, ladies'. This had happened in the far past, early in what we call the fifth century B.C.[21] And the event which the dedication was popularly and erroneously believed to commemorate was the most sensational and distinguished act that women ever performed in the service of Rome. It occurred in the interval between the tragedy of Lucretia and the tragedy of Verginia, a little after 490 B.C.[22]

In 493 Cn. Marcius had won his glorious victory over the Volsci and had captured the town of Corioli; to mark his achievement his name thereafter was Coriolanus—Cn. Marcius Coriolanus. He was a patrician of the most reactionary sort, despising the civilian proletariat, scorning the tribunes, and a man, in the internal politics of the city, so arrogant that, despite his military glory, he was banished. He placed his unrivalled military genius at the service of the enemy and at the head of their army marched on Rome. Resistance was unavailing, and from his camp at the Fossa Cluilia, at the fourth milestone from Rome, he had only to advance, and the city was his. Deputations from the Roman government he either insulted or refused to see. Then at last a deputation of women arrived, with his mother Veturia—or Volumnia, according to the tradition which Plutarch followed, and Shakespeare adopted—and his wife Volumnia—in the other tradition, Vergilia—at their head. His mother chastened him and, where appeals to patriotism had failed, consciousness of a son's duty to his parent (*pietas*, which was Aeneas' own sense of duty) triumphed. Coriolanus turned about and marched the Volscian army home. There were two stories of his end. Either, reasonably enough, the Volscians, whom he had cheated of an easy conquest, killed him (as Plutarch and Shakespeare believed) or he lived on, and made an epigram:[23] 'the older you get, the harder an exile's life becomes'.

The Senate at Rome marked the women's triumph by decreeing the erection of a temple to Fortuna Muliebris on the spot. This in 487, or thereabouts.

It is all nonsense, of course. Marcius was not a patrician; he was not even a Roman. He was a Latin from Ardea, and the army which he led was a Latin, not a Volscian army. The story of concessions made in the hour of victory was the Latin account of the background of the *foedus Cassianum*, the great treaty of Rome and the Latins made in 493. Romancers in the fourth century and the Roman historians of the second century B.C. between them have invented the whole of this splendid story. So discriminating modern scholarship has established. It is a case where truth is poorer by far than fiction.[24]

v. Sacrifice and Service

In the fourth century history begins to get the upper hand of legend, but still women are found in the wings, if not in the centre, of the main historical stage.

The woman poisoner, for instance, a recurrent figure in the annals of Rome (as in those of other cities, ancient and modern, before the physical causes of gastric disorders were understood) made her conspicuous début in 331, the year of the first recorded poison trial at Rome.[25] The prominence of the citizens who died in this year was too great, and the gruesome circumstances of their deaths too similar to allow the simple diagnosis of an epidemic; a slave-girl gave evidence, and led the authorities to a place where a number of married women were found to be busy brewing a concoction which, they asserted, so far from being poisonous, was a health-giving tonic. The proof of the tonic was in the drinking, and twenty of them, all women of high social standing, were called on to substantiate their claim. They drank, and died on the spot. A hundred and seventy of their associates were arrested and condemned—whether to the same penalty, we are not told. Livy gives us the story, but qualifies it engagingly with the remark, 'This story is not in all the history books, only in some; so I hope it may not be true.'

Later, in 180, there was another *cause célèbre*. A consul died, and was found to have been poisoned by his wife Hostilia, who wished to create a vacancy in the consulate for her son to fill. In 154 two distinguished men—one Postumius Albinus, a consul—were poisoned by their wives. The ladies' families lost no time in having them strangled.[26]

The erection of the second oldest temple to Venus—Venus Obsequens—in 295 was not without a certain macabre humour. A number of married women were found to be trading as prostitutes. They were fined, and the proceeds employed in the erection of the temple.[27]

But other women were capable of better things. There is a pleasing —even if, according to scholars, unhistorical—record of a dedication to Venus the Bald (Venus Calva), which was said to have been made in honour of Roman women who gave their hair for bowstrings when the Gauls beseiged the Capitol in 390 B.C.[28] And there were a number of occasions when women made the State a present of their gold, first in this same year 390 B.C., when under Brennus the Gauls had captured and sacked all Rome but the Capitol and, according to the story, demanded a thousand pounds of gold as ransom before they would depart.[29] The second time was at a desperate stage in the second Punic war in 215, the year after the disaster of Cannae, when Hannibal and his army were at large and victorious in Italy. Then the tribune C. Oppius passed a bill by which women were allowed to keep only half an ounce of gold; they were forbidden to wear dyed clothes; and, except for priestesses in the course of their religious duties, they lost the privilege of driving in carriages in the streets of Rome, a privilege which, some believed, had first been granted in acknowledgement of their patriotic contribution to the ransom of 390.[30]

In a war like the second Punic war, where casualty figures are very high, women are the silent sufferers. But to some the war brought glory. Indeed the beginning and end of the war produced, in the view of the elder Pliny later, the two chastest Roman women of all time.[31] The first was Sulpicia, wife of Fulvius Flaccus, who was four times

consul; she was selected to dedicate a statue of Venus in accordance with
the bidding of the Sibylline Books. Recourse to the Sibylline Books
was a desperate device, frequently employed, in this seemingly endless
war. The books, consulted in 205 B.C., when—admittedly—the fortunes
of the war were changing fast, announced that Hannibal would be
forced to leave Italy if the Great Mother was brought from Pessinus
in Phrygia.[32] Delphi was consulted; the King of Pergamon in Asia
Minor co-operated; and on April 4th, 204 B.C.—a day commemorated
annually thereafter by great games, the Megalensia—the goddess
arrived by sea; she was a black stone. The young P. Scipio Nasica was
chosen as the Roman of highest moral character to bring the goddess
ashore; after which the matrons carried her in turn to Rome, to the
temple of Victory on the Palatine. This is Livy's account. But, as Livy
knew, there was an embellishment to the story which the poets—and
the family of the Claudii—reasonably stressed. According to this, the
ship carrying the goddess ran aground near the mouth of the Tiber
and by no physical expedient could it be moved. Then Claudia
Quinta came forward—a married woman, evidently, and not a Vestal
Virgin—and prayed aloud that it would follow her if—and only if—her
chastity was beyond question. For there had been dark rumours about
her morals. In a moment those rumours were refuted; the ship moved
forward on its course. When the goddess's temple on the Palatine was
dedicated in 191, Claudia's statue was placed in the vestibule and shared
Claudia's own miraculous reputation. Twice the temple was burnt
down; on neither occasion was the statue even singed.

Of the goddess's journey up the Tiber to Rome, Sir James Frazer
wrote, 'Popular tradition naturally favoured the miraculous version
of the story . . . but we may surmise that Livy's version is the truer to
history.' However regretfully, we must agree.[33]

vi. Moral Decline in a Post-War Period

From 200 B.C. onwards the history of current events was being written
by contemporary Roman historians; and though their works have not
survived, they were available to Livy and other writers whose books
we ourselves can read. At last out feet are—very nearly—on firm
ground.

Among the historians who wrote towards the middle of the second
century B.C. and whose work has perished, was that self-confident and
boorish embodiment of austere moral rectitude, the elder Cato. It was

his view, and the view of other Roman historians too, that they lived in a period of increasing moral decline. Opinions differed only as to the moment at which the rot set in. Some traced its origins to the relief and relaxation which followed the defeat of Hannibal in 202 B.C., the end of the anxious years of the second Punic war. Others thought the defeat of Macedon in the third Macedonian war at the battle of Pydna in 168 to be the critical moment, since the victorious armies on their return infected Roman Italy with a taste for the art and civilized luxury of the Greek-speaking world. Others were to think that 146 was the vital date, for then Carthage was utterly destroyed and Rome was left without a rival in the Mediterranean world whose power she needed any longer to fear.

The increasing emancipation and self-assertion of women was symptomatic, and in 195 B.C. a tremendous issue was made in the Senate of the repeal of the Oppian law. Passed twenty years earlier under the critical stress of war, it appeared to women and to those who shared their views to have lost its *raison d'être*. Women even went as far as to behave like early twentieth-century suffragettes—to demonstrate publicly in the streets at the time of the debate. This in itself was enough to persuade the recalcitrant Cato, consul in this year, to believe that, as a matter of principle, a firm stand should be made. He was the man who once said bitterly[34], 'All men rule their wives, we rule all men—and who rule us? Our wives.' Livy gives the text of the long and pompous speech which he made.

Cato's History (*Origines*) included the period of his own career and in it he is known to have inserted the texts of his own public speeches; so, as Cato's History was used by the historians on whom Livy depended, and indeed read by Livy himself, it might be hoped that in Livy we could read the speech which Cato actually made in the Senate in 195; and scholars of repute have argued that this is indeed the case. On the whole, however, the view prevails that this is not a genuine speech, but is the invention either of Livy or of the historian (probably Valerius Antias) on whom he depended.[35] But if it is fiction, it is good fiction, for the speech is one which, however deplorably, Cato would have been happy to have composed. So, with a few adaptations, would many an eminent Victorian.

'If every married man had been concerned to ensure that his own wife looked up to him and respected his rightful position as her husband, we should not have half this trouble with women *en masse*. Instead, women have become so powerful that our independence has been lost in our own homes and is now being trampled and stamped underfoot in public. We have failed to restrain them as individuals, and now they have combined to reduce us to our present panic. ... It made me blush to push my way through a positive regiment of women a few minutes ago in order to get here. My respect for the position and modesty of them as individuals—a respect which I do not feel for them as a mob—prevented my doing anything as consul which would suggest the use of force. Otherwise I should have said to them, "What do you mean by rushing out in public in this unprecedented fashion, blocking the streets and shouting out to men who are not your husbands? Could you not have asked your questions at home, and have asked them of your husbands? Or have you a greater appeal in public than in your homes, a greater appeal to other women's husbands than to your own?" And at home if women were modest enough to restrict their interests to what concerns them, they should properly be completely uninterested in knowing what laws were being passed or rescinded in this House. ...

'Woman is a violent and uncontrolled animal, and it is no good giving her the reins and expecting her not to kick over the traces. No, you have got to keep the reins firmly in your own hands; otherwise you will find that this present issue is quite a minor one compared with the other restrictions, whether of convention or of law, whose impositions women detest and resent. What they want is complete freedom—or, not to mince words, complete licence. If they carry this present issue by storm, what will they not try next? Just consider the number of regulations imposed in the past to restrain their licence and to subject them to their husbands. Even with these in force, you still can hardly control them. Suppose you allow them to acquire or to extort one right after another, and in the end to achieve complete equality with men, do you think that you will find them bearable? Nonsense. Once they have achieved equality, they will be your masters. ...

'For some of their dissatisfactions I can see neither rhyme nor reason. It might perhaps seem natural for one woman to feel ashamed or angry if she was denied some possession which another woman was allowed; but now that the regulations about dress apply universally, how can any one woman be frightened by the thought of the finger of scorn being pointed at *her*? Living economically or being poor are the last things that anyone should feel ashamed of; but, thanks to the law, you need not feel ashamed on either account. What you have not got, you are not allowed by law to have. This very equality, of course, is what the rich woman resents. Why, she asks, can she not be a woman who attracts everybody's attention because of the gold and purple that she is wearing? Why can other women who could not afford such splendour shelter behind this law and create the impression that that is how they would themselves be dressed, if only it was legal? I ask you, do you want to inaugurate a period of dress-competition—rich women wanting clothes which nobody else in the world can afford, poor women spending beyond their means, because otherwise they would be looked down on? Once you start to feel ashamed without proper cause, you cease to feel any shame at all when you should. When a woman can afford something, she will buy it; when she can't, she will go to her husband for the money. Pity then the poor husband, whether he capitulates to his wife, or whether he does not. If *he* does not find the money, some other man will. . . .'

The speech made on the other side by the tribune L. Valerius was no less spirited.

'While everybody else is to enjoy the recovery of our national prosperity, our wives alone, it seems, are to receive no benefits from the restoration of peace-time conditions. Men, of course, will have purple on their togas if they are magistrates or priests; so will our sons; and so will the big-wigs of the country towns and, here in Rome, even the district officials who, after all, are not the cream of society. To that we shall raise no objection at all—not in their lifetime merely, but even to the extent of their being cremated in their purple when they are dead. But women, if you please, are to be forbidden to wear purple. You, being a man, can have a purple saddle-cloth; the lady who presides over your household will be forbidden to wear a purple cloak; and so your horse will be better turned out than your wife.

'Still, purple wears out and is perishable, and here I can see some grounds, unfair though they are, for your obstinacy. But what about gold? You may have to pay a goldsmith for the work he does, but gold itself never loses its value. And both for the private individual and for the state—as recent experience has shown—it is a useful form of capital.

'But—to take Cato's next point—in a state where nobody possesses gold, no jealous rivalry exists between one woman and another. And what is the present state of affairs? One in which every single woman feels distressed and angry. They look at the wives of our Latin allies, and what do they see? These women are allowed the ornaments which Roman women are forbidden; these women are a striking sight in their gold and purple; these women drive through Rome, while *they* have to walk, as if it was the Latin allies, not Rome, that ruled the Empire. This is an experience which men would find distressing enough. What of women, whom even trifles can upset? Women cannot be magistrates or priests, celebrate triumphs or acquire decorations or the gifts or spoils of war. Elegance, jewellery and beauty-culture— those are the distinctions that a woman prizes; those constitute what an earlier generation called 'a woman's toilet'. What is it that women leave off when they are in mourning? Purple and gold. And when they go out of mourning, these are what they wear again. How do they mark festivities and holidays? By changing their dresses, and wearing their best clothes for the occasion.

'I turn to Cato's next argument—that, if you repeal the lex Oppia, you will never be free to impose a single one of those restrictions which the law now imposes; and that you will find that you no longer have the same control over your daughters, your wives and even your sisters. To this I answer that, as long as her menfolk are alive, a woman never seeks to escape from her dependence. The independence which they acquire if they lose their parents or if they are left widows is a thing from which they pray to be spared. Where their personal appearance is concerned, they would rather accept your dictation than the law's. And you on your part should not make slaves of your women and be called their masters; you should hold them in your care and protection and be spoken of as their fathers or as their husbands.'

For good or ill, the liberal view prevailed. Valerius Maximus, writing more than two centuries later at the time of the emperor Tiberius, looked back on this as a black day in the history of Rome:[36] 'The end of the second Punic war . . . encouraged a looser way of living—when married women did not shrink from blockading the tribunes M. and P. Junius Brutus in their houses because they were prepared to veto the abrogation of the Oppian law . . . They succeeded, and the law which had been continuously effective for twenty years was rescinded. This was because the men of the period had no conception of the extravagance to which women's indomitable passion for novelty in fashion[37] would lead or of the extremes to which their brazenness would go, once it had succeeded in trampling on the laws. Had they been able to foresee the sort of fashions which would appeal to women, hardly a day passing without the invention of some further expensive novelty, they would have set their faces firmly against the devastating spread of extravagance at the moment of its introduction. But why speak of women? Lacking strong mental powers and being denied the opportunity of more serious interests, they are naturally driven to concentrate their attention on creating more and more startling effects in their appearance. What of men? ...'

VII. The Bacchanalian Scandal

Nine years later: 186 B.C.

* P. Aebutius, whose father had served in the cavalry, was left a ward and, on the death of his guardians, was brought up by his mother Duronia and T. Sempronius Rutilus her second husband, with whom she was infatuated. Unable to produce proper accounts of his stewardship of his young stepson's property, Rutilus was faced with the alternatives of securing his death or of getting an absolute hold over him—the one way of corrupting him being that of the Bacchanalia. So Duronia sent for her son and told him that when he was ill she had vowed, if he recovered, to initiate him into the Bacchic ritual, and that, since her prayers had been answered, she wanted now to do her duty and discharge her vow. He must spend ten days in complete abstinence, then dine and, after ritual ablution, she would introduce him into the sanctuary.

Now there was a girl, who had once been a slave, called Hispala Fecenia, by nature far too good for the profession which she followed. She was a courtesan of distinction, who had been introduced to this way of life when she was a slave and had not changed her habits after she was freed. She lived near young Aebutius and was his mistress, but she was not an expensive mistress, and she did no harm to him or to his reputation; for she was genuinely devoted to him and, since his own relations made no provision for him, it was only her generosity which kept him alive. She was so fond of him, in fact, that when her patron died and left her independent, she applied to the authorities for a 'tutor' and made a will leaving Aebutius her sole heir. With their affection so deeply pledged, they had no secrets from one another; and the boy told her with a smile that she must not be surprised if she did not see him for some nights because for religious reasons he wished to be initiated into the Bacchic cult, in discharge of a vow taken when he was ill.

'God forbid,' she said, horrified by the news. 'I would rather we were both dead. May curses and destruction rain on the head of whoever has persuaded you to this.'

* What follows, to page 41, is a free translation of Livy 39, 9, 2, to 14, 3.

'You can dispense with your curses,' he said. 'It is my mother who has told me to do it, and my stepfather supports her.' For he could not understand why she should talk so wildly.

She said, 'It would not be right for me to criticize your mother; but I will say this—your stepfather is doing his best to destroy your morals, your reputation, your prospects and your life.'

This surprised him the more, and when he asked her what it was all about, she begged the gods to forgive her if, because she loved him so well, she revealed what ought not to be told. When she was a slave-girl she had accompanied her mistress to the sanctuary, but she had never gone to it once she was free. She knew that it was a regular stew of corruption and that for two years nobody had been initiated who was over the age of twenty. On introduction, like a sacrificial victim, a man was handed over to the priests, who conducted him to a spot where the din of howling, incantation, cymbals and drums drowned his cries as he was forcibly debauched. She refused to let him go until she had exacted a promise from him that he would abandon any thought of initiation.

He returned home. His mother explained the ritual that he must observe on that and following days; and then he said in his stepfather's presence, 'I refuse to do any such thing. I do not intend to be initiated.' At this his mother shouted, 'I know what it is. You can't bear to be separated from Hispala for ten days. You are so much under the in-fluence of that poisonous bitch that you have lost all respect for your mother and your stepfather—even for the gods.' Losing all control of themselves, his mother and his stepfather drove him with four slaves from the house, and he went to his aunt Aebutia, explained why his mother had turned him out and, on her advice, told the whole story in confidence the next day to the consul Postumius, and was instructed by him to come back in two days' time.

The consul went to his mother-in-law Sulpicia, a woman who was held in great respect, and asked her if she knew an old lady called Aebutia who lived on the Aventine. Sulpicia said certainly, she knew her as an old-fashioned lady of great integrity. So he said that he must meet her, and asked Sulpicia to send someone to fetch her. Aebutia arrived and soon afterwards in a seemingly casual way the consul mentioned her nephew Aebutius. At this Aebutia burst into tears and began to speak pitifully of the young man's misfortunes—robbed of his property by those who should have been the last to harm him, driven out by his mother and living now in her house—all be-

cause he was a good young man and—god forgive her for saying so—
was refusing to be initiated into a cult which, if you believed what
people said, was one of sheer obscenity.

After this the consul decided that Aebutius was to be trusted. So he
said good-bye to Aebutia and asked his mother-in-law to lose no time
in sending to the Aventine and getting hold of the freed slave-girl
Hispala, who was evidently well known in the neighbourhood, because he wanted to ask her some questions too. At the news that for
some unknown reason she was summoned to the house of such a distinguished and respectable lady, Hispala was in a state of great consternation and, when she arrived and saw the bedels in the hall, the retinue
of a consul, and the consul himself, she all but fainted. She was taken
to a room in a remote part of the house and interviewed by the consul
in the presence of his mother-in-law. He told her that if she could
screw herself up to tell the truth, she could be assured on Sulpicia's
word and on his own that she need not feel any fear. All that she need
do was to tell him what actually happened when the Bacchanals celebrated after dark in the grove of Semele.

At this she shivered with panic and could not even speak; but after a
while she pulled herself together and said, 'I was only a girl when I
was initiated, with my mistress. But for some years now, since I have
been free, I have known nothing of what goes on there.' The consul
said he was glad that she admitted to being an initiate, and urged her to
show the same openness in telling the rest of her story. When she said,
'I've told you all I know', the consul told her that she could not expect
to receive the same generous treatment if the truth was forced out of
her under cross-examination that she would receive if she made a
voluntary confession; that in fact somebody had already revealed the
whole of the information that he had received from her.

Guessing—rightly—that it was Aebutius who had revealed her
secret, she fell on the ground at Sulpicia's feet and begged her not to
let the chatter of a one-time slave-girl with her lover be taken so
seriously that it might even involve a capital charge. She really knew
nothing, and had only spoken to Aebutius as she did in order to
frighten him.

At this Postumius lost his temper and said, 'You seem to think you
are playing the fool with your lover, and you forget that you are in the
house of a lady of distinction and in the presence of a consul.' But
Sulpicia raised the panic-stricken girl to her feet and encouraged
her, and at the same time she calmed her son-in-law. So at last when

Hispala recovered her confidence, she had many bitter things to say of Aebutius' treachery in repaying her generosity to him in this way, and said that she was terrified of the gods if she revealed the deep secrets of their rites, and more terrified still of their worshippers who, if she gave the information, would tear her apart limb from limb. She begged Sulpicia and the consul to smuggle her out of Italy to some place where she could spend the rest of her life in safety. She was given the consul's assurance and his personal undertaking that she would be able to remain in absolute safety in Rome.

After this Hispala explained the origin of the rites. It had at first been a women's shrine, to which men were generally not admitted, and there were three festivals a year at which the Bacchic rites were celebrated by daylight and married women took it in turns to act as priestesses. It had all been changed, under a pretence of divine revelation, by a Campanian priestess called Paculla Annia. She had been the first to initiate men—her own sons, Minius and Herennius Cerrinius; and she had changed the daylight ceremony to one which took place after dark, and had increased the number of initiation days from three a year to five a month. Since the introduction of such promiscuity, with men worshipping side by side with women, with the further licence which the darkness afforded, every kind of crime and debauch had been practised. There was greater prevalence of unnatural than of natural vice. Reluctance on a man's part to indulge in such vicious practices meant death. They recognized no moral standards whatever, and that was the very bond of their religion. The men behaved as if possessed, their limbs out of control, uttering gibberish; married women dressed as Bacchae, with their hair down their backs, ran to the Tiber, plunged burning torches into the Tiber and withdrew them fully alight (because of the live sulphur mixed with the lime).[38] Men fastened to a machine which whisked them away into deep caves were said to be snatched away by the gods; they were men who had refused to take part in conspiracy, crime or debauch. The number involved was enormous, almost a second populace, and included men and women of the most distinguished families. Two years earlier they had made a rule that no initiate should be accepted above the age of twenty, for young people were easier to corrupt and vitiate.

That was her evidence and, having given it, she fell at their feet again, begging once more to be sent away somewhere. But the consul asked his mother-in-law if she could give up part of her house so that Hispala could live there, and an upstairs room was put at her disposal, the outside stairs being firmly barred, so that the room could be reached only from inside the house. No time was wasted in bringing her baggage and fetching her slaves. Aebutius was told to move to the house of one of the consul's dependents.★

Here was the first great religious scandal in Roman history and, as was to be the case in subsequent religious scandals, women were seriously involved.

Already the political opponents of the Scipios, of whom Cato was one, and of Flamininus (who had defeated Philip of Macedon in the second Macedonian war and had 'freed Greece' in 196) regarded their passion for Greek culture as a dangerously unroman affection;[39] and here, in the consul's revelations about the Bacchic cult, was evidence of the demoralizing effect of a religion which had come from Greece. Hard-headed men like Cato already appreciated the dangerous appeal which Eastern cults might have for Romans; such cults were at the best emotional and at the worst orgiastic, involving experiences which, by the Roman conception of religion, were no proper part of religion at all. Hardly had the cult of the Great Mother (Cybele) been installed in Rome (and the necessary provision made to ensure that public celebrations in her honour, the Megalensia, should be of a conventional Roman type, and to forbid a Roman citizen from becoming one of her castrated over-ornamented priests) when this second warning bell was sounded. One can imagine the speech that Cato made; unfortunately no more survives of it than a single word.

Instructions were given to the consul and to the appropriate magistrates for the immediate rounding-up and, if they were found guilty of the criminal activities for which the Bacchic cult was alleged to have been the cloak, the execution, of the Bacchic-worshippers.[40] This was a lengthy business, for the cult already spread through many of the Italian towns. The alarming news was broken to the people by the consul at a public meeting.

That 7,000 people were involved in what was known as 'the conspiracy' is no doubt an exaggeration by the Roman annalists, who always liked big figures.[41] Men found guilty were executed summarily; women were handed over to their families for execution. And, when the first crisis had been surmounted, the Senate—on October 7th—made regulations for the future, prohibiting the practice of Bacchic-worship except under licence from the urban praetor (confirmed by a meeting of the Senate at which a quorum was present),

★ From page 37 has been a free translation of Livy 39, 9, 2 to 14, 3.

and even then with a maximum number of no more than five worshippers[42] (three women and two men). Copies of the decrees were
then circulated officially to the allied communities in Italy, which were
politely invited—constitutionally they could not be instructed—to
observe them. A copy survives on bronze, published in the south,
somewhere between Nicastro and Catanzaro, and discovered in 1640.[43]
That is how, in this uncertain period, we come to have the exact date of
one of the Senate's decrees.

But what of the story of the informants? What of P. Aebutius to
whom, according to Livy,[44] the Senate now voted 100,000 sesterces
and exemption from military service, and what of Fecenia, who by the
same account received 100,000 sesterces too, together with exemption
from all the handicaps from which a woman suffered if she was not
free-born? She could now marry the highest in the land.

Grave historians will have none of this. This is not history, they
assure us; it is romance. The character of the generous-minded
prostitute is drawn, we are told, from comedy, from the Greek play-
wright Menander.[45] If it is romance, it is a romance with the background set for a splendid climax, but the climax itself is missing. Why
did Aebutius and Fecenia not marry and live happily ever after?

But when the inscription proves that Livy has recorded at least two
of the Senate's decrees with complete accuracy, it is sheer wilfulness to
discard his account of the decree by which the two informants were
rewarded.[46] So we have got to believe that the greatest credit for the
exposure of the 'plot' lay with a young man of military age called
Aebutius and a former slave-girl, young and marriageable, called
Fecenia—a name which is unexampled, and commands the more belief
on that account.

In more than one crisis in Roman history it is certain that authority
was only able to act because of information supplied by slave-girls and
prostitutes. In 63 B.C. a woman of singularly loose morals called
Fulvia went on her own impulse to the consul M. Tullius Cicero and
gave him the information which made possible the exposure of the
Catilinarian conspiracy.[47]

Livy's account of the Bacchanalian 'conspiracy' may, indeed, owe
something to the later conspiracy of Catiline. It is noticeable, for instance, that, while the offences of the Bacchic-worshippers, according
to Fecenia's evidence, lay within a monotonously small range of sexual
depravity, the criminal offences for which men were executed by the
consul were the very practices in which Catiline's young men were

indoctrinated:[48] 'debauch, murder, false witness, forging signatures, and forging wills'.

But there is no reason in the world why we should not believe the story of Aebutius and Fecenia—unless, of course, we start history with the assumption that nothing romantic can ever be true.

VIII. Noble Women

The most important women in republican history, however, avoided notoriety and their names did not get into the books. These were the women of the small number of the aristocratic families—both patrician and plebeian—by whose menfolk Rome was governed for centuries. Their marriages cemented the political unions of the great families.

The best-of such women, like Cornelia herself, brought up their children well. They endured hardship without complaint, like Papiria, the first wife of the great Aemilius Paullus, whom he divorced and who lived in very great poverty until one of her sons, Scipio Aemilianus,* inherited a tremendous fortune from his aunt (who was also, by adoption, his grandmother), the widow of the elder Africanus, and gave all the rich jewellery and ornaments of the dressing-table, all the household extravagances, to her.[49]

There were unpleasant women among them, naturally. There was a very famous Claudia, daughter of the great Appius Claudius, the censor of 312. Her brother lost not only a naval battle but an entire fleet off Drepana in 249 in the first Punic war. Three years later, as she emerged from the games at Rome and was crushed by the crowd, she was heard to say, 'What would the crowd be like if it included all the men who went down in my brother's fleet? I only wish this crowd could be put aboard another fleet and that excellent Admiral, my brother, raised from the dead to lose it.' This kind of arrogance was a tradition in the Claudian family; but, tradition or no tradition, the aediles, to whom the remark was reported, fined her heavily for her indiscretion.[50]

The Claudii, men and women alike, were always a law to themselves. A hundred years later, Ap. Claudius Pulcher, consul of 143 and father-in-law of Tiberius Gracchus, the tribune, provoked a war with the Salassi—in the area of the Val d'Aosta—and, after losing seven thousand of his own troops, managed, in a second engagement, to kill,

---

* He was an Aemilius Paullus by birth, but was adopted by the son of Scipio Africanus. See page 210.

as he claimed, five thousand of the enemy. For this qualified success he asserted his right to celebrate a triumph at Rome; and, unmoved by the Senate's refusal to give permission, he prepared to celebrate it at his own expense. His second daughter, Claudia, was a Vestal Virgin and, when she found that a tribune would intervene and by his veto prevent the celebration, she threw herself into her father's arms and, clutching him, was carried in his chariot in the triumphal procession. Under her sacred protection he was safe from interference by a whole College of Tribunes. Among Roman triumphs this, a demonstration of Claudian *hauteur*, was surely unique.[51]

Most insufferable of all noble women was the wife of a consul some time in the second century B.C.—her name is happily not recorded—whose insolence was publicized in a speech of Gaius Gracchus. Travelling with her husband, she arrived at Teanum Sidicinum in Campania, and decided to bathe in the men's public baths. The chief magistrate of the town was instructed to clear the men out; but because this took time, and there was no opportunity of cleaning the baths before she arrived, she complained to her husband and caused the chief magistrate to be led to the stake, stripped and given a public whipping.[52]

II

FEMALE EMANCIPATION

AT NO time did Roman women live in the semi-oriental seclusion in which women lived in Greece. The wife was mistress of the household—*materfamilias domina*; and shared with her husband responsibility for the supervision of the religious cult of the family. In early Rome, if she was loving and obedient to her husband, a good Hausfrau and an attentive mother, she led by Roman standards—as by the later standards of the Victorian age—a full and complete life. She had no legal personality. As a girl she had lived in absolute subjection to her father; as a married woman she lived in absolute subjection to her husband, as inseparably bound to him as his own daughter. Women should have been blissfully contented with their lot: so the elder Cato and his like would have assured you.

That they were not all content is clear from the fact that by the third century B.C. the old forms of marriage which bound them in subjecttion to their husbands* had generally given place to a free form of marriage in which the wife remained in the power of her father, and after she was twenty-five years old, subject only to formal supervision by her guardian (*tutor*), she retained possession of her own property and was able with no trouble at all to free herself by divorce from her husband. The period in which the change occurred is one on which, in a matter of this sort, we have next to no evidence at all. By the last fifty years of the Republic, when we have plenty of contemporary evidence—for good or ill—in the smart, corrupt society of Rome itself, the New Woman has arrived. Her interests lie outside the four walls of her home. In politics she is a power in her own right. She is, perhaps, the centre of notorious public scandal. She may have no more sinister ambition than to escape from domesticity into the world of cultured and clever Bohemianism. Or she may wish nothing more than to share her husband's—or her son's—public interests and to help him in his public career.

* See pages 179 f.

At the same time—subject, of course, to the greater independence which they enjoyed under the system of free marriage—the majority of married women even in the higher social class were probably still contented—or forced to content themselves—with the duties and responsibilities of domestic life. This was certainly true of society in the country towns of Italy; and it was true, too, of many a woman whose husband played a prominent part in politics at Rome. More than nine hundred of Cicero's letters survive, including twenty-four to his wife Terentia,[1] but there is nothing in them to suggest that she shared his literary or political confidences; she evidently tolerated him for the egotist that he was and, until in the end he became obsessed with the idea that she was stealing his money[2] and he divorced her, she kept a home for him. Her cross-grained sister-in-law, difficult wife of a difficult husband (Cicero's brother Quintus) nursed her grievances or, more often, embarrassed other people by expressing them; but the marriage survived more than twenty years before breaking up.[3]

When the Greek historian Polybius lived in Rome in the middle of the second century B.C., among all the dignified formalities of public life, few ceremonies impressed him more strongly than the ceremonial of a statesman's funeral, the parading of the death-masks of his distinguished ancestors, and the funeral oration in which his public achievement was commemorated.[4] It would probably have surprised him greatly to know that within half a century it would be conceded that a woman might be entitled, on her death, to such public recognition. It was in 102 B.C. that the first public funeral oration was pronounced in honour of a woman. This was spoken by the consul Q. Lutatius Catulus, in memory of his mother Popilia.[5] The precedent was followed and in the last period of the Republic more than one distinguished woman was publicly honoured at her death. The most famous speech of all was that delivered in honour of Julia, the widow of Marius, by her nephew Julius Caesar, in 68 B.C.[6] It started in this remarkable fashion: 'My aunt Julia was descended on her mother's side from Kings, on her father's from Gods. Her mother was a Marcia, and the Marcii Reges go back to Ancus Marcius; our own family, the Julii, traces its descent from Venus. She combined, therefore, the sanctity of Kings and the holiness of Gods, who have Kings for their servants.'

We can be certain that if, instead of invading Britain in 54 B.C., Caesar had been in Rome when his mother Aurelia died, he would have delivered an even more remarkable oration in her memory. For his father had died when he was young, and she had played a notable part in her son's upbringing, and was closely attached to him as he laid the foundations of his career.[7]

Women of the bluest blood had never been without their importance in Roman politics; for their marriages (arranged, of course, by their parents) cemented the powerful alliances of the great families—the 'nobility'—which, in the third and second centuries B.C., were at the very foundation of Roman politics and policy. Such were the marriages of the great P. Scipio Africanus, who defeated Hannibal, to Aemilia, sister of L. Aemilius Paullus who was to be consul in 182 and 168 and to win the third Macedonian war, and of his daughter Cornelia to Tiberius Sempronius Gracchus, the marriage from which the two revolutionary tribunes, Tiberius and Gaius Gracchus, were born. Marriage was the means by which the political dynasts of the crumbling Republic sought to control affairs. Caesar could have been one of 'Sulla's young men', if he had been prepared to divorce his wife, Cinna's daughter, and make a different marriage. When Caesar, Pompey and Crassus made their political alliance in 60 B.C., Servilius Caepio* was told that he could not after all marry Caesar's daughter Julia, to whom he was engaged, as she was required to marry Pompey. When Julia died in 54, Pompey resisted Caesar's suggestion for a new set of marriage connexions and, as an indication of his changed political alignment, married Cornelia, whose father, Metellus Scipio, became his colleague in the consulship of 52.

What was novel in the late Republic was the self-assertion—often, not always, vulgar self-assertion—of certain of these women once they were married. The most startling of such characters, despite her evident breeding and culture, was Sempronia, wife of the consul of 77 B.C., an agent of Catiline in his conspiracy to overthrow the government in 63 B.C., if Sallust is to be trusted. This is how he described her:[8]

'In addition to men of every kind, Catiline was said at this time to have attracted a certain number of women who, to support their prodigious taste for extravagance, had at first sold their favours; but

---

* This may have been Q. Servilius Caepio, brother of Servilia and uncle of M. Junius Brutus, who murdered Caesar in 44 B.C. But this Caepio died in 59 B.C., adopting his nephew who, though generally still called M. Brutus, was really after this Q. Caepio Brutus, and it may well have been this M. Brutus who was engaged to Julia. For the elder Caepio (see page 56) may well have been a married man.

now, while their extravagance was unabated, they were growing old and could no longer support it, and they had run heavily into debt. Catiline believed that they could be used to demoralize slaves in Rome, to set the town on fire and to bring their husbands into the conspiracy, or perhaps to kill them.

They included Sempronia, whose numerous outrages would not have disgraced a hardened criminal.

Well-bred, handsome and with children of her own, she had little of which to complain. She was well-read in Greek literature as well as in Latin; her singing and dancing were rather too professional for a lady, and she had many other accomplishments which made for dissipation.

Self-retraint and chastity ranked lowest in her scale of values; and it was hard to say which she thought less of squandering, her money or her reputation.

Often before this she had broken her word, lied to escape a debt, even had a hand in murder; and with no money left to pay for her extravagance, she had gone utterly to the bad. Yet she had a good brain; she wrote verses; she was amusing; and, whether in the language (*sermo*) of the drawing-room or the brothel, she was a good talker, full of wit, even of charm.'

Sallust himself, as an evil-doer who had seen the light, and had re-formed, had an obsession with morality which was all but patho-logical; yet even when account is taken of this fact, the passage defies explanation. That there was in Rome a cohort of bankrupt, high-class (married) prostitutes, by this time past their prime; that such women were likely to be good instruments for suborning slaves to make good incendiarists, is the figment of a wildly disordered imagina-tion. And that Sempronia herself played any part at all in the actual conspiracy is disproved by the silence of Sallust himself and by the fact that she is never mentioned in any of the other detailed accounts of the conspiracy which survive.

How, then, is this poisonous picture of Sempronia to be explained? Was she the last descendant of a once-distinguished house, daughter and last surviving child of C. Gracchus the revolutionary tribune of 123 B.C.? Or was Decimus Brutus, one of Caesar's murderers in 44 B.C. her illegitimate son by Caesar himself, and not her husband's son at all? These are the desperate suggestions to which scholars have been driven in their efforts to explain Sallust's description of her.[9]

Whatever the explanation, it is an unforgettable portrait. Tacitus thought so highly of it that he borrowed from it for his own description of the empress Poppaea.[10] Sempronia was, be it remembered, the wife of an ex-consul who was alive still in 63 and, for whatever reason had not thought fit to divorce her. So she was perhaps as talented as Sallust was forced to admit; and she was not, perhaps, by any means as vicious.

There was another woman of high birth called Fulvia—whether she was married, or had ever been married, we do not know—who played a not unimportant part in Catiline's conspiracy.[11] She was mistress to Q. Curius, a man who did little credit to one of the best of Roman names. He had been evicted from the Senate by the censors of 70 B.C. and, like other disappointed and unsuccessful men, he joined Catiline in 63. Of Fulvia it can at least be said that she considered the plot to murder the consul Cicero incautious. So she induced Curius—for the prospect of high remuneration, which his enemy Caesar in the end persuaded the Senate not to pay—to turn King's evidence. In an ideal world Fulvia would have learnt her lesson and after that would have gone straight; but, alas, history meets her again eleven years later as one of the chief exhibits at a brothel party to which Pompey's father-in-law, Q. Metellus Scipio, consul in 52, was invited as a guest.[12]

Better the genuine than the debased coin; and in the public life of the late Republic there were a number of splendid women. Another Fulvia was such a one.

She is perhaps the earliest Roman woman whose face we can recognize, for it is in all probability the face of Victory on a coin of Antony's which survives.[13] This Amazon of a woman was, in succession, the wife of Clodius, young Curio and Mark Antony. In each marriage she proved a good wife and became the mother of children.★ If, during the last four years of her life she developed into a virago, she was at least an infinitely loyal virago. After Caesar's murder in 44 B.C. she was at Antony's side, squandering Caesar's treasure. She was at Brindisi with him in the autumn, watching as the heads of mutinous centurions were lopped off.[14]

★ By Clodius, of a son and a daughter Claudia, who was engaged to Octavian from 43–41; by Curio, of a son who fought for Antony at Actium and was executed by Octavian after the battle; by Antony, of two sons: M. Antonius, whom Octavian selected to marry Julia and be his son-in-law in 36 and killed in 31, after Actium; and Iullus Antonius, who lived to marry Octavian's (Augustus') niece Marcella, to be consul in 10 B.C. and to perish on account of his association with Julia, as a dangerous conspirator in 2 B.C. See pages 74, 86.

In the winter, when Antony was in Gaul, she was in Rome, a suppliant at the powerful politicians' feet, to prevent their declaring her husband a public enemy. When the triumvirate was formed in 43 B.C., she refused to champion the fourteen hundred wives of the proscribed, from whom the triumvirs demanded an exorbitant levy.[15] Before and after Philippi she was Antony's agent in Italy; and subsequently, with her brother-in-law, who was certainly her subordinate, she commanded the army of the discontented whom Octavian had to fight. We can still decipher, scratched on the sling bullets which they shot into Perugia, the obscenities of the troops in Octavian's besieging army; and we can read, reproduced in Martial, the unattractive obscenities of Octavian himself, on the subject of the Amazon who commanded the besieged.[16] But, once the war had ended, she was well treated and rejoined Antony in Athens. Almost at once he crossed to Italy to confer with Octavian; and at Brindisi in 40 B.C. he learnt that she had died in Greece.

It is not surprising that the writers of her own and later ages treated Fulvia with scant sympathy. What language other than obscene vituperation could Cicero employ in description of a woman who had Clodius for her first husband and Antony for her last? Modern historians are scarcely more generous. Yet her importance is not to be denied;[17] she was the first woman to enact the rôle of ruler's wife in Roman history, and Shakespeare perhaps appreciated her greatness better than any historian, either ancient or modern:

> As for my wife
> I wish you had her spirit in such another;
> The third of the world is yours; which with a snaffle
> You may pace easy, but not such a wife.

So Antony speaks; and Domitius Ahenobarbus adds, 'Would we had all such wives, that the men might go to wars with the women.'

The extreme republican party in its death throes itself produced two very remarkable women. The first, appropriately enough, was the younger Cato's daugther Porcia,[18] married happily to M. Calpurnius Bibulus, Caesar's unco-operative colleague in the consulship of 59 B.C. But by 45 her happiness had vanished. She had lost all but one of her sons and, fighting Caesar in the civil wars, she had lost her father, her husband and her brother. That summer M. Brutus astounded Roman society by divorcing his wife and marrying her. She was her father's daughter and did much to steel Brutus' resolution for the murder of Caesar on the Ides of March. Suddenly, as they were talking, Brutus noticed that she was bleeding profusely; it was a self-inflicted wound, her melodramatic way of showing him that he could trust her with his secrets. Later, when Caesar was dead, and the tide had turned against his murderers and her husband was overseas, she was carefully watched by her friends who suspected that her mind was set on suicide. Steel being denied her, she took coals from the fire, swallowed them, and died. She was forerunner of the martyr-wives of the martyr-Stoics who opposed the rule of the Caesars later.

Of all the women in late Republican politics Servilia is the greatest. She was Cato's elder and deeply respected half-sister; she was twice married, and in 59, perhaps, came very near not merely to marrying again, but to marrying Caesar. They had been living in close association and it may well be that the only reason for which Calpurnia was the woman whom Caesar married in that year was that she was eighteen years old, while Servilia was forty, and Caesar was obsessed with the desire to father a son. His regard for Servilia was a motive, among others, for his generosity in pardoning her son Brutus who had fought against him at Pharsalus in 48 and in trusting him so warmly up to the moment when Brutus killed him.

It is in the following fifteen months that, through Cicero's correspondence, we see Servilia at close quarters and appreciate her importance in the world of Roman politics.

On June 5th, some three months after the Ides of March, the two chief heroes of the Ides, the praetors Brutus and Cassius, who would have been lynched if they had shown their faces in Rome, were insulted by the offer of trifling administrative posts in the provinces, corn-commissionerships in Asia and in Sicily. On the eighth there was a family council at Anzio, to decide whether they should accept the appointments.[19] Brutus and Cassius were there; Servilia, her daughter Junia Tertia (Cassius' wife) and Brutus' wife Porcia—and, as a friend of the family, Cicero. Cassius, his eyes agleam, was 'a second Mars'; but it was Servilia who controlled the meeting. When Cicero started to make a speech about missed opportunities, she interrupted him and said—said to Cicero—that she had never heard such nonsense. And when Cassius refused to swallow the insult of the corn-commissionership, she said, 'Right. We will get the senatorial resolution rescinded. I will see to that.'

From the time when Brutus and Cassius went overseas to the East in summer 44 and Octavian, the adopted son of the man whom they had murdered, was embraced with increasing affection by the government at Rome, Servilia's anxiety for the future must have grown greater with every moment. A year later she had cause for still worse alarm. When Lepidus, another of her sons-in-law, deserted the Republican cause in Gaul and joined Antony, he was declared a public enemy at Rome, on June 30th, 43. If his property was impounded, as was likely, what then was to happen to her daughter and to his sons, her grandsons? And what advice should she send to her son Brutus in the East? Was this the moment to advise him to return with the army which by now he commanded, to Rome? Servilia summoned a meeting in Rome, which Cicero attended, on July 25th, to discuss the question.[20]

We know from Brutus' letters to Cicero, and from Cicero's letters to him, of her unremitting anxieties; she was, as Cicero said, 'as untiring as she was sagacious'—'*prudentissima et diligentissima femina*'.

'You are the centre of all her thoughts,' Cicero told Brutus. And, after Philippi, his victor showed his generous appreciation of that fact. Antony sent home to her the ashes of her son. How long she survived his death, we do not know.

For the aristocracy and commons of Rome and Italy the forties of the last century before Christ constituted one horrifying succession of war (Pharsalus, Thapsus, Munda, Philippi and the Perusine war) and of murder—the assassination of Caesar in 44, the blood-bath of the proscriptions a year later. And at the end of the decade peace was as remote as ever; Octavian in Italy was estranged from Antony who was in the East, and Sextus Pompeius, in command of the sea-approaches to Italy, strangled the import of food to Rome.

There was still no hope of peace unless the three great commanders could reach an accommodation; and this, it seemed, was achieved when Octavian and Antony came to terms at Brindisi in 40 B.C. and made an agreement with Sextus Pompeius at Misenum a year later. Though the peace was short-lived, its achievement was a diplomatic triumph, and was due in large part to the patient efforts of two highly respected women, the mothers of Antony and of Sextus Pompeius. In both cases this success crowned lives which had known more than enough of hardship and of tragedy. Antony's mother Julia (a distant relation of the dictator) married again after the death of Antony's not very distinguished father; her second husband was executed on Cicero's instruction as an associate of Catiline in December 63. The mother of

Sextus Pompeius was Mucia, whom Pompey had divorced on his return from the East in 62; she had married again, and had a son, Aemilius Scaurus, by her second marriage.

Julia, who had worked hard in the interest of the victims of the proscriptions of 43, her own brother included, was kindly treated by Sextus Pompeius, with whom she took refuge after the Perusine war, and she showed her gratitude by negotiating an alliance between him and her son. At Brindisi she assisted in the reconciliation of Antony and Octavian, and she was probably instrumental—together with Mucia, who played a very large part—in the agreement which Antony and Octavian reached with Mucia's son Sextus Pompeius at Misenum in 39. Octavian did not forget Mucia's goodness, and showed his gratitude for it when, after Actium, he spared her son Aemilius Scaurus who had fought against him and was taken prisoner.[21]

All these were women of breeding. But in the murkier patches of political life—and the decade which followed the death of Sulla in 78 B.C. was such a period—there were powerful women of far less attractive stamp. There was Praecia, a woman of no breeding at all, the most powerful member of whose *salon* was Cornelius Cethegus, a turn-coat in the civil wars of Sulla and the Marians in the eighties, who lived on as a powerful and unprincipled *éminence grise* in the politics of the seventies. Plutarch did not describe her kindly:

'Among those notorious for their good looks and wanton behaviour was a woman called Praecia. She was in fact no better than a common prostitute; but from the fact that she turned her contacts and conversations with people to the political advantage of her friends, she enhanced her personal attractiveness by acquiring a reputation for looking after her friends' interests effectively. And since Cethegus, whose reputation and influence were then at their height, was her lover, she was all-powerful in Rome. No public decision was taken unless Cethegus backed it, and Cethegus took his orders from Praecia.'

So L. Lucullus, consul in 74 B.C., a man whose own life was by no means blameless, could only secure his great command to fight Mithridates through Cethegus' support and, to win this, he had to pay Praecia her price.

Less sinister, if sinister at all, was the influence of the lovely actress Volumnia Cytheris (mistress both of Antony and of M. Brutus) whose presence as a fellow-guest at dinner once shocked Cicero badly—for he had not known that it was to be that kind of a party at all.[22]

There were at the end of the Republic other women—beautiful,

intelligent and altogether immoral—who, without any interest at all
in politics, set out to exploit their charm to the full, while that charm
lasted. Clodia was one, Fausta was another. In the veins of both ran
the distinguished blood of the Metelli, a family whose history was a
whole showground of distinguished consuls. On her father's side
Clodia sprang from the Appii Claudii, who appeared prominently in
every chapter of the Roman history books from the fifth century B.C.
onwards. Fausta was Sulla's daughter. Both had husbands who were
prominent in Roman public life. Clodia's husband was a snob of a
man, Metellus Celer, who became consul in 60 and died a year later;
Fausta was married to Annius Milo who, like Clodia's brother (whom
he killed in 52 B.C.) was a noisy and dangerous gangster, a politician of
no merit, a man admired by Cicero but by no one else at all.

Clodia was thirty-three years old in 61 B.C. when the poet Q.
Valerius Catullus of Verona, six years her junior, fell wildly in love
with her; they loved passionately, and quarrelled as violently.[23]
Thanks to the survival of the poems which he wrote to her—his
'Lesbia'—a mere three years of ecstasy has never since died or been
forgotten. '*Vivamus mea Lesbia atque amemus*'—'Lesbia, let us live,
and let us love'. In 59 B.C. her husband died suddenly, poisoned—
gossip said—by his wife. She was certainly anything but an inconsolable widow, for in that same year Catullus was supplanted as her lover
by a man younger still, M. Caelius Rufus, the son of a knight, who was
bent on a senatorial career. He was twenty-three; 'Lesbia' was
thirty-five. Caelius was Catullus' friend, and Catullus' bitter protest
to him survives.[24]

Caelius had recently left home and set up his own establishment on the
Palatine, with Clodia's brother as his landlord. His life with Clodia was
full of pleasure:[25] 'fondling, loving, Baiae'—the Roman equivalent of
Brighton—'bathing parties, dinner parties, drinks parties, sing-songs,
musical parties, boating parties'. But by 57 Caelius found the strain too
great; Catullus had stood it for three years; he survived two. But while
it is the privilege of such a woman to abandon her lover when she
wishes, she does not expect to be abandoned by him. In April 56
Caelius found himself in the courts, answering fantastic charges which
Clodia had instigated. He spoke first in his own defence; he called her
Clytemnestra—for Clytemnestra killed her husband—and, more vulgarly, he called her a cheap tart: '*quadrantaria Clytemnestra*'. Less vulgarly, but no less effectively, Cicero flayed her with invective. She
lived like a prostitute (*meretrix*); her house was 'disreputable, savage,

criminal and ridden with lust'; it gave cover to 'lust, extravagance, and every kind of unheard-of vice and outrage'.[26]

The speech is one of Cicero's shortest and best. In defending the right of Youth—his client—to sow its wild oats, and in ridiculing the weakness of some of the prosecution's allegations, he was light-hearted, amusing, gay. It is easy to forget that for Clodia, from whose humiliation and resentment the case arose, the verdict was a crushing tragedy. She was thirty-eight, and losing her hold. We never hear of her again.

At no time in his life did Caelius' moral qualities deserve admiration; but he was clever, witty and highly intelligent, as we can tell by reading the letters which he wrote to Cicero, and which survive. Catullus had those qualities too and, for all his coarse virulence, he was tender, sensitive and lovable. That, with her striking eyes, Clodia was very beautiful, and retained her beauty is beyond dispute. But, more than this, she was witty, intelligent and highly educated. She could not otherwise have cast such a spell over those two men, both considerably younger than herself. Sempronia, whose character Sallust—himself as smugly moral as Mr Pecksniff—sought to demolish, was older still; she too, by Sallust's own account, was an intelligent woman, a stimulating conversationalist. Clodia was a consul's widow; Sempronia was an ex-consul's wife. They were both rebels against the staid limitations of conventional society, seeking amusement and stimulation where it was to be found. They took risks, and lived dangerously. Anything to escape the boredom of respectability.

As for Fausta, her husband Milo is said to have found her in bed with Sallust the historian—this in Sallust's unregenerate days—and to have thrashed him within an inch of his life and to have taken a large sum of money off him before he let him go. But Milo did not divorce her, and the colourful story may not be true.[27] A woman of more distinguished birth still was Caecilia Metella, daughter-in-law of P. Lentulus Spinther, consul in 57 B.C. and Cicero's benefactor.[28] Her lovers included Cicero's infamous son-in-law P. Cornelius Dolabella; and when in 45 B.C. her husband was driven to divorce her, she married the dissolute son of the actor Aesopus and helped him to squander the vast fortune which he inherited from his father.[29]

Women of wealth, birth, charm and talent, unfettered by any moral restraint, hungry for animal pleasure or hungry for power—hungry, perhaps, for both. The large stage of late Republican society had room for them. With the establishment of the Empire, their display on the grand scale was curtailed, unless they belonged to the imperial family or were accepted into it. In that event their opportunities were greater than ever—so also, as Julia and Messalina both found, were the risks involved.

The accounts of the notorious women of the late Republic, mostly from hostile sources, reveal, however unintentionally, the high standard of their education and culture. And we can snatch odd glimpses of other women too—women who are not mentioned for abuse— where the same truth is plain.

There was no more tragic woman in the late Republic than Cornelia, daughter of Metellus Scipio, the consul of 52 B.C. Her first husband P. Crassus, a charming and gifted man whom for different reasons both Caesar and Cicero greatly liked and admired, was killed with his father in the disaster of Carrhae in 53 B.C. In the following year she was married for political reasons, as has been seen, to Pompey, whose wife Julia had died two years earlier. This her second marriage was more tragic even than her first; it lasted for four years, two of them years of civil war, and at the end she was a spectator of Pompey's murder when, in flight after his defeat at Pharsalus, he landed in Egypt. This is Plutarch's description of her:[30]

'Her youth was by no means her only charm. She was widely read, she played the lyre, was good at mathematics and capable of making a useful contribution to a philosophical discussion. At the same time there was nothing unattractive, nothing of the bluestocking, about her, as is so often the case with this kind of sophisticated young woman ...'

The culture which Propertius admired in an educated woman—a *docta puella*—was of a literary sort.[31] And it is evident, that, from the late Republic onwards a number of women in Rome were very well educated indeed. The distinguished orator Q. Hortensius, who died in 50 B.C., had a daughter who was perhaps the wife of Q. Servilius Caepio, who adopted M. Brutus.[32] Despite the fact that women could not plead at the Bar at Rome, she interested herself in her father's profession to such a degree that at a critical moment in Roman history she pleaded, and with success. This was in 42 B.C., when Antony's wife Fulvia refused to champion the cause of the wives of the proscribed on whom the triumvirs had imposed a crippling burden of taxation. Hortensia argued their case in a memorable speech which posterity preserved and read[33]—'because it was a good speech, and not just because it was made by a woman'.

Vanity, extravagance, immorality and a superstitious addiction to religious cult are by tradition the charges which a satirist brings against the female sex; and early in the second century A.D. Juvenal, in his sixth satire, attacked women on all these counts—and on others too.[34]

There was the bluestocking, and there was the gossip, the woman with a finger in every pie, neither of whom is unknown in present-day society. The dinner-table conversation of the first was a tedious ranting lecture on whatever subject came into her head. It might be literature; it might be philosophy. The experts had no chance against her; she shouted them down. If her women friends managed to get a word in, she turned pedagogue and corrected their pronunciation, even attacking her husband for the way in which he spoke. As for the gossip, she was always first with the news—which, often enough, she had invented—of catastrophic floods, an extraordinary comet, the latest reports from China or from Thrace. In the company of generals, it was she, not her husband, who did the talking. She was feminine only in her domestic curiosity; she knew and retailed the secrets of every Roman bedchamber.

This is a satirist's picture, not a portrait but a caricature. Its implications are evident. The society of imperial Rome included many women who were capable and more than capable of holding their own in educated conversation with men, both about literature and about current affairs.

The close association of married women with their husbands' interests was revealed in a melancholy fashion in the Empire in all the cases where, when a husband was struck down for allegedly treasonable activities, his wife was involved in his disaster.

At the end of Nero's principate a woman was to be seen in Rome with a complexion so startlingly white that she might almost have been a corpse.[35] This was Seneca's widow, Pompeia Paulina, who had made a suicide pact with her husband, when the moment came in 65 A.D. for him to die; but she had been revived, recalled from the gates of death by Nero's orders—not unwillingly, according to malicious gossip; but malicious gossip is not always to be believed.

Seneca was a philosopher as well as a politician; and the loyalty of his wife was matched by the loyalty of the wives of other philosopher-politicians of the Stoic-Cynic school of the early Roman Empire, men who dreamed about republicanism and were 'agin the government' on the ground that, if Rome must have an emperor, he should be someone who was elevated by merit, not by birth or arms. These men chose their wives well—women who shared their convictions and were prepared, if necessary, to share their fate.

About one family in particular there was a kind of hagiology—the elder Arria; her daughter, the younger Arria; her grand-daughter Fannia.[36] The last two were close friends of the younger Pliny, and Tacitus must have known them too. So that we, in our turn, can know about them.

The elder Arria, married to Caecina Paetus, consul in A.D. 37 and, inexplicably, a friend of the Empress Messalina,[37] had already shown her quality when, during a desperate illness of her husband, she kept from him the news that their boy had died, talking of him as if he was still alive, until her husband passed the crisis. After the abortive rebellion of the Illyrican legions against Claudius in A.D. 42, Caecina Paetus was recalled, under arrest, to Rome; since she was refused leave to accompany him, she chartered a private boat and arrived in Italy as soon. When her anxious friends withheld from her the instruments of suicide, she dashed her head against a wall and, on recovery, pointed out that nothing could impede the will of a determined woman. When for Caecina the alternatives were suicide or execution, she plunged a dagger into her breast and handed it to him, telling him that it did not hurt: 'Paete, non dolet.'[38]

(This fearless resolution in suicide is one of the most remarkable of Roman qualities, and one which women shared with men. Tacitus, indeed, describes the case of a senator whose doom was pronounced by Nero, whose mother-in-law and daughter joined him in cutting their veins. The three died in sight of one another.)[39]

Thrasea was consul in A.D. 56 and an ostentatious critic of Nero from then until he was forced to suicide in A.D. 66 after the Pisonian conspiracy. His family was single-minded, devoid of waverers: his wife Arria, their daughter Fannia, Fannia's husband, Helvidius Priscus and her stepson (a son of Priscus' earlier marriage), the younger Helvidius Priscus. The younger Arria, like her mother, knew no stronger duty than obedience to her husband; his prohibition alone prevented her suicide in 66. She was banished with the rest of her family, recalled under Galba, banished again and again recalled. By the time of Vespasian's death she and her daughter were both widows, for the elder Helvidius had been executed. His son was put to death by Domitian in A.D. 93 and, once again, the two women were banished. Nerva recalled them. Fannia's death was as self-sacrificing as her life. She volunteered to nurse a Vestal Virgin who had tuberculosis, contracted the disease herself, and died.[40]

The biggest change of all which came with the Roman Empire and deeply affected the lives of women whose husbands' careers lay in public life arose from the fact that they were no longer compelled to remain in Rome during their husbands' tours of duty in the provinces. Women had fled overseas with their husbands during the civil wars and, after that, the wisdom of the Republican rule was challenged. The regulation, sensible enough in the early days when pro-consuls and their staffs were actively occupied in campaigning through most of the year, could well have been relaxed as early as the second century B.C. in the case of provinces whose government was in the main a matter of civil administration. It was unreasonable, surely, to expect that magistrates' wives as a class would behave like the consul's wife whose ill-tempered act at Teanum Sidicinum in Campania Gaius Gracchus had ensured that posterity should not forget.[41]

In a man's public career there might well be more than three occasions when he had to leave Rome to spend at least a year and sometimes much longer in administrative or military duties in one of the provinces; and during these periods his family was broken up. Boys of twelve or older usually accompanied their fathers and, if they survived the experience (Porcia never saw again the two boys who left her with her husband Bibulus for Syria in 51 B.C.), their morals were not always greatly improved. In Cilicia, for instance, in 51–50 B.C. young Quintus Cicero was taught by his uncle Marcus to open the letters written by his mother in Rome to his father (who was out in Cilicia on his brother Marcus' staff), to show them to his uncle to read, and then to reseal them and to replace them in his father's mail.[42] More serious still were the disasters which might occur at home where the grass widow, if she was attractive, was the prey of every accomplished seducer. Lurid accounts of her misbehaviour, sometimes true, sometimes untrue, trickled out to her husband in his province. So, when he returned to Rome, his first act often was to divorce his wife. L. Lucullus divorced his wife Clodia ('Lesbia''s sister) when he came back from his Eastern command in the late sixties;[43] his successor Pompey divorced his wife Mucia on his return to Italy in 62 B.C.[44] To escape temptation, a woman must be another Penelope-like Aelia Galla, whose husband left her in Rome when he went off to fight the Parthians in 20 B.C. and was elegantly rebuked by Propertius for his heartlessness.[45]

After the civil wars it would have been difficult for Augustus to

revive the earlier practice, had he wished to do so. He was in fact too
wise to think of reviving it at all.

No longer were marriages broken up, as they were broken up so
frequently under the Republic. More than this, wives now had a
larger part to play in their husbands' careers. There was a danger, of
course, that the part might be overplayed; and in the early years of
Tiberius' principate two women came near to dominating their husbands, pushing themselves forward even where their husbands' command of the troops was concerned. These were the elder Agrippina,
wife of Germanicus, and Livia's friend Plancina, wife of Cn. Piso,
governor of Syria. The public rivalry of the two women in Syria was a
part of the background of the tragedy of A.D. 19—Germanicus' ordering of Piso out of his province, his subsequent death and Piso's death
in Rome on a charge of treason.[46]

So, not unreasonably, the question of women's presence in the
provinces was discussed at a meeting of the Senate in A.D. 21 at which,
as consul, the Emperor's son Drusus presided. It was an interesting
debate, opened by a Severus Caecina, whose 'Victorian' outlook on
women was that which the elder Cato had expressed in his opposition
to the repeal of the Oppian law more than two centuries earlier.* But
the reactionary was no more successful now than then in reversing the
progressive tendency of the times.

†After a long preamble about his happy relations with his wife,
who had borne him six children, and after stating that in all his forty
years of service abroad in one province and another he had always
insisted on her remaining in Italy—this in order to show that he himself had always observed the rule which he was now proposing—he
moved that no wife should be allowed to accompany her husband on
administrative service in the provinces. He underlined the wisdom of
the rule which had once existed, forbidding the presence of women on
diplomatic or administrative missions abroad, on the ground that in
peacetime they had to be entertained and so the business of administration suffered, while if war broke out, they interfered with its efficient
conduct because they panicked and made a Roman army on the march
look like the progress of a barbarian monarch. The trouble, he pointed
out, was not merely that women as a sex were weak and not tough
enough for such a strenuous life, but that if discipline was relaxed, they
were cruel and schemed to get power in their own hands. 'They move

---

* See pages 33-5.
† From here to page 62 is a free translation of Tacitus *Annals*, iii, 33f.

about the troops, and have officers at their beck and call. There has been an occasion recently when a woman was actually in command of a cohort parade and legionary manœuvres. Members of the House do not need to be reminded of the number of cases of prosecution for corrupt administration in which, though it was the husband who was prosecuted, it was the wife against whom most of the charges were levelled. It is the wives who from the first moment of their arrival attract the worst type of settler, and become involved in scheming and intrigue. In fact you have two official escorts, two Government Houses, not one, and the unreasonable and domineering instructions are those which come from the women—the women whom the Oppian and similar laws once kept in their place, but who in these modern emancipated times control households, lawcourts—even armies.'

Only a few Members applauded this speech, which had been subject to general interruption on the ground that it was out of order and that Caecina was not the man to make a pronouncement of public policy on a matter of such importance. In the end Valerius Messala, who had inherited something of his father's talent as a speaker, answered the points which Caecina had raised, pointing out that a number of the severe regulations of the past had been most beneficially relaxed, times having changed. Once there was war at the gates of Rome, and the provinces were enemy territory; but those days were now over. He thought that the concessions made to feminine comfort were trifling, a small cost to the family budget, and no expense at all to the provincial taxpayer; otherwise women simply shared their husbands' lives and there was nothing in such association to interfere with normal peace-time administration. When war broke out, it was obvious that husbands had to put on their uniforms and leave them; but when the husbands returned from their strenuous fighting, could anything be more honourable than that they should relax in the company of their wives? In answer to the charges of power-seeking and avarice which Caecina had brought against women, he said that, though a large number of officials had demonstrably succumbed to a wide variety of temptations, the sending out of officials to the provinces had not for that reason been brought to an end. 'If you claim that husbands are often corrupted by their wives' evil communications, I reply with this simple question: are all bachelors impeccable? The Oppian laws were all right once because the conditions of those days left no alternative; if concessions and relaxations have been made subsequently, it is because it was to the public interest that they should be. It is no good excusing our own weakness by euphemistic talk. If a wife misbehaves, it is her husband who is to blame.* One or two people may be weak; but it is wrong to make that a ground for robbing husbands and wives of their common partnership in good times and bad. Women are naturally weak; and Caecina is proposing that they should be deserted by their husbands and left victims to the temptations of their own flesh and the lusts of other men. When you consider that, with husbands present to keep watch on their wives, marriages are only just saved from running on to the rocks, you can easily imagine what will happen if for a number of years on end they are annulled by what to all intents and purposes amounts to a divorce. In our zeal for effecting reforms in outlying parts of the Empire, it would be a mistake to shut our eyes to the scandals which occur here in Rome.'

Drusus made a short speech in the same sense. He pointed out that members of the imperial family were frequently called on to visit distant parts of the Empire, and referred to his own marriage and to the number of occasions when Livia had accompanied Augustus on his imperial tours, both in the West and in the East. He spoke of his own visit to Illyricum and to the visits to other parts of the Empire which in the public interest he might be called on to make in the future. 'I should undertake them with very great reluctance indeed,' he said, 'if they involved separation from my wife whom both for herself and for the sake of our children I love so dearly.'†‡

It is true that in the first century A.D. it was still an unusual thing for a province to be visited by a reigning Emperor with his consort, but the following centuries saw a big change. When Trajan went out to the East, his wife and niece went with him. Sabina journeyed with Hadrian up the Nile. The younger Faustina died in Cappadocia; Julia Domna was with Septimius Severus when he died at York.

* In A.D. 24, three years later than this speech, the law was altered, and a Roman official in the provinces became legally responsible for any offence committed in the province by his wife.[47]

† She was called Livia, that dear wife of his, and was a daughter of Drusus and Antonia Minor. Two years after he had spoken of her with such great affection, she was seduced by Sejanus and, with her seducer, conspired to murder him.

‡ From page 60 to here has been a free translation of Tacitus *Annals* iii, 33f.

III

INTRODUCTION TO THE EMPIRE

✦✦✦

FROM THE restoration of peace after the civil wars by Augustus in 27 B.C. to the death of Nero in A.D. 68 was just short of a century. The five emperors who ruled in this period were men of marked and diverse individuality; their womenfolk were in many cases sensational.

Augustus was seventy-five when he died in A.D. 14; Livia was his wife when the civil wars ended and she was his wife still when he died. She was one of the women of whom he could feel proud; the others were his sister Octavia and his two nieces, daughters of Mark Antony, both called Antonia.

Tiberius was fifty-four and a widower when he became Emperor in A.D. 14, and seventy-seven and a widower still when he died in A.D. 37. His mother Livia survived, a powerful dowager, to die at the age of eighty-five in A.D. 29.

With the accession of Gaius Caligula at the age of twenty-four in A.D. 37, youth was at the helm; he survived less than four years, and had three sisters (one of them, the younger Agrippina) and, in succession, four wives.

When, to his own surprise and the world's, Claudius was proclaimed Emperor in A.D. 41, he was in his fiftieth year, and he ruled until A.D. 54. His wives, when he was Emperor, were, in succession, Valeria Messalina and the younger Agrippina, his niece. Messalina was lovely, gay, lascivious and foolish; Agrippina was as ambitious as her mother and, at the start, more fortunate; her son Nero became Emperor in A.D. 54, at the age of sixteen. Five years later, though with amateurish ineptitude, he contrived her murder. Nero's first wife was his step-sister, the frigid Octavia. She was killed too, and for three years, from 62 to 65, he was married to Poppaea. Statilia Messalina was his third wife, this being her fifth marriage.

There were powerful women with strong political interests and ambitions: Livia, and the two Agrippinas, mother and daughter. There were self-indulgent women, assisted by immense wealth in the exploitation of their great charms: Julia, Valeria Messalina, Poppaea.

Corruption, intrigue, cruelty and flamboyance pervaded the life of the upper classes in Rome during this century. Even so, there is an extravagance, which is often hardly credible, in the recorded history of the men and women of the imperial house, and for this there are two causes. The first is to be found in the salacious imagination and the scurrilous gossip of a Roman society which was untroubled by the fear of prosecution for libel or for slander. What was old Tiberius doing on Capri at the end of his life, if he was not indulging in unexampled orgies of sexual indulgence? How should Gaius Caligula show such great affection to his sisters, if he was not living in incest with them?

If contemporary gossip was the first cause, the historians' lack of integrity was the second. Instead of rejecting the scandal, they repeated it. They were moralists by profession, epigrammatists and satirists by upbringing and indeed by instinct. And so their portraits are not so much portraits as brilliant caricatures. After the Julio-Claudian orgy—or nightmare—was over, when the Flavians—and then Nerva and Trajan—succeeded, and social respectability became the fashion, the modes of the Julio-Claudian court appeared more *outré* and more shocking than ever. That was when Tacitus—and Juvenal—wrote; and no history of the Julio-Claudians will ever be uninfluenced by their brilliant and satirical picture of the manners of an age which they were as delighted to describe as they would, one hopes, have been shocked to experience.

Though Augustus made a profession of 'restoring the republic' in 28 and 27 B.C., when the civil wars which followed the murder of Julius Caesar were at an end, it was clear to him and to others who thought realistically that, without an Emperor at the helm, the 're-stored republic' could not survive. When he died, there must be an Emperor to succeed him.

From Augustus onwards every responsible Emperor knew that though, under the system, he could not nominate a successor, it was his responsibility to ensure that at his death a fit successor would be available and, if possible, already trained to take over his powers. In this he knew that he could rely on the loyal co-operation of his trusted friends; equally well he knew that there were other parties who were plotting and conspiring in the hope of a succession other than that which he might intend.

It was natural for an Emperor to hope that he would be succeeded by his son—at the best, a son of his body; at the worst, a son whom he had adopted. In this way the succession worked smoothly in the case of the Flavians (for Vespasian was succeeded in order by his elder and his younger son), and it worked smoothly from Nerva onwards, in four successive cases through adoption, until Marcus Aurelius was succeeded by Commodus, his son.

In the case of the Julio-Claudians, the succession after Tiberius, though it produced three Emperors who might well have seemed, at their accession, to have no qualifications at all to rule, was surprisingly untroublesome in itself. Tiberius died leaving two grandsons, one of his blood, one by adoption; of these the latter, Gaius Caligula, having the necessary political and military support, succeeded, and quickly rid himself of his only rival. When Gaius was murdered, his uncle Claudius was found to succeed him; when Claudius died, he left two sons, one of his blood, one by adoption, the latter being his step-son and great-nephew, Nero. Thanks to his mother, the younger Agrippina, Nero had the more powerful military and political backing; he succeeded, and his stepbrother Britannicus was put out of the way. Yet it cannot be pretended that in any of these three cases the future Emperor had been groomed at all for his imperial responsibilities.

During the long principates of Augustus—forty years, from 27 B.C.—and of Tiberius—twenty-three years from A.D. 14—the prospect of the succession was a nightmare which bedevilled the public life of Rome and the private life of the Emperors themselves and of their numerous relations, not because there were no fit candidates, but because they all died young.

Tiberius at his accession had two grown and able sons, Drusus by birth and Germanicus, his nephew, by adoption. If conflict between them could be resolved, either, it seemed, had the makings of a responsible ruler. Yet, because it was assiduously fomented by interested parties, the conflict could not be resolved; and in consequence of two grim tragedies both were dead before the rule of Tiberius was nine years old.

In Augustus' case the tragedy had been even greater. His own health was not good, and it seemed from the start that his rule might not be a long one. At the same time the inevitability of the imperial system was not yet commonly accepted; and he could not do more than indicate—and that only with the greatest caution and delicacy—who might be qualified, if he died, to take his place. This was a daunting responsibility.

It was made the more difficult for him on account of the fact that he had no son. Yet, aware that he owed his own elevation in the main to his relationship to Julius Caesar (his great-uncle and adoptive father) and to the loyalty of Caesar's troops which he had inherited, he knew that his successor must, if possible, be a man of Julian stock. That meant that he must be a son or grandson of his sister Octavia or of his own daughter Julia, for they were his only close relations, the only women who had Julian blood. Hence the dynastic importance of Octavia's marriages, and of Julia's.

It is this fact which explains the intricate complication of the family life of Augustus and his relations, and the importance which attached to the women of his family in connexion with his plans for the future government of Rome.

M. Marcellus was Octavia's only son, offspring of her first marriage, and when Marcellus married Julia in 25 B.C., there was every hope that a successor would be found either in Marcellus himself or in one of his sons. Instead, he died after two years, and left no children. Augustus then married Julia to his contemporary, M. Agrippa, a man who, despite the obscurity of his origins, was a distinguished soldier, a loyal friend and, to a large degree, the architect of Augustus' own supremacy. This time expectations were fulfilled. Before long there were two grandsons whom, in 17 B.C., Augustus adopted as his own sons, Gaius and Lucius Caesar. Augustus might reasonably hope that one or other of these boys held the future of Rome in his hands.

Julia had been born to Augustus from a marriage which ended before he became Emperor; and during the whole period of his rule he was married to Livia. Had this marriage produced even a single son, the future would have been a great deal brighter. It might have been brighter, too, if Livia was not already the mother of two sons, Tiberius and Drusus, by her former husband. Tiberius was reserved and difficult, Drusus an open and attractive person; both were to show themselves to be soldiers and administrators of quite remarkable talent. Both had entered on manhood before Gaius and Lucius Caesar were born. But they were not Julii. So, given their talents and their personalities, they were, from the point of view of a Julian succession, something of an embarrassment.

In 9 B.C. when Gaius Caesar was eleven years old and Lucius Caesar eight, Drusus died. He had married Antonia, the younger daughter of

Octavia (by her second marriage to Mark Antony), and of the three children of that marriage, the eldest, Germanicus, then six years old, inherited to the full his father's charm and popularity.

The stars in their courses, it seemed, were working to frustrate Augustus' reasonable plans. By A.D. 4, Gaius and Lucius Caesar were dead. Had a popular vote been taken at this moment, there is little doubt that Germanicus, then nineteen years old, would have been the people's choice. But Augustus realized that he had no alternative now but to adopt Tiberius, then forty-five years old and an experienced soldier and administrator, and to associate him in his government in such a way that, when he died, Tiberius would be his successor. Though Tiberius had a son of his own (another Drusus), Augustus insisted that he should adopt Germanicus.

All Augustus' hopes for a successor of Julian blood had failed; and there was a singular lack of graciousness about his capitulation to the inevitable; there was no graciousness, either, when the time came, about the language of his will: 'Since an unkind fate has robbed me of my grandsons, I make Tiberius my heir.'

Octavia's life ended in sadness; her hopes were swept away when Marcellus died, and she never recovered from her prostration at his death. Julia's life, as will be seen, ended in disaster. Only Livia emerged triumphant. The race for the succession had been won by the outsider, her able and enigmatic son Tiberius. It was tempting to make a Machiavellian figure out of her, to make her responsible for the elimination of the whole series of fancied 'successors', to picture her sweeping piece after piece off the board as she cunningly advanced her own pawn. The Julian part of the family and their supporters did this, and Tacitus regrettably followed their lead.

This is to anticipate, at the cost of some repetition, the history which will be told in greater detail in the chapter which follows. But it is hoped that, together with the genealogical tree which is printed on page 286, it may help to elucidate the complicated relationship of members of Augustus' family, the significance of their marriages and the importance in all this dynastic planning, which events so cruelly frustrated, of the women of the family—in particular, Octavia, the younger Antonia, Julia and Livia.

THE WOMEN OF AUGUSTUS' COURT

THE EMPEROR Augustus who founded the Roman Empire and so made Rome and, after Rome, western Europe his debtor, was born, a C. Octavius, in 63 B.C. Adopted by the will of his great-uncle Julius Caesar, he became a Caesar—Julius Caesar Octavianus (modern historians call him Octavian)—when he was eighteen in 44 B.C. Seventeen years later, after the successive dispatch of Julius Caesar's murderers at Philippi and of Antony and Cleopatra after Actium he took the name Augustus. When he died in A.D. 14 at the age of seventy-five, his last words were spoken to his wife Livia, urging her not to forget the happiness of their married life.[1] They had been married fifty-one years, since 38 B.C. Two years earlier than that he had been married, for political reasons, to Scribonia, a relative of the Pompeys who had already been married twice, and she was mother of Julia, his only child. Soon after Julia was born in 39 B.C. he divorced Scribonia, exasperated by her 'moral perversity'.[2]

This 'moral perversity' lay in her refusal to tolerate one of Octavian's mistresses. At the same time, Octavian fell so passionately in love with Livia that he had not the patience to wait even for three months until after the birth of the child (Drusus, younger brother of Tiberius) with whom she was pregnant. They lived together, and on January 17th, 38, three days after the child's birth, they were formally married.[3] Respectability professed itself shocked; but priestly officials were easily persuaded to approve the unconventional haste. Her former husband, Tiberius Claudius Nero, obligingly played the part of the bride's father, and gave her away.

Tongues wagged of course. Was Augustus perhaps the child's father? They were to wag again later, about his association with the wife of his minister Maecenas. It was said too that he enjoyed deflowering virgins, of whom, like the good housewife that she was, Livia ensured that there should always be an ample supply.[4] If the fetid indelicacy of Roman imagination could think of no greater scandals than these with which to tax him, it may safely be assumed that, judged by contemporary standards, he was a reasonably moral man. He was also, in his relation with the women of his family, a remarkably insensitive and a remarkably unfortunate man.[5] The fact that there were no children of his marriage with Livia was his first misfortune and has, indeed, been seen as the origin of the whole tragedy of the family history of the Julio-Claudians.[6] The Julian part of the family, descended from Augustus' daughter Julia, hated and despised the purely Claudian part of the family—Livia, her son Tiberius and his descendants, who had no Julian blood at all. What by Republican tradition was the bluest blood was, in fact, despised by blood which was by no means so blue.

Augustus' sister Octavia, born in 69 B.C. and six years older than himself, enjoyed a moral reputation even more unsullied than his own. She was a prodigy among women of the new imperial family, even at its beginnings, in that she had not a single critic. This was not only because in the propaganda which represented Octavian's war with Antony as a crusade, it was convenient to depict her as a deeply wronged woman, the chaste Roman foil of the voluptuous foreigner Cleopatra; it is evident that she was in fact as good as she was beautiful.[7]

In 54 B.C. she was married to a man more than twenty years her senior, C. Claudius Marcellus, whose hysteria as consul in 50 helped to provoke Caesar's invasion of Italy and the civil war. Their children were born late in the forties, a son M. Claudius Marcellus and two daughters, each called Claudia Marcella.

When through the patient efforts of the statesmen at Brindisi in the autumn of 40 the immediate danger of war between Octavian and Antony was, as it seemed, averted and Antony assumed responsibility for the eastern part of the Empire, Octavian for the west, no better means existed of sealing the new reconciliation than a political marriage; and it must have appeared a double kindness on fortune's part that, with Octavia only recently a widow, news should arrive from Athens that Antony's wife Fulvia was dead.[8] Octavia could hardly wish for a more attractive husband or Antony for a more desirable wife or for a kinder stepmother for Fulvia's children. Whether he told her that he was the father of two more children, the twins Alexander Helios and Cleopatra Selene, recently born to the Queen of Egypt, is not to be known.[9] Cleopatra, anyhow, was a foreigner with whom by Roman law he could not contract a legitimate marriage. Octavia did not worry overmuch, perhaps, at the news that her husband had had a Queen for his mistress. It was to Fulvia, after all, not to herself that he had been unfaithful.

Antony struck a coinage to celebrate his wedding to Octavia. It was an issue which made numismatic history, for it was the first time that a woman's portrait head appeared on a Roman coin.[10]

Their marriage at first was neither unhappy nor unfruitful. There were two daughters, Antonia maior and Antonia minor, children who were destined, one to be mother and grandmother, the other to be grandmother, of Roman emperors; Antonia minor was to inherit the full measure of her mother's gentleness and charm.

The winter of 39/8 Octavia spent with Antony in Athens, unable and unwilling to do what Cleopatra had done in 41 and was to do again later, to play the part of Aphrodite, to match, in the East, the antics of Antony as the New Dionysus. In 37 her conciliatory influence was felt at Taranto where, once again Antony and Octavian were reconciled and, in forlorn hope of an abiding concord, Octavian's two-year-old daughter Julia was betrothed to M. Antonius Antyllus, the son of Antony and Fulvia.

In the autumn of 37 Antony belatedly strapped on his armour and went off to fight the Parthians—and to enjoy his vacations from fighting in the company of the Queen of Egypt. Octavia, who had come out as far as Corcyra, received instructions to return to Octavian's protection, taking their daughters and her stepchildren with her. In Italy in 36 she received the startling news that her husband and the Egyptian Queen were married. The lawyers assured her that, since Cleopatra was not a Roman, this was, by Roman law, no marriage at all and, credulous and forgiving, she travelled East again in 35, bringing the troops and gold which, after his disastrous Parthian campaign, her husband so badly needed. At Athens she found a letter. She was to send on the troops and the gold and to return, herself, to Rome. Three years later, in 32, Antony sent her a formal notice of divorce.[11]

The year 27 marked ostensibly the full restoration of peace—the 'pax civilis'. Actium had been fought in 31; Antony and Cleopatra were dead, and Octavian, now honoured with the name Augustus, had surrendered his extraordinary powers which, inoffensively disguised, had been returned to him. There was time at last to survey his family which, however little the fact may have been appreciated by contemporaries, was to be the imperial family of the new Roman Empire. It was a very young family indeed.

Augustus himself was thirty-six and his wife Livia thirty; they had been married eleven years, and they were by this time accustomed to the sad prospect of a marriage without issue. There were three children in the house, Julia now twelve years old, and with no immediate prospect of marriage, for Antony's son Antyllus, to whom she was betrothed in infancy had been put to death on Augustus' orders after Actium. Julia's upbringing, a foretaste of what her own children were in due course to suffer, was closely supervised by Augustus himself and would have merited Queen Victoria's austere approval. She was taught spinning and weaving (Augustus liked wearing clothes which had been made by his womenfolk), and she was encouraged to avoid flippancy in her conversation; young men who called, even when the family was on holiday, received a letter from the Emperor, and did not repeat the indiscretion.[12]

Of Livia's two sons by her earlier marriage, Tiberius Claudius Nero (Tiberius) was fifteen and betrothed to a girl of six or seven. This was Vipsania Agrippina—daughter of the marriage of Augustus' friend and lieutenant M. Agrippa to Caecilia, the daughter of Cicero's friend Atticus. By 28 B.C. Caecilia was either dead or divorced, for Agrippa had married again. His new wife was Octavia's daughter, the younger Marcella. Livia's younger son Nero Claudius Drusus (Drusus) was eleven years old. Both brothers had lived with their father until his death in 33. They had since joined their mother and lived in Augustus' house.

Octavia's household was full of young people, her own children by two marriages and Antony's children by three. There was her son by her first marriage, M. Claudius Marcellus, now aged sixteen; he had discarded the toga of boyhood and, by Roman standards, was of marriageable age; of his sisters one certainly and both probably were already married. There were her two daughters by Antony, the elder Antonia being twelve years old, and the younger nine. Older than any of them was Iullus Antonius, Antony's son by Fulvia. Finally there was Cleopatra Selene, one of the twins born in 40, the only survivor of Antony's liaison with the last Queen in the line of the Ptolemies. Shadowed by the grandiloquent mockery of her names, the child was brought to Rome with her brother to walk as captive in the great triumph in which Octavian celebrated his victory over her parents. Her brother had evidently died; and she had found a home in the house of her generous stepmother.

Augustus' nephew Marcellus and his stepson Tiberius had shared prominently in the glory of his triumph in 29. Marcellus rode one

trace horse and Tiberius rode the other, of the chariot in which
Augustus himself stood. Both were to accompany him to Spain to
receive their blooding at the end of this same year 27. It requires little
imagination to recapture the anxious concern of the two mothers.
The two youths could not ride side by side for ever; with no son of his
own, Augustus must promote one or the other of them to the chief
place in his favour. In 25 B.C., after he had seen them both at close
quarters in Spain, he made his choice. Marcellus married Julia and
became the Emperor's son-in-law.

There seems little doubt that Augustus always disliked Tiberius[13]
(who in Spain had shown a great fondness for the bottle); anyhow
Tiberius was already betrothed to Vipsania Agrippina, and it would
have been difficult to disturb that arrangement without offending her
father Agrippa,[14] who was Augustus' intimate, influential and singularly touchy friend.

Most important of all, Marcellus was his nephew and, through his
mother, a Julian; and it is most unlikely that, even had he liked Tiberius
greatly, Augustus' choice would have been different. Her father's
choice would certainly have been Julia's own; for while Tiberius was
sombre and deeply reserved, Marcellus was all openness and charm.[15]
Whether Julia's mother Scribonia, who had not committed the imprudence of a further marriage since Augustus divorced her, was
present at the wedding, we do not know. Julia was given away by M.
Agrippa, since her father had not yet returned from Spain. Ill-health
detained him—and, it has been suggested, an element of cowardice;
he was frightened of meeting Livia and of explaining why he had not
preferred her son.

In the event, the marriage was one on which Fortune frowned.
After two years Marcellus was dead, victim of an epidemic, a patient
who did not respond favourably to that cold-bath and cold-drinks
treatment of the doctor Antonius Musa, by which only a few months
earlier Augustus' life was saved.[16] There were no children of the
marriage.

Despite the Schadenfreude of Agrippa and of many of the senatorial
nobility, who considered that Marcellus had been in a little too much
of a hurry to assume the prerogatives of a favoured Prince Charming,[17]
Marcellus' death was portrayed as being—and in many quarters was
genuinely felt to be—a national disaster. Augustus spoke the funeral
oration, a handsome panegyric. And poets indulged the theme of
youthful promise cut short, Propertius in an elergy[18] which, even if its

text were more certain, would still perhaps be stigmatized as 'an obscure and difficult poem'—

> quid genus aut virtus aut optima profuit illi
> mater et amplexum Caesaris esse focos?*

and Virgil, destined himself to survive Marcellus by four short years,
in splendid verse:[19]

> Ostendent terris hunc tantum fata neque ultra
> esse sinent.†

Horace, who had noticed the marriage of Marcellus in an earlier
ode,[20] wrote nothing that has survived about Marcellus' death.

It is chiefly the women who must weep. Octavia, so courageous in
facing her earlier hardships, was inconsolable. In the remaining twelve
years of her life she never discarded her mourning garments. She built
a library in memory of her son; but for the rest, if Seneca is to be
believed, she overplayed the part of the sorrowing mother:

'She refused to have a portrait of her son whom she loved so dearly,
and she never allowed his name to be mentioned in her presence. She
conceived a hatred for all other mothers which, in the case of Livia,
amounted to a frenzy; because Livia's son, as she thought, now inherited the happiness which *she* had been promised. Spending more
and more of her time alone in the dark, with no regard even for her
brother, she refused to listen to poems and other compositions in
honour of Marcellus' memory, and to every attempt of consolation
she simply closed her ears.'[21]

She cannot have taken such leave of her reason as to believe the
mutterings of the scandalmongers, that Livia was Marcellus' murderer; [22] and she need hardly have given herself the luxury of hating
Livia, for even in her grief and prostration she had the satisfaction of
seeing Livia's ambitions—if, indeed, Livia had such ambitions—crushed
for the second time. Having lost a son, Octavia was prepared in succession to surrender a son-in-law rather than see Julia married—as by
all reason she should now have been married—to Tiberius. To marry
Julia, Agrippa must divorce his wife, Octavia's daughter, the younger
Marcella; both on her own and on her daughter's behalf the sorrowing

---

* 'Good birth, good character, a splendid mother, marriage into Caesar's house—what
good did these things do him?'
† 'Fate will give the world a glimpse of him—no more than that.'

Octavia was prepared to make the sacrifice.[23] Revenge can be very sweet indeed.

It would be nice to believe, with a German scholar, that Livia fought back and that she suggested to Augustus that, rather than marry Agrippa, Julia should marry C. Proculeius whose stepsister Terentia was married to Augustus' minister, Maecenas. Though admittedly a prominent figure, and a close personal friend of Augustus, Proculeius was not even a senator; so that, when it came to the succession, the children of such a marriage could never challenge the claims of Tiberius. Such—it is suggested—were Livia's dark and sinister thoughts.[24] But if it is true that Augustus ever thought of C. Proculeius as a possible son-in-law, it cannot have been at this moment, when Proculeius' stepbrother Murena had recently been executed as a serious conspirator and the power of Maecenas was in serious decline. To advocate such a *mésalliance* would have been sheer stupidity; and nobody has ever suggested that Livia was a stupid woman.

So Julia married her first cousin's husband, Agrippa. Agrippa, indeed, may have put strong pressure on Augustus to approve the marriage—at which, once again, Augustus was not present. He was in Sicily, and too busy to return. We know nothing of Julia's feelings, or of Marcella's. Was Julia as inconsolable as her mother-in-law when Marcellus died? Was Claudia Marcella altogether sorry to lose a husband of forty-two in favour of one nearly twenty years younger— Iullus Antonius, Mark Antony's attractive son?

Tiberius' marriage to Agrippa's daughter by the first of his three marriages, Vipsania Agrippina, still hung fire, and they were not married until after Tiberius returned from accompanying Augustus to the East in 20 B.C. Of the young women of Octavia's—now sorrowing—household, Antonia maior, now eighteen years old, married L. Domitius Ahenobarbus; Antonia minor did not marry Tiberius' younger brother Drusus until 16 B.C. Cleopatra Selene was off Octavia's hands in 20; her background warranted an exotic marriage, and the arrangement which Augustus made, if not exotic, was at least colourful. She married King Juba of Numidia and Mauretania, a man ten years older than herself, to whom she had been betrothed in the year after Actium.[25] They had much in common. Juba had marched, a captive, in Caesar's triumph in 46, Cleopatra Selene in the triumph which followed Actium. Both had been educated in Italy, and both had responded well to a Roman upbringing. She was the last of the Ptolemies and proud of her ancestry; he was a scholar and historian of distinction. Their daughter was one of the three queens who were privileged in due course to be, in succession, the wives of the Roman freedman Antonius Felix.[26]

Julia's marriage to Agrippa achieved its vital object, the procreation of imperial grandchildren. A son was born in 20, a second son in 17. In 17 Augustus adopted them both; the elder was now called C. Caesar, the younger L. Caesar. Together with the sisters who appeared in due course, Julia and Agrippina, they were brought up in the palace, under the Emperor's personal supervision.[27] The girls were given an education similar to that from which their mother was still considered to have received benefit; the boys were taught literature and swimming by their grandfather; also, curiously, to imitate his handwriting. There is no record of the part which Livia played in their upbringing.

With the future prospects of his family, as it seemed, now well established, and with so remarkable an example at the very apex of Roman society of a model, healthy and fruitful marriage of the traditional old-fashioned type, the year 17 was aptly selected for a great propaganda to encourage, indeed enforce, the reintroduction of the good morals of fabled antiquity. The first of Augustus' laws for the improvement of morals had been passed already, probably in 19/18. Indeed this legislation had been hanging like a threat over the gay dissipation of licentious youth for about ten years earlier than that.

Ever since the second century B.C. thoughtful Roman gravity had been obsessed with the nightmare of a falling birth-rate, seeing the problem from one point of view only, the provision of an ample supply of recruits for the Roman legions. How could men and women be persuaded to marry and produce more sons, who would grow up to become good Roman soldiers?

Warning was sounded in the preface to Livy's History:

'I hope everyone will pay keen attention to the moral life of earlier times, to the personalities and principles of the men responsible at home and in the field for the foundation and growth of empire, and will appreciate the subsequent decline in discipline and in moral standards, the collapse and disintegration of morality down to the present day. For we have now reached a point where our degeneracy is intolerable— and so are the measures by which alone it can be reformed.'[28]

Strong words.

Ten years earlier, in 28, Propertius among others had received a jolt.[29] Legislation was proposed, to enforce a strict code of marriage but, in the face of strong opposition, it was abandoned. A change in the law might force Propertius to abandon his mistress and become a respectable married man, a father of soldiers. But the threat passed away, something to be laughed at in elegant elegiacs:

> *Unde mihi patriis natos praebere triumphis?*
> *Nullus de nostro sanguine miles erit.*

Sons to win triumphs how should *I* beget?

In 19/18 the bills went through the Senate, a law on marriage between the social classes (*de maritandis ordinibus*) and a law for the restraint of adultery (*de adulteriis coercendis*). Both were Julian laws, introduced by Augustus and called after him. The programme was one which Cicero had recommended to Julius Caesar over quarter of a century earlier:[30] 'less lust, and larger families'. In more graceful language, Modesty was to be recalled from the distant past, and Virtue was to emerge from neglect.[31] All possible steps were to be taken to ensure that men between twenty-five and sixty should be married men, and women between twenty and fifty should be married women.[32]

Though there were republican precedents for such *mésalliances* it would have been commonly agreed that the ladies of a senatorial household should carry a certain stamp of good breeding; they should not, in fact, have started life as slave-girls—or, what was even worse in Roman eyes, as actresses. But in other sections of Roman society, a man might be inclined to marry his mistress and even raise a family from her, if it was made clear that a Roman could legitimately marry a slave-girl who had been freed. That—outside senatorial families—such marriages were legitimate, the new law stated explicitly, beyond any possibility of doubt.[33]

For the rest it was thought best to proceed by a system of rewards and punishments. The mother of three children* was rewarded by the grant of independence in the administration of her property; the father of three children was privileged to advance more expeditiously through the stages of his public career. Bachelors—*caelibes*—were debarred from receiving inheritances from outside a very narrow circle—the third grade—of their own families; spinsters and childless women were similarly debarred. More drastic and far less defensible was the infliction of penalities on the childless—she might well be a barren—woman who became a widow or was divorced. The widow

---

* See, for further details, page 202.

was given twelve months, the divorced woman six, in which to find another husband.[34]

There was one more gateway to be barred. An ingenious admixture of rewards and punishments might produce a great increase in the number of marriages. But how could the integrity of married life be ensured? What laws should exist for the punishment of adultery?

The republic had no such laws at all. A husband might take summary justice if he caught his wife in the act of adultery. Otherwise she was returned to her father, who presided over the family council which fixed her fate.[35] Her husband divorced her, of course, and retained a portion of her dowry.*

By the Julian law on adultery jurisdiction was taken from the family and became, in a public court, the responsibility of the State, banishment being the normal punishment for both the guilty parties. The wronged husband—who henceforth could retain only one-sixth of his wife's dowry, if there were no children—must first divorce his wife before witnesses. He was then allowed sixty days in which to bring a prosecution for adultery against her. If, after the divorce, he failed to prosecute, she could be prosecuted by any member of the public above the age of twenty-five. If the husband had not divorced her, she was immune from prosecution, but self-righteous members of the public shouldering the self-imposed burden of responsibility for public morals, could prosecute him and seek to show that he had discovered her in the act and had not minded, or, alternatively, that he himself derived an income from her infidelities.[36] (More than a century later, under Trajan, no less important a body than the Emperor's own Cabinet, considered the case of a junior army officer whose tender-heartedness prevented him from divorcing his wife though she had committed adultery with a centurion. The Cabinet did his duty for him.)[37]

If adultery was proved, the wife and her paramour were banished to different islands for life; the man lost half his property; the woman lost a third of her property, and half her dowry, in addition to the further amount which the husband retained if there were children, and she might not be married again to a free-born Roman.

Adultery (*adulterium*) was, or now became, restricted to a *liaison* of a man with a married woman; and if the offender was married, he had nothing to fear from his wife for, however extensive her knowledge of his misbehaviour, the law did not allow her to initiate a prosecution. For unnatural vice, however, now perhaps first defined as *stuprum*, a

* See, for greater details, page 188.

man could be prosecuted by any other man who wished; this crime embraced *liaison* with a free unmarried girl (unless she was a registered prostitute or a recognized concubine)* or with a widow; it also embraced male homosexuality.

Historians of the modern world have commended Augustus for his moral legislation. 'This *lex Julia de adulteriis coercendis* was an outstanding piece of legislation, and one which endured as the basis of Roman law on the subjects with which it was concerned. By bringing the family as an institution under public protection it marked a notable advance in the conception of the proper functions of the State, and, by penalizing the practices of an age when men and women had begun to seek their own pleasure alone, it opened the way for a return to the ancient view of marriage as a union '*liberorum quaerundorum caussa*'— for the procreation of children.'[38]

Against this pronouncement, let it be said that it opened the way also to a recurrence of vexatious charges (many of them demonstrably false) and, no doubt, to widespread practice of blackmail.[39] Whether the standard of public morals was raised is doubtful in the extreme. Man can as little be made moral as honest by an Act of Parliament.

In introducing his law Augustus claimed to have discharged a function laid on him by the Roman Senate, and without doubt the *epigoni* of the younger Cato approved. A larger section of the Senate, however, made no secret of its disapproval. Augustus decided to teach them a lesson in Roman history; and so their patience was further exhausted while they listened to the reading of the speech 'On increasing the birth-rate', which had been delivered over a century earlier, in 131, by one of the censors.[40] It contained such improving sentiments as this: 'If it was possible to live without wives, gentlemen, we should all save ourselves that bother. But Nature has ordained that, while life with them is not easy, life without them is quite impossible, and so we must act with a view to our lasting well-being, not to the pleasure of the moment.'

There were disorderly scenes in the Senate when—as did not often happen—Augustus was caught off his balance.[41] In some irritation he told the senators that they were responsible for their wives' good conduct; and unwisely he added, 'as I am for mine'. 'Tell us,' they shouted, 'how you control her.' Lamely Augustus said that he laid down certain rules concerning her dress and concerning her appear-

---

* See pages 231 f. Concubinage may, in fact, first have become an officially recognized status by virtue of Augustus' legislation.

ances in public. The occasion was not one of his parliamentary triumphs.

From June 1st to 3rd, 17, after an interval of more than a century, Rome celebrated the Secular Games, the inauguration of a Brave New World, which was to be characterized not by progress in any modern sense but by the restoration and revival of the religion and good manners which had characterized Rome's golden past.[42] Had the reception of Augustus' moral legislation been more whole-hearted and had it not been necessary to postpone the operation of much of it for three (and later for two more) years, the Secular Games would have set an even more conspicuous seal on the new regulations about class-marriage, adultery and unnatural vice. A hundred and ten matrons were involved in the celebration, and choirs of twenty-seven boys—an innovation, this—and twenty-seven girls sang a commissioned song of Horace, the *carmen saeculare*, first before the temple of Apollo on the Palatine, later before the temple of Juppiter on the Capitol.

One part of his commission must have made Horace shudder; he was to refer explicitly to Augustus' recent legislation. This he did in the fifth stanza (lines 17–20) of the poem:

> *Diva producas subolem patrumque*
> *prosperes decreta super iugandis*
> *feminis prolisque novae feraci*
> *lege marita.**

Generous criticism has suggested that the Romans perhaps, unlike ourselves, liked poems about acts of parliament;[43] a reasonable judgement dismisses the lines as 'prosy'[44]; an outspoken English scholar wrote dryly,[45] 'If as in stanza 5, even Horace halts, we may well pity the genial bard who finds himself compelled to invoke a poetical blessing on legislation which his tastes must have led him to dislike, and his common sense must have despised as visionary.'

12 to 9 B.C. were years of mourning in the imperial family. Livia lost her younger son, the handsome and popular general Drusus, in 9; he died in Germany from an accident on campaign, already father by Antonia minor of two sons and a daughter. The sons were Germanicus, who was to die young and grow into a legend and Claudius who,

* 'Goddess, produce children and give success to the Senate's decrees about the marriage of women and the marriage law which aims at increasing the birth-rate.'

in a transformation scene beyond all anticipation, was to turn when nearly fifty from a buffoon into a Roman Emperor. Livilla was the daughter, destined to marry Tiberius' son (her first cousin) and to be seduced by an ambitious schemer 'from some town or other in Tuscany'—by Sejanus.[46]

Drusus had already won, and after his death retained, a popularity which his brother Tiberius never succeeded in earning. The popularity of Drusus' son Germanicus was to be greater still; and when under the melancholy rule of Tiberius people counted their losses, their imagination constructed a happy world of make-believe in which Drusus succeeded Augustus as Emperor or, if not Drusus, Germanicus—a world of which they had been cheated. Drusus should never have died; or Germanicus either. And, since imagination takes no account of facts, imagination went further. Why did Drusus die, it asked? Why did Germanicus die? The answer was easy; both had been murdered, Drusus on Augustus' instruction, Germanicus on the instruction of Tiberius.[47]

What of Livia? Was Drusus *her* favourite son too? When he died, we know that outwardly she exhibited all the stoicism of a Roman matron of the old school. And we can read the 474 lines of a verbose elegiac poem of consolation addressed to her—written, if the manuscripts are to be believed, by Ovid. But Ovid never wrote such awful poetry as this. It is a prize composition of a later age and not, happily, a poem which Livia had to read.[48]

It was in 9 B.C. that Drusus died. Two years earlier death had brought an end to the long melancholy of his mother-in-law Octavia. And in 12 B.C., on his return from a tour of duty in the East, Agrippa had died in Campania, leaving a family of four children (the two adopted sons of Augustus and their sisters Agrippina and the younger Julia), and his wife Julia pregnant with a fifth (the later Agrippa Postumus). Their marriage had been true to the spirit of the new legislation. Whatever Agrippa did, he did well; and—so far—Julia was a daughter of whom to be justly proud.

How are we to explain the consummate folly of Augustus' decision that without delay Julia should marry again—and should marry Tiberius?[49] For Tiberius himself, and in the end for Rome, the marriage was disastrous; he was forced to divorce his wife Vipsania Agrippina (mother of his son Drusus) to whom he was deeply attached. Never a genial character, he was, as a result of his experiences in the following ten years, to grow more morose and more embittered in the long span of his remaining life. It is an easy and altogether implausible hypothesis that, if the one child of his marriage to Julia (born probably in 10 B.C.) had lived, happiness was in store for them all, because it was for the part of stepfather, not for the part of father, that Augustus cast him. Self-sacrificingly he was to assist in the upbringing of Augustus' successor—Gaius Caesar or, if anything happened to Gaius, Lucius. Livia—'third time lucky'—can hardly have sponsored an arrangement which conflicted so violently with her son's own wishes. Had Augustus a better understanding than is commonly supposed of his daughter's character?[50] Did he expect her to be steadied by her third marriage, as she had been steadied by her first and second? No feeling of affection recommended Tiberius as a son-in-law; he was chosen because, at whatever cost to himself (and that to Augustus did not matter), he might well prove useful.

Choosing, for whatever purpose, to forget the extremely undistinguished origins of Agrippa, Julia is said to have considered that, in marrying Tiberius, she married beneath her.[51] Her father—so competent in the ordering of other people's lives—had relieved her of much of the responsibility for the upbringing of her children. Her new husband, on perpetual call for military service on the frontiers, as good as abandoned her; and her spiteful attempts, understandable in a woman who thought herself publicly slighted, to persuade Augustus to take some action against Tiberius, were unsuccessful.[52] She was not the woman to sit in the dark and mourn. She decided instead to enjoy, while she still could, the raffish and bohemian pleasures of the younger set in society at Rome.

More interested—just as he was more skilful—in controlling the public life of Rome than the private life of his family, Augustus was absorbed in preparations for the introduction to public life of his two grandsons—his adopted sons—Gaius in 5 B.C., when he was fifteen years old, and Lucius three years later. To assist them, and him, over the period of their political adolescence, he looked to Tiberius, and in 6 B.C. Tiberius received for five years the grant of tribunician power, the instrument of Augustus' own control of the central government in Rome; and, on top of this, he was commissioned to go out to the far eastern frontier to deal with trouble which had arisen in Armenia.

For this flattering recognition of his value, however temporary, to the commonwealth, some modest expression of gratitude was to be expected. Instead, Tiberius rehearsed the unexpected part which he

was to play on a far larger stage some thirty years later; he announced
that he wished to abandon public life and to devote himself to the
study of philosophy. What was the explanation of his contrariness,
people asked? The scandalous conduct of his wife? Jealousy of his
stepsons? The hope that Rome would discover in his absence the value
of his public services, which were too easily taken for granted? Wiser
judges perhaps discerned a fundamental instability in his character.[53]

Augustus protested in the Senate; Livia appealed to her son in
private. But he was inexorable. So leave of absence was granted, and
he slipped quietly out of Rome on the Ostia road; from Ostia he sailed
for Rhodes.

Tiberius' behaviour was not allowed to affect the pomp and circum-
stance with which in 5 and 2 B.C. the young Caesars, Gaius and Lucius,
were introduced to public life and launched on careers in which, as it
seemed, nothing less was at stake than the future imperial government
of Rome. It was indeed a clear and tranquil sky from which in 2 B.C.
the storm suddenly broke. Julia was exposed.[54]

She was thirty-seven years old. That she had lovers is not to be
doubted. But when it comes to describing the infamies which led to
her exposure, our sources are either coy or dumb: she had taken part
in revels and in drinking parties—at which she became very drunk—
in the forum and even on the rostra; she and her friends had placed
crowns of flowers on the head of the statue of Marsyas—this is all that
we are told that is credible. That she had plied for hire as a prostitute,
and used the uncomfortable platform of the rostra for a brothel,
merely 'adds artistic verisimilitude to an otherwise bald and uncon-
vincing narrative'.

This is the point at which we begin to realize that we have no conception at all of Julia as a person. None of the writers to whom we
might naturally look for evidence thought her worth describing—or
dared to describe her—in any but the crudest terms; and for a picture
of her we must jump four centuries ahead to Macrobius. For in the
extraordinary hodge-podge of Macrobius' *Saturnalia*, amid questions
of literary criticism, discussion of heat in human bodies and investiga-
tion of the question whether the hen came before the egg, there are
chapters on the memorable sayings of Cicero and others, on the witticisms made by Augustus and made by others at Augustus' expense and,
finally, a chapter on the witticisms and manners of Julia. This part of
Macrobius was derived in part from a book *On Urbanity* by Domitius
Marsus, written at the time of Augustus, in part from a similar book

written not much later.[55] The source, then, is not contemptible. Here is the passage:[56]

'She was in her thirty-eighth year—that is to say if her mental qualities had still been sound, she was on the verge of old age;* but she abused the advantages which she derived from her good fortune and her good father. She enjoyed literature and, as with her background was natural, she was very well informed. As a person of gentle humanity, altogether devoid of cruelty, she possessed great charm, and people who came to know her failings were amazed at the conflict in her character. Time and again, with a mixture of indulgence and seriousness, her father had suggested that she should behave less extravagantly and choose quieter friends; yet when he reflected on his numerous grandchildren, all of whom took so closely after their father Agrippa, he was ashamed to think of his daughter as anything but a faithful wife. So he lulled himself into imagining that, for all her gaiety and her outward flouting of the conventions, she was innocent, and he used to tell his friends that he had two children whose idiosyncrasies he must humour—the Roman government, and his daughter.'

She clung, like any other sensible woman, to her youth. She was not very old when her hair started to go grey. One day—the act was typical of him—Augustus came on her as her servants were plucking out her white hairs. He said nothing at all at the time, but some days later this conversation took place:

Augustus: Would you rather be bald or white-haired?

Julia: White-haired, of course.

Augustus: Why, then, are your servants at such pains to make you bald?

There is a dreadful probability about it as conversation.

Of the instances of Julia's wit which Macrobius gives, one is adroit, but singularly coarse. The others are amusingly light-hearted. One day, dressed with extreme severity, she embraced her father with severe formality. On the previous night when he had been shocked by her costume, he had said nothing; on this occasion he complimented her on her dress. She answered, 'Last night I dressed for my husband, this morning for my father.'

Shocked at a gladiatorial show by the difference in character between the men by whom Julia was surrounded and those who were in

---

* Forty was the age when, by Roman notions, a person passed from youth to old age.[57]

attendance on Livia, he wrote Julia a letter on the subject. She answered, 'But one day my friends and I will be old too.'

In 2 B.C. the storm broke. Taking full advantage of the encouragement which the Julian laws had given them, the informers were active. Augustus learnt about the parties in the forum. He was told—truly, no doubt—of Julia's numerous lovers.

The scandal could have been hushed up, Julia being sent to live a certain distance away from Rome. Augustus decided, however, to accord it all possible publicity. He behaved with a kind of hysteria, violating the law—even his own laws—at every move. As Tiberius was not accessible, Augustus acted on his behalf and divorced his daughter in Tiberius' name.[58] Assuming the truth of all that he had been told, he gave himself the morbid pleasure of writing a letter to the Senate, in which he described her transgressions in detail.[59] Denied the opportunity of self-defence, Julia was banished to the island of Pandateria (Ventotene) off the Campanian coast.[60]

Instructions were given that, when she died, she should not be buried in the mausoleum of Augustus at Rome,[61] and Augustus complained that, if only Maecenas or Agrippa had been alive, he would have known the truth about his daughter earlier.[62] When one of her freedwomen called Phoebe committed suicide, perhaps from fear of interrogation under torture, he said, 'I wish *she* had been my daughter'.[63]

Julia's two promising sons, Gaius and Lucius, were no doubt as greatly shocked as was their grandfather. So, perhaps, was her promising daughter Agrippina. Only two of her relations showed charity. Tiberius wrote from Rhodes, begging Augustus to allow her to retain her personal property.[64] And Scribonia, by this time quite an old lady, left Rome of her own free will to live on Pandateria with her daughter.[65] Scribonia's moral standards were anything but lax; it was, indeed, because she was so strait-laced that Augustus had divorced her. She was a *gravis femina*, and *gravitas* was the quality above all others which marked the traditional Roman matron.[66]

Pandateria (today Ventotene) is an island less than two miles long and never as much as half a mile wide, which lies thirty-one miles due west of the extreme north-west tip of the bay of Naples. All that we know of the island in antiquity is that it was plagued with field mice which nibbled the sprawling grapes.[67] This indicates that the island was cultivated more intensively in antiquity than it is today, when few trees fruit plentifully except the prickly pear.

The island had a small harbour, which the Romans had cut out of the tufa and, perched on the extreme northern point of the island, like a fortress, was the imperial villa, doubtless not without its comforts then; now it lies in ruins, as much regarded as a municipal rubbish dump. There were slaves; and there was a garrison of attentive warders.

What, in Pandateria, was there for Julia to do? It cannot have been long before she tired—as her own daughter Agrippina and other distinguished Roman women later exiled to the island would one day tire—of its volcanic geology and the theatrical magnificence of its cliffs, of the warmth of the sun and the complexion of the sea; and before she wearied of the relentless wind, which gives the island its modern name. On clear days the sight of Italy on the horizon was a reminder of better times; and on good days and bad alike the giant rock of S. Stefano (today a convict settlement) little over a mile away, suggested that there might be prisons worse even than hers.

For company she had her mother; but before visitors were allowed, they had to satisfy the rigorous police check which Augustus had instituted. No man was admited unless he was politically safe and physically unattractive. And—even in this island which grew grapes— her vindictive father had insisted that she should be allowed no wine.[68]

The Roman world could not fail to contrast her mother's generosity with her father's harshness; and it is not surprising that Julia's punishment was felt to be too stern. Popular protests were at first unavailing, Augustus remarking that fire and water should sooner mix than his daughter be restored; so people threw firebrands into the Tiber, and Augustus was not amused.[69] But after a time he gave way, and Julia was allowed to leave Pandateria and to live at Reggio in the South of Italy. And he even confessed to regretting the language which he had used in the letter which he wrote about her to the Senate.

Having disregarded the law in his treatment of his daughter, Augustus went further, and pronounced that illicit association with her— and, by implication, with any women of the Julian house—was high treason. 'Reprehensible as adultery might be, it was not uncommon; by bringing it under the serious heading of sacrilege and treason, Augustus departed a long way not only from traditional Roman generosity in such matters, but even from the wording of the law itself,' as Tacitus wrote later.[70]

Julia's lovers were brought to book.[71] Iullus Antonius, son of Mark Antony, the most prominent of them, an ex-consul and husband of Julia's cousin Marcella, committed suicide. Others were banished.

That is the story of Julia's fall, which the ancient writers give.

Her admirers—or at least her sympathizers—among historians have endeavoured to show that she was the victim—few would say the completely innocent victim—of the scheming of other people. It has been suggested that the enemies of Tiberius contrived her downfall since, once Tiberius divorced her, as he must do, he would cut the only cable by which he was connected to Augustus, and would lose whatever small prospects he had—and in 2 B.C. they were very small indeed—of succession to the Empire.[72] The contrary suggestion is that her exposure was contrived by Tiberius, Livia and a clique of conservative senators, and that the object of the blow was Augustus himself—Augustus, who must either take no action against his daughter or, alternatively, must expose the scandal, and in either case must bring great discredit upon himself.[73]

These are both bad guesses, because, if she was guilty of no more than sexual aberrations, nobody could possibly have anticipated that, once the facts of his daughter's loose-living were revealed to him, Augustus would behave as in fact he did. It would have been reasonable for him to banish Julia quietly. It could not have been expected that he would act with such wild intemperance and give the affair a quite startling publicity. His behaviour, indeed, is explicable only on one of two assumptions. Either, at the age of sixty-one, he had lost all sense of proportion in the matter of moral behaviour, or Julia was exposed as being something more serious than an adulterous woman. She was exposed as a dangerous political adventuress.

This last, as the elder Pliny indicates, was the truth.[74] Her associates, who were involved in her downfall, were men with important family names—a Quinctius Crispinus, a Sempronius Gracchus, an Appius Claudius Pulcher, a Cornelius Scipio and, cornerstone of the whole sinister edifice, Iullus Antonius himself. Already, as Augustus' nephew by marriage, he stood fourth in relationship to Augustus, for the moronic Agrippa Postumus can be left out of account. First came Augustus' two grandsons, whom he had adopted with every indication already that Gaius Caesar was being groomed for the succession. Next came Tiberius, now in deep disgrace in Rhodes. Antonius stood next.

Humiliated by the contempt which her husband Tiberius felt for her and resentful against her father for his treatment of her in the matter of her marriages ever since she was a child, Julia must have gone too far in her encouragement of Antonius' ambitions. She may have agreed that Tiberius would have to be eliminated. Her father was old, and it is to be hoped that Antonius gave her the impression that he was ready to wait for nature to take its course. As for her sons, she was perhaps persuaded that they were as yet too young for the succession. This, perhaps, was what Augustus came to believe when, with the passage of time he regretted the intemperance of his behaviour. At the first moment of the exposure, he evidently thought that she was involved in a plot to murder her father, her husband and both her promising young sons.

Accepting this, the plausible reconstruction of a distinguished German scholar,[75] a French historian of distinction has gone farther.[76] He has suggested that Julia, not Antonius, was the driving force behind the conspiracy; that the idea of murdering her father and her sons was one which she had proposed earlier to Tiberius and that it was because of his horror at the suggestion that Tiberius took himself off to Rhodes. So Julia added Tiberius' name to the list of her prospective victims, and hitched her wagon to Antonius' star instead. It is even suggested that the stories of her intoxication were false, an embroidery on the true fact that, with Antonius and the other conspirators, she drank, perhaps on the Rostra, from a loving-cup which contained human blood. Catiline and his associates, after all, are said to have behaved in such a way.

But there is a point, even in history, where, however brutally, imagination must be curbed.

After five years of philosophy on Rhodes, Tiberius was prepared once again to confront the responsibilities of public life, and the prospect of returning to Rome was no doubt the more attractive from the fact that Julia was his wife no longer. He asked, and Livia asked, if he might return. At first Augustus was no more merciful than at any other time; but in the end, in A.D. 2, permission was granted.

But now the Fortune of Augustus' house, which was never a kindly Fortune, struck again. Lucius Caesar died in A.D. 2, Gaius Caesar two years later. Neither left widow or children for, though Gaius was twenty-five and Lucius twenty, neither was married. Augustus was now faced with the prospect which at every stage he had sought to avert—the prospect that Tiberius would be his successor. Augustus

was in his middle sixties, Tiberius twenty years younger. It would be
nice to believe that Julia wrote, interceding on Tiberius' behalf, as
Tiberius had done on hers.[77] Anyhow, in A.D. 4 Tiberius was adopted
by Augustus, and his name changed from Tiberius Claudius Nero to
Tiberius (Julius) Caesar. He also received administrative powers far
larger than those which he had as good as rejected when he behaved so
cavalierly nine years earlier. At the same time Augustus adopted his
surviving grandson Agrippa Postumus, who was fifteen years old;
and he required Tiberius to adopt his nephew Germanicus, Drusus' son.

Within Augustus' family the monotonous story of scandal and disappointment was still incomplete. Of Agrippa's two daughters by Julia,
Agrippina was at every stage of her life a true daughter of her father;
her sister Julia was her mother's child. Deriving no benefit from those
tedious hours which Augustus had devoted to her education, she was
not prepared, when her husband died, to enjoy the restricted life of a
widow with two young children. Her husband L. Aemilius Paullus
had been executed, perhaps in A.D. I, for participation in an obscure
conspiracy.[78] After this she was banished, but then recalled. Heedless
of the warning, 'she devoted herself to vice'. Once again, in A.D. 8,
the informers pounced. On Julia herself a sentence of perpetual exile
was pronounced; she was sent to the small island of Trimerus (S.
Domenico) in the Adriatic(north of the promontory of Gargano), and,
on Augustus' instruction, the bastard child to whom she gave birth,
was exposed.[79] D. Junius Silanus, named as her adulterer, was merely
declared a *persona non grata*, Augustus making formal renunciation of
their 'friendship', which meant that Silanus could no longer expect to
be admitted to his morning levées. Silanus took the hint, and retired
into voluntary banishment (from which, under pressure from the
Senate, Tiberius, when he was Emperor, allowed him to return).[80]
Julia's young brother Agrippa Postumus shared in her disgrace; a
crude, ill-tempered lout, who possessed abnormal physical strength,
he was banished first to Sorrento, then to the island of Planasia (Pianosa,
southwest of Elba). Scandalmongers shook their heads and muttered,
'incest'; it was a very natural thing for a Roman scandalmonger to
mutter.[81]

Augustus' daughter, his grand-daughter and the last of his grandsons
were now banished to different points, distant from Rome and from
one another. This was the time when, with a tasteless appearance of
wit, he referred to them as his boils and his ulcers.[82] He even adapted a
line from the Iliad:[83]

Would that I never had wedded or bedded,
Would that I never had fathered a child.

However, of the victims of the purge of A.D. 8 the most famous by
far was no relative of Augustus, but a mere knight, the poet P. Ovidius
Naso. The facts are anything but certain, for we have no evidence but
the abject and pitiful defence of himself which he made later in a
poem to the Emperor:[84] 'two crimes destroyed me, a poem and a
blunder'.

The blunder, it seems, lay in his having abetted in some way or other
the intrigue of the younger Julia and Silanus. The poem was *The Art
of Love*—love in this context having little to do with conjugal affection;
it was a light-hearted, if didactic, poem on the technique of the successful lover and on the art of the successful courtesan.[85]

Augustus, in fact, had reached the inevitable climax of the moral
reformer; he had decided to institute a literary censorship. And
against the doctrinaire self-assurance of the censor of literature the
defence of Ovid was pathetically inept. It rested on two grounds. The
first was that he could not be held responsible if the book had corrupted
the morals of staid Roman matrons, because he had at the start explicitly
warned respectable women off the field, telling them that his book was
no book for them to read. 'Far from me, ye narrow fillets, badge of
modesty, and thou, long ruffle, covering half the feet.' In fact, of
course, as he knew and Augustus knew, this was an open invitation to
respectable women to read the book. His second defence rested on the
previously unchallenged Roman tradition of erotic poetry and the fact
that there were few stories mythological or legendary which did not at
some point or other offend the censor.[86]

Little, of course, was to be gained by such a defence, for Ovid was a
convenient scape-goat in a larger cause; literature was to be recognized
as a compartment of the Augean stables which the new Hercules was
determined to sweep clean. A Hercules, indeed, with a perverted
sense of humour. While the islands to which his descendants and their
adulterers were banished, though they might have the character of
prisons, were on the periphery of the Italian world, Ovid was sent to
pursue love in a very remote and (in winter) very cold climate indeed—
to Tomi (Constanţa) on the west coast of the Black Sea.

In the following year, A.D. 9, the purge was consummated. The
moral legislation of 19/18 B.C. was consolidated and in some respects
modified in a law—the *lex Papia Poppaea*—introduced in the names of

the two consuls.[87] The irony of their both being bachelors did not escape the notice of caustic contemporary wit.

The general principle of rewards and punishments was the same as before—rewards for parents, punishments (in the form of prohibition to inherit) for the unmarried. In as far as account was now taken of the fact that married people cannot have children by the simple act of wishing to have them, and married people without families were no longer treated, in the matter of acceptance of inheritances, as if they were unmarried, the legislation of A.D. 9 marked an advance. Childless widows and divorced women between twenty and fifty were given a longer period of grace—two years and eighteen months respectively—before they must marry again, and unmarried men, debarred by that fact from accepting an inheritance, were given a short period of time in which to find a wife and inherit, as if married all the time.[88]

Few women of real nobility have received such venemous treatment from historians as Livia has received, in particular from Tacitus. Little account was taken of the large contribution which she made to the achievement of Augustus; no account at all was taken of the fact that she was the mother of Drusus, whom posterity idolized, and the grandmother of Germanicus, who was a greater idol still. In the tradition which Tacitus followed and, to which he added his own poisonous distortions, her crime lay in the fact that she was Tiberius' mother. But for his mother, Tiberius might never have been Emperor: that was the fantasy. And, as fantasies take no account of facts, she was described as a Lucrezia Borgia of a woman, who secured the Empire for her son by removing those who stood in his way—Lucius Caesar, Gaius Caesar, Germanicus, and Agrippa Postumus. It was even suggested that she hastened Augustus' end in A.D. 14. All these allegations were as untrue as they were malicious.[89] Gaius and Lucius Caesar and Germanicus certainly died natural deaths; and, if Agrippa Postumus was murdered, Livia had no part in the murder. Tacitus, at his irresponsible worst, reported the slanders, careless whether he described them as rumours or as facts.[90]

If regard is had to the indisputable facts of her life, a very different picture emerges. It is one which Claudius by his acts and the less sensational writers, Valerius Maximus and Velleius Paterculus and Seneca, by their writings confirm.[91]

Livia's devotion to Augustus, and his devotion to her, were beyond dispute.[92] In their younger years she tolerated, even encouraged his acts of unfaithfulness, whether it was a stray virgin or Terentia, the wife—and, indeed, one suspects from Horace's account, the highly-sexed wife—of his minister Maecenas, who was needed to satisfy his fancy.[93] She nursed him in his numerous and, in his early years, serious illnesses.[94] In a great part of his life he depended on her, and occasions must have been numerous when he sought her advice, even, on serious matters, arriving with written notes of the subjects which he wanted to discuss.[95] This was a subject, naturally, on which Augustus gave no information to the world; and so, in accordance with its own nature, the world made guesses. The sinister critics who, after more than a century, satisfied Tacitus' venomous taste, were prepared to state for fact that Augustus had decided to build up Germanicus and not Tiberius as his successor in A.D. 4, but that Livia persuaded him to change his mind. Wiser people realized that throughout her life her influence on Augustus was likely to have been a humanizing influence; and at some time or other, after they were both dead, this topic was made the subject for free imaginative composition by some educationalist or other. The result was a long discussion, in fact almost a monologue, in which Livia's part was Portia's, her pleading that 'the quality of mercy is not strained'. Forestall a conspirator by winning his respect and affection, not by cutting off his head. This plausible composition was happily preserved and served up for consumption as a piece of true history. It is recorded by Seneca in his De Clementia and, at inordinate length, by the loquacious Cassius Dio.[96]

It is, in reverse, a conversation of Mrs. Proudie with her husband; for it happened in bed as Augustus tossed sleepless, disturbed by the thought of yet another conspirator to be dispatched. This was Cn. Cornelius Cinna, grandson both of Cinna, the opponent of Sulla, and of Pompey the Great, consul later in A.D. 5. He was detected but, thanks to Livia's intervention, his life was saved. According to Seneca (whose dating is certainly wrong) this happened in Gaul between 16 and 13 B.C.: according to Dio's even more dramatic account, Cinna was arrested in Rome in A.D. 4.[97] Next morning he appeared before the Emperor to receive his sentence. Augustus said, 'I will not only spare you, but will show my confidence in you by making you consul for this very next year.' He should have added, 'You have my wife to thank for this.'

Livia's beauty, which she retained, became with time a somewhat austere beauty; and, though in private she relaxed to a greater degree than convention would once have allowed, she encouraged austerity as well as traditional Roman decorum in the household over which she presided; and she paid high regard to dignity in her public appearances.[98] 'She has the beauty of Venus, the character of Juno'; and for once Ovid's flattery was not altogether inept.[99] Within the family and outside it, she displayed imaginative generosity; for all her brusqueness, she was kind—and even, when she restrained one of his rash literary projects, helpful—to her singularly unprepossessing young grandson Claudius, and she perhaps realized that the boy was not the fool that others thought him.[100] For it is not without significance that, in marrying Plautia Urgulanilla, he married the grand-daughter of one of her most intimate friends. She lived on affectionate terms with her daughter-in-law Antonia, who moved into her house when her husband Drusus died.[101] She even showed pity to her stepdaughter Julia, and did all that she could to alleviate the harsh conditions of her exile: a fact which Tacitus felt bound to record but, naturally, not without a vicious comment.[102] When her son was Emperor, she intervened more than once to save her friends whose husbands were in trouble.[103]

She had, it must be admitted, little interest in culture, and she had no sympathy with emotional weakness. When her son Drusus died, she acknowledged the help which she received from Augustus' philosopher Areus; but her own native stoicism perhaps counted for as much as his good advice.[104] She had despised Octavia's parade of sorrow when Marcellus died; Livia trampled on her own grief, and showed a smiling face to the world. She was a tough woman, in fact; and so were the women whom she made her friends.

That the public, while finding much in her to respect, never took her to its heart, is understandable. She never sought popularity for herself; she was content to live in the shadow of her husband.

In A.D. 14, when she was seventy years old, he died. Fifteen years of life lay ahead for her, and a new part to play, the part of Dowager-Empress, of Empress-Mother.

She left the palace, naturally; but she had in Rome two houses of her own. One on the Palatine, the so-called 'house of Livia', is still open to tourists, who can even gaze at her pictures on the walls—of Hermes, Argus and Io and of Polyphemus and Galatea.[105] Her name, IVLIAE AVG., is perhaps to be read on one of the drainpipes.[106] It is a modest house, and perhaps it came to her from Augustus. Her other house was a villa at Prima Porta on the way to Veii, nine miles north of Rome on the via Flaminia, known as 'ad Gallinas ad primam portam'. This was where the laurel twig held in the beak of a hen (gallina) which an eagle dropped in her lap in 37 B.C. had been planted and had grown into a splendid shrub, from which on triumphal days the laurels were plucked for Augustus'—and indeed for his successors'—wearing.[107]

Thanks to the genius of Italian archaeologists, the wall-paintings of her dining-room have been skimmed off and re-set in the Museo Nazionale in Rome. Here is a woodland glade round four sides of the room, green and bosky, with flowers and with birds galore. But they are small birds, not hens; and the trees are fruit trees, not laurels. There is a lot of fruit on the trees and that—it is made clear—explains the birds. Nowadays the cacciatori would have had them, every one.

She was accustomed to a life of intense business activity, for she was immensely rich, owning property in Asia Minor, Gaul and Palestine as well as in many parts of Italy, and she had complete independence in its administration, for she had been freed from *patria potestas* in 35 B.C., granted the rights of a mother of three children in 9 B.C. and, on Augustus' death, was exempt from the operation of the law (*lex Voconia*) which restricted the amount which a woman might receive in inheritance.[108] Her personal staff of over a thousand included Burrus, who was later to hold office as Commander of the Praetorian Guard under Claudius and Nero. The extent of her wealth is indicated by the fact that her bequest to Galba (the later Emperor), when she died, was one of fifty million sesterces.[109]

In Roman society she preserved her status as First Lady, for the Emperor Tiberius was a widower.

What of her position in the state?

First of all, she was adopted into the imperial family, and she became not merely Julia but Julia Augusta. The adoption and the title were Augustus' last gifts to her, under his will.[110] And when Augustus was consecrated, she was appointed first Priestess of his cult and given the right, in that capacity, to be accompanied by a public servant (*lictor*) when she appeared in public in Rome.[111]

For the rest, a protocol had to be established; and in the first meeting which the Senate held after Augustus' funeral and consecration, specious flattery and a mischievous desire to embarrass Tiberius combined in a series of awkward proposals: that, as Augustus had been given the title of 'Father of his Country', his widow should now be called 'Mother of her Country' (*Mater Patriae*); that the Emperor himself, already called 'the son of divine Augustus' should be called, too, 'the son of Julia'. Tiberius acted correctly in refusing to accept these suggestions; he did not want the Julian family at Rome to model itself on the practices of the defunct Hellenistic kingdoms.[112]

Augusta's position, of course, called for recognition. She held levées in her own right, and the names of those who attended them were published.[113] The various priestly colleges celebrated her birthday, and her name was included in the annual vows which were taken for the welfare of the Emperor.[114] Before Augustus had been dead many months, a request came from Gytheion in the Peloponnese for permission to institute an extensive cult to divine Augustus and to living members of the imperial house. Tiberius gave a ruling on the application except in as far as his mother was concerned; in that case he left the decision to her. In A.D. 23 the province of Asia was allowed to erect a temple to a curious and unexampled trinity: Tiberius, his mother and the Senate.[115]

In public the relations of Augusta and the Emperor were studiously correct.[116] Tiberius always spoke of his mother with respect and in public he deferred to her wishes. Nor have we any reason to think that in private she sought to impose her will on him and to determine public policy, or that she even claimed a right to be consulted by him on affairs of state.[117] There is no evidence whatever to support the allegations which Tacitus repeats so smoothly: that she wanted a share in the government, or that she claimed that Tiberius was under an obligation to her, since it was to her that he owed his title of Emperor.[118]

It must not be forgotten that Augusta was becoming a very old lady, and she may never have recovered completely from the serious illness which she suffered in A.D. 22.[119] She was never effusively affectionate and it may well have been the case that even she could not penetrate the hard shell of Tiberius' reserve. Up to the time of her illness in 22, Tacitus himself admits that they got on well together; after this the growth of Tiberius' infatuation for Sejanus—an indication in itself of his personal loneliness—may have injured his close relationship with his mother. We hear nothing of Livia's attitude to Sejanus, or of his attitude to her; and this silence of our sources is interesting, and may well be significant. Certainly Augusta must have been aware that, as the years passed, Tiberius was growing more and more unpopular at Rome, and that she inevitably shared a part of his unpopularity. Whether she tried to warn him, and whether his self-imposed relegation to Capri had, from Sejanus' point of view, the advantage that it broke contact between them, we cannot know and we should be unwise even to guess. Tacitus' suggestion that Tiberius went to Capri with the object of escaping from her dominating influence is both poisonous and silly.[120]

She must have derived great comfort from the affection of her daughter-in-law Antonia, a woman as busy as herself and occupied, like herself, both in the administration of her private property and in attending to the interest of innumerable clients and friends.

Within the family, tragedy descended from generation to generation. The elder Julia died in banishment in A.D. 15 at the age of fifty-three, and her daughter died, in banishment still, in A.D. 28. Of Augusta's three grandsons, Germanicus died tragically in the East in A.D. 19 and Drusus, Tiberius' son, died four years later. Their widows were sources of acute embarrassment. Rumour—this time uncomfortably near to the truth—suggested that Drusus' wife Livilla (herself the sister of Germanicus and a grand-daughter of Augusta) had been a party to the murder of her husband and that she was mistress of the equestrian upstart Sejanus. Agrippina dispensed with rumour; she informed the world as a plain matter of fact that her husband Germanicus had been murdered in Syria, poisoned by Augusta's friend Plancina, wife of the governor of Syria, and poisoned on Augusta's and the Emperor's direct instruction. She was, like Plancina, a masterful woman; both in their time had taken a large part in the command of the troops which were nominally under their husbands' orders. And now Agrippina was a deeply resentful woman, clutching her six surviving children, and fighting to preserve their safety in face of a conspiring world. She began to develop obsessions; when she dined with the Emperor, she ostentatiously refused food, making it clear that she expected it to be poisoned. 'Do you really think that you are being insulted whenever you are not allowed to behave as a queen?' Tiberius was driven once to ask her.[121] Sejanus she knew for the powerful enemy that he was, and after six years of militant widowhood she even thought—it was the only sign of weakness that she ever gave—of marrying again.[122] But when she made the suggestion to the Emperor, he was unsympathetic. The youngest of her three boys, Gaius Caligula, was taken to live for a short time in his great-grandmother's house. It is easy to understand how greatly he resented its discipline. With that wit which was his second nature he called her 'a Ulysses in Roman petticoats'.[123]

His ordeal was a short one for in A.D. 29 Julia Augusta died, an old lady of eighty-five. Twelve years later she became a goddess, for one of Claudius' first acts on his accession was to secure her consecration. She was not the first Roman woman to be so honoured; she was anticipated by her great-grand-daughter Drusilla, sister of Gaius Caligula and consecrated by him on her death in A.D. 37.

'She was a good match both for her husband and for her son: as cunning as the one, as two-faced as the other.' This is her obituary in Tacitus.[124] The truth would not have sounded half as smart: that she belonged by birth to two of the greatest Roman families, the Claudian and the Livian, and that there was no more distinguished woman in the history of either house.

Soon after Augusta's death, Agrippina and her elder son were denounced in a letter from Tiberius to the Senate; they were removed to the islands, Nero to Pontia (Ponza), Agrippina to Pandateria, which once was Julia's prison. No relief came to them when Sejanus was struck down in 31, after Antonia had conveyed from Rome to Tiberius on Capri her suspicions about the dangerous nature of Sejanus' ambitions.[125] Livilla's part in her husband's death was exposed when the truth about Sejanus was revealed, and she was forced to commit suicide.[126] Agrippina, who had been treated with the utmost physical brutality by her guards on Pandateria, starved herself, or was starved to death.[127] She died on October 18th, A.D. 33, two years to a day after Sejanus' violent death. Four years later, on his accession, her son Gaius Caligula sailed out to the island and brought her ashes home to Rome.

At Rome in the eight catastrophic years in which Tiberius survived his mother, people thought and spoke of her with a generosity which was long overdue. They suggested that she had been a restraining influence on her son, and that the horrors of Tiberius' administration in its last stages were due to the removal of that restraint. Tacitus even repeats such comments, unconcerned by their contradiction of all that he had written earlier about her relation to her son.[128]

Antonia ended her life as she had lived it—well. She took her grandson Gaius Caligula into her house after Livia's death, and he stayed there happily until Tiberius sent for him to come to Capri. On his accession Gaius wished to honour her, as Livia had been honoured, with the title of 'Augusta', but she modestly declined it; she became, however, a priestess of the divine Augustus. She might, indeed, have restrained Gaius in some of his excesses, had she lived, for his respect for her was very evident. But she died on May 1st, A.D. 37, only six weeks after his accession.[129]

MESSALINA, AGRIPPINA AND POPPAEA

'What woman will not take an Empress for her model?'★

++

1. The Death (in A.D. 48) and Life of the Empress Messalina

†ADULTERY was such an everyday affair as to hold no further interest for Messalina, and pressure from Silius that they should abandon their concealment came at a moment when she was herself ready for some unheard-of scandal. Silius may have been fated to take leave of his senses; alternatively he may have calculated that a risk was worth taking for the sake of avoiding greater risks still. He pointed out that, as they had plenty of associates with as much to fear as themselves, they need not wait for the Emperor to die of old age; that while people were innocent, no harm could come to them from long-term planning, but that blatant crime called for shameless audacity. He emphasized that, having neither wife nor child, he was ready to marry Messalina and adopt Britannicus‡ as his son. Violent as were Claudius' outbursts of anger, he was the last man to be on the alert against deception; so that, if they forestalled him, Messalina's anxieties would disappear, while her power would remain as great as ever.

It was not through any love for Claudius that Messalina hesitated to accept these overtures; she was afraid that, once he had achieved supreme power, Silius might assess at its proper value a *liaison* which as long as it was dangerous had seemed attractive, and scorn her for the adulteress that she was. On the other hand, because of its utter out-rageousness—the last pleasure for anyone so completely abandoned—she had a passion to be called Silius' wife. So as soon as the opportunity

---

★ '*Quae non faciet quod principis uxor*', Juvenal 6,617 (of Caesonia, wife of Gaius Caligula who—so scandal declared—gave him an aphrodisiac which, since it was far too strong, drove him out of his mind).

† What follows, to page 103, is a free translation of Tacitus *Annals* xi, 26–38.

‡ Son of Claudius and Messalina.

arose—a visit by Claudius to Ostia for some sacrificial purpose—she went through the formal ceremonial of a marriage service.

I appreciate that this will seem like a story which only a novelist could have invented: that in a city where everything that happened was known and broadcast, anyone at all should have felt such blind assurance—more than this, that a consul-designate and the Empress should fix a day, invite witnesses to sign the marriage contract and meet together as if, 'for the procreation of children'; that she should listen to the words of the ceremony, assume the veil and sacrifice to the gods; that they should have taken their places at the wedding breakfast, have kissed and embraced, and finally should have spent the night as a freshly married couple. But the facts as I give them are what people of an older generation than mine have been told and have described; without one element of sensationalist invention.

The Palace staff was aghast, in particular the holders of the most powerful—and, if Claudius were unthroned, most dangerous—posts. Earlier scandals, like the occasions when the ballet dancer Mnester took the Emperor's place in bed, had not threatened the Emperor's life. A young man of good family, handsome and intelligent, already on the verge of holding the consulship, was something different. He was playing for bigger stakes, and after this marriage it was easy enough to see what the next step would be. The courtiers no longer spoke in whispers, but vented their fury openly; without any doubt at all, they were frightened men: Claudius was so feeble, clay in the hands of his wife, and plenty of men were dead on her instructions already. As against this, they based their hopes on the Emperor's pliability and thought that, if they could make the first move, and stun him with the outrageousness of her crime, they might destroy her by getting her condemned before ever a charge was brought against her. It would be fatal to give him the opportunity of listening to her defence; his ears must be stopped even against hearing her full confession.

Discussions were therefore held between the freedmen Callistus, Narcissus and Pallas, whose influence was then at its greatest height, at which they discussed the possibility of concealing what they knew and proceeding by a series of quiet warnings to persuade Messalina to abandon her passion for Silius. They abandoned the idea on account of the danger to themselves—Pallas, because he was a coward, Callistus because he had learnt from experience of the rule of Gaius Caligula that power is more safely preserved by cunning than by foolhardiness. Narcissus alone refused to let the matter drop. He changed his ground merely to the extent of deciding that nothing must be said to warn Messalina of the charge being made against her or of the person of her accuser. During the Emperor's long absence at Ostia he awaited his opportunity and in the end selected Claudius' two favourite mistresses and by bribery and promises induced them to inform Claudius of the facts. If Messalina was out of the way, their own power would be all the greater, as Narcissus pointed out to them. Their names were Calpurnia and Cleopatra.

The first time they were alone, Calpurnia fell to the ground at Claudius' feet and cried out, 'Messalina is married to Silius', and then turned to Cleopatra, who was waiting there ready, and said, 'Have you heard about it?' When Cleopatra said 'Yes', she insisted that Narcissus should be sent for. Narcissus arrived, profuse in apology for having pretended to know nothing about Messalina's affaires with men like Vettius and Plautius. 'As for this present matter,' he said, 'I am not going to make any charges of adultery, because then you might ask him to return the palace, slaves and all the other perquisites of empire that she has given him. You can let him keep them, but you must make him give back your wife and rescind his marriage to her. Because I suppose you know you have been divorced? Silius is married to her. The ceremony has been witnessed by the Senate, the troops and the crowds in the streets. There is no time to lose. Her husband is master of Rome.'

Claudius immediately summoned his most powerful counsellors, first the Minister of Food (Praefectus Annonae) and then the Commander of the Praetorian Guard, and questioned them. They told him that the report was accurate, and other people crowded round with advice. 'Go to the barracks. Make sure you can rely on the Guard. Your life is the important thing. There will be time to think about punishment later.' Claudius, it appears, was in such a panic that he kept on asking people, 'Am I still Emperor? Is Silius still a private citizen?'

It was now late autumn, and in a wild orgy of extravagance Messalina was celebrating a mock vintage in Silius' house. The presses were at work, with the wine pouring out. Women clad in skins were dancing like Bacchae in sacrifice or frenzy. Messalina was brandishing a wand, her hair flying loose down her back, and Silius was beside her, his brow wreathed with ivy, wearing buskins and rolling his head, surrounded by a disreputable and yelling chorus. It is said that Vettius Valens* climbed for a joke to the top of a huge tree and when he was

* He was Messalina's doctor.

asked what he saw, he replied, 'A dirty storm blowing up from Ostia.'
It is possible that there really was a storm. If not, he spoke at hazard,
and his words acquired an ironical significance in the light of later
events.

On the arrival of messengers with the news that the secret was out
and that Claudius was on his way, determined on vengeance, Messalina
disappeared into the gardens of Lucullus,* while Silius, to disguise his
fear, left with apparent nonchalance to perform his duties in the forum.
The others made off in different directions, but on the appearance of a
party of centurions any of them discovered, whether in public or in
hiding, was arrested and handcuffed. Messalina's courage did not
desert her and, though the suddenness of the disaster gave no time for
thought, she determined on a course which had often saved her before
—to meet her husband and let him see her; she also sent instructions
that their children Britannicus and Octavia should go to their father
and throw their arms around him. In addition she asked the senior
Vestal Virgin, Vibidia, to petition the Emperor as Pontifex Maximus,
and to beg mercy.

With three companions only—so suddenly did her friends desert
her—she went on foot the whole way across Rome and on the road to
Ostia she secured a lift on a refuse cart. Nobody felt any pity for her;
her scandalous outrages had made too deep an impression for that.

The Emperor and his party were equally frightened, for Geta, the
Commander of the Guard, was utterly unprincipled, and they felt no
confidence in him. Narcissus, therefore, with the backing of those
who shared his apprehension, told the Emperor that the only safe
course was to appoint a freedman Commander of the Guard for that
one day only; he offered himself for the post. And to ensure that
Claudius was not persuaded by L. Vitellius or Largus Caecina to
change his mind on the drive to Rome, he succeeded in securing a seat
for himself in their carriage.

Claudius, it was widely said later, showed little consistency, criticiz-
ing his wife's misconduct at one moment, recalling his marriage and
the extreme youth of his children the next. As Vitellius would do no
more than exclaim, 'Shocking business', 'Disgraceful affair', Narcissus
tried to induce him to speak less ambiguously and to say what he really
thought. In this he had no success; for Vitellius persisted in giving

---

* They were on the Pincio, between the present Via Due Macelli and the Porta Pin-
ciana and had been acquired by Messalina from the property of Valerius Asiaticus, after
she secured his arrest and suicide in the previous year, 47.

vague answers on which conflicting interpretations could be placed; and Largus Caecina followed Vitellius' example.

When Messalina appeared, crying out that he must listen to the mother of Octavia and Britannicus, her accuser shouted her down, referring to Silius and her marriage; and to divert Claudius' attention from her, he waved in his face incriminating documents bearing on her crimes. Soon after, just as they reached the city, Claudius would have been confronted by his children if Narcissus had not given orders for them to be withdrawn. The Vestal Virgin Vibidia, however, he was not powerful enough to remove; and she, with many reproachful expressions, insisted that his wife must not be executed before her defence was heard. Narcissus replied that the Emperor would hear the case and that she would be given every opportunity of answering the charge; the reverend lady might therefore return to the discharge of her sacred duties.

It was an extraordinary scene. Claudius might have been dumb; Vitellius' attitude was that of a man utterly in the dark as to what was happening; the freedman was in complete control. He issued his orders. The house of the adulterous Silius was to be opened, and that was where the Emperor was to go. As soon as they were in the house, he pointed to the portrait of Silius' father which by a senatorial regulation had no right to be there, and to the heirlooms of the Emperor's own family, the Nerones and Drusi, which Silius had acquired as a reward for his infamous conduct. Claudius was by this time both angry and threatening. Narcissus took him to the barracks, where a group of soldiers had been detailed to crowd round and, after preliminary admonition from Narcissus, Claudius made a short speech to them. He was indignant, and with reason, but could hardly express himself for shame. After this a great roar of noise came from the troops, demanding to know the names of the offenders and insisting that they be punished. When Silius was brought on to the platform, he made no attempt at defence or at delay; he simply asked to be put to death quickly.

A large number of other accomplices were executed summarily, Mnester being the only one to cause any delay. He tore his clothes off and shrieked to Claudius to look at the weals on his body, and not to forget that it was on Claudius' own instruction that he had placed himself under Messalina's orders. It was not for money or power, like the others, but from simple necessity that he had become involved; and if Silius' plot had succeeded, he would have been the first victim to be eliminated. The Emperor was impressed by this and inclined to grant a pardon, but the freedmen persuaded him that it would be a mistake, after executing so many members of the nobility, to show sympathy with a ballet dancer. The man was a criminal; whether he acted voluntarily or under compulsion was quite irrelevant. . . .

All this while in the gardens of Lucullus Messalina spun out her life, putting the finishing touches to her prospective appeal, in a mood of reasonable optimism, even of occasional resentment; so well did she preserve her arrogance to the very end. Indeed if Narcissus had not had her killed quickly, the tables might have been turned, and he might well have been the victim. For after Claudius had returned to the Palace and, under the influence of an early meal and a glass of wine had relaxed and was mollified, he told someone to go to 'the poor creature' and tell her to appear to plead her case on the following morning. On the news of this Narcissus' apprehensions were roused by the thought of the Emperor's anger cooling, his affection for his wife returning and his remembering in bed that night the conjugal pleasures that he was missing. He therefore went straight out and, finding some centurions and an officer, said simply, 'The Emperor's orders. She is to be executed immediately.'

A freedman Euodius who was detailed to prevent her escape and to see the execution carried out, went straight to the gardens and there found her lying on the ground, with her mother Domitia Lepida sitting beside her.

Though Lepida had always been on bad terms with her daughter in the days of her daughter's grandeur, she was overcome with pity for her in her last extremity, and was trying to persuade her to forestall the executioner.

'Your life is at an end,' she said. 'Your only aim now should be to die honourably.'

But Messalina was vitiated by the lascivious life that she had led, and she had no spirit left. She was crying and indulging in vain self-pity when the gates were forced open. The executioners had come. Their officer stood there, saying nothing. The freedman reviled her, letting loose a torrent of indecent abuse.

It was only now that Messalina realized that there was no hope. She accepted the dagger, but her hand was shaking so violently that she could not pierce her throat or her breast. So the officer dispatched her. Her mother was allowed to take charge of the corpse, and the news was given to Claudius at the dinner-table that Messalina was dead. It was not clear from the account whether she had been killed or had committed suicide, and Claudius did not ask. He called for a drink and went on with the party. Nor did he show any normal emotion—hate, satisfaction, anger or distress—in the days which followed, as little moved by the jubilation of her accusers as by his children's grief. In fact he forgot about her; and in this he was helped by the Senate's resolution that her name was to be erased and her statues removed from all public and private sites.*

This is Tacitus' account of Valeria Messalina's end.[1] It happened in A.D. 48.

Her origins were distinguished, for she sprang from the Domitii on one side and from the Valerii Messalae on the other; and on both her father's and her mother's sides she was the great-grand-daughter of Octavia, the sister of Augustus. Claudius was her mother's first cousin. She was very beautiful[2] and still very young—no more than twenty-three years old when she died. She had married Claudius in 39 or 40, when she was only fourteen. He was thirty-four years her senior, forty-eight when she was fourteen. They had been Emperor and Empress for over seven years, since Gaius Caligula was murdered in January 41, and she was the mother of two children, Octavia and Britannicus. In view of her notorious immorality, it is remarkable that nobody seems even to have suggested that anybody but Claudius was their father.

She was lascivious, cruel and avaricious. It was perhaps not simply a sign of her rank that she made the advances always and did not receive them. She loved passionately and, when she tired of a lover she liked to see him dead: Polybius, the imperial freedman, for instance, in 47. Her rivals—like Gaius Caligula's sister Julia Livilla, with her alleged paramour, the respectable Seneca—she dispatched to banishment† or, if they had pained her deeply, as did Poppaea Sabina, 'the most beautiful woman of the age'—and an older woman, too, to increase the insult—when she stole her lover, the pantomime actor Mnester, they had to die. The elimination of Poppaea Sabina[3] was her greatest triumph of all for, by concealing Mnester's name and alleging that the distinguished consular from Gaul, Valerius Asiaticus, was Poppaea's seducer, she secured death for him and (for a year's short enjoyment) his splendid gardens for herself.

---

* From page 97 has been a translation of Tacitus *Annals* xi, 26–38.

† Julia Livilla was recalled from Ponza by Claudius on his accession; so this, her second, banishment followed hard on the heels of her first.

Without the active assistance of the imperial freedmen she could not have triumphed at such fever pitch. And she had the flabby connivance of the sycophantic and avuncular L. Vitellius, whom the Emperor trusted. How much the Emperor himself knew of her doings is one of history's secrets.

The truth, one might have thought, was scandalous enough. But in a world in which salacious imagination ran riot, in which the mysterious 'dossier of her crimes' handed by Narcissus to Claudius was an irresistible provocation to speculation and one historian, at least, Fabius Rusticus, was Seneca's friend and by his pen could avenge her treatment of him, stories spread by contrast with which the truth paled into insignificance: how she concealed her black hair under a flaxen wig and, under the name Lycisca, was regularly and inexhaustibly employed in a smoky brothel (Juvenal knew most of the salacious details, and the elder Pliny knew more); how she set up a brothel in the Palace, with women of the highest social standing for prostitutes and their distinguished husbands for pimps (Cassius Dio described it all). But, blind as Claudius was, he was not as blind as all that. And the fact that Tacitus, when he referred to her misdemeanours, made no allusion at all to such scandal is enough to prove it fiction.[4]

Her passionate attachment to C. Silius was no more than a year old; so short a time was it since she drove him to divorce his wife Junia Silana and to accept her as his mistress. 'Silius appreciated the danger; but refusal of her advances meant certain death, and he hoped that the liaison might be kept a secret. He was amply rewarded, and philosophically decided to enjoy the present and let the future take care of itself. On Messalina's part there was no concealment at all. She would come to his house attended by a huge crowd of followers; she would cling to his side when he went out, and she poured wealth and honours on him. In the end you might well have thought that the Empire had changed hands. The Emperor's slaves, his freedmen, even his heirlooms were to be found in the adulterer's house.'[5]

The handsomest man of his day, Silius belonged to a family which first achieved eminence under Augustus and in just over half a century produced five consuls and was made patrician.[6] His father, a friend of Germanicus and the elder Agrippina, commanded the Upper German armies from A.D. 14 to 21, and was driven to commit suicide in A.D. 24. Among the honours which the younger Silius owed to the influence of his imperial mistress, no doubt, was his nomination to one of the consulships of 48. He was in his early thirties (perhaps, indeed, exactly the same age as the younger Agrippina); and it was not in fact unexampled for the member of a patrician family to achieve the consulship as young as thirty-two, ten years earlier than men whose origins were less distinguished.[7]

Silius possessed more than his good looks. He was an accomplished orator; he had made a good marriage; he had the assurance of a distinguished career ahead. He had, however, the taint of ambition; and that perhaps explains the fact of his being caught in Messalina's net. Once caught, he had not a chance. That Claudius should have known nothing of their intrigue would seem incredible if there were not the example of Julia, whose brazen excesses were known to the whole of Rome before they were discovered by Augustus. When they had got away with so much, even the insanity of the marriage may have seemed a fair risk to take.

Little good did his good looks do him. That was Juvenal's theme in his tenth satire, on the vanity of human wishes:

> *Choose what thou would'st advise* Him, whom the Great*
> *Empress resolves to Marry. This so Neat*
> *Good, Noble Youth is hal'd, poor wretch, to Fate*
> *By Messalina's Eies. She Dress'd does wait*
> *In Crimson veil: The Tyrian Marriage-bed*
> *Is in the open Gardens richly spread.*
> *Ten hundred thousand Sesterces, as due*
> *Portion by Ancient Rite, she'l make good too.*
> *The South-sayer, with those that Seal, attends.*
> *This thou thought'st known but to some trusty friends.*
> *She'l marry in all Form. Now advise right:*
> *Unless he yields, he dies e're Candle-light.*
> *If thou committ'st the Crime, the Delay's small:*
> *Till the Fact's known to Rome, Rout, Prince and all.*
> *The shame of's House He shall know last: mean-while*
> *Obey: unless a few days—life seems vile.*
> *Choose yet the best, thy judgment can afford,*
> *This fair, white Neck must feel the sharp-edged Sword.†*

Even in the dissolute world of early imperial Rome the marriage of an Empress to a commoner during the lifetime of the Emperor and without his knowledge was so bizarre and fantastic that it caught the

---

* As if this was a *suasoria*, a school exercise in imaginative composition.
† Juvenal x, 329–345, tr. Barter Holyday, D.D., and late Archdeacon of Oxon., 1673.

general imagination. Two generations or so later Juvenal told the
story and moralized about it. And at least one person found it incredible, and moulded it into what he thought a more plausible form.
He suggested that Claudius knew all about the marriage, and was
indeed a witness and signatory to the contract for the dowry. This he
did—on the rationalist's ingenious hypothesis—because there had been
portents of imminent disaster such as could only be averted by this
marriage ceremony which, Claudius was assured, was a mock marriage
and nothing more. Suetonius, who repeated the story, rightly rejected
it.[8] To have had Claudius there would have spoilt the fun.

The marriage with Silius was important because it gave Narcissus
and the other freedmen who, perhaps because of Polybius' death, had
turned against her, the chance to strike. Even so, success was not
assured; and Narcissus needed to play his cards with care. Had there
been even the smallest ground for alleging that Messalina and Silius
were in conspiracy to murder Claudius or to dispossess him of the
Empire, that allegation would certainly have been made. It was not;
and several days may well have lapsed between the marriage ceremony
and the carefully planned breaking of the news to Claudius. It is clear
from Tacitus' account that, without Narcissus' hysterical incitement,
not only Claudius but his counsellors, men like Vitellius, might
easily have taken the view that this new adventure of Messalina was
not really more serious than her customary peccadillos, of which they
knew already.

In no sense did the ceremony constitute a 'legal marriage'. It was for
Messalina just a new excitement and Cassius Dio may not have guessed
badly when he wrote that Messalina had decided to go through the formality of a marriage service with her future lovers as a regular practice.[9] The social world of early imperial Rome, after all, was one which
witnessed mockeries even more fantastic. For in Nero's principate a
patrician Sempronius Gracchus, a man who demeaned himself by
fighting as a *retiarius* in the arena, was formally married to a boy, a
cornet-player, paying a dowry of 400,000 sesterces.[10] In A.D. 64 Nero,
wearing the flaming veil of a bride, was one party in a formal marriage
service; some dissolute young man from among his friends was the
other.[11]

Messalina's death brought sorrow to her two young children, but to
nobody else. That on the day after her death her absent-minded husband noticed her absence from the dinner-table and asked where she

was, is hardly to be believed. The story is an echo of the time when, ignorant of the fact that Messalina had driven Poppaea Sabina to suicide a few days earlier, he asked Poppaea's husband at dinner why he had come without his wife.[12] To which the husband replied smartly that he was sorry to have to tell the Emperor that his wife had died.

It may well be true, however, that in an address to the Guard, Claudius said, 'Since my marriages have been so unsuccessful, I shall remain unmarried; and if I break my undertaking, you have my permission to stab me to death.'[13] Yet already he felt the need for a new wife, and the freedmen were in competition to make the choice for him. There were three candidates for his bed: Aelia Paetina, to whom he had been married before, and by whom he had a daughter, Antonia; Lollia Paulina, who had been married to Gaius and knew already what it was to be an Empress; and Julia Agrippina, his niece, Nero's mother.[14]

With the strong backing of the freedman Pallas, Agrippina was selected. The marriage was ominously incestuous; but the Senate exerted decorous pressure, and the Emperor made a decorous show of submission.[15] The definition of incest was amended, and others were free to follow the Emperor's lead. Two men availed themselves of the opportunity—a centurion, whose marriage the Emperor and the new Empress attended, and a freedman's son.[16] So Suetonius records; *se non è vero, è ben trovato*.

II. The Death (in A.D. 59) and Life of the Empress Agrippina

*C. Vipsanius and C. Fonteius entered on their consulship and Nero now committed the crime on which he had been brooding for a considerable time. He had been Emperor long enough† to acquire a confident audacity, and his passion for Poppaea grew ever greater as the days passed. Knowing that, as long as Agrippina remained alive, Nero would never divorce Octavia and marry her, Poppaea often taunted him and sometimes made fun of 'the baby prince', as she called him, on the ground that he took his orders from other people and, so far from being a ruler, was not even independent.

'Why do we not get married? Is it my looks that you object to? Or, despite its triumphs, is my eminent family not grand enough for you? Are you afraid of my not having children? Or of my not really loving

* What follows, to page 115, is a free translation of Tacitus *Annals* xiv, 1ff.
† Since 54.

you? I know what it is: you are terrified that, once I am your wife, I shall open your eyes to the injuries which members of the Senate have suffered from your mother and to the universal detestation felt for her arrogance and greed. If the only daughter-in-law that Agrippina can tolerate is one who works against her son, then I should like to be allowed to return to Otho; after all, he is my husband. I would rather live miles from Rome and hear reports of the insults to which the Emperor is exposed than witness them with my own eyes and be involved, like him, in danger.' By bursting into tears she ensured, like the clever adulteress that she was, that her words struck home. Nobody discouraged her, because everybody wanted to see Agrippina's power smashed, and it occurred to nobody that Nero's hatred would go to the length of murder.

Agrippina's determination not to relinquish her hold on him was such—according to the historian Cluvius—that on a number of occasions in broad daylight when he was tipsy after dinner she appeared before him elaborately made up, with the unmistakable suggestion of incest. She kissed him with indecent passion, and wheedled him to her criminal purpose. Other people at the table noticed and, when one woman so employed her wiles, Seneca sought help from another, the girl Acte, whose father had been a slave and who shared his concern both because of the danger to herself and because of the danger in which Nero was involved. He got her to tell Nero that everybody was saying that he had committed incest, that his mother was boasting about it and that the troops were not prepared to tolerate that kind of an Emperor. Fabius Rusticus confirms that it was by this ruse on the part of the slave's daughter that the scandal was averted; but according to his account Nero, not his mother, planned the outrage.[17]

Other writers confirm Cluvius' version of the story, and that is the general tradition. Agrippina may in fact have entertained this outrageous project; or perhaps, on her past record, no sexual novelty on her part seemed incredible. Ambition had driven her to become Lepidus' mistress when she was a young woman; for a similar purpose she went to any length to satisfy Pallas' wishes; and marriage with her uncle was a training in abomination.

Nero was careful therefore never to be alone with her; and when she went off into the parks or into the country—to Tusculum or to Antium (Anzio)—he expressed his approval of her taking a holiday. But in the end he realized that she was an intolerable nuisance, wherever she was, and decided that she must die. The only question was whether to use poison, the knife or some other form of violence. To his first idea—poison—there were a number of objections. It must either be administered at an imperial dinner party and there, in view of the way in which Britannicus had died, it could hardly appear an accident; or else the woman's own servants would have to be seduced, which would be difficult since her own criminal experiences had taught her to forestall attempts on herself; and, anyhow, she was immune, having dosed herself regularly with antidotes. To dispatching her by cold steel there were two objections: nobody could think of a way in which it could be done quietly; and in the case of a murder of such importance there was the fear that an assassin might shrink from obeying his instructions.

In the end the freedman Anicetus, who was in command of the fleet at Misenum, applied his brains to the problem; he had tutored Nero as a boy and hated Agrippina as heartily as she hated him. He explained that it would be possible to build a ship part of which could be made by a contrivance to come loose when out at sea. She would be thrown into the water, with no idea of the cause. 'At sea,' he said, 'any mishap is possible. If she perishes in a shipwreck nobody in the world will be so malignant as to place a criminal interpretation on a mischance attributable to wind and wave. As Emperor, you will naturally dedicate a temple and altars to her as soon as she is dead and in other ways make an ostentatious display of the devotion you felt for her.'

This ingenious suggestion was accepted; it came at just the right moment; he always went to Baiae for the festival of Minerva* and now he persuaded his mother to join him. To spread belief in a reconciliation which Agrippina with optimistic feminine credulity might swallow, he went about saying that when a man's parents were angry he must submit and be reconciled. She arrived by sea from Antium, and Nero went down to the landing stage, gave her his hand, embraced her and escorted her to Bauli, a villa between Cape Misenum and the bay of Baiae, right on the sea. One of the ships at anchor was better turned out than the rest, giving the impression that this too was a mark of honour for his mother, who had normally travelled in a warship manned by marines.

She was then invited to dinner, so that, perpetrated in the darkness of night, the crime might go unobserved. At this point it is reasonably certain that somebody revealed the plot to Agrippina, but she could not make up her mind whether to believe it or not. However, she travelled to Baiae by chair. There the warmth of her reception banished her

* March 19–23.

fear; Nero greeted her affectionately and placed her in the place of honour at table. Conversation was animated, Nero sometimes talking with boyish affection, sometimes in a grave manner as if he was confiding important matters of policy. The party broke up late, and he accompanied her as she left, gazing into her eyes and embracing her tenderly. He played his part to the bitter end—unless, of course, for all his inhumanity, he was genuinely affected by the knowledge that his mother was going to her death and that he would never see her again.

As if with the deliberate purpose of exposing the crime, Providence ordained that the night should be clear and starry and the sea calm. Two friends were in attendance on Agrippina, Crepereius Gallus, who stood near the helm and Acerronia, who sat leaning over Agrippina's feet. The ship had not travelled far and Acerronia was talking happily about Nero's change of heart and the reconciliation between him and his mother when, at a given signal, the roof, which carried a heavy weight of lead, collapsed on top of Crepereius, who was squashed and killed immediately. Agrippina and Acerronia were saved by the raised sides of the couch, which, as it happened, were strong enough to take the weight. The ship itself did not break up because in the general confusion the large number of those who were not privy to the plot got in the way of those who were.

The oarsmen decided to move over to one side of the ship and so topple it over; but, acting on the spur of the moment, they did not agree quickly enough to do this, and there were others who balanced them by going over to the opposite side; so it was possible to drop more gently into the sea. Acerronia was unwise enough to cry out, 'I am Agrippina. Help for the Emperor's Mother'; she was bashed to death with poles, oars and any other naval tackle handy. Agrippina, who kept her mouth shut and was therefore unrecognized, escaped with a single wound in the shoulder; she swam until she was picked up by small sailing boats which arrived on the scene. They took her to the Lucrine Lake, and from there she was carried back to her villa.

Agrippina now appreciated the full significance of the deceitful invitation and of the high distinction which she had been accorded, as of the fact that, only just offshore, without being struck by a gust of wind or running on to a rock, the ship had collapsed from the deck downwards, like a contrivance on the stage. In view of Acerronia's death, and her own wound, her best precaution against a further attempt was to conceal what she had discovered. So she sent a freedman Agerinus to tell Nero that by the grace of god and thanks to his own good fortune she had escaped a serious accident and, because immediate rest was what she needed, to request him, for all his alarm at her danger, to wait before he called. She herself was careful to betray no anxiety; she dressed her wound and took a restorative. As far as Acerronia was concerned, no pretence was necessary; and Agrippina gave orders for her will to be brought to her and for her possessions to be placed under seal.

Instead of the news for which he was waiting—that the murder had been successfully accomplished—the information which reached Nero was that she had escaped with a slight wound, having been near enough to danger to be left in no doubt where the responsibility for it lay.

Nero was panic-stricken, crying out, 'She will be here at any moment, set on revenge, I swear she will. She will arm her slaves. She will incite the troops to mutiny. She will appeal to the Senate and People. She was shipwrecked and wounded and her friends were killed: that is the charge that she will make. What can *I* do against her?' Burrus and Seneca were his only hope.

Whether or not* they were privy to his plot, he had them woken and summoned immediately. For a long time neither of them spoke. There was no point in trying to dissuade him, if they were bound to fail; and they may have believed the situation so desperate that, if Agrippina was not dispatched, Nero would have to die.

Seneca spoke first. He looked Burrus in the eyes, and asked a question. Should the troops be given orders to kill her? Burrus replied, 'The loyalty of the praetorians is to every member of the imperial family. They remember Germanicus and will certainly refuse to lift a hand against his daughter. Anicetus made a promise; he had better perform it.'

Without wavering Anicetus called for leave to direct the murder. Nero then said, 'Today I become Emperor; and for this great promotion I am indebted to a freedman. Go quickly and take men who obey orders and waste least time about it.' Then, hearing that Agerinus had come with news from Agrippina he deliberately staged the ground for a charge by dropping a sword at his feet as he was delivering her message. As if the man had been caught red-handed, he ordered his arrest. The false account which he proposed to publish was that, humiliated by the detection of the crime, she had committed suicide.

As the news of Agrippina's—assumedly accidental—mishap spread, people came running down to the shore as soon as they heard it. They

* Obviously not; or why were they asleep?

clambered on to the harbour works, even into boats at anchor; some even waded into the sea until they were almost out of their depth; and some stretched out their hands. The shore was packed with people asking every kind of question and giving answers which were no answers at all—wailing, praying, shouting; and a large crowd came flocking down with lights. Then the news spread that she was safe, and they prepared to go and congratulate her; but then they saw the troops, armed and menacing, and scattered.

Having posted soldiers round the villa, Anicetus forced the front door, arrested every slave he saw and so reached the door of her bed-room, where a few servants were standing, the rest having fled in terror when the troops broke in. Inside the bedroom, which was poorly lit, Agrippina was alone with one of her slave-girls; she felt increasingly worried by the fact that no one, not even Agerinus, had come from her son, and reflected that, if things had gone well, the atmosphere would have been different; this sudden tumult, following on her abandon-ment, portended the worst. Then the slave-girl went and as she was saying, 'Are you deserting me too?', she looked behind her and saw Anicetus and his escort, a ship-captain called Herculeius and a naval officer called Obaritus. She said, 'If you have come to inspect me, please report that I am feeling better. If you have come to kill me, I refuse to believe that my son has given orders for his mother's death.' The murderers stood round her couch and the captain hit her on the head with a club. When the officer drew his sword to kill her, she pointed to her womb and said, 'This is the place to strike.'

She was struck repeatedly and died.

The facts about her death are in no doubt; but on the question whether Nero looked at his mother's corpse and praised her figure, divergent views have been expressed. She was laid out on a dinner couch and cremated that same night in the cheapest manner; and as long as Nero was emperor her ashes were never given decent burial. She had her servants to thank for the fact that later she was given a humble grave in the hills near the road to Misenum and the villa which be-longed to Julius Caesar the dictator, and looks down on the bay.

When the pyre was lit, a freedman of hers called Mnester stabbed himself to death, either because of his devotion to his patroness or be-cause he feared execution anyhow.

For several years Agrippina had anticipated this violent death, but she had not been worried by the prospect. For, when she consulted astrologers about Nero, she had received the answer, 'He will be

Emperor and will kill his mother.' She said, 'He is welcome to kill me, as long as he becomes Emperor.'

The crime had been committed before Nero appreciated its full import. The rest of the night he spent partly in petrified silence, though several times he jumped up in a panic, and he was out of his mind, waiting for the day to break, as if it would bring his own death-sentence with it. His restoration to hope and strength he owed to Burrus, at whose instigation the centurions and officers were first in the field with their flattery, shaking him by the hand and congratulating him on his escape from sudden danger and from his mother's attempt on his life. Next his friends started to go to the temples* and, following this lead, neighbouring towns sacrificed and sent deputations to him in expression of their delight. He was their match in insincerity —plunged into mourning, weeping over his mother's death and angrily disappointed, as it seemed, in the fact of his own survival.

Places do not wear false expressions, like people; and, confronted by the sinister sight of the sea and coast where it had all happened—it was even believed by some that trumpets sounded from the surrounding hills and wailing from his mother's grave—he moved to Naples. From Naples he sent a dispatch to the Senate to the general effect that one of Agrippina's most trusted freedmen had been discovered with a weapon and that, conscious of her guilt on account of her intended crime, she had paid the penalty.

He raked up further charges from the past, claiming that she had aspired to partnership with him in imperial rule, and had intended that the guard should take the oath to her—a woman—and that Senate and people should be similarly humiliated; that, once her claims were frustrated, she had turned against the army, the Senate and the plebs, had tried to persuade him against any act of public charity and had plotted against the lives of distinguished statesmen. It had required considerable efforts on his part to prevent her from forcing her way into the Senate and dealing on her own with the requests of foreign embassies. He managed indirectly to criticize the administration of Claudius by attributing to his mother the responsibility for the abuses of that authoritarian régime. Her death, he said, was Rome's good fortune. He even gave an account of the shipwreck—as if anyone could be foolish enough to believe that this was an accident, any more than that a plot to destroy the imperial cohorts and fleet was to be

---

* At Rome the Arval Brothers met, having received the news, but did not sacrifice, on March 28th; they sacrificed in thanksgiving for his escape on April 5th.[18]

detected in the dispatch with a weapon of a single man by a half-drowned woman. Though Nero's brutality was beyond all terms of remonstrance, it was not against him but against Seneca that criticism was directed; the speech was an open confession of guilt, and Seneca was assumed to be its author.

In the Senate at Rome there was hot competition among the politicians; they decreed thanksgivings before all the gods, the institution of annual games to commemorate the detection of the plot during the festival of Minerva, the erection of a gold image of Minerva side by side with a portrait statue of the Emperor in the Senate House, and the degradation of Agrippina's birthday* to be a day of ill-omen. Previously when sycophantic honours were decreed, Paetus Thrasea had either declined to speak or had passed them over with curt assent; but on this occasion he involved himself in future trouble, without bringing freedom any nearer to other people, by what he did. He got up and walked out of the House.

There were a large number of quite pointless prodigies. One woman gave birth to a snake, another was killed by a thunderbolt in bed with her husband. There was a sudden eclipse of the sun and all fourteen districts of Rome were struck by lightning. So far were these events from showing the hand of god that Nero's criminal rule continued for many years to come.

To aggravate his mother's unpopularity and to show his own greater tender-heartedness now that she was dead, he brought home people whom Agrippina had had banished: two women of good families, Junia Calvina and Calpurnia, and two ex-praetors, Valerius Capito and Licinius Gabolus. He even gave permission for the ashes of Lollia Paulina to be brought back and enclosed in a tomb. He reprieved two men whom he had banished recently, Iturius and Calvisius. Silana whose disgrace was attributed to Agrippina's hostility, had fallen ill and died at Tarentum, on her way back from her remote exile, at the time when Agrippina was losing her power, or at least her vindictiveness.

Nero stayed in Campania because he could not decide in what style to enter Rome, and wondered whether he would receive an obsequious welcome from the Senate and an ovation from the people. The most discreditable of his courtiers—and such men abounded as in no other reign—assured him that the name of Agrippina was detested and that

---

* November 6th. The Acts of the Arval Brothers for A.D. 57 and 58 record sacrifices to Juppiter, Juno, Minerva, Salus publica, Concordia (ipsius), on both occasions.[19]

his own popularity had increased as a result of her death. They urged him to discard all fear and to go and see for himself what it was like to have Rome at his feet. They demanded the right to walk in front of him. *They found greater enthusiasm than they had promised— people drawn up by tribes, the Senate in gala dress, wives and children arranged in formation, the children according to their ages, boys and girls separately. Tiers of seats had been erected on the route, just as if it was a triumph.

In proud arrogance, celebrating his triumph over the servility of Rome, he proceeded to the Capitol and paid his vows. After which he gave free play to those gross appetites which respect for his mother, however slight, may not have suppressed before, but had at least impeded.†

This is Tacitus' account of Agrippina's end, derived from historians who wrote not long after the tragedy occurred. The scandalous suggestion of incest is not to be taken seriously for, from the Republic onwards, this tasteless imputation was made too commonly about prominent people to carry any conviction; what salacious gossip tediously invented, uncritical—or unprincipled—historians, like so many parrots, repeated.

Other historians add little to Tacitus' story. If Nero survived to rule for another nine years, at least—Suetonius records—he suffered from bad dreams.[21] Anicetus did not suffer at all. He rid Nero of his mother and, three years later, with the same sinister competence he rid Nero of his wife; after that he retired in comfortable prosperity, and died a natural death.[22]

That it was at Poppaea's suggestion and for Poppaea's sake that Nero killed his mother, may at first appear unlikely; for why did he wait another three years before he divorced Octavia and married her? Yet, as will be seen, the suggestion may well be true.

In Messalina and Agrippina Claudius had, for his third and fourth wives, two outstandingly beautiful women. There is greater refinement, perhaps, in Agrippina's more sharply drawn features than in the fuller face of the lascivious Messalina. In the matter of sex Agrippina may not have inherited the exemplary moral character of that model wife, her mother; but her indiscretions were premeditated, committed

* From the records of the Arval Brothers, it seems that he was thought in Rome to be returning on June 23rd, and was back in Rome on September 11th.[20]

† From page 107 to this point has been a free translation of Tacitus, *Annals* xiv, i–13.

only in the interest of a consuming political ambition which itself was a part of her inheritance from her mother. Germanicus was her father; she inherited neither the weakness of his character nor the strength of his great personal charm.

Of the eight children of Germanicus and the elder Agrippina, six survived infancy—three boys and, born after the boys, three girls. Gaius Caligula was the youngest of the boys. Agrippina, born in A.D. 15, was the eldest of the girls. The name of Cologne perpetuates her birthplace; called Ara Ubiorum or Oppidum Ubiorum (capital of the Ubii) since its foundation by M. Agrippa, her grandfather, it was made a Roman colony and called Colonia Agrippinensis in her honour when she had become consort of the Emperor Claudius in A.D. 50.[23]

She was only four years old when her father Germanicus died so tragically in Syria in A.D. 19. Her home for the next ten years was as unhappy as any in Rome; with her brothers and sisters, she was nurtured on stories of her mother's real and imagined wrongs. The Emperor Tiberius was no friend of the family; his powerful minister Sejanus was its open enemy. The blow fell in 29, when her mother Agrippina and her eldest brother were banished. Her brother Drusus was arrested a year later.

By this time Agrippina was emancipated from her family. She was married in A.D. 28, at the normal age of thirteen, to Cn. Domitius Ahenobarbus, a man who so little resembled his distinguished father, the consul of 16 B.C., as to be described, fairly enough, as 'a man who was in every aspect of his life utterly detestable'.[24]

By A.D. 32 Sejanus was dead; but so were Agrippina's mother and her two elder brothers. Then, after five more gloomy years, the clouds lifted. On March 16th, 37 Tiberius was dead and two days later Agrippina's brother Gaius Caligula was Emperor. Five years too late, their mother's ambition was achieved.

Gaius was bound to his three sisters by the closest ties of affection. This understandable and happy outcome of their sad upbringing provoked, in Roman *salons*, monotonously salacious talk of incest. The sisters received unusual public honours. One distinction which cannot but appear bizarre, since all three were married, was the status of 'Honorary Vestal Virgins'. Agrippina was even pregnant; and on December 15th, 37 she gave birth to Nero. It may or may not be true that, in answer to his friends' congratulations, her husband replied that 'any child of Agrippina and himself must be a loathsome object and a public disaster.'[25]

Agrippina, happily, was not to be long troubled by such coarse-mindedness; for Domitius contracted dropsy and in two years' time was dead. For Agrippina the all-important fact was that she had achieved what neither the Emperor nor her sisters had achieved; she had a son. For the next fourteen years she re-lived her mother's ambition, to be mother to an Emperor.

At the start she made a bad false step. In as far as Gaius (himself only twenty-six years old) had indicated a prospective successor, it was M. Aemilius Lepidus, husband of his favourite sister Drusilla. Drusilla died in A.D. 38; and nothing was more natural than that Agrippina should want Lepidus for a husband. Though her husband Domitius was still alive, she became Lepidus' lover. Whether or not she was involved in his plotting to overthrow Gaius Caligula, is not to be known. The Emperor was forewarned; and in A.D. 39 at Mainz, to which Gaius had gone with Lepidus and his two surviving sisters, the plot was exposed. Lepidus was executed and, with cynical and adroit brutality, Gaius handed Agrippina the urn containing his ashes, with the instruction that she should carry it back to Rome. She and her sister Julia Livilla were banished to the islands—to Ponza—and Gaius gave himself the amusement of auctioneering their possessions at Lyons.[26] This in the winter of 39/40. In 40 Ofonius Tigellinus (twenty-two years later Nero's prefect of the praetorian guard and one of his most disastrous intimates) was banished on the allegation that Agrippina had been his mistress.[27]

This was disaster; and, had Gaius not been murdered at Rome in January 41, it would have been a final disaster. But Claudius recalled her and restored her the value of her property. Domitius was dead, and she looked round for another husband. She would have liked, it was said, to marry Galba; and, had she succeeded, Roman history would have taken a different course.[28] In the end she married Passienus Crispus, consul for the second time in 44. He was a wit and, with a fortune of 200 million sesterces, a wealthy wit. His wife Domitia, whom he now divorced, was Agrippina's sister-in-law. So, as he had no children of his own, it might be hoped that he would share Agrippina's interest in the promotion of her son—his stepson and his nephew.

Nero's prospects were less bright than they had been once; for the Emperor Claudius had a son of his own, Tiberius Claudius, later to be called Britannicus, one of the two children of his marriage with Messalina. Britannicus had been born in 41 and so was three or four years younger than Nero. For him and for his sister Octavia life was to hold little but tragedy. They were both, perhaps, cowed children. Nero, though anything but cowed, was not an attractive boy; in the search for popularity his strongest asset was the fact that he was grandson of Germanicus. For there was in Germanicus some romantic quality which people remembered even a generation after he was dead.

Messalina's mother Domitia Lepida was sister to Domitius Ahenobarbus; so Messalina was Agrippina's niece. There was no open rupture between them, perhaps because Agrippina was perspicacious enough to anticipate, and patient enough to await, Messalina's ultimate downfall. When it came she was ready with intrigue, prepared to accept the powerful freedman Pallas as her paramour for the sake of his influence with her uncle Claudius. Pallas succeeded; Passienus was disposed of; the law of incest was disregarded; and she married her uncle in A.D. 49. Claudius and his court felt again the domineering influence of a powerful woman.

'From this moment the country was transformed. Complete obedience was accorded to a woman—and not a woman like Messalina who toyed with national affairs to satisfy her appetites. This was a rigorous, almost masculine despotism. In public, Agrippina was austere and often arrogant. Her private life was chaste—unless power was to be gained. Her passion to acquire money was unbounded. She wanted it as a stepping-stone to supremacy.'*

Within a year of the marriage Nero had been adopted by Claudius and was Claudius' elder son; and he was married to Claudius' daughter Octavia. Agrippina had become 'Augusta'—the second woman in Roman history to carry this honourable name in her lifetime, the first to carry it in the lifetime of her husband.[29] In no time at all her career was open to all her talents; and the personal support that she was likely to need was at her disposal. She trusted Pallas; the respectable Seneca (banished in 41 on the allegation of adultery with her sister Julia Livilla) was recalled in 49, to be Nero's tutor (who was tutor to Britannicus?); and Burrus—well aware to whose influence he owed his promotion—was given the command of the praetorian guard without a colleague in 51. She used, and despised, them both. Two years later as a precaution—unnecessary perhaps—her sister-in-law, Messalina's mother, Domitia Lepida, was put out of the way on a trumped up charge.

'First, however, out of feminine jealousy, she destroyed Domitia

* Tacitus *Annals* xii, 7, 5ff., tr. M. Grant (Penguin Classics).

Lepida, who regarded herself as Agrippina's equal in nobility. In beauty, age and wealth there was little between them. Moreover both were immoral, disreputable and violent, so they were as keen rivals in vice as in the gifts of fortune. But their sharpest issue was whether aunt or mother should stand first with Nero. Lepida sought to seduce his youthful character by kind words and indulgence. Agrippina, on the other hand, employed severity and menaces—she could give her son the empire, but not endure him as Emperor.'*

Claudius himself was already doomed when Narcissus, whose power Pallas had already usurped, sought to open Claudius' eyes and to persuade him to interest himself in the future of his own son. It was too late; for—the historians tell us—Agrippina by now was prepared to dispose of her tediously unnecessary husband. Poison was to be the means. A professional female poisoner, a Gallic woman called Locusta, was engaged. The poison, it is said, was administered in a dish of mushrooms. 'Claudius ate the mushrooms after which he ate no more.' Exercising that wit which the most dissolute of the Julio-Claudians inherited as a part of their birthright, Nero called mushrooms 'the food of the gods'. For, once dead, Claudius was officially consecrated; he was now a god.[30]

In a comic masque, however, written by Seneca for the amusement of Nero and the Court and called 'Claudius into Pumpkin' (*Apocolocyntosis*) the playful suggestion was made that he did not become a god at all; instead, when he reached Heaven and sought admission, he was blackballed by the gods and sent shambling down to hell instead, and there he was put on trial and condemned to be a slave to his nephew and imperial predecessor Gaius. As for his dying—the Fates had ended his life because they thought that the Roman world had suffered too much from him already. There is no mention of poison. But this, after all, was a merry piece of buffoonery; it was not composed with any sinister purpose, like the play in *Hamlet*.[31]

There is a grim irony about the thought of Agrippina's dispatching Claudius by poison. For it had been the obsession of her mother Agrippina, and no doubt impressed by her on her children, that Germanicus, who was Claudius' elder brother, had been poisoned.

If Claudius really was poisoned. . . . The gruesome accounts vary. The most detailed of the stories is told by Tacitus and by Suetonius, but by no other author. By this account, the professional poisoner failed. Claudius was sick enough to be safe. So a second poisoner was

* Tacitus *Annals* xii, 64, 4–6, tr. M. Grant (Penguin Classics).

quickly pressed into service—the doctor—who tickled Claudius'
throat with a feather drenched with a second and more insidious
poison.[32]

That, from the moment of his death, it was commonly assumed in
Rome that Claudius had been poisoned by his wife, is not to be doubted.
But in societies like that of the early Roman Empire the cause of anybody's death had only to be intestinal for poison to be the common,
ill-informed diagnosis on the part of the scandal-monger.[33] It is not
impossible that, so far from being murdered, Claudius died a natural
death. He was always disgustingly greedy. Too many mushrooms for
dinner, perhaps? Bad indigestion? A weak heart? Who can tell?

Poison or no poison, Nero's champions—Agrippina and Burrus—
acted with determination and speed. Nero was acclaimed by the
Guard; he was accepted by the Senate. Nobody has recorded what
Britannicus thought or felt.

Nero's accession should have been the journey's end for Agrippina's
ambition. But, once exercised, power—and vengeance—is not so
easily relinquished. Narcissus was her next victim. He was imprisoned
and dead before Nero was given the chance to interfere. And after
that, in the streets, even when he received the Senate in the palace,
Agrippina was always at Nero's side. Had she been taxed with this, it is
easy to imagine her reply. Nero was so young still, and she was not
sure that she really trusted either Seneca or Burrus . . .

Nero made his first protests. With no little courage, he dismissed
Pallas. Alive to her own danger, Agrippina sought to frighten Nero by
threatening to reveal the sinister facts which lay behind his own
accession to the Empire; she was prepared to come out in public in
support of Britannicus' just claims. Nero took heed. He re-engaged
Locusta, and Britannicus was poisoned at an imperial dinner party.
This—in 55 A.D.—was his first imperial triumph; his second was the
eviction of Agrippina from the Palace to live in a private house in
Rome.

Her fall from power was manifest. She was vulnerable now, and
the attack came quickly. It was launched by two women as unscru-
pulous as Agrippina herself. The wealthy Junia Silana was one;
Agrippina's sister-in-law Domitia (sister of Domitia Lepida) was the
other. They had the satisfaction, both of them, of repaying long-
incurred debts of malice. Domitia had Agrippina to thank for the loss
of her husband Passienus Crispus. Junia had been the wife of C. Silius
until Messalina wrecked their lives as well as her own; after that Agrip-

pina had contrived by her slander to prevent her from making a second marriage. Their plot was a simple one: to persuade Nero that Agrippina was now conspiring to replace him as Emperor by C. Rubellius Plautus, the great-grandson of the Emperor Tiberius.

The scheme came near to success for, unnerved with hysteria, Nero all but ordered his mother's immediate execution. Burrus saved her, calming the Emperor and pointing out to him that his mother must be given the opportunity of defending herself against the charge. He was sent, with Seneca, to take her evidence.

'Agrippina displayed her old spirit. "Junia Silana has never had a child," she said, "so I am not surprised that she does not understand a mother's feelings. For mothers change their sons less easily than loose women change their lovers. If Silana's dependants Iturius and Calvisius, after exhausting their means, can only repay the hag's favours by becoming accusers, is that a reason for darkening my name with my son's murder or loading the Emperor's conscience with mine?

'"As for Domitia, I should welcome her hostility if she were competing with me in kindness to my Nero—instead of concocting melodramas with her lover Atimetus and the dancer Paris. While I was planning Nero's adoption and official career and making all the other preparations for his accession, she was beautifying her fish-ponds at her beloved Baiae.

'"I defy anyone to convict me of tampering with the city police or provincial loyalty, or of inciting slaves and ex-slaves to crimes. If Britannicus had become Emperor, could I ever have survived? If Rubellius Plautus or another gained the throne and became my judge, there would be no lack of accusers. I should then be charged, not with occasional indiscretions—outbursts of uncontrollable love—but with crimes which no one can pardon except a son."'*

This was, perhaps, her finest hour. And, not content with this outburst, she demanded an audience with the Emperor himself. The plot had failed. Junia Silana was sent into exile; from which she returned four years later in 59, to die a natural death at Taranto, only a little too early to know that Agrippina herself was dead. Nero's aunt Domitia escaped in 55; he eliminated her—by poison, it was said—four years later.[34]

Agrippina survived four more years; and then, at Poppaea's instigation Nero decided that the time had come for her to die. It was in this interval, perhaps, that she wrote her book, an autobiography with

---

* Tacitus *Annals* xiii, 21, tr. M. Grant (Penguin Classics).

notes on the misfortunes of members of her family. It was a bitter book, no doubt. The elder Pliny read it, and so did Tacitus.[35] Even as she wrote, she must have had a shrewd suspicion of the worst misfortune of all, which was still to come.

We have many records in the early part of Nero's rule of the sacrifices of that select little body of priests, the Arval Brothers. On Agrippina's birthday in 57 and 58 and on Nero's birthday in 58 they sacrificed, among other deities, to Concordia, an object of devotion at no other period in their known history. We need no better evidence to indicate the anxiety felt in Rome generally on account of the rift between Nero and his mother.[36]

Concordia turned a deaf ear to the Arval Brothers' prayers.

On the anniversary of his accession, October 13th, in 58 the Arval Brothers made an offering to Felicity (the gods' bountiful reward to the virtuous). They sacrificed to Felicity again on June 23rd, 59, when news came that Nero was returning to Rome from Campania after his mother's death. Later in that same year on Nero's birthday (December 15th), they substituted Felicitas for Concordia. It is to be feared, indeed, that sycophancy persuaded him to accept references to the loss of his mother as 'his Felicity'. This is the point, evidently, of the greeting which Nero received: 'Your provinces of Gaul urge you, sir, to bear your Felicity like a man.'[37]

III. The Daughters of Claudius and the Womenfolk of Nero

After two betrothals, neither of which ended in marriage, Claudius married, and then divorced, Plautia Urgulanilla; she came from a distinguished Etruscan family and her grandmother had been a friend of Livia. There were two children, a boy who died of an accident and a girl born after the divorce and disowned by Claudius on the ground that he was not her father.[38]

His second wife, Aelia Paetina, he divorced 'for trifling reasons', but not before she had given birth to a daughter, Claudia Antonia. Born in about A.D. 28, Antonia was at the right age for marriage when Claudius became Emperor in 41. Her two successive husbands had curious similarities. Both carried republican names of the utmost distinction; the first was a Pompey[39] (Cn. Pompeius Magnus), the second a Sulla.[40] The claim of Pompey to his name derived from the extraordinary pretentiousness of his father, M. Crassus Frugi, consul in A.D.

27, who, because his wife Scribonia was grand-daughter of a grand-daughter of Pompey the Great, named his son in this extraordinary manner. It was necessary to go back four generations—and on his mother's side—to find the last male Pompey. Gaius Caligula had forbidden Pompey to ape his remote, if distinguished, ancestor, and stopped him calling himself 'the Great' (Magnus). Claudius restored the name, and married him to his daughter Antonia. They were married for six years; then, early in 47, pretentious father, well-bred mother and eminently-named son, all three, were executed by Claudius as dangerous persons.[41] Antonia was then married again, this time to the lethargic Faustus Cornelius Sulla Felix (half-brother of Valeria Messalina), about whose name there was no pretentiousness at all; his great-grandfather was grandson of Sulla the dictator.[42] Sulla was father of Antonia's son—to whose birth, since he had a son of his own, Claudius paid little attention—and, having survived Claudius' principate and indeed been consul in 52 and having, together with Burrus and Pallas, escaped a trumped-up charge in 55, he retired to banishment in Massilia in 58 and there was executed on Nero's orders in 62.[43]

In 62, then, Antonia—whose son died young—became a widow. In that same year her half-sister, the Empress Octavia, was ignominiously divorced by Nero and, with scarcely an interval, murdered. That frightened child of Claudius and Messalina was born in 40, a Claudia. She was given the second name—which she used—of Octavia to commemorate the fact that Augustus's sister Octavia was, by both lines of descent, her mother's great-grandmother.[44] Of her young life down to her mother's disgrace in 48, little is known beyond the fact that long before she could understand what marriage was, she knew that she was to marry the attractive L. Silanus, great-great-grandson of Augustus, to whom she was betrothed in 41, when she was one year old and he was fifteen. The period which followed was one of deceptive calm. Claudius, for all his eccentricities, was, to his daughters at least, a fond father, and Antonia's husband and the child Octavia's *fiancé* enjoyed his favour and with it the prospect of distinction. For Pompey the blow fell early in 47, for Silanus a year later, when Messalina was dead and he stood in the way of Agrippina's ambition for her son. The child, Octavia, stunned at the age of seven by her mother's disgrace and death, can hardly have comprehended the stories that she was told when, a year later in 48, by the machinations of Agrippina and that *éminence grise*, the Emperor's friend L. Vitellius, her betrothal to Silanus, then almost at the end of his praetorship, was annulled after

scandalous allegations, which even Claudius cannot have believed to be
true, of his incest with his sister.* In 49 Octavia acquired a stepmother,
Agrippina; Silanus had committed suicide on the day of Agrippina's
marriage to Claudius; and she was herself once again betrothed, this
time to her detestable cousin and now stepbrother, Nero. Already the
child had learnt to wear a mask, where her true feelings were concerned.
She was married to Nero in 53. Her father died in 54, her brother
Britannicus in 55, the first—it was said—poisoned by her stepmother,
the second by her husband.

Nero hated his cold, unemotional wife and adopted for his mistress
the freedwoman, Claudia Acte, who had been brought once as a slave
from Asia. His responsible counsellors lent their connivance for fear
that, if they discouraged him, his ardour might find even more scandalous outlets. There was even a moment of reconciliation between
him and his mother. With every appearance of condoning his irregularities, she told him that youth must have its fling and he, unasked,
sent her splendid gifts of clothing and jewellery from the imperial
wardrobe. Before long, however, Agrippina, with greater propriety,
championed the claims of her unhappy daughter-in-law. For reward,
she was evicted from the palace.[45]

In 58 occurred the event which stamped Agrippina's doom, and
Octavia's. Nero met Poppaea Sabina. For seven years he was her
passionately devoted lover.

Born probably in A.D. 31, this beautiful, intelligent, ambitious and
unprincipled woman was nine years older than Octavia and six years
older than Nero himself.

Her grandfather, C. Poppaeus Sabinus, consul in A.D. 9, and governor
of Moesia for twenty-four years, from 11 to 35, under Augustus and
Tiberius, was her only ancestor of note. Her father, an undistinguished
knight called T. Ollius, shared in Sejanus' disgrace in 31; and died
perhaps before her birth. That enabled her mother to spare the child
the dreadful name of Ollia, and to call her Poppaea Sabina instead.

Even so, she did not marry well. Her husband—in about 44, presumably—was a knight, Rufrius Crispinus[46] who, as prefect of the
praetorian guard, was agent in the arrest of Valerius Asiaticus in 47.
Her mother, the elder Poppaea Sabina (married for the second time to a
Scipio, and allegedly Asiaticus' mistress) was involved in Asiaticus' fall
and driven to suicide. In the eyes of Messalina—who had engineered

* See page 130.

the whole catastrophe—Poppaea, not Asiaticus, was the real offender. And her offence? She had supplanted the Empress in the affection of the handsome pantomime actor Mnester.*

For her daughter the years that followed were uneventful enough, except for the fact that in 51 her husband was displaced by Agrippina's influence from the command of the Guard. Then, in 58, events moved quickly. The handsome young senator M. Salvius Otho fell in love with her; so she divorced her husband and married him. He was twenty-six years old, and she was twenty-seven. It is evident that she had never moved, as her mother had moved, in the best Roman society, for Nero had never met her. Otho was fatally happy in marriage. His weaknesses were far more venial than those of others who in the early Empire rose to be Caesars, and lack of reticence was one of them. He spoke lyrically of Poppaea's charm, and Nero asked to meet her. Soon she was Nero's mistress, calculating her chances of becoming Empress.[47]

Her husband was easily removed. Though he had held no higher office than that of quaestor, Nero sent him to govern one of the most distant provinces in the Empire, Lusitania. The remaining obstacles were women, like herself: Nero's mistress Acte, Octavia, his wife and, most formidable of the three, his mother Agrippina. Agrippina despised Poppaea's birth, and hated her into the bargain.

Tacitus took pains over her description.[48] 'She had every asset except goodness. From her mother, the loveliest woman of her day, she inherited distinction and beauty. Her wealth, too, was equal to her birth. She was clever and pleasant to talk to. She seemed respectable. But her life was depraved. Her public appearances were few; she would half-veil her face at them, to stimulate curiosity (or because it suited her). To her, married or bachelor bedfellows were alike. She was indifferent to her reputation—yet insensible to men's love, and herself unloving. Advantage dictated the bestowal of her favours.'

This is a curious passage, a close reproduction of that purple passage in which Sallust[49] had described Sempronia.† So the picture is perhaps more startling than true. In particular, there is no evidence of such promiscuity in Poppaea's love affairs. Ambition led her to discard Otho in favour of Nero, but that was all. Otho never lost his love for her; Nero never tired of her.

She was beautiful, and she was smart, she was fair, and enhanced the

---

* See page 103.
† See pages 47 f.

attraction of her light auburn hair[50] by the new style of coiffure which she helped to make fashionable. Her skin was soft, thanks to the herd of five hundred wild asses, kept for her bath-milk, and to the 'Poppaean unguents' which remained in fashion long after she was dead.[51] She was intelligent and talked well. Among remarks of hers which were remembered was her wish to die before she ceased to be attractive, a wish which the gods, unkind in all else, granted to her. And, apart from conventional fascinations like astrology, she had unexpected interests—for example, Judaism.[52] Though the legend that she was a Jewish proselyte is not true, it is certain that she met Josephus at Puteoli in 64, made presents to him and used her influence to secure the release of Jews from Judaea who had been sent under arrest to Rome. She may even have used her influence at Jewish instigation for a sinister purpose; it was she perhaps who suggested to Nero in 64 that the Christians should be accused of responsibility for the fire at Rome.[53]

Agrippina was put out of the way in 59; yet, despite Poppaea's nagging—so imaginatively described by Tacitus that it might be authentic fact[54]—he was in no hurry to marry her, not because he minded her pedigree but because he wanted to be certain that she would bear him children. At last in 62 the moment came; Poppaea was pregnant.[55]

Though Nero, like other rulers in the world's history, might excusably be obsessed by the necessity of fathering sons, nothing could excuse the tasteless brutality with which Octavia was dispatched. To divorce her on the ground of sterility was not enough; it was alleged that she had committed adultery with a slave, a flautist from Alexandria. The infamous Ofonius Tigellinus, who had succeeded to the command of the Guard in this very year, inaugurated his sinister office by taking evidence from Octavia's outspoken slaves; he cannot have relished what they told him—about himself. The false allegation of misconduct was prudently forgotten and proceedings stopped short at the formalities of a civil divorce.[56] As restoration of her dowry, Octavia received Burrus' house and the estate of Nero's latest victim, Rubellius Plautus, sinister gifts both of them. She left Rome for Campania under military guard. Nero and Poppaea were married twelve days after the divorce.[57]

But now the populace, with whom Octavia was as popular as in her own household, showed its affection for her and its hatred of Poppaea. Rioting broke out in Rome. Octavia's statues were garlanded, Poppaea's overthrown. A mob even broke into the palace.[58]

In despair Nero summoned the resourceful Anicetus who, if he had failed to remove Agrippina by his ingenious ship-carpentry, had at least dispatched her in the end by cruder methods. All that was required of him now was a public statement that Octavia was his mistress.[59] In no further need of evidence, Nero ordered her removal to the island of Pandateria, and there she was at once dispatched.[60] On June 9th her veins were cut; she was suffocated in the hot chamber of a bath; her head was chopped off and sent to Poppaea. In Rome, since protests could avail no longer, sycophancy came into its own. Religious thanksgivings were held as if it was not a timid and friendless little mouse but some formidable revolutionary that had been killed.[61]

By January 21st, 63 the child had been born—at Antium—and the colleges of priests in Rome were offering their dutiful thanks to the gods. It was a daughter, called Claudia. The adulatory Senate marked the occasion by a profuse gift of honours. Poppaea was given the name 'Augusta'; so was the child. A temple was decreed to the goddess Fecundity.[62]

The echoes of popular excitement and rejoicing had hardly died before, at the age of four months, the child was dead. The Senate knew its duty; it accorded the 'divine infant' consecration.[63]

Two years later, in 65, Poppaea was expecting a second child. It was the year of the second celebration of the quinquennial games which, with the title 'Neronia', Nero had instituted in 60: contests in music, gymnastics and horse-racing. He was flushed with pride—for naturally he was victor in every contest in which he had personally engaged—and, after all the effort, understandably tired and irritable when he returned to the Palace. Rebuked by his wife for coming back late, he kicked her. A miscarriage ensued, from which she died. In defiance of all Roman tradition, she was embalmed, and her body was placed in the mausoleum of Augustus. But there was a funeral too, and Nero himself spoke the necrology. After which, like her daughter, she was declared by the Senate to have become a goddess.[64]

Though Nero never ceased to love Poppaea and was in no sense her murderer because he caused her death, he had not finished with marriage yet. There is a story that he now proposed marriage to his surviving adoptive half-sister Antonia and, insulted by her refusal, procured her death; that, perhaps, was when the story was invented which Tacitus refused to believe, that Piso, leader of the abortive conspiracy against Nero in 65, planned to divorce his wife and marry her.[65] The youthful Sporus, whose face reminded Nero of Poppaea's, he is said to have had castrated, and then to have married[66] and to have

taken as his wife to Greece in 66. If so, he took two wives; for he had
married the rich and cultured Statilia Messalina, herself the survivor of
four earlier marriages, the last of which was concluded, in Nero's best
manner, when he wanted to marry her, by the arrival of soldiers and
a quick suicide for her husband.[67] Like Nero himself, she was honoured in Bocotia with the attributes of godhead.[68] She was a woman
who managed her affairs with such prudence that she survived Nero's
débâcle in 68. Indeed there is nothing to show that she was ever in any
danger. Otho might even have married her, it was said, if he had
survived.[69]

By 66, then, the women in whose lives Nero had played his sinister
part were dead, except for Acte. She was not important enough to be
killed; and, as she was the first woman to awaken Nero's passion, she
was, appropriately, the last to show him any love. For it was she who
saw to his burial. At least Nero had brought her a fortune. One of her
freedmen, it seems, was a Christian. Some even have asked: was Acte,
before she died, a Christian convert herself?[70]

Poppaea, though she was never loved by the Roman mob, was
remembered with kindly charity by the romantic husband whom she
had discarded. For in the short period in which Otho was emperor in
69, he restored her statues.[71]

The luckless Octavia received more lasting distinction. She was
made the subject of a tragedy, the *Octavia*, which survives with the
tragedies of Seneca. Seneca cannot in fact have been its author, for the
play shows knowledge of the circumstances of Nero's death, which
occurred three years later than his own. The style, however, resembles
that of Seneca's tragedies and the play was certainly written by someone who was alive at the time of the events on which the tragedy was
based, and even a witness of them: a pupil of Seneca, perhaps, writing
early in the Flavian period.

The play was reminiscent—and consciously reminiscent—of more
than one Greek tragedy. Octavia was a second and unhappier Electra,
for her stepmother, like Electra's mother, had killed her father. But
while Electra had been able to save the life of her brother Orestes and
share in the splendidly fateful act of retribution when he murdered
Clytemnestra, Octavia had had no power to save Britannicus, that he
might avenge her wrongs. She was a second Hermione too, a barren
woman supplanted in her husband's love by the interloper Poppaea
who, like Andromache, was capable of bearing children.

Little action occurs, but a number of characters make speeches:

Octavia, sad and spiritless, waits for death, wondering why Juppiter does not strike Nero with a thunderbolt; her nurse counsels patience on the ground that Juno was rewarded for turning a blind eye to Juppiter's countless *amours*—for in the end she kept him as a patient and devoted husband; Seneca denounces the habits of contemporary society, sighing like a good Stoic for the simple innocence of primitive man. Nero gives orders for execution, like the Red Queen, to an officer of the Guard, declaring that the best emperors have always found it necessary to kill people, and that it is a sign of weakness in a ruler to pay attention to the wishes of the populace (he also rebuts Seneca's contention that passionate love exhausts itself with the mere passage of time); the ghost of Agrippina, who has broken out of the underworld, prophesies Nero's ultimate doom. Poppaea's nurse tells her that she is Thetis to Nero's Peleus; Poppaea is distraught by a horrible nightmare; a messenger announces that the people are in rebellion; so Nero gives the order, and Octavia is led off to her death.

The play has been described,[72] and with justice, as 'one of the most bizarre documents which have reached us from antiquity'. It is crude, and sometimes almost comic. Yet in parts it is deeply moving, telling of the conflict in which three frightened people are involved: Octavia, Poppaea and—here, if anywhere, the author shows his skill—Nero, who is as badly frightened as any of them.

iv. Epilogue: The Last of the Julian Ladies

Despite all this marrying and inter-marrying there was, ten years after Nero's death, only one woman alive who had the blood of the Julii in her veins. This was Junia Calvina; and there is no little irony in the fact that she was the grand-daughter of the younger Julia (who had been banished in A.D. 8, and had died twenty years later) and the great-grand-daughter of the elder Julia, who had met her doom in 2 B.C. She inherited their charm and their spirit; she was, according to Tacitus, 'handsome and shockingly unconventional'—'*sane decora et procax*'; by Seneca's description, she was infinitely gay: '*festivissima omnium puellarum*'.[73] And she inherited the misfortune of her family too; for she also was banished; though, more fortune than either Julia, she was recalled.*

She was married to L. Vitellius, brother of the later Emperor; and, for what reason we do not know, divorced. Her brother, to whom she

* See page 95.

was devoted, was the Junius Silanus to whom Octavia was betrothed. In A.D. 48, when Messalina was dead and that arch-sycophant, the elder L. Vitellius, until recently Julia Calvina's father-in-law, had decided to nail his colours to Agrippina's mast, he was charged with a double duty: to break off the engagement of Octavia and Silanus, so that Octavia could marry Nero, and to prepare the Roman public for the marriage of Agrippina to Claudius. The marriage of an uncle to his niece being by conventional Roman standards incestuous, it was not particularly imaginative of him to make incest the ground for cancelling the engagement of Silanus to Octavia, particularly as it was certain that Silanus' relations with his sister were not incestuous at all.[74] But, as is seen over and over again in the history of the late Republic and of the Empire, there was such a salacious vulgarity in the Roman mind that, where there was ostentatious affection between brothers and sisters, the word incest had only to be mentioned to command belief. So, by allegation of 'incest', which was no incest at all, the ground was prepared for, among other things, an imperial marriage which, without any question, was itself incestuous. Silanus, whose courage was as great as his charm, committed suicide on the day when Claudius and Agrippina married.* His sister had already been banished.

But, even in human affairs, the tide turns. When Nero had rid himself of his mother, he knew no better way of spiting her for the immoral scheming of which, with Octavia as his wife, he regarded himself as the chief victim, than to recall Junia Calvina.† It was too late to make amends to her brother. So she returned to Rome, saw the whole dynasty out, left a record—on a stone which survives[75]—of her great devotion to one of her freedwomen, her 'delicium', and gave Vespasian an opportunity (as other events did also) of showing on his death-bed that his sense of humour had not deserted him.[76] When it was reported to him as a sinister portent that the mausoleum of Augustus had suddenly gaped open, he replied, 'I expect that it is making room for Junia Calvina.'

* See page 124.
† See page 114.

FROM THE FLAVIANS TO CONSTANTINE

+++

1. The Flavians: Women of the Court

NERO'S death and the civil war which followed it put an end to a court whose atmosphere was one of perversion, immorality and vicious intrigue. With the accession of Vespasian the municipal upper class of Italy and even of the western provinces rose to the surface of Roman society; and the bourgeois virtue of parsimonious respectability became the fashion. No one could pretend that the reform was not long overdue.

As concerned the Court, the Flavian period is dull, as no period before or after it was dull; it contains not one single interesting woman.

Vespasian reigned without a consort. His homely wife Flavia Domitilla had died, and his only daughter had died, when he was still a commoner.[1] He kept a concubine (concubina*) in the Palace, an example which more than one of his imperial successors who were widowers in the following century were to follow. She was Antonia Caenis, a freedwoman of Antonia minor. She had been a mature woman in A.D. 50, and at Vespasian's accession she was anything but young. She liked money and she liked the power which her position gave her. Though Domitian treated her without courtesy, other people found her useful; and Roman society was never embarrassed by the fear that Vespasian might commit the imprudence of marrying her. She died in 75, and her successors, who administered satisfactorily to Vespasian's needs inside the Palace, were inconspicuous outside it.[2]

His younger son Domitian reigned from 81 to 96 and, though he may not have been a faultless ruler, he was a remarkably long-suffering husband. His wife, Domitia Longina, was the daughter of the distinguished general Corbulo, whom Nero had put to death; in 70 Domitian snatched her from her husband L. Lamia Aelianus, made her his mistress and subsequently married her.[3] She gave birth to a son

---

* On the status of a 'concubina', see pages 231 f.

who died in infancy. Rumour alleged falsely that she gave her favours to her brother-in-law Titus; and there was ample evidence, soon after Domitian's accession, that she was infatuated with the ballet-dancer Paris. Paris was executed, but Domitia's life was spared. She was banished from the Palace, but Domitian soon missed her and, ostensibly in response to public feeling (which was more effective in her case than in that of Nero's wife Octavia), he recalled her two years later, probably in 84. So successful were they in patching up their married life that in 90 there was some anticipation—unhappily unfulfilled—that she was about to have another child.[4] She rewarded her husband's forgiveness meanly, for she was a party to the conspiracy by which in 96 he was murdered. She survived another forty years, and must have been a very old lady indeed when she died, and one of her freedmen built a temple in her honour at Gabii, giving 10,000 sesterces to the town council on condition that it should hold an annual *festa* on her birthday.[5]

Domitian's elder brother and predecessor, Titus, Emperor from 79 to 81, was the only one of the Flavians whose susceptibility was the cause of anxiety at Rome. By the time of his father's accession in 69 he had buried one wife (Arrecina Tertulla) and divorced a second (Marcia Furnilla). Had popular opposition not expressed itself so strongly, his third wife—and Rome's empress—might have been a middle-aged Jewess, thirteen years older than himself. .

This splendid, loose and wealthy woman was Julia Berenice,[6] before whom and her brother Agrippa—with whom she was living in sin— Paul so eloquently described his conversion to Christianity[7] in Festus' presence at Caesarea in A.D. 60. Mommsen described her, not ineptly, as a miniature Cleopatra.

She was the daughter of King Agrippa i, born in A.D. 28, twice married (the second time to one of her uncles, by whom she had two sons) before, from the age of twenty onwards, she lived as the unmarried consort of her brother Agrippa ii. Both were involved in the Jewish troubles in Judaea under Nero; when their palace was burnt to the ground, they went over to the Roman side and, on the arrival of Vespasian, she paid her first court to his son Titus.[8] In 69, when she was a widow of forty-one, he was a widower of twenty-eight. When Vespasian became Emperor and Titus was left to finish off the Jewish war, she, with Agrippa, was in Titus' camp.[9]

In 75 she paid her first visit to Rome. Though her beauty may have begun to fade, her immense wealth was unimpaired and Titus, perhaps, was not unaware of its attraction. He was her lover, and it may even be true that he proposed marriage to her. But she presumed too fast and too far; philosophers preached against her, and the Roman populace expressed its disapproval. So she was asked to leave. But on Vespasian's death and Titus' accession she was back again. Once again she was disappointed. And that is the last that history records of her.[10]

From within the Flavian family itself only one woman has left any mark at all on history. This, tragically enough, was (Flavia) Julia, daughter of Titus by his marriage to Marcia Furnilla.[11] Sculpture perpetuates her handsome features and her magnificent coiffure; literature tells the sad story of her life.[12] Her uncle Domitian refused to take a leaf from Claudius' book and to marry her; but, once she was married to her cousin (Domitian's first cousin) T. Flavius Sabinus, who was consul in 82, he was happy to seduce her. When her father was dead—in whose lifetime she received the title 'Augusta'—and her husband, by Domitian's sinister agency, was dead too, and in the period, particularly, when Domitian was estranged from his wife, they lived freely together until, sadly, she died; then, probably in 91, she was consecrated and became a goddess, 'diva Julia Augusta'. Slander declared that, finding herself pregnant, she was forced by Domitian to resort to abortion; and that this was the cause of her death. If this was Juvenal's account alone, we might hesitate to believe it; but the younger Pliny, too, tells the same story. So, if not true, it is at least what the contemporary world believed.[13]

ii. The Womenfolk of Trajan and Hadrian

There were four of these women: Plotina, strong-minded wife of the Emperor Trajan[14] and Ulpia Marciana, his most satisfactorily affectionate sister; Matidia, who was Marciana's daughter and Vibia Sabina, daughter of Matidia and, since some time before 101, Hadrian's singularly unsuitable wife. It was the women who mattered; neither Marciana's husband nor Matidia's was a man of any consequence at all. They are distinguished, as a group, by their high moral integrity and so, as a group, they were perhaps just a little dull—dull even to look at, were it not for the fantastically complicated fashion in which they chose to dress their hair.* Virtue came into residence, however belatedly, on the Palatine in Rome. Not since Livia and the younger Antonia—for Sextilia, the mother of Vitellius, for all her exemplary

---

* See page 256 and plate 13.

modesty, was a bird of very swift passage[15]—had such women lent decorum to the imperial house.

This is what, in the tedious outburst of flattery with which he smothered Trajan in the Senate in 100 (the *Panegyricus*), the younger Pliny had to say of Trajan's wife:

'Many men of importance have incurred discredit because they rushed into marriage with too little thought, or because they were too complaisant in tolerating a wife whom they would have done well to divorce; the discredit incurred in their private lives effaced the distinction of their public careers and, because they were unable to control their wives at home, they were thought to fall below the highest standard of the perfect Roman.

Your wife, on the other hand, has brought you nothing but renown and distinction. No woman alive has greater integrity or represents more perfectly the best tradition of Roman womanhood. If the High Priest had to choose a wife, she—or some woman like her—would be his certain choice.

"Some woman like her," do I say? But where is there such another woman?'

In a letter to a friend Pliny called her 'the most irreproachable of women'—'*sanctissima femina*'; and Cassius Dio declared her blameless.[16] But she deserves better epithets than these; in the first two centuries of the Empire Livia is her only rival in greatness.

Sixty years or so after the event, as we know from the father of the historian Cassius Dio,[17] people in Cilicia were talking of the death there, at Selinus, of the Emperor Trajan in early August 117. It was Selinus' great moment of history; it was a moment, too, when the future government of Rome may well have depended on the strong mind and quick wit of the Empress Plotina.

The imperial party had left Rome for the East four years earlier, in September 113: the Emperor, Plotina, Matidia and Matidia's son-in-law Hadrian, who was a remote relative of the Emperor, a Spaniard like himself, a man of thirty-eight who from the time of his marriage twelve or more years earlier was not unjustified in thinking that he was being groomed for the succession. Indeed, if Trajan's successor was to come from within the family, he was the only possible choice. Yet he was not Trajan's kind of man. He was a scholar, in particular a devotee of Greek culture, while Trajan was a military man, no scholar and, indeed, no great friend of culture. On personal grounds, indeed, Hadrian was Plotina's choice, not Trajan's.

Plotina, who had been born at Nîmes and belonged to a family which, by provincial standards, was reasonably distinguished,[18] was nothing if not modest—when she first set foot in the Palace, she said, 'I hope that, when the time comes to leave this building, I shall be the same woman that I am today'—but, besides possessing a strong will, she was a clever woman, interested in religion and philosophy, with a particular attachment to Epicureanism. Wholehearted and loyal as was her devotion to her husband (who was considerably older than herself), he was not capable, as Hadrian was capable, of stimulating her mind. Her interest in Hadrian was widely known and, as was natural, grossly misconstrued by Roman gossip.[19] Trajan, on the other hand, detected qualities in Hadrian which, understandably enough, he distrusted. It was said that he had not been wholeheartedly in favour of Hadrian's marriage to his great-niece[20] but that he had given way to the persuasion of Plotina—indeed to the unanimous will of all the women by whom he was surrounded, for Marciana and Matidia warmly approved of the marriage too. And, when they set out for the East in 113, Trajan was still procrastinating; he had not adopted Hadrian or given any unmistakable indication that he wanted Hadrian to be his successor.[21]

There was a background of sadness to the departure of the imperial party for the East. A year earlier, in 112, Marciana had died. She had been married to a man called Matidius, of whom nothing is known; she had lived in the palace with Trajan and Plotina and in the *Panegyricus* was next after Plotina to be the target of Pliny's extravagant praise:

'She is your sister, and she never forgets the fact. Her qualities are your qualities: sincerity, openness, candour. Anyone who compared her with your wife and tried to decide whether, in order to live a good life, it was better to have a good training or to be well born, would have to admit that he could not decide. In the case of women particularly, rivalry is the most effective source of ill feeling. This starts from their living together, it is increased by the equality of their status, it is brought to a head by jealousy, and ends in their hating one another. All the more reason, therefore, for admiring the fact that in this case, though the two ladies live in the same house and share the same

rank, there is never a dispute or a quarrel between them. They respect
each other, they defer to each other; both are so deeply devoted to you
that neither thinks it of the slightest consequence to her which of the
two you love better.'[22]

One is bound to feel that Plotina was a very remarkable woman
indeed to live with her sister-in-law on such terms as these. Both
women, indeed, had been offered the title 'Augusta' by the Senate but,
speaking with a single voice, they both at first refused the honour. By
A.D. 105 they had accepted it. In Marciana's case the distinction was
remarkable indeed; never before had the title been accorded to any
woman who was not an emperor's wife or daughter. In 112 both
Plotina and Marciana were given the right to issue coins.[23]

Marciana's daughter Matidia was equally a favourite of Trajan. She
had been married to L. Vibius Sabinus, and had been left a widow with
two daughters, the elder called Vibia Matidia, the younger, Vibia
Sabina, being Hadrian's wife. She was, indeed, an inconsolable widow,
devoted to her husband's memory and determined not to marry again.
She, in succession to her mother, was honoured with the title 'Augusta'.

She, then, and Plotina and Hadrian accompanied Trajan to the East
in 113. Why was Sabina not one of the party? Were her relations with
Hadrian already so bad?

The Emperor himself, at the age of sixty, felt in fine fettle when they
left Rome. After all, he could well have described himself as a plain
soldier; and now, after an interval of seven years, he was on his way once
again to the front, to command the most ambitious enterprise of un-
provoked aggression in the East that there had been since the disaster
of Crassus in 53 B.C. Historians are at a loss to explain what seems a
simple act of megalomania. Hadrian would hold a command in the
fighting, of course; whether he was already critical of the whole
undertaking cannot be known.

The journey out was naturally a triumphal progress. There were
statues, statues all the way, erected with dutiful loyalty at places where
they stayed, some to Trajan, some to Plotina.[24] After all, if the early
months of the upstart Vespasian are excepted, this was the first time
since Augustus that a ruling Emperor had been seen in the provinces
east of Greece.

Once Syria was reached, Trajan left his womenfolk and moved to
the front. All went well at first. In 114 and 115 Armenia and Upper
Mesopotamia were overrun and preparations were made to hold and

administer both territories as Roman provinces. In 116 Trajan captured Ctesiphon and his army progressed, without meeting any serious resistance, to the Persian Gulf.

What next? News came of revolts in the lands which he had conquered a year or two earlier, not all of which were suppressed; and, with sinister consequences in store, a widespread revolt of Jews broke out in Egypt, Cyrenaica and Cyprus.

In the winter of 116/7 the last blow fell. Trajan, who had perhaps suffered from high blood-pressure for some years, had a stroke.[25] Though he recovered sufficiently to talk of resuming military operations, he was forced to realize—perhaps persuaded by his womenfolk—that he must take things more easily, in fact return to Rome. Hadrian was left behind as governor of Syria. With his wife and niece and with an entourage which included the Prefect of the Praetorian Guard, P. Acilius Attianus, and his intimate personal attendant, M. Ulpius Phaedimus, Trajan started on the journey home.

Plotina's anxiety must have increased as the days passed. So far from improving, Trajan's health deteriorated. This was cause enough for distress to a loving wife. But, as a prudent and patriotic woman with a stronger personality than Pliny's account suggested, she had an acute sense of personal responsibility in an issue which concerned the whole future welfare of Rome.[26] Trajan still had not adopted Hadrian, and she was determined that this should be done. On August 9th the news reached Hadrian in Syria that he had been adopted, and a declaration to this effect, witnessed by Plotina, was sent to the Senate at Rome. On August 11th Hadrian received a second dispatch, with the information that Trajan was dead. The news was made public and the army in Syria at once proclaimed Hadrian emperor. On the 12th, by sad coincidence—if sad coincidence it was—M. Ulpius Phaedimus died too.[27]

There were many who deplored the adoption and its consequence, the elevation of Hadrian to the purple, and a number of men distinguished in public life paid for their opinion with their lives. The atmosphere of Roman political life was one in which gossip, scandal and insinuation flourished, and after a hundred years there was revived the kind of poisonous slander by which Tiberius' accession and the part supposedly played in it by his mother Livia had been discredited.

Had Trajan in fact adopted Hadrian at all? Or was the report a false one, and were the supposedly confirmatory documents a forgery? Was it all a base contrivance on Plotina's part? This is what Hadrian's critics were soon saying in Rome; it was the story which, sixty years later, the father of Cassius Dio was told when he was governor of Syria.[28] When Trajan was already dead, it was said, his body was removed and there was substituted someone who from under the bed-clothes, imitating the tired voice of a dying man, made the declaration of adoption. Was it coincidence that Trajan's personal attendant, M. Ulpius Phaedimus, himself died a few days later than his master? Or did he die because he knew too much?[29] Why was Plotina's signature on the certificate of adoption which was sent to Rome? Was it true that the document was not signed by Trajan himself?[30]

Nobody knew the truth at the time, and though scholars have argued this way and that, nobody can know the truth today. In as far as the rule of Hadrian and of the two emperors who succeeded him, both men of his choice, marked the last period of contented stability that the Roman world enjoyed, Plotina's deception—if, indeed, she prac-tised a deception—was one which neither she nor Rome had any reason to deplore.

The two ladies, escorted by that formidable figure, Attianus, Prefect of the Guard, carried Trajan's ashes home to Rome. Matidia survived to see two years of Hadrian's rule; Plotina lived only two or three years longer, until 121 or 122. When Matidia died, Hadrian spoke her funeral oration, and a copy, part of which survives, was appropriately erected at his favourite Tivoli.[31] Plotina who in her time had not been afraid to tell Trajan that he should be more severe in the punishment of corrupt practices on the part of his stewards[32] and, when there was a dispute between Greek and Jewish legations from Alexandria, had won him over to the side of the Jews before the hearing had even started,[33] retained her interest in public affairs. As we know from inscriptions, she was successful in persuading Hadrian to relax the rule by which the person nominated for succession to the headship of the Epicurean school in Athens must be a Roman citizen.[34] This was the kind of matter in which she could know that she would have no difficulty in rousing Hadrian's interest. In speaking her funeral oration, Hadrian said, 'She often made requests of me, and I never once refused her anything.'[35]

Matidia, of course, became a goddess when she died; so, by Had-rian's act did her mother Marciana,[36] who had died in 112. When Plotina died, she was consecrated too, and a temple was erected in her honour.[37] There had been no serious and reputable consecration of women at Rome since Claudius had secured this honour, years after her death, for Livia; now, suddenly, Olympus was invaded by three imperial goddesses. They kept in death that close association which had marked their lives, association with one another and with—the now divine—Trajan himself.

As far as his contemporaries were concerned, Hadrian, in contrast to his adoptive father, was anything but a lady's man.[38] The women who suffered from his ungraciousness were two: his sister Domitia Paulina[39] and Vibia Sabina, his wife.[40]

Domitia Paulina's husband, L. Julius Ursus Servianus, was at least thirty years older than herself. The marriage produced a daughter Julia, who married, and there was a grandson, born in about 118. Relationship between the two families was frigid, if not openly hostile. Julius Servianus, who regarded his young brother-in-law as an extravagant spendthrift, had done his best to set Trajan against him.[41] Hadrian retorted in similar spirit. His sister was never given the title 'Augusta'; when she died in about A.D. 130, no significant honour was paid to her memory; no favour was shown to her son-in-law in his public career (though, in the next generation, he was the only man in the family) and finally, six years after her own death, her husband (by then ninety years old) and her grandson, who was eighteen, were both put to death as men of dangerous ambition.[42]

Sabina was only about twelve years old when she married Hadrian, who was thirteen years older, in about 100. There may not be any truth at all in the remarks which he and his wife are alleged to have made on the subject of their marriage; but those remarks illustrate well enough the very real unhappiness of the marriage itself. She is said to have remarked that, rather than perpetuate a character as inhuman as his, she had taken care to ensure that she should not bear him a child.[43] He, on the other hand, is said to have described her as a tiresome and irritable woman whom in any other walk of life he would not have hesitated to divorce.[44] Suetonius Tranquillus, the biographer, was discharged from his post as private secretary to the Emperor—and Septicius Clarus was dismissed from the prefecture of the Guard at the same time—because they consorted with her on what Hadrian thought far too familiar terms.[45] When in A.D. 136 she died, slanderous tongues declared that Hadrian had poisoned her.

Yet she was given the title 'Augusta' when he took the title 'Pater Patriae' in A.D. 128; she probably accompanied him on several of his imperial tours and certainly was with him in Egypt in A.D. 130. It was indeed a remarkable party which travelled up the Nile and stayed at Thebes in the autumn of that year, to be rewarded after sunrise on November 21st and 22nd by the 'song of Memnon'. There were the Emperor and his unaffectionate consort; there was the handsome boy Antinous, by whom Hadrian was infatuated and with whom—to his credit and hers—Sabina seems to have been on perfectly good terms. And there was a poetess.

Of all the millions of people who have defaced monuments with their *graffiti* there is none to whom anyone with a frolicsome affection for the past can feel greater gratitude than to the poetess Julia Balbilla[46] who, not content with composing poems in the most grotesquely artificial language—Aeolian Greek—cut them (or commissioned their cutting) on Memnon's left foot.[47] Apart from ecstasy over the joyful sounds of Memnon which had excited Emperor and Empress alike, she has perpetuated her own pedigree. The blood of kings ran in her veins (through bastard children of the royal house of Commagene) and, more recently, she must have descended either from Balbillus, the astrologer, to whom Nero resorted or from Tiberius Claudius Balbillus who, after a career—in Egypt—in the personal service of the Emperor Claudius, became Prefect of Egypt under Nero. We know from Seneca that the latter was a highly talented literary figure; all the more fortunate was it, therefore, that it should have been he who witnessed—because he could describe it as it deserved to be described—the extraordinary sight of a battle between dolphins and crocodiles at the mouth of the Nile[48] (a battle which, by diving and attacking the weak underbellies of the crocodiles, the dolphins won). He surely, rather than the astrologer, was the grandfather of the intimidating poetess. Who, one wonders, had invited her to join the imperial party? That it was Sabina, is commonly assumed. Yet it is hard to believe that Hadrian did not find her a poetess after his own heart.

They were as happy, no doubt, as a party of tourists can be—with tragedy unsuspected, but very near. For it can only have been a few days later than Antinous was drowned.[49]

III. The Women of the Antonines

In his last years a very sick man indeed, Hadrian was forced to choose a successor and, by the act of adoption, to make his choice known. In this he showed himself both a deplorably bad and at the same time a penetratingly good judge of character. His first choice, made in 136, of L. Ceionius Commodus who, on adoption, changed his name to L. Aelius Caesar, was at the time, and still remains, incomprehensible.* The man was an idle good-for-nothing. Fortunately he died before Hadrian himself died, in 138.

After that Hadrian acted with genius, and his action gave Rome its last golden age. He adopted a man of fifty-two whose family, coming from Nîmes, had a distinguished record in administration, T. Aurelius Boionius Arrius Antoninus, whose name was now changed to T. Aelius Hadrianus Antoninus. When in this same year 138 Hadrian died, there was a startlingly close repetition in Rome of the outburst of popular fury which had occurred at Tiberius' death almost exactly a century earlier. So far from giving the slightest encouragement to such behaviour, Antoninus acted with dignity and, indeed, insisted that Hadrian should be consecrated. For this commendable behaviour he won the name of 'Pius'. Hence the name by which he is commonly called, Antoninus Pius.

He had at the time of his adoption advantages which neither Trajan nor Hadrian had possessed. Not only was he married, but he possessed that most useful asset in Roman public life, a daughter. His handsome wife, ten to twelve years younger than himself, was Annia Galeria Faustina (the elder Faustina) and her family, distinguished too, on both sides, for its political and administrative record, came from Spain. They were married probably between 112 and 115.

Hadrian attached two conditions to the adoption of Antoninus, one good, one bad. Antoninus was to adopt his seventeen-year-old nephew (son of Faustina's brother), M. Annius Verus (whose name on adoption became M. Aelius Aurelius Verus—he is known to history as Marcus Aurelius); but he was also to adopt L. Ceionius Commodus, a boy of eight, son of the L. Aelius Caesar who had been Hadrian's deplorable first choice as his own successor; he, on adoption, became L. Aelius Aurelius Commodus (and is the man known to us as L. Verus).

Even this was not enough. Hadrian insisted on tying up the future more tightly still. L. Verus—at the age of eight—was to be betrothed to Antoninus Pius' daughter, the younger Faustina, perhaps by this time his only surviving child; L. Verus' sister Ceionia Fabia, then aged fifteen, had been engaged at Hadrian's wish in 135/6 to M. Aurelius. There was no end to Hadrian's inexplicable devotion to the family of the Ceionii.[50]

* Unless—see page 199—he was Hadrian's natural son.

On Hadrian's death—perhaps with Hadrian's agreement, secured shortly before his death—Antoninus Pius altered these arrangements.[51] Ostensibly because L. Verus was so young, Antoninus' daughter, the younger Faustina, was engaged to M. Aurelius instead; and in the event L. Verus did not marry until he was thirty-four, in A.D. 164; and then he married Annia Lucilla, daughter of the marriage of M. Aurelius and the younger Faustina.

In the public life of Rome, as judged by the official acts both of the Emperors and of the Senate and by the record of inscriptions and of coins, the elder and the younger Faustina, consorts of Antoninus Pius and of M. Aurelius, were treated with the utmost propriety and accorded every conceivable honour and distinction.

Whereas Sabina had to wait ten years for such an honour in the principate of Hadrian, the elder Faustina became 'Augusta'—Faustina Augusta—on her husband's accession; this by the formal vote of the Senate, which her husband approved.[52] She also received the right to coin. When three years later, in 140/1, she died, she was buried in the Mausoleum of Hadrian (Castel Sant' Angelo). She was consecrated, to become 'diva Faustina Augusta'—and a temple was built and a priestess created for her cult. The temple, at first dedicated to her and after Pius' death dedicated jointly to him, survived intact, to be converted in the seventh or eighth century into the church of S. Lorenzo in Miranda.[53] Its columned front stands still in the forum, facing the *Via Sacra*, and on the architrave and frieze its original dedications can be read.

In addition to the voting of a temple, a large coinage was issued in her name as a goddess, with the legend AETERNITAS; for this was a consecration to be taken seriously.[54] Good emperors and good empresses who earned consecration were to be seen as part of the tradition of Eternal Rome (the nine hundredth anniversary of whose foundation was on the point of being celebrated). Her memory was happily commemorated further by the establishment of an endowment for maintenance allowances to poor girls, the 'puellae Faustinianae'. This was in the good tradition of Trajan's alimentary scheme.[55]

The marriage of M. Aurelius to his first cousin, the younger Faustina, was celebrated with tremendous pomp[56] in the year 145, and after their first child was born a year later, they both received outstanding public honours. M. Aurelius was associated in the rule of Antoninus Pius, and Faustina was granted, in 146 or 147, the title of 'Augusta' and the right to coin.[57]

This after the birth of a single child. But it soon became evident that this was a fabulous marriage, one without precedent in the whole history of the imperial house in Rome. Even the record of the elder Agrippina was soon beaten. Year after year—except for a gap between 152 and 156—children arrived. This achievement was fitly recognized in coinage—FECVNDITAS AVGVSTAE—one type of which showed Faustina draped by four children.[58] By the end she had given birth to twelve children, perhaps even more. Many of them, naturally, did not survive infancy; but some survived, though not always for the good of Rome, in particular the future Emperor Commodus (L. Aelius Aurelius Commodus) born in 161 and his older sister Annia Lucilla, who was to marry L. Verus.

Antoninus Pius would perhaps have been happier if he had been allowed to live a farmer's life at his villa at Lorium, north of Rome on the via Aurelia. Not for him that Versailles of a fantasy which Hadrian had built below Tivoli. It was perhaps because he did not greatly enjoy ruling that he ruled so well. And fortune was kind to him; there were no bad crises on the frontiers.

In 161 he died, and M. Aurelius, a philosopher by inclination and a ruler perforce, succeeded and, modelling himself on the example of Antoninus, to which he paid such handsome tribute in his *Meditations*,[59] he ruled until he died in 180. He made L. Verus his fellow-ruler—until in 169, at the age of thirty-nine, Verus died of a stroke. In 177—for the intelligence of a philosopher cannot be matched against the blind affection of a father—he associated his son Commodus in his government.

The tranquillity of the frontiers under Antoninus Pius proved to have been the deceptive quiet which precedes the storm. At the very start of Marcus' rule the Parthians attacked in the East; in 166 Germans from north of the river overran the Danube provinces and even penetrated into north-east Italy as far as Aquileia. L. Verus was sent to the East and thanks to good officers, in particular to the commander-in-chief, a Syrian who had just held the consulate, C. Avidius Cassius, a successful campaign was fought. To confront the German invaders, M. Aurelius and L. Verus took the field together and negotiated an agreement (the first of many such in Roman history) by which the invaders retired. But after Verus' death Marcus had to campaign from 170-4 on the Danube; in 175 he received the frightening news that Avidius Cassius, left as governor of Syria by Verus and subsequently promoted to be supreme Roman commander in the East, had revolted and set himself up as Emperor. Marcus had no alternative but to go East himself; but before he arrived, Avidius Cassius had been murdered by his troops.

Faustina was in every respect the perfect Emperor's wife. Having given him a splendid family of children at home, she did not shirk her duties abroad. She was at Sirmium on the Save with one of her small daughters from 170–4 during the German wars and, after Marcus' victory over the Quadi, she was hailed as 'Mother of the Army' (Mater Castrorum).[60] She accompanied M. Aurelius to the East, when Avidius Cassius rebelled and in 176 she died suddenly at Halala, at the foot of the Taurus mountains in Cappadocia.

In death she was as greatly honoured as her mother had been.[61] At M. Aurelius' request, the Senate consecrated her. Temples were erected in her honour both in Rome and at Halala where she died. Halala was made a colony, Faustinopolis. There was a further endowment for poor girls, the 'puellae Faustinianae'.

So much for the public life of Antoninus and of Marcus and of their consorts. Of their private life we secure an intimate glimpse in the surviving letters of M. Cornelius Fronto, who was at first tutor in rhetoric to Marcus Aurelius and, when his instruction ceased and Marcus' interests turned to Stoicism, remained on terms of close friendship with him. Fronto corresponded in the main with Marcus, but also with L. Verus and with Antoninus Pius. Antoninus Pius once wrote to Fronto, 'The part of your speech in which you did honour to my Faustina gave me great pleasure. It was a distinguished piece of writing; but, more than that, absolutely true. I would rather face banishment with her on Gyaros than life without her in the Palace.' But perhaps—for this may have been written when the elder Faustina was dead—this was a reference to his daughter, not to his wife.[62] However, there *is* a nice story of Antoninus and his wife, which does credit to him, without reflecting any great discredit on her.[63] When he was adopted by Hadrian in 138 and she criticized him for being ungenerous, he answered, 'Silly (*Stulta*). We had some money of our own before; but now that we have become royalty, we have lost even that.'

In his *Meditations* Marcus reveals from time to time intimate details of his private family life; he pays tribute, for instance, to his wife as 'obedient, loving and devoid of affectation'.[64] Fronto's references to the younger Faustina and to the children in his letters to M. Aurelius— no less frequent than his references to his own physical ailments—are

what would be expected of a man writing to a friend who enjoyed a
happy and a tranquil married life. And from Faustina herself there is
the charming record on stone of her happiness when Galen succeeded
in curing an illness of Commodus: SALVO COMMODO FELIX
FAUSTINA.*

It may even be thought a tribute to their wives that neither Antoninus
nor Marcus married a second time—Marcus, as he said explicitly, so
that his children should not have a stepmother to bully them. It was
said, indeed, that Ceionia Fabia, whose early engagement to him was
broken off so many years ago, was anxious after all this time to marry
him, when he became a widower.[65] Both Antoninus and Marcus did
what Vespasian had done, and kept concubines, once their wives were
dead. Antoninus' concubine was Lysistrata, a freedwoman of his wife;
Marcus' was daughter of a procurator.[66]

How is the historian to reconcile this pleasing picture of the elder
Faustina and her daughter with the hostile accounts of the ancient
biographers who wrote more than a century later than the events?
In the case of the elder Faustina, the slander is no more than a single
sentence, that 'she was much criticized for being too free and loose in
her way of living; criticisms which caused her husband great distress,
but which he kept to himself.' This, given the writer's venom, is as
good as a confession that he had no evidence at all to bring against
her.[68] 'Antoninus showed at once that his affection and honour for his
wife were above all the malicious gossip that gathered around her
name. The historian might well follow his example.'[69]

The case against the younger Faustina, at first sight, is more substantial. There is an extraordinary story that in 174 she was so anxious
about her husband's health—and it is true that, from their correspondence, he seems to have been almost as great a valetudinarian as
Fronto himself—that she wrote to Avidius Cassius urging that, if
Marcus died, he should make a bid for empire (at the expense, naturally, of her own son Commodus)[70] and that she should then become his
wife. As embroidery to the story, it was alleged that her death in
Cappadocia after Avidius Cassius' failure was not due to natural causes
at all, but was suicide; she was afraid of what would happen when
Marcus discovered what she had done.[71] Is it conceivable that, if she
had in fact communicated with Avidius Cassius, Marcus would not
have known the truth long before? Even historians who are so credulous as to believe this nonsensical story have to admit that the alleged

* 'Commodus is well again, and Faustina happy.'[67]

correspondence between Faustina and Cassius reproduced by the bio-grapher is the most self-evident of forgeries.

For the rest, there are in the *Lives* of the *Historia Augusta* a fantastic series of allegations concerning the irregularity of her moral life. Messalina herself could never have hoped to be credited with such a list of lovers: gladiators and pantomime actors *en masse*, men of eminence, her relations with whom, it was said, were a rich source of jokes on the common stage; and finally her son-in-law L. Verus, of whom in the end she is alleged to have freed herself by means of a dish of poisoned oysters, because the fool had confessed the truth to her own daughter, his wife.[72]

The story of Commodus' birth in the *Life* of Marcus in the *Historia Augusta* is the most startling of all.[73]

'There is a story, in itself not improbable, that it was not Marcus Aurelius, but some lover of his wife's, who was father of Commodus, the son by whom he was succeeded. According to one story, while she was once watching a procession of gladiators, Faustina fell violently in love with one of them and, in the course of a protracted illness, confessed the truth to her husband. He consulted Chaldaean experts, who advised that the gladiator should be executed, and that Faustina should take a bath in his blood and afterwards retire to bed with her husband. This certainly put an end to her infatuation, and it was after this that her son was born—Commodus, who was far more like a gladiator than a prince. . . . At the same time there is much support for the view that someone other than Marcus Aurelius was his father; for it is common knowledge that at Gaieta Faustina used to pick out sailors and gladiators and encourage them to make love to her.'

These stories of Faustina's loose conduct have several weaknesses. Marcus evidently adored his children and there was no thought on his part—or on Fronto's—that he was not their father. So that it is of a model and most fertile wife that these infidelities are asserted. And how explain the uninterrupted affection of Marcus for his wife in her lifetime, and the high honours which he secured for her at her death? Either, in his absent-minded philosophical way, he knew nothing of what was going on, or he pretended not to know. This is not convincing. Or, when told, for instance, of Faustina's behaviour with the gladiators and sailors at Gaieta, he was content to dismiss the matter with a sar-donic joke.[74] 'The Empire, which I owe to my marriage is, in a sense, her dowry; I could not divorce her without giving up that dowry.'

As for the fantastic account of Commodus' origins in the *Historia Augusta*, it is hard to know how far it is the invention of the author of that extraordinary work (produced either at the time of Diocletian and Constantine, as it claims, or at the time of Julian, or in some other part of the fourth century),[75] and how far he discovered a foundation for it in his earlier sources. In any case it was a story told with a purpose—to ensure that the reputation of Marcus Aurelius, who for the author of the *Lives* of the Emperors was the hero of the whole series, should not be damaged by the fact of his having such a man as Commodus for his son. The nonsensical story, therefore, can be dismissed; it is not history, but fiction.

From Cassius Dio, a contemporary, we have no more than this statement:[76] 'Other people's misdoings, in particular his wife's, he tolerated, making no fuss and exacting no punishment.'

Which is no more than to say that in much that she did the younger Faustina was open to criticism. What woman—what man—is not?

Marcus Aurelius, who would have preferred the sheltered life of a Professor of Philosophy, was succeeded by his son Commodus who—and the world too—would have been happier if Fate had cast him for the crude and bestial role of a professional gladiator. However inexplicably, the best of families are sometimes cursed with such a son; Roman gossip being what it was, it is easy to understand the currency of the insinuation that Commodus had not Marcus but a gladiator for his father.

His disaster was the greater for the fact that he first tasted power at far too tender an age. He was the survivor of twins born to Faustina in 161. At the age of five he received the name of 'Caesar'; he was consul at the age of sixteen and an associate already in his father's rule; he reigned as Emperor from 180 (when he was nineteen years old) until he was murdered in 192, at the age of thirty-one. After Gaius Caligula and Nero he was the third example of youthful irresponsibility and ineptitude at the Roman helm; after the toy-autocrat, the aesthete; after the aesthete, the gladiator.

We know of three women of significance in Commodus' life: his sister Annia Lucilla, his wife Bruttia Crispina and, after her death, the concubine Marcia—'in all respects but the formalities, his wife'—who organized the plot to kill him.

Annia Lucilla married L. Verus in 164 in romantic circumstances. He took leave from the Eastern front to meet and marry her at Ephesus.

She had travelled out from Rome escorted, as far as Brindisi, by her
father and after that escorted by a relation (perhaps Ceionia Fabia), her
father having instructed that she should not be given any official recep-
tions on her journey.[77] The marriage lasted until Verus' death five
years later. After which Lucilla (at daggers drawn always with her
sister-in-law Ceionia Fabia, who evidently nurtured her grievance at
having been cheated out of marrying Lucilla's father) was left with a
small daughter and forced against her own will and her mother's to
marry again with almost indecent haste. This time she married the
elderly and highly distinguished Ti. Claudius Pompeianus, a man whom
she detested, by whom she had a son.[78]

Neither she nor Bruttia Crispina long survived the nightmare of
Commodus' rule; but there was no element of injured innocence in
either woman's death. Lucilla, 'a woman whose character was no
better than her brother's', and whose elderly and unambitious husband,
troubled by bad eyesight, lived a retired country life, could not forget
that, as L. Verus' wife, she had once shared with her mother the position of First Lady at Court.[79] Though she was treated with the greatest
courtesy by Commodus, she despised her sister-in-law the Empress as
greatly as she despised her second husband. She had much in common, evidently, with the elder Agrippina. Unable to submit to the
precedence of another woman at Court, she drove Ummidius Quadratus, who was her first or second cousin, to conspire against her
brother's life. This in 182. The actual murder was to be done by
Claudius Pompeianus Quintianus, a relation, perhaps the nephew, of
her second husband; but he was anything but a perfect murderer,
coming on Commodus with a knife, proclaiming 'This is a present to
you from the Senate', but sustaining his brave part no farther than that
before he was arrested. Lucilla was banished to Capri and, after an
interval, dispatched. Her despised sister-in-law survived a few
years longer, probably until after 187, but was then found guilty of
adultery and banished—also to Capri—and afterwards executed.[80]

Commodus did not marry again; instead he took as concubine
Marcia, who had been concubine of the Quadratus who conspired
against him and was killed in 182. She was a woman who evidently
cared for him and might have made something of an emperor out of
him, had she been given the chance. Instead, in order to save her own
life, she was driven to take his. If the account of Herodian is to be
believed, she behaved from the beginning of the enterprise to the end

with intelligence and intrepidity. She was, in fact, the first great concubine in Roman history.[81]

Commodus had decided in his eccentric way that on the first of January 193 he would abandon the traditional and dignified formalities of the Roman New Year's Day and would present himself to his people not in the purple of an emperor, but in the equipment of a gladiator, and instead of appearing from the palace, he would emerge with a professional escort of gladiators from their barracks.

On the last day of the old year—192—Marcia, concerned alike—as we are assured—with the dignity of the State and with the kind of company that the Emperor kept, tried to dissuade him, but failed. He simply summoned the Prefect of the Guard, Q. Aemilius Laetus[82] (a forceful character who once fought him in a mock gladiatorial fight and at another time, according to popular rumour, had prevented him, when in a frolicsome Neronian mood, from setting Rome on fire) and the Groom of the Bedchamber, Eclectus, an Egyptian, so that the necessary preparations might be made for him to spend the night in the gladiators' barracks. They, like Marcia, did their best to dissuade him from such folly and, like Marcia, they failed.

Commodus now retired for his siesta, but first made a list on a writing pad of people whom he proposed to have executed that very night. He put it on a sofa and, not expecting that anyone would come into the room, he left it there when later he went out to the baths. His favourite slave-boy came into the room, picked up the pad and still had it in his hands, playing with it, when he came out of the building and encountered Marcia. She took it from him and, seeing that the writing was in the Emperor's hand, she read it, to see if it was of any importance.

She was horrified by what she saw—a list of people due to be executed that night, with her name at the top, followed by the names of Laetus and Eclectus. Next came the names of distinguished senators who had been the friends of Commodus' father and who seemed to him to constitute a standing reproach to his irregularities, and of wealthy senators whose money could, he thought, be better employed if it was distributed among his soldiers and his gladiators.

It is perhaps no more than the historian's imagination that at this moment she cried out, 'Well done, indeed, Commodus. Here is a fine return for the benevolence and affection which I have lavished on you and for the drunken insults which I have endured from you all these years.'

Eclectus and Laetus were shown the document and the three decided that, to save their own skins, Commodus must be put out of the way that night. Marcia, in her efficient manner, took the business in hand and, as soon as Commodus returned from the baths, he was handed a cup of particularly fragrant and heavily poisoned wine. After which, in his intemperate way, he fell sound asleep. However, he woke quickly enough, and was very ill indeed—so ill that, from fear that he had got the whole of the poison out of his system, the three secured a strong man called Narcissus who, on the promise of adequate remuneration, took the Emperor by the throat and throttled him to death.

He was not the last survivor of the family of Marcus Aurelius and Faustina. Three of his sisters survived him: Fadilla, Cornificia and Vibia Aurelia Sabina.[83]

Unlike so many assassins, Marcia and her associates kept their heads, once the deed was done. They went to the house of the admirable Publius Helvius Pertinax, a veteran of sixty-six, who was accepted by the Senate and army; and after a blameless rule of three months, he was murdered by the soldiery, to whom Didius Julianus offered the promise of better money. Inevitably the king-makers were involved in their candidate's fall: Marcia, Eclectus, Laetus—all three of them were killed.

There was one section of society in which the name of Marcia was long remembered with affection. She had been a friend of the Christians and in her powerful days in the Palace she had done her best to help them.[84]

IV. The Achievement of Julia Domna and her Sister

Spain and Gaul had given Rome its second-century emperors. It was now the turn of Africa and Syria. Septimius Severus came from Lepcis Magna in Tripolitania (from a family so little romanized that his sister embarrassed him in Rome and had to be sent home because she could scarcely speak a word of Latin);[85] his wife Julia Domna and her great-nephews, the emperors Elagabalus and Alexander Severus, came from Emesa in Syria.

The shocking murder of Pertinax and the contemptible interlude of Didius Julianus invited the commanders of the great provincial armies to stake their own claims, and the disaster of A.D. 69 happened all over again. The ultimate victor in the conflict was L. Septimius Severus, who was proclaimed Emperor at Carnuntum in April 193. He ruled until his death at York in 211. He was a successful Emperor in that he preserved the frontiers, succeeded by extortionate taxation in raising the income that he needed, and did not fail to retain the loyalty of his troops. He was an effective, but not particularly enlightened, ruler, as is illustrated by the advice which he gave on his death-bed to his sons: 'Avoid quarrels. Pay your soldiers well, and do not bother about anybody else.'

He was a fantastically superstitious man; while still a commoner, he enjoyed a variety of dreams, all of which could be interpreted to suggest that he had a distinguished future ahead; and he was also an enthusiastic astrologer.[86] After the death of his first wife Paccia Marciana (of whom we only know that in his autobiography he did not mention her name),[87] he happily remembered at Lyons in his Residence as Governor of the province of Gallia Lugdunensis, that when he had done service in Syria, commanding legion iv, he had visited the temple of the Sun (Elagabalus) at Emesa, made the acquaintance of Julius Bassianus the priest who, as his office showed, was a man of breeding, and of his daughter Julia Domna.[88] Either then or later he had learnt that she had a horoscope which matched the promise of his own dreams. She was destined to be a ruler's wife.[89] So he sent for her and married her. This in 185. A year or so later their first son Caracalla was born at Lyons;[90] in Rome in 189 she gave birth to a second son, Geta. Not that they needed for long to be content with such simple names. Septimius Severus performed the unexampled feat of adopting himself into the defunct house of the Antonines. So his sons and, in a more extraordinary way still, Julia's great-nephews—the future Emperors Caracalla, Geta, Elagabalus and Alexander Severus—were all Antonines, Aurelii or Aurelii Antonini.

Julia's round face and Syrian features did not constitute beauty of the first order; but she had great intelligence and great courage, and her influence and personality pervaded the whole Empire. The record of no other Empress survives on so many inscriptions and on so many coins.[91] She was a more powerful figure even than Plotina, and was the most masterful Empress that Rome had yet experienced. An abundance of titles, mostly without precedent, were devised for her, and appear frequently on inscriptions and even on coins.[92] Already in 196 after Septimius' defeat of the Adiabeni, she was 'Mother of the Army' (Mater Castrorum), as the younger Faustina had been. But she was ultimately to be 'mother' of far more than that. In the dedication of the arch of the money-changers in the forum Boarium at Rome, as set up in 204, she was 'Mother of the Augusti'—Caracalla and Geta—

'and of the Army.' When the inscription was revised after Geta's death, she was described as 'Mother of our Augustus'—Caracalla— 'and of the Army and of the Senate and of the Country'—'*Matri Aug. n. et castrorum et senatus et patriae*'.[93]

After some years of increasing tension she fought and lost her first big fight. The council chamber of the Emperor was too small to contain both her and the immensely powerful Prefect of the Guard, C. Fulvius Plautianus, who started with the advantage of being a fellow-national of Severus, perhaps even a relation.[94] He was a curiously unbalanced man, who insisted that his wife should live in purdah. To establish his influence at Julia's expense, Plautianus took what he must have known to be a very great risk—and succeeded. In 201— probably—he either launched or allowed it to be believed that he was on the point of launching, a prosecution against the Empress for adultery—which, in view of her rank, was, by Augustus' definition, the same as high treason.[95] Except for that poor tormented creature Octavia, wife of Nero, no Empress had been so grossly insulted, and it is easy to imagine the consternation which the affair produced. If the case actually reached the courts, Julia was acquitted—as Plautianus had probably expected and intended all the time—but for the moment her power over her husband was broken. Plautianus' star was in the ascendant; in the following year his daughter Plautilla was married to the Emperor's son and prospective heir, Caracalla. It was small consolation that Caracalla's hatred for Plautilla as a wife was as great as Julia's hatred for her as a daughter-in-law.[96]

Indomitable woman as she was, Julia now turned to assert her personality and patronage in a sphere in which she was unlikely to encounter the jealous competition of the Prefect of the Guard. Surrounding herself with literary men and philosophers, she founded a *salon*. Cassius Dio was one of the writers in whom she was interested; and it was therefore ungenerous as well as inaccurate of him to write of her as a woman of low birth.[97] Philostratus was her secretary, and it was she who commissioned him to collect what records survived, and to publish a *Life* of that mixture of fanaticism, asceticism, miracle-mongering and austerity, Apollonius of Tyana, who had lived a century earlier.[98] 'The account given is founded on the diary of Apollonius' disciple Damis, which purports to have got into Julia Domna's hands and to have been handed by her to Philostratus for re-editing. It bears striking resemblances to the New Testament, except that the style is more pretentious, and indeed better, the general tone infinitely

more erudite, and the matter still more miraculous.'[99] For Philos-
stratus the Empress was 'Julia the philospher'.[100] Among his letters is
one which he wrote to her. 'We must not forget that the superim-
position of Western culture upon a character essentially Eastern won
for the Empress such a world-wide popularity as would ensure everywhere the publication and acceptance of her opinions. In private life
she must have been a woman of strong and imperious character, deeply
imbued with that rather credulous mysticism so typical of the East, yet
not without the ballast of calm reasoning which a philosophical training gave her. " The philosopher Julia"is probably no idle or unmerited
compliment.' So a modern biographer of her husband writes.[101]

Her political eclipse may have lasted as long as three years. But by
204 she took a personal part in the celebration of the Secular Games
such as no Empress had taken before;[102] and in the following year a
check was called to the avarice, the cruelty and the intemperance of
Plautianus, whose standing in the State was by now no lower than that
of the Emperor's sons.[103] Information against him was laid by the
Emperor's brother, P. Septimius Geta, on his death-bed; Caracalla
followed up the accusation and, charged with treason, Plautianus was
murdered in the Palace on January 22nd. 'And somebody plucked out
a few hairs from his beard, carried them to Julia and Plautilla, who were
together, before they had heard a word of the affair, and exclaimed,
"Behold your Plautianus".'[104] Whether Julia had any pity at this
moment for Plautilla, who is to say? Plautilla's husband certainly had
none. She was divorced and banished to Lipara.

A strong emphasis in the Roman coinage on the concepts of 'Aeternitas'—hope for the continuance of the reigning family, which was
reasonably based on the fact that the Emperor had two sons—and on
'Concordia' could not conceal what to Julia must already have been
the cause of acute alarm, the hatred which Caracalla and Geta felt for
one another.[105] When the whole family left in 208 for Britain, where
Septimius would be on campaign, it was in the forlorn hope that the
brothers might be reconciled. Their father on his death-bed in 211
consigned the Empire to them both (an act of signal folly) and urged
them to patch their quarrels up; but neither was moved by sentimental
piety. They carried his ashes back to Rome, but there was no reconciliation. People speculated, Herodian says, on the possibility of dividing
the Empire into two parts, so that each might rule half.[106] Then, surprisingly, in February 212 Caracalla suggested that he should meet his
brother in his mother's presence and should settle the quarrel. Geta

came. So did centurions, commissioned by Caracalla. When Geta ran to his mother for protection, they stabbed him to death in her arms, and in the confusion they managed to wound her as well. Geta's memory was publicly condemned, and his name was erased from innumerable laudatory inscriptions which had been set up to him together with the other members of his family. He was in his twenty-third year when he was killed. Perhaps in fact he was a character little more amiable than his brother; and Julia, knowing that she was under close observation, had, for her own safety, to appear to share Caracalla's satisfaction in the murder.[107] When one of Marcus Aurelius' surviving daughters, Cornificia, called to offer Julia her condolences, this seemed to Caracalla—who should have considered himself by the curious process of adoption to be her nephew—good enough cause for her execution. We are told of her last words—words which Hadrian might have spoken: 'Go forth, poor little soul, for whom this vile body is a prison; be free, show that you are Marcus' daughter, whether they like it or not.'[108] Caracalla also sent orders to Lipara that his wife should be put to death. Julia, however, was safe. Vile as Caracalla was, he was not as vile as Nero.

Caracalla survived to be Emperor for six years, and his rule is memorable for the act by which in 212 all free inhabitants of the Roman world were made Roman citizens. For the rest, administration and its problems were distraction from his real interests, the army, the gladiators and the charioteers, and he was not dissatisfied as Julia, who did her utmost to persuade him to take his imperial duties more seriously, established over him that ascendancy which Plautianus had tried once to prevent her from establishing over her husband. In consequence their relations were good; so good, in fact, that the poisonous talk of the Roman gutter, in its monotonously unimaginative way, spread whispers of incest. At other moments, having regard to the fact that Caracalla had lived without wife or concubine since he was nineteen years old, it declared that he was impotent.[109]

The terrible sycophancy of the times is indicated by the records of the Arval Brothers for 213. This highly respectable company of men, all of considerable distinction in Roman life, whose corporation had survived continuously since its refoundation by Augustus, sacrificed on anniversaries and other important occasions of state. They also dined—in this year, three times—and after dinner they opened their mouths and shouted. This, in 213, was what they cried out:'Bravo, bravo. You'—Caracalla—'are safe and victorious. Bravo. Happy are

we who see you Emperor. May god take years from our lives and add
them to yours. Germanicus the most great, god preserve you. Britannicus the most great, god preserve you. If you are safe, then *we* are
safe and sound. Lucky senate, to have you for Emperor. Augustus,
god preserve you for ever. You are young in your triumphs, yet a
general wise as a veteran. A greater than Augustus, god preserve you.
Augustus! Augustus! Bravo, Julia Augusta, mother of Augustus.
Thanks to you, Augusta, we set eyes on Augustus. God preserve you
both for ever, Augustus, Augusta.'[110]

Julia was in Bithynia when Caracalla was in the East in 214/5 and in
the following year, during his Armenian and Parthian war. So great
was the trust which he placed in her that she was allowed to receive
petitions and to answer most of the official correspondence addressed
to him. His dispatches to the Senate were sent in her name as well as in
the name of himself and the army.[111]

In April 217, when he was on his way from Edessa to Carrhae to
sacrifice, Caracalla was murdered. Julia received the news in Antiocheia and, unable—as L. Verus' wife Lucilla had been unable—to face
descent from the position of First Lady at the Roman court, she contemplated suicide. Nobody insulted her by suggesting that she had
ever felt any affection for Caracalla, or that she felt any grief now at his
death. However, when Macrinus, who had supplanted Caracalla,
wrote to her graciously and allowed her to retain her guards and other
marks of rank, her spirits revived; and Macrinus may well have been
right in starting to suspect that she was playing with the idea of making a bid for power on her own account. That was why his gracious
communications ceased and, instead, he sent a curt dispatch, ordering
her out of Antioch. At this her brave and proud spirit broke. The
world was full of inscriptions which declared her past glory, her
portrait was stamped on the coins which still jingled in innumerable
pockets. Yet what happiness had come to her from a life so full of
fighting and determination? She had done a little, perhaps, to help the
literary men. And there may have been a grateful philosopher or two,
for whom she secured a Chair. Yet her horoscope had not lied. It had
promised her husband power; it had not promised her a happy life.

Already she had a cancer. But that was too slow. So now she
starved herself to death.[112]

History preserves the fragment of this Syrian woman's conversation
with another woman, in whom she met her match.[113] This was the

wife of a Scotsman, Argentocoxus. Julia was talking to her in Britain, after peace had been made, inquiring into the habits of the Caledonians like a good anthropologist, and passing sweeping judgements on them like a bad one. When she criticized the promiscuous sexual relations of the Scots, Argentocoxus' wife retorted, 'In satisfying the needs of nature, our behaviour is a great deal better than yours. We pick up the best men and consort with them openly. At Rome you select the worst, and are debauched by them in secret.' It is a pity that Tacitus had died a hundred years earlier, for the retort would have given him the greatest satisfaction. Indeed, he might have invented it.

Julia Domna had a younger sister, Julia Maesa whose husband, Julius Avitus, was consul in 209 and died, it seems, when Caracalla was Emperor. They had two daughters, Julia Soaemias and Julia Mamaea, both of whom were widows and each was the mother of an only son. The son of Soaemias was Varius Avitus, an abnormally good-looking boy, fourteen years old when Caracalla was killed and already, treading in his great-grandfather's footsteps, priest at Emesa of the baal, the sun-god Elagabalus, whose image was a black conical stone. His cousin, Gessius Bassianus, son of Mamaea, was a boy of ten. Nothing could have seemed more impossible then than that either of them should become a Roman emperor. Yet it happened—thanks to the resolution, the imagination and the wealth of their grandmother and of their mothers. These three women[114] (of whom, avarice apart, Soaemias alone is less than completely admirable) determined, at first for bad and then for good, the history of Rome in the eighteen years which followed Caracalla's death.

Julia Maesa had lived for a long time in Rome and had evidently received visits there from her two daughters, both of whom lived in Syria, for both of them had married Syrians. When Macrinus was proclaimed Emperor in succession to Caracalla out in the East, he sent Maesa curt instructions. She was to leave Rome and return to the East, taking all her possessions with her.[115] Those possessions, happily, were very extensive indeed. But after Rome Emesa was a poor place; after her own house in Rome and the imperial palace of her sister, even the expansive quarters of a family of such great wealth and local distinction as hers were cramping. She felt an acute nostalgia for life—indeed for palace life—in Rome.[116]

The opportunity was at hand, for the big army which Caracalla had assembled in the East had not been dispersed, and it was well enough known in Emesa that Macrinus was already unpopular with large numbers of the troops who had proclaimed him. Troops were easily bought, if you had—as Maesa had—the necessary money. Indeed the purchase of soldiers' loyalty was a subject which she had no doubt discussed more than once with her realistically-minded brother-in-law, Septimius Severus, when he was alive. In default of anybody better, her elder grandson would have to be her candidate;[117] and—here was the stroke of genius—because, all things being equal, soldiers fight better for having a good cause as well as good cash to fight for, what better cause could there be than the avenging of Caracalla's murder? What better cause than to secure for Caracalla's young son the just succession of which he had been cheated by Macrinus. The young priest must cease to be the son of his worthy but not outstandingly distinguished father, now conveniently dead. Soaemias, with whom royalty counted for more than a reputation, was proud to confirm the story. Varius Avitus, it appeared, was not the son of her husband, but of Caracalla. Which being the case, the boy's name by rights was not Varius Avitus at all; he was M. Aurelius Antoninus.

The boy must, even in his long silk robes and his tiara, have been singularly attractive (though there is little that is attractive in his coin-portraits), and he was evidently well known to the numerous soldiers who came into Emesa on leave.

So the incredible project was achieved. The boy was smuggled into the camp. That this happened without the knowledge of his grand-mother and of his mother, as Dio says, we may take leave to doubt.[118] The troops proclaimed him. To Macrinus the thing at first appeared a joke; it was less of a joke when, sending the new Prefect of the Guard to bring back his head, he received back the Prefect's head instead; it was no joke at all when his troops and the boy's joined battle. The women—Maesa and Soaemias—stopped the beginning of a rout, jumping from their chariots and appealing to the troops. The boy himself, on horseback, fought with inspired courage. It was the single creditable achievement of his, admittedly short, life. The date was June 8th, 218.

Macrinus, adopting a disguise which was anything but effective, hoped to get back to Rome and to rally support there for himself and for his son Diadumenus. He was conveniently murdered on the way. The Senate which unhappily had acted on Macrinus' information— that the boy was not quite right in the head—and had declared war on him, his cousin, their mothers and their grandmother, received its first information of the true state of affairs in a communication from the new Emperor, who described himself as 'Imperator, Caesar, son of Antoninus (Caracalla), and holder of both the proconsular and the tribunician power'. He did not know, perhaps, that by centuries-old convention, an Emperor waited to receive such powers and titles by the Senate's decree.[119]

The women, who knew their Rome, reasonably wondered what would happen when Rome first saw in the flesh the fantastic and pretentious youth who had now declared himself to be Rome's Emperor.

The long progress to Rome started, and the world can never have witnessed a more extraordinary cortège. As centre-piece there was the new Emperor Elagabalus (for he had taken the god's name as his own), the boy with his stone. There were the three ladies—for his aunt Mamaea was not the woman to be left behind. There was his young cousin. And there were the king-makers, the chief architects of the victory which had been won in the field: Gannys, an inferior member of Maesa's household who had got on so well that he combined the parts of tutor of the boy and paramour of his mother,[120] and a more extraordinary character still, P. Valerius Comazon, who had started life as an actor, but had then joined up in the ranks, a man for whom there was a startling career in store.[121]

Their journey was interrupted by the season, and they settled down to enjoy the winter in Nicomedia in Bithynia. Perhaps the boy was ill for a time; a nervous breakdown would be more than understandable. But, with his stone, he was happy; he organized complicated celebrations of its worship and was regularly costumed in his priestly outfit, wearing silk, a nightmare of purple and gold, with necklaces and bangles and, on his head, a richly bejewelled mitre. So costumed, he announced his entry on his second consulship and his second year of tribunician power. His grandmother and his mother conferred with the military chiefs, Gannys and Comazon, and decided that, with Rome ahead, they must endeavour to make at least a passable Roman of him.[122] When they explained that it was a mark of decadence in Rome to wear silk, he simply replied that there was something cheap about wool, and that he could not wear it. He was developing a will of his own. When Gannys continued to play the heavy tutor, Elagabalus, who at an earlier stage had thought of creating him a Caesar and marrying him to his mother, decided that the time had come for him to die. 'To be sure, Gannys was living rather luxuriously and was fond of accepting bribes, but for all that he did no one any harm and bestowed many benefits upon many people.' Such was the temperate judgement of Cassius Dio.[123]

The boy's grandmother who, after all, spoke from long experience of social life at a high level in Rome, told him that by Roman standards he looked more like a woman than a man; but so far from taking a lesson from her, Elagabalus commissioned a vast picture of himself in the act of sacrifice to his stone (which was in the picture also). This was sent ahead to Rome with instructions that it should be hung prominently in the Senate-House. It would enable senators to familiarize themselves in advance with his appearance. It was unlikely to please them, for all its beauty; the instruction that they should sacrifice before it would please them even less.[124]

In early July 219 the imperial party reached Rome. The Romans looked at him and at his extraordinary clothing, and called him the Assyrian. A youth who was circumcised and did not eat pork could not by any stretch of imagination be thought of as a Roman.[125]

The most commendable of his emotions was his pious devotion to his stone; and he may well have believed in simple sincerity that, in bringing the sun god to Rome, he was one of Rome's greatest benefactors. Temples were built to the sun god Elagabalus, the largest and most important of them on the Palatine, and to this temple the Emperor sought to remove objects of traditional veneration like the palladium, which the Vestal Virgins preserved and which Aeneas, it was believed, had brought from Troy. There was, too, a 'holy marriage' between his god and a goddess, the Carthaginian Juno Caelestis, whose statue was brought to Rome for the purpose.[126] As priest of Elagabalus, he was 'the highest priest of all', 'Sacerdos amplissimus'; and in his ingenuous manner he thought that, in this capacity, he should marry a sacred and dedicated woman.[127] So he rid himself of his first wife and married instead Aquilia Severa, who was a Vestal Virgin. It is hard to know how much offence was given by this act, though it was intended, no doubt, to flatter, not to insult, the native religion of Rome. Indeed he had the boldness to say, 'I did it in order that godlike children might spring from me, the high priest, and her, the high priestess.' 'He ought to have been scourged in the Forum,' Cassius Dio observed, for that was traditionally the punishment of anyone who violated the chastity of a Vestal Virgin.[128]

The worship of his god was extravagant and orgiastic and at first, no doubt, had for the Romans the attraction of a splendid and altogether novel carnival.[129] Once a year, at midsummer, the black stone was taken through Rome from the Palatine to its temple outside the walls; it was carried in a car drawn by six white horses, and the Emperor would perform the difficult exercise of running and walking backwards in front of it, so as not to take his eyes off its splendour. In case he fell, the streets were sprinkled with gold dust.

To the womenfolk who, with Gannys and Comazon, had established him on his dangerous and dizzy pinnacle, he showed the greatest deference and respect in public. He did his duty to his great-aunt Julia at the start; she was consecrated when his 'father' Caracalla was consecrated. His mother received such public honours as were thought once to be the ambition of Livia and of Agrippina, but which no woman had ever before enjoyed. Soon after his accession she was introduced to a session of the Senate, given an official seat beside the consuls, and even invited to put her signature to a decree, as if she were a bona fide member of that body.[130] It may be that this happened no more than once.

Julia Maesa and Soaemias were accorded the right to coin from the start of his rule, and retained the right to the end. Both received the title 'Augusta'. His three wives, during the short period of their marriages, had the right of coinage also. In laudatory language Julia Soaemias was called 'Mother of Augustus' and 'Mother of the Army', Julia Maesa 'Mother of the Army and the Senate'.[131]

He thought—or perhaps his grandmother persuaded him—that, as Rome had a Senate of men, it should also have a Senate of women. This body was set up and met on the Quirinal. Its only known achievement and one which, perhaps, was not altogether useless, was the issue of a complicated code of etiquette for women in Rome: 'What kind of clothing each might wear in public, who was to yield precedence, and to whom, who was to advance and kiss another, who might ride in a chariot, on a horse, on a pack animal, or on an ass, who might drive in a carriage drawn by mules or in one drawn by oxen, who might be carried in a litter, and whether the litter might be made of leather, or of bone, or covered with ivory or with silver, and lastly who might wear gold or jewels on her shoes?'[132]

It is possible that in early days priestesses had held meetings as a body; and, though Elabagalus' 'Parliament of Women' was dissolved at his death, it was revived later by the Emperor Aurelian, and perhaps on other occasions also.[133]

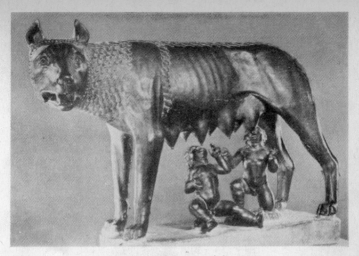

1 The She-Wolf (*Lupa*) and the Twins
(a) In bronze on the Campidoglio at Rome
(wolf 5th century B.C.; twins of Renaissance date)
(b) In mosaic from Aldbrough, Britain (probably 4th century A.D.)

2(a) Vestal Virgin

2(b) Roman Matron

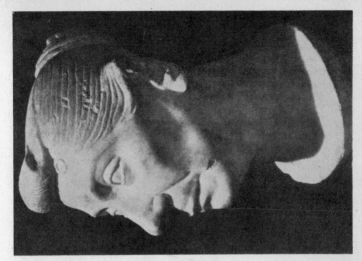

3(b) An old woman

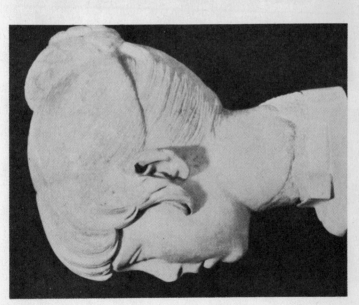

3(a) A young woman

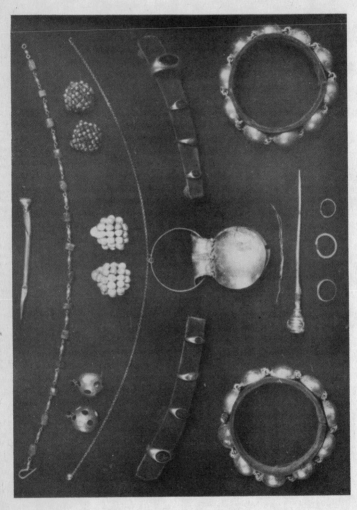

4 Jewellery from the House of the Menander, Pompeii (showing hair-pins [*acus*] necklaces, ear-rings, bracelets, rings)

5(a) Antony and Octavia

5(b) Livia

5(c) Agrippina i

5(d) Agrippina ii

Coins: Ashmolean Museum, Oxford

5(e) Messalina and her children

6 Head thought to be a portrait of Octavia

7(a) Plotina   7(b) Sabina

7(c) Faustina i after consecration, with reverse, Faustina sitting on a
low chair under a kind of shrine in a *biga* drawn by elephants
ridden by mahouts

7(d) Faustina ii, with reverse, Concordia
Ashmolean Museum, Oxford

8(a) Septimius Severus, Julia Domna, Caracalla (Geta defaced),
painting on circular wooden panel from Egypt.

8(b) Julia Maesa   8(c) Julia Mamaea

8(d) Julia Soaemias   8(e) Helena

Coins: Ashmolean Museum, Oxford

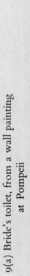

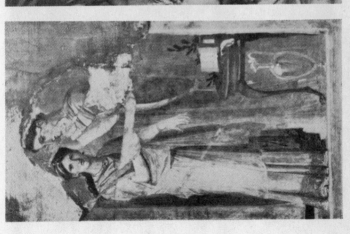

9(a) Bride's toilet, from a wall painting at Pompeii

9(b) Wedding scene, from a stone relief at Mantua

10 Husband and wife
(a) Etruscan, from Cerveteri (6th century B.C.)
(b) Roman (Republican period)

11(b) Portrait of a baker (or perhaps a student of law) with his wife, from Pompeii

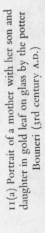

11(a) Portrait of a mother with her son and daughter in gold leaf on glass by the potter Bouneri (3rd century A.D.)

12 Dancing girls (not women athletes), mosaics of 4th/5th century A.D. from Piazza Armerina, Sicily

13 Various coiffures

(a) Five heads (imperial period)

(b) Julia, daughter of Titus

(c) Flavian woman

(d) Woman from
Herculaneum

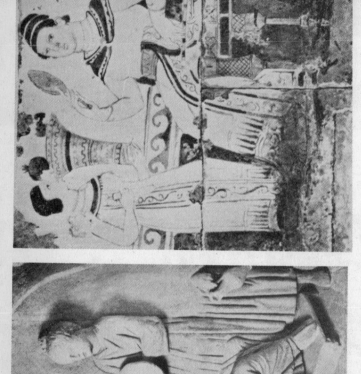

14 (a) Stone relief from Neumagen, 3rd century A.D.

14 (b) Wall painting from a grave at Cumae, 4th/3rd century B.C.

15(a) A Gallic soap factory
(or pharmacy)

15(b) Shopping: buying
belts and pillows

16 Girl decanting perfumes, from the Farnesina house in Rome
(late Augustan period)

While Soaemias was content to enjoy, for the short time that they lasted, the extravagant pleasures of a disordered life, her intelligent mother realized that this wild extravaganza could not last much longer. Two facts had to be faced; first that (except in a project which was grandiose and theatrical, like the completion of Caracalla's Baths) Elabagalus had as little interest in administration as he had talent for it; secondly, that he had now revealed himself as a homosexual pervert of quite abnormal delinquency. 'He performed such acts,' Cassius Dio wrote, 'as I should be ashamed to describe.' He proceeded to describe them.[134] The *Historia Augusta* devours the scandals with the avidity of a dung beetle. Much that is recorded as fact was, no doubt, the imaginative invention of the disordered minds of the narrators. But much was true. And when Elagabalus' devotion to the fair-haired charioteer Hierocles, by origin a Carian slave, reached the point of sending for his slave-mother and giving her the rank of a consul's or an ex-consul's lady, and when he spoke of making Hierocles a Caesar, the limit was reached. 'He worked with wool, sometimes wore a hair-net, and painted his eyes, daubing them with white-lead and alkanet. Once, indeed, he shaved his chin, and held a festival to mark the event; but after that he had the hairs plucked out, so as to look more like a woman.' His grandmother took him to task, and begged him to lead a normal life, but he was deaf to her pleading.[135]

Maesa was a realist. The boy was incorrigible and would have to be sacrificed; his mother would have to be sacrificed too.[136] How fortunate that she had an excellent candidate for the succession—her other grandson. Mamaea naturally welcomed the prospect of a larger part than that of Emperor's aunt, and blushed no more than her sister had blushed in confirming the rumour which was now assiduously circulated, that she too had been unfaithful to her husband, that her boy had no right to the name Gessius Bassianus, for he too was really Caracalla's son. The boy was happily of a very different disposition from his cousin, and did credit to the care which his mother had taken over his education. He was untainted by Elagabalus' abnormalities. People liked him; in particular—and this mattered—the soldiers of the Guard.

As it was never wise to disregard the formalities, it was desirable that Elagabalus should be persuaded to adopt him; and his first reluctance was overcome when it was pointed out to him that, with a Caesar to attend to the tedious business of administration, he would be free to devote the whole of his time to his religion. So the adoption was

performed; a boy of sixteen adopted another of twelve. Elagabalus
even marked the occasion with a certain wit. 'I seem,' he said, 'to have
acquired a very large son.' Bassianus became M. Aurelius Severus
Alexander.[137]

Not long after the adoption, Elagabalus suspected its purpose and,
jealous of his cousin's greater popularity, sought to rid himself of him.
But Alexander had his mother's protection—she never allowed him to
eat food which had been sent by the Emperor—and also his grandmother's. In the end Elagabalus was murdered by the Guard at Rome;
they killed his mother too.[138] Not content with killing them, they
stripped their bodies and dragged them through the streets of Rome;
his they threw into the river.

So at the age of thirteen and a half Alexander Severus succeeded to
the Empire, and he was Emperor for over twelve years, dying at the
age of twenty-five in A.D. 235. At last Mamaea came into her own.
She received the title 'Augusta' at her son's accession.[139]

Though Alexander was no Elagabalus, neither his mother nor his
grandmother was willing to take any risk. 'The title and dignity of
Empire was his, but the control of affairs and the administration of the
Empire rested with his mother and grandmother; and they tried to in-
troduce everywhere a new element of seriousness and responsibility.'[140]
Two important steps were taken to mark the change of climate.
In sharp contrast to the antagonism which had prevailed between
Elagabalus and the Senate, a council of sixteen senators was set up,
to advise his successor. This was the women's doing. And the god
Elagabalus, after his brief Roman holiday, was prudently returned to
Emesa.

Four years later Maesa died and was consecrated.[141] Her brave and
venturesome life had brought its disappointments. But at the end she
could afford to reflect on the success with which, time and again, she
had foreseen danger and had forestalled it. Her courage she shared
with the other women of the family, her sister and her two daughters.
Her death, in its surprising peacefulness, was her own. She was not
murdered, as both her daughters were murdered. She had not, like her
sister, to take her life.

Having, with his grandmother, created her son's career, Mamaea,
thanks in part to her good intentions, came very near to destroying it,
once Julia Maesa was dead.[142] It is perhaps no accident that in this

family of strong women, the men were conspicuously weak. Alexander soon found that he was so well guarded against temptation by his mother, and that his days were so fully occupied in profitable learning, that he was left with little opportunity to manœuvre independently, in however innocent a fashion. Worse still, he discovered that his mother's life was anything but a model of innocence; she was behaving in the tradition of the women of her family, and hoarding money in a shameful fashion; his integrity was too great to be satisfied with her explanation—that she was doing this in order to ensure that he would have money, should he ever need it, to bribe the troops.

At this point he challenged her and married—a lady with the elaborate name of Gnaea Seia Herennia Sallustia Barbia Orbiana, the daughter of Sallustius Varius Macrinus, or perhaps Macrinianus.[143] It is all too easy to imagine the consternation which ensued. Among the strong-minded women of this family there was none who liked the notion of a daughter-in-law, particularly if the daughter-in-law, as consort of the ruling Emperor, would usurp her mother-in-law's position of first lady at Court. But this is what now happened. Faced with the crisis, Mamaea called up all her reserves of strength. She tried to prevent her son from giving his wife the title 'Augusta', and in this, naturally enough, she failed. But that was not the end. After a year or two (by autumn 227) she had achieved her object, and wrecked the marriage. The Empress was banished to Africa; her father was executed.[144] Alexander married again, perhaps even twice more. If he had children, they died in childhood.

It is hard to know how seriously to take the *Life* of Alexander in the *Historia Augusta*, according to which, because of the respect which he showed to senators, he was a paragon of all the virtues.

His fond mother never deserted him. When he left Rome to campaign in the East against the Persians in 231, she went with him; when he was forced to go North to deal with trouble on the Rhine two years later, she went too. It was dislike of Mamaea and her avarice, as well as of the favouritism which she and Alexander showed to the soldiers who had come from the East,[145] which encouraged the troops on the Rhine to murder both him and her at Mainz on March 18th or 19th, 235. To succeed him, after all these years of petticoat government, the troops selected C. Julius Verus Maximinus for their Emperor. He was, until recently, a centurion, a man who had started life as a Thracian peasant. He possessed prodigious physical strength and had no education at all. He ruled three years without ever visiting Rome, or indeed Italy, and then he in his turn was killed.

It is surprising to find a woman as avaricious and as dominating as Mamaea described by the monk Zonaras as 'a woman of exemplary devotion'. She was interested in Christianity, and so curious to know more about it that, when she was at Antiocheia—before Elabagalus' proclamation, and the family's move to Rome—she had Origen brought under military escort and, at her wish, he preached her a sermon.[146] Her son was evidently brought up to be not unsympathetic to Christianity, for his private chapel included, side by side with the statues of a small number of deified emperors, images of Apollonius of Tyana, Christ, Abraham and Orpheus.[147] This, then, for Christians, was a comforting period on which to look back at the time of the terrible persecutions which came early in the following century. It seemed no real exaggeration to declare that Mamaea had been a Christian. But this was to go some way beyond the evidence.[148]

v. The Mother of Constantine and the Daughter of Diocletian

In the period of exactly half a century which divided the death of Alexander Severus in 235 from the accession of Diocletian in 284, there were something like forty men who, in some cases only for a few days, enjoyed the illusion of being Roman Emperor. The armies chose and proclaimed an Emperor; then they killed him, and chose and proclaimed his successor. The frontiers were breached by terrible invaders, with names that were new—Franks, Goths, Alamanni, Persians. In 260 the Emperor Valerian was taken prisoner by the Persians, and treated with signal ignominy. The period produced but one woman of real distinction, Zenobia.

Some three hundred years after Cleopatra's death, in Aurelian's triumph in A.D. 274, the Roman populace enjoyed the unprecedented spectacle of a woman who, before she was made captive, had, in a letter to the Emperor, given herself the title of 'Queen of the Orient'. This was Zenobia (Bat Zabbai) the Palmyrene, dark, beautiful, weighed down in the triumph by an abundance of jewellery whose burden, for all her toughness, she could scarcely support. This woman claimed Cleopatra for an ancestress and, in the days of her freedom, she had dressed in what she imagined to be the costume of Dido. She was a paragon of chaste womanhood and after 267 was the widow—and perhaps, also, the murderess—of that Odaenathus of Palmyra who had restored Roman power in the East after the débâcle in which Valerian was taken prisoner by the Persians. An active widow, Zenobia conquered Egypt and most of the Eastern Empire; but when she proclaimed her son Augustus, the Emperor Aurelian came East and fought her. He captured Palmyra, and his cavalry were too fast for the camels on which she sought to escape. So she was taken, and brought to Rome, and exhibited at his triumph. And then she was allowed to retire into private life and given a villa at Tivoli, up on the hill or down on the plain, near Hadrian's. With her outlandish Roman accent, she must have been a startling acquisition for local society. Greek, Aramaic and Egyptian were the languages in which she felt herself at home.[149]

Despite all the disasters, the Empire survived, thanks to the clear-headed genius of Diocletian, whose Dalmatian orgins were of the humblest. He was, perhaps, at the start of his life, a slave-boy.

He restored safety to the frontiers, and reasonable administration to the Empire, through his appreciation of the fact that the Empire was too large to be governed by a single man, even with the co-operation of a Caesar. There must be two Augusti and two Caesars. And the Empire, instead of being adminstered from Rome, must be administered from two more strategically sited centres, from Milan in the West, which should be the residence of one Augustus, and Nicomedia in Bithynia, which should be the residence of the other. Rome's day as capital of the Roman Empire was over. So was a system of government which, in some of its essentials, still recalled the settlement of Augustus. Government henceforth was to be monarchy of the most absolute kind. In 293 the new system was set up. The first Augusti were Diocletian himself (at Nicomedia) and his old friend Maximian (at Milan); the Caesars were Constantius in Gaul and Britain, Galerius on the Danube. It was clear that dynastic marriages would play the same important part in such government as they had played, for in-stance, at the time of Julius Caesar's association with Crassus and Pompey and at the time of the triumvirate which followed Julius Caesar's death. So, for a start, Galerius was to marry Valeria—Dio-cletian's daughter, of whom he was evidently fond—and Constantius was to discard his concubine and marry Theodora, the step-daughter of Maximian, to whom he had in fact been betrothed since 289.

The history of the last period which this book covers can be told in terms of two of these three women. The concubine of Constantius, and mother of Constantine, was a splendid intrepid woman, who travelled to Jerusalem at the age of seventy-three, and survived the experience by some years. The other was Diocletian's daughter Valeria, 'whose melancholy adventures might furnish a very singular subject for tragedy'.[150]

Helena was Constantius' concubine. Romance, passing for history, has made her a king's daughter; has even clutched at a sentence in a panegyric and made her a Briton; has even believed her to be Constantius' married wife. She was, in fact, probably Dalmatian, and her father an inn-keeper.[151] Constantius, whose social origins were more distinguished than those of his colleagues, evidently encountered her in one of those journeys between frontiers which officers so often made. At the end of her life, naturally, when she was 'domina nostra Flavia Augusta Helena' and confronted the world as the Emperor Constantine's distinguished mother, a powerful patroness of the Christian Church (and Christianity did not at all like the idea of concubines), people flattered her, even in public inscriptions, by calling her Constantius' wife, 'divi Constanti castissima coniunx'.[152]

Constantine was five years old when, in 293, Constantius discarded Helena, became a Caesar, and married Theodora. There were three sons and three daughters of the marriage.

Valeria married Galerius, whose ancestry was no more distinguished than her father's, for he had started life as a herdsman. The marriage lasted until Galerius' death in 310. There were no children, but she was a good mother to her husband's bastard son Candidianus. Like her mother Prisca, she was in sympathy with the Christians; perhaps, though not baptized, they were members of the Christian Church.[153]

On May 1st, 305, Diocletian surprised the world, as Sulla had once surprised it, by resigning his power and by persuading his fellow-Augustus, Maximian, however unwillingly, to follow his example. His reason may have been the same as Sulla's, that his health was failing. He was fifty-nine years old and enjoyed, in retirement, a further nine years of life. His splendid palace at Split was already built and waiting for him; the pleasure of growing cabbages lay ahead.[154] Maximian retired to a villa in Lucania.

The new Augusti were Constantius and Galerius (Diocletian's son-in-law); the Caesars were Maximin Daia (nephew and adopted son of Galerius) and Severus. Little over a year later Constantius, who had

recovered Britain after its revolt under Carausius, died at York, and
Constantine was acclaimed by the troops in Britain as his successor.
Galerius accepted this news with little grace, but recognized him as a
Caesar, and it was as a result of the political confusion of the ensuing
years that Maximian, who had emerged from his retirement, decided
that he would acquire a powerful ally if he bound Constantine to
himself by marriage. So Constantine found himself, at the age of
nineteen in 307 in the same predicament which had confronted his
father fourteen years earlier. He had to part with his concubine
Minervina, who was already the mother of his attractive boy Crispus,
and to marry Fausta (Flavia Maxima Fausta, younger daughter of the
Emperor Maximian, and sister of Maxentius). The wedding took
place at Arles early in 307, and we possess a panegyric allegedly written
for the occasion.[155] It speaks of the honourable estate of marriage and
of the importance of children, who may grow up and become soldiers,
in language which would have commended itself as much to the censor
Metellus Macedonicus as to the Emperor Augustus; it flatters the bridegroom in language which could hardly be surpassed as sycophancy
except, perhaps, by the language in which it flatters the bride's father.
The bride it scarcely mentions at all. But that was natural perhaps. It
is very difficult to say much about a little girl of nine.

She was, by Roman tradition, three years too young for marriage.
But Emperors need not observe the regulations which bind the lives
of lesser men; and, in any case, Constantine and Fausta were engaged
already, and there was a picture of the pair of them, in token of the fact,
in Maximian's palace at Aquileia.[156] The marriage would have taken
place in any case; its date—a pure formality—had merely been advanced by a few years. So it might have been pleaded.

Some time elapsed, not unnaturally, before their first child was born.
There were, in the end, three children, all sons—Constantine ii, Constantius and Constans.

Acting, perhaps, under the persuasion of his mother, who was an
enthusiastic pagan, Galerius induced Diocletian to consent, however
unwillingly, to the issue on 303 of the edicts which authorized the
persecution of the Christians. Diocletian's retirement followed not
very much later, together with the elevation of Galerius to be Augustus,
and of his wife Valeria to be 'Augusta', 'sacratissima ac piissima Augusta, materque castrorum'. In 311, when he was a dying man, Galerius
revoked the edicts by the issue of an Act of Toleration; and there were
four imperial women, all strongly attracted to Christianity if, indeed,

they were not Christians already, who will have known a deep relief—Fausta, Helena, Prisca and Valeria. It was, perhaps, the last moment of happiness that these last two women were ever to know; for it was from now that misfortunes broke over them fit, as Gibbon said, to make a tragedy.

Galerius on his death in 311—which was horrid, like Sulla's and Herod's, and is therefore described circumstantially by the historians—committed his wife and son to the care of Licinius, who had been his fellow-Augustus since 308; but they mistrusted Licinius—unwisely, perhaps, in the event—and took refuge with Maximin Daia, who had become Caesar in 305. The boy Candidianus, who fell into Licinius' hands, was well received at first, and then put out of the way.

In the fight for personal mastery which ruined the effectiveness of Diocletian's reorganization of the government of the Empire, Maximin's first thought on the arrival, in deep mourning, of Galerius' widow, was that it would suit his book well to divorce his wife and marry her.[157] 'The vile animal was inflamed with passion. The lady was still in black, and not yet out of mourning. He sent and begged for her hand, undertaking to rid himself of his present wife, if she agreed. Valeria was perfectly open, and gave him the only possible answer. While she was still in mourning, she could not possibly think about marrying, when the ashes of her husband, his father,* were not yet cold. And it was monstrous of him to divorce a faithful wife. That, no doubt, was the way in which, in the course of time, he would treat *her*.' But there was, no doubt, more of politics in the proposal than, as Lactantius would have it, lust.

He responded harshly. Many people were put to death, for no other reason than that they were her friends; and Valeria and Prisca were banished to a remote part of Syria. Diocletian sent protests from his retirement at Split, but they were not answered. Diocletian did no more; he was, after all, an old man, tired of the world, interested only in his garden. Then, when Maximin's army was defeated by Licinius in 313 at Byzantium, and he died in Cappadocia, Prisca and Valeria set out once more in their wanderings. For fifteen sad months they moved from place to place in the East, their identity disguised, these two women who had been imperial consorts in their time; they started, perhaps, with the illusive hope that somehow in the end they would find their way to Diocletian, but it was not long before that hope was extinguished by the news of Diocletian's death. At the end of fifteen

---

* Galerius was Daia's uncle, and had adopted him.

months' wandering, in Thessalonica, they were recognized. They were publicly beheaded, and their bodies thrown into the sea.[158]

Helena's was not merely a happier, it was by absolute standards a splendidly satisfactory, life. In the early days of Constantius' marriage to Theodora she might reasonably have felt a little bitterness, a little jealousy. But when it was her son Constantine, not Theodora's sons, who won the satisfying distinction of power, she can have enjoyed the pleasure of revenge; for Theodora was sent with her sons to the obscure retirement of Toulouse, from which she seems never to have emerged.[159] Not that such mean emotions would have become so devout a Christian woman; for after 312, with Constantine, she was a Christian convert of immoderate zeal.[160]

She also enjoyed the comfort of extreme wealth, and she had property in various parts of the world. She owned considerable property in the city of Rome itself, at the eastern juncture of the Caelian and Esquiline, on both sides of the Aurelian wall, from the present-day site of St. John Lateran to that of Santa Croce in Gerusalemme, an area in which three inscriptions have been found, set up in her honour.[161] Inside the wall was her Roman residence, the 'palatium Sessorianum'.

There was no end to her generosity; the Christian Church, her friends, the troops, all were her beneficiaries. She contributed largely to the construction of her son's new capital, Constantinople which, naturally, contained a number of her statues.

Christianity for her embraced more than charity and ritual; it included doctrine. So, responding no doubt to Eusebius' teaching, she was a rabid Arian, as—also under the strong influence of Eusebius— was Constantine's half-sister Constantia,[162] who in 313 married Licinius and was present in 325 at the Council of Nicaea, giving all her support to the Arian cause. It was under this feminine influence, perhaps, that Constantine supported the Arians in the controversy.

After the official 'foundation' of Constantinople in 330, the intrepid Helena set out on her journey to Jerusalem, resolutely deposing Eustathius the Bishop as she went through Antioch[163] (because he was on the other side in the controversy, and so she regarded him as a dangerous theologian). She built two churches, one in Bethlehem, one on the Mount of Olives,[164] and, on returning to Constantinople, she built a couple more. She died there in her son's presence, and her body was taken for burial to Rome.

There was little in her life that she had cause to regret—except, perhaps, her part in securing the death of her daughter-in-law Fausta,

Constantine's wife, in 326. The facts of this sorry story are all too uncertain. Constantine himself reversed the process by which Augustus had grown from a lustful, ambitious, cold-blooded young murderer into a grave and revered statesman, and since Constantine had his new religion to improve him, it was the more deplorable that, towards the end of his life, his rule degenerated so badly. By no blot is it stained worse than by the murder of his son Crispus, to whom he was devoted. Crispus was married—to another Helena—in 321, and his first child was born a year later. He had an admirable public career, even though in 326, when he was poisoned, he was no more than twenty years old. Perhaps he had been indiscreet. Perhaps he was in fact conspiring against his father. That he was as innocent as Hippolytus and that his stepmother Fausta was as passionate as Phaedra, and behaved as Phaedra behaved, is recorded, but is hardly to be believed.[165]

That Fausta was held to be in some way responsible for Crispus' death is evident, and in 326 Helena induced Constantine to put her to death in a singularly horrible fashion. She was roasted—or scalded— to death in the baths.[166]

Helena is gloriously commemorated in Rome today. That in Jerusalem she in fact acquired fragments of the true cross, the cynic may take leave to doubt; and, in view of the fact that there is no mention of this in Eusebius, he will have the historian on his side. But Helena may have been assured that some object which she had acquired in Jerusalem was of such a kind; Constantine may have shared her illusion and that may have been the reason why he had built, on land belonging to his mother, the church which was the original of the surviving Santa Croce in Gerusalemme.

Next to the church of Sant'Agnese, which Constantine or his daughter first built, is the church of Santa Costanza on the Via Nomentana, with mosaics on the barrel-vaulting of the encircling ambulatory, of birds and fruit, the vintage and the glory of the countryside, which in Rome has no equal in loveliness. This was built by Constantine to be a mausoleum for his daughter Constantia.[167] When she died in 354, seventeen years after him, this was the spot to which her body was brought, as he intended.

PART TWO

✦✦✦✦✦✦✦✦✦✦✦✦✦✦✦✦✦✦✦✦✦✦✦✦✦✦✦✦✦✦✦

HABITS

VII

THE WEDDING CEREMONY

‹•••›

1. Choice of a Husband

THE GLAMOUR of a woman's first marriage can never be recaptured; and in describing a Roman marriage, it is of a girl's first marriage (which was more often than not her husband's first marriage too) that a modern writer, like an ancient writer before him, naturally thinks. With the steady increase of divorce under the Republic and with the penalizing later, by Augustus' legislation,* of a childless widow or divorced woman under fifty who did not marry again, second and third marriages became common. Juvenal, indeed, with the exaggeration of a satirist, speaks of a woman who married eight times within five years.[1]

Romans were evidently precocious, even by modern Mediterranean standards, and a girl was held to be ready for marriage at the age of twelve, a boy at the age of fourteen. Though marriage did not always take place so early (particularly among the lower classes, where there was difficulty in finding the dowry), the evidence of literature and of inscriptions alike establishes that fourteen was the average age of a girl at her first marriage.[2] By Augustus' stern legislation the ages at which men and women were penalized for not being married were twenty-five and twenty respectively; and it was certainly the case that many women were in their late teens when they married, and many men in their early twenties. Marcus Aurelius was twenty-four years old when he married Faustina.

In the higher social classes, in which marriages were generally arranged marriages, a son was expected to defer to his father's wishes in the choice of a bride, provided that his father did not choose some one of notoriously bad character.[3] Though a daughter, too, would naturally defer to her father's wishes, it was with her mother that her confidences were shared; and a mother felt justified in turning angrily on

* See page 221.

her husband if he had gone behind her back in arranging their daughter's marriage. There was a story that in the second century B.C. the marriage of the elder Tiberius Gracchus to Cornelia, daughter of the great Scipio Africanus, was arranged at a male banquet;[4] that when Scipio returned home and told his wife that he had arranged a marriage for their daughter, 'she was angry, as only a woman can be, because he had not consulted her about the girl, who was her daughter as much as his. She said that even if he was marrying the girl to Tiberius Gracchus, she, as a mother, ought to have been consulted'. Exactly the same story was told of the circumstances in which in the next generation the younger Tiberius Gracchus became engaged to the daughter of Appius Claudius.[5] The first story is certainly untrue, and the second story may not be true either. But the sentiment expressed in both cases was, by Roman standards, right and proper. Only in an establishment like that of the younger Cato at the end of the Republic, where women were disciplined into an old-fashioned subservience, could a proposal of marriage from Pompey, the greatest Roman alive, have been turned down by the master of the house, and the decision meekly accepted by his womenfolk.[6]

In looking for a suitable young man, a girl's parents or guardian often turned for advice to their friends. Junius Mauricus asked the younger Pliny at the turn of the first and second centuries A.D. if he could suggest a suitable match for his niece, daughter of Arulenus Rusticus, whom Domitian had put to death in A.D. 93. As always, Pliny was ready to oblige.[7] He had the very man, Minicius Acilianus of Brescia, who was about forty and, one may suspect, a little on the old side—but we do not know the lady's age.

'His face, with its highly-coloured complexion, shows breeding. He is a handsome fellow, every inch a senator. Things of this sort ought, I think, to be mentioned, for they are the qualities to which a well-behaved young woman has a right to feel entitled. Should I mention that his father is an exceedingly wealthy man?'

He should indeed. As Juvenal pointed out: if you were poor, you had little chance of succeeding as a suitor to a rich man's daughter.[8]

Husband and wife must have achieved puberty—they must conventionally be fourteen or twelve years old respectively—at the time of marriage; or the marriage was legally null. Marriage of close relations was a crime—*incestum*—punishable orginally by death, later by deportation; but in the definition of close relationship for this purpose, the rules were relaxed with time. Once marriage of second cousins was forbidden, but by the second century B.C. the marriage even of first cousins was not unusual. In the Empire Marcus Aurelius and his wife, the younger Faustina, were first cousins. When in A.D. 49 Germanicus' daughter Agrippina was selected to succeed Messalina and to be the fourth wife of the Emperor Claudius, her uncle, public opinion was reasonably shocked.* In the fourth century the marriage of an uncle with his niece was once again forbidden by law.[9]

Youth (below the age of puberty) and blood relationship within the prohibited degree, then, were absolute obstacles to marriage.

There were, in addition, marriages which the law refused to recognize. It did not recognize the marriage of a Roman and a foreigner. A Roman woman might not marry a slave. Before 445 B.C. a plebeian and a patrician might not marry. Just as a senator or a descendant of a senator through males to the third degree could not (after the *lex Julia* of 18 B.C.) marry a freedwoman, so the daughter, grand-daughter or great-grand-daughter of a senator through male descent could not marry a freedman—a prohibition which must often have seemed unreasonable when, in the early Empire, the children of a man who rose to the consulship might have the children of a freedman as their, sometimes immensely wealthy, first cousins.[10]

Until Septimius Severus altered the law, a Roman woman might not marry a ranker in the legions;† and, if she lived in a province, she might not marry an official in the Roman administrative service in that province. Nor, very sensibly, if she was a ward, might she marry her tutor or guardian or his son or grandson.[11]

In none of these cases could the law forbid a marriage from taking place; what it did was to refuse to recognize its validity. Neither party could litigate in any matter arising out of the marriage or receive any public benefits which were accorded to those who were legally married. The union was not a *matrimonium iustum*. If children were born, they were illegitimate.

Where none of these prohibitions applied and a marriage was valid by Roman law, a Roman girl's husband was either a full Roman citizen or a territorial subject of Rome who was not a Roman citizen (*peregrinus*), and in this latter case the man either possessed or did not

---

* See page 107.

† In the French Foreign Legion today legionaries may only marry after twelve years service, but an N.C.O. can marry after six years.

possess the right of marriage with a Roman (*conubium*). This right belonged, before the unification of Italy in 90 B.C., to most Latin communities in Italy; it belonged after 90 B.C. by special grant to Latin colonies. When 'conubium' was granted together with citizenship—to auxiliary troops on discharge, under the Empire; to whole communities, as it was by Claudius to the town of Volubilis in Mauretania, or to individuals—its meaning★ was wider; for it entitled men to contract a fully valid marriage with any non-Roman woman, a marriage where children would be Roman citizens.[12]

The law differentiated in these various cases as concerned the status of children of the marriage. The marriage of a Roman woman to a Roman man was, of course, a *matrimonium iustum* in the fullest sense; the children were Romans, like their parents. When a Roman woman's husband was not a Roman citizen but possessed *conubium*, the children followed their father and were not Roman citizens; if he did not possess *conubium*, they followed the mother, and were Roman citizens; but the practice changed with the passing of the *lex Minicia* (whose date is uncertain); after that, if a Roman woman married a peregrine husband who did not possess *conubium* their children did not acquire Roman citizenship, but inherited the inferior status of their father. Hadrian altered the law, so that children of a Roman mother and a Latin father were full Roman citizens.[13]

Since parents always want the best possible marriages for their children, and a girl could not marry without the consent of her father or guardian (though she could appeal at law against any refusal as being unreasonable), she had little opportunity, if she wished, of contracting a *mésalliance*. And even if her husband died and she wished to marry again, but was under the age of twenty-five, her relatives could bring pressure to bear, even to the extent of appealing to a magistrate, to prevent her from a marriage which they thought undesirable. So that if marriages took place on which the law frowned, they were marriages, no doubt, in which the bride was no longer a very young woman.[14]

Despite the fact that marriages were arranged, they succeeded often; often, because of it, they failed. A good marriage was one which satisfied both families; a successful marriage, in addition, satisfied the public

---

★ The *lex Aelia Sentia* of A.D. 4 allowed a *Latinus Iunianus*—a slave who was partially, not fully, manumitted—to secure Roman citizenship one year after the birth of his first child, provided he had married a Roman or Latin woman with the appropriate formality.

needs of the State by producing sons who in the course of time grew up and became soldiers. From the beginning of Rome's history to its end the anxious state was alive to the problem of manpower, to the need for sufficient recruits to feed its hungry legions. There can be only a limited number of families in any country today whose service tradition is so strong that a wedding is regarded as the prelude to the birth of a future soldier; in Rome the thought was one which even poets stressed.[15]

II. Betrothal

Betrothal in infancy sometimes happened; but it was general practice, no doubt, before late in the Empire it became law, that children must be able to understand what was said, when an engagement was being made; that is to say, they must be at least seven years old.[16] Indeed Augustus legislated that, for certain purposes, an engagement should not be recognized in law if the girl was under the age of ten when it was made.[17] Yet even after this, Octavia, daughter of Claudius, can have been little more than a year old when she was betrothed to L. Junius Silanus, then a youth of fourteen or fifteen.[18]

The formalities of the engagement were conducted between the future husband (or, if he was too young, by his father or tutor) and the father or guardian of the girl. In early times it was, as the lawyers say, 'bilaterally actionable'; either party could sue the other for breach of promise.

Before the end of the Republic such formality had vanished (and actions for breach of promise had vanished too) in favour of a looser system, by which the engagement was an informal agreement to marry,[19] made in writing or before witnesses, easily renounced by either party with the mere formula, Condicione tua non utor. Betrothal-gifts were exchanged, but were not of such significance as normally to warrant proceedings for restoration if the engagement was broken off. The man, however, made a substantial gift to his fiancée—donatio ante nuptias—some time before the marriage, the gift being generally recoverable, and after Constantine legally recoverable, if the engagement was broken off.[20] The sum was normally given back to him at marriage, as an addition to his bride's dowry, so as to increase the amount which would revert to her, if she became a widow. The reason why the gift was made before the marriage was that Roman law forbade the exchange of substantial gifts between husband and wife after marriage. This curious prohibition may be no earlier than Augustus; it survived to the time of Septimius Severus and Caracalla.[21]

In the turbulent political world of the late Republic and of the civil wars an engagement which had appeared satisfactory at the moment when it was arranged might, because of a change in the political situation, become unnecessary or even undesirable. Julius Caesar's daughter in 59 B.C. was on the point of marriage to a Servilius Caepio (perhaps M. Brutus) when, in Caesar's political interest, the engagement was broken off and she married Pompey.[22] The first engagement of the young Octavian—to Servilia, daughter of Julius Caesar's colleague in the consulship of 48 B.C.—was broken off when the triumvirate was formed in 43 B.C., and, in order to cement his new association with Antony, he became engaged to Antony's step-daughter (Clodia, daughter of P. Clodius and Fulvia); but before they married,[23] it became more important that he should establish a family connexion with Sextus Pompeius; so his second engagement was broken off in its turn, and he married Scribonia, sister of Sextus Pompeius' father-in-law, a woman much older than himself, already twice married and the mother of children.

The engaged couple were *sponsus* and *sponsa*. The engagement was sealed with a kiss, and by a custom which had come, perhaps, from the East and which was in origin an earnest of the payment of purchase money (*arra*), the man placed an iron ring[24] (*anulus pronubus*) on the third finger of his fiancée's left hand.* Relatives and friends were invited to a party to celebrate the happy occasion: *sponsalia* it was called. It was an indication of Augustus' friendly informality when he was Emperor that, until he was very old, he would accept invitations to such parties. Gaius Caligula, too, appears to have attended quite undistinguished engagement parties.[26]

While it may be assumed that the proceedings were very strange and hardly comprehensible to the two chief parties, if they were still children, the older people no doubt enjoyed themselves with family talk and family reminiscence and, if the engagement was a really satisfactory one from the point of view of both families, they were happy in anticipating the advantages which would follow the union, in business, perhaps, or in politics. The Romans, after all, were an extremely practical people.

---

* This finger was in direct nervous communication with the heart. So, at least, on what he considered good scientific authority (Egyptian autopsies) Aulus Gellius would have us think.[25]

Cicero's daughter Tullia was twelve years old when she became engaged in 67 B.C. to her first husband.[27] The marriage took place four years later, and, when it was ended by his premature death in early 57, she was once again in the marriage market. A year later, then aged twenty-three, she was engaged to Furius Crassipes. We have the letters which her father wrote to her uncle Quintus in Sardinia[28] in late March, to say that he hoped that Crassipes was safely hooked; in April, to say that the betrothal formalities were completed on the 7th and that he had given an engagement party on the 8th. When the marriage was dissolved in 51, Ti. Nero (father, in the event, of the later Emperor Tiberius) travelled all the way to Cilicia, which Cicero was governing, to sue for her hand. Cicero gave him his blessing, and sent agents to Rome to report his wishes; but they arrived too late. Tullia (now twenty-nine years old) and her mother had made their own disastrous choice. The betrothal party had already been celebrated; she was going to marry the infamous Dolabella.[29]

III. Forms of Marriage[30]

There were three different forms of marriage in the early days of Rome and in every case the wife passed out of the authority of her father and owed all but inescapable submission to her husband; in fact, she exchanged one dependence for another; she changed her family. Well before the end of the Republic women rebelled against such servitude and, though the original forms of marriage were still recognized in law, they were rare in practice. The 'free marriage' had taken their place.*

The first (*coemptio*) was a survival of primitive bride-purchase. In the presence of five witnesses the bridegroom made a fictitious purchase. He paid a penny (*nummus unus*) to the father or the guardian (*tutor*) and, in exchange, received his bride. The second was marriage in virtue of simple cohabitation (*usus*), but must obviously have involved some declaration of honourable intention at the start, or there would have been no way of distinguishing between a man and his wife on the one hand and a man and his concubine on the other. In this case the husband did not acquire full authority (*potestas*) over his wife until the conclusion of a year's continuous association, and as early as the fifth century B.C., feminine wit had devised a means of avoiding such submission; by an ingenious and simple device, wives absented

* See page 45.

themselves from their husbands' company in each year for three days on end.[31]

The third form of marriage (*confarreatio*) was the most picturesque and interesting.[32] The Pontifex Maximus and the Priest of Juppiter (Flamen Dialis) presided at the Ceremony, at which ten witnesses were present. There were extensive sacrifices: a sheep, spelt-bread (*farreus panis*), fruits, salt cake (*mola salsa*). The bride and groom sat on adjoining chairs, over which a fleece—the skin, perhaps, of the sheep which had been sacrificed—was spread. It is not certain that this form of marriage was restricted to patricians, but it is certain that it was, and continued under the Empire to be, the only form of marriage which was legitimate in the case of the holders of four of the highest priesthoods of the State—the Rex Sacrorum and the Flamen Dialis (whose wives were automatically priestesses), the Flamen Martialis and the Flamen Quirinalis. No one was eligible for any of these priesthoods whose parents had not been married by *confarreatio* and who had not himself been married by the same ceremony. Divorce (*diffarreatio*) being in such cases an immensely complicated and difficult achievement and one in which the husband alone could take the initiative, emancipated womanhood objected to the ceremony. Indeed, the Flamen Dialis and his wife could in no circumstances whatever be divorced;* death alone could part them, and if she died first, he had at once to resign his priesthood. Not surprisingly, the office remained unfilled from 87 B.C. for seventy-five years, and when Tiberius was Emperor, the law was altered so as to restrict the absolute submission of the wife of the Flamen Dialis to the sphere of her religious duties.[33]

As early as the third century B.C. free marriage had become the general practice. By this the wife retained her property and, as she did not pass under the absolute authority of her husband, divorce was easy.

iv. Fixing the Day

Not all days are marrying days. According to the tradition of the Russian Orthodox Church weddings might not take place between Christmas and Easter; and in the various branches of the Western Christian Church marriage in Lent and even in Advent is discouraged. Similarly, among all the superstition of ancient life, only the foolhardy

---

* A single exception—by special permission of Domitian—does not disprove this rule; see page 216.

would invite misfortune by marrying on an inauspicious day. The Roman calendar was full of such days. It was fatal to marry at a time when the spirits of the dead were at large—potentially so mischievous and so vindictive, particularly (for former husbands were involved) when widows married. For this reason February 18th–21st, the feast of the dead (the *Parentalia*) was avoided. So were August 24th, October 5th and November 8th, days when the *mundus*, an opening to the underworld in the Forum, was open; also the month of May, when the Latins sacrificed to the dead. There was a saying 'Wed in May and rue the day'. The first half of June likewise was an inauspicious period—until on June 15th the spring-cleaning of the temple of Vesta was completed and its scourings thrown into the Tiber. March (especially the 1st, 9th and 23rd) was an unlucky month for a different reason, because in this month the *Salii*—the dancing priests of Mars—'moved the shields'. 'Arms mean fighting, and fighting is alien to the spirit of marriage.' Festival days were inauspicious for first marriages, but were suitable for widows who remarried. The superstitious reason was curiously indelicate, but the distinction was easily rationalized; a first marriage, it was said, should be attended by a large wedding party and, in view of all the distractions, it was difficult to be sure of a big attendance at a wedding on a festival day. Second or third marriages, on the other hand, were the better for being quiet affairs. Days which commemorated national disasters were avoided for obvious reasons; so in each month were the Kalends (1st), the Nones (5th or 7th) and Ides (13th in some months, 15th in others)—for a variety of reasons, not least because the following days were black days and therefore not fit days for a bride to inaugurate her domestic and religious duties as mistress of her new home.[34]

The wedding must be held, then, on an auspicious day,[35] a *hilaris dies* —best of all, in the second half of June, in Nature's season of abundant fruitfulness, at harvest-time. For superstitions about weddings, like the ceremonial of weddings, were survivals from early times when Romans were farmers living on and from the land. The deities of marriage— Ceres, Tellus, Picumnus and Pilumnus—belonged, all of them, to Nature and the land.

v. The Wedding[36]

Though there was a complicated and conventional succession of ceremonies, first in the bride's home, then in procession to the bridegroom's house, and finally at the bride's entry to this, her new home, and though something very like a marriage contract was signed by witnesses, neither individually nor in association did these acts constitute marriage. Whether the parties had observed every detail of the ceremony or, on the contrary, had dispensed with ceremony altogether, the law's definition of marriage was the same. It was the state of a man and a woman who lived together with mutual consent (*consensus*) as husband and wife (*adfectus maritalis*). In the absence of such consent and relationship, evidence that the ceremonial had been complied with, or indeed that the marriage had been consummated, counted for nothing.[37]

Religion and superstition—which, though no longer understood, were the basis of established tradition—account for most of the ceremonies: the expulsion of influences, the appeasement of spirits, which might do harm, and the encouragement, in particular, of powers capable of engendering fertility. By the end of the Republic the ceremonial had lost its religious significance for the participants, and the Roman world had to wait for its conversion to Christianity before the religious aspect of marriage was, ever again, of primary importance. The ceremony was a civil ceremony; and there was, of course, the question of the dowry; for it was as much to the interest of the bride's father (or *tutor*) as to the interest of the bridegroom (and, perhaps, his father) that on this very important subject there should be no opportunity of a quibble later on.

The young bride surrendered her childhood's toys, dedicating them to her household gods, and she surrendered too her childhood's dress, which until late in the Republic was a toga (*toga praetexta*). Then she was dressed for the ceremony.[38]

First of all, her hair. Before this her hair had not been parted and had been gathered up at the back of her head, tied by a ribbon or fastened by a pin, before it fell back over the neck in the style of a 'horse's tail'.

For the wedding it was parted into six locks (*sex crines*), which were fastened together with woollen fillets (*vittae*) at the top of her head in the shape of a cone (*meta*), called *tutulus*. This was a primitive coiffure which, except for certain priestesses, survived only for brides on their wedding day.

The parting of the bride's hair must be done with a bent iron spearhead (*hasta recurva, hasta caelibaris*). There was a welter of speculation about the reason for this practice; modern anthropology suggests that its original object was to dispel the evil spirits which reside particularly in the hair. A spearhead with which a gladiator had been killed was thought particularly efficacious; but to speak of 'the application to the bride's tresses of a spear still dripping with the blood of a stabbed gladiator', as Sir James Frazer does, is to assume, somewhat fantastically, that, whenever a Roman wedding took place, a freshly-killed gladiator was always available.[39]

The bride's 'wedding veil' was oblong, of thin transparent fabric, such as georgette or voile and, in fact, a scarf rather than a veil, covering her head, but leaving her face exposed. It was of brilliant orange or flame-colour and matched by the colour of her shoes. Upon her head was placed a wreath of marjoram (*amaracus*). Her wedding dress was a *tunica recta* (a *tunica* which had been woven on an old-fashioned upright loom), made of white, fine flannel or loosely woven muslin. Like a modern wedding dress, it would never be worn, in its original form, again. For the future, as a matron, she would dress in a *stola*. The tunic was fastened about her waist by a woollen girdle knotted with what was called 'the knot of Hercules', a kind of talisman to avert ill-fortune.[40]

The guests assembled, friends and clients of the families, for whom attendance was a social obligation (*officium*). The bridegroom arrived and, dispensing with the religious preliminaries, the taking of the auspices, which had been customary in early Republican times, the bride declared herself his wife with the words, '*Ubi tu Gaius, ego Gaia.*'* This did not mean that she adopted his name, for in fact her name did not change.[41] It meant: 'To whatever family or clan you belong, I also belong.' And now she was led by a bridesmaid (the *pronuba*) to join hands with her husband. A sacrifice took place, generally of a pig. If the marriage was by *confarreatio*, the couple sat on two chairs on which a fleece had been placed, and ate spelt-cake.

Next, anyhow from the earliest days of the Roman Empire, the marriage contract, the *tabulae nuptiales*. The *auspex*—who was a cross between a family priest and a best man—pronounced the necessary formula, performing a function which had once been discharged by a real priest. And the marriage contract, which contained the agreement about the dowry, was signed by a number—probably ten—of the wedding guests. Two such contracts survive on papyrus, both from Egypt and both, probably, from the first century A.D. In both cases the

---

* It is not absolutely certain that the declaration took place at this moment. It may have been made later, when the bride first entered the bridegroom's house.

bride's jewellery, and in one her clothing, is itemized and the value of each article is recorded.[42]

The contract being signed, the moment had come for the guests to wish the couple good luck. They cried, 'Feliciter.' By this time everybody must have been ready for the 'cena', the wedding breakfast, at which the bride reclined beside the bridegroom—who, it would appear, met the expense of the entertainment. This was not allowed to exceed a certain sum: after Augustus, a thousand sesterces.

So the first part of the wedding ceremony reached its festive conclusion.[43]

In the evening the bride was formally removed from the arms of her mother[44] (an act which may, or may not, have symbolized the original Rape of the Sabine Women) and, with a display of reluctant modesty, she was escorted to her new home. Her friends accompanied her, joining with the onlookers in shouting, 'Talasio', with little idea what the word meant* and also in shouting and singing a great deal of ribaldry, whose meaning they understood very well indeed.[45] The Romans approved of this kind of public obscenity, and for ensuring a fruitful marriage its magic effect was thought to be considerable. Walnuts were thrown by the bridegroom and by others, which children scrambled to collect.[46]

The escorting of the bride to her new home (the *domum deductio*) was a fundamental part of the marriage ceremonial, and occurred even when, as could happen legally, the bridegroom was absent and played his part by letter or by messenger. Still in such a case the procession to his house took place.[47] These, however, were abnormal occasions.

Three young boys, sons of living parents,† played an important part in the procession.[48] One held the bride's left hand, another her right hand. The third, who went in front, carried a torch which had been lit at the hearth in the bride's home. It was of whitethorn or of pine, and was one of five torches which lit the procession. Attendants carried spindle and distaff.

As the procession reached the bridegroom's house, further traditions were observed. The boy threw away the torch (as, today, the bride may throw away her bouquet), and there was a scramble to secure it,

---

* See page 25.

† In weddings of the Greek orthodox church today the boy and the girl who hold the candles on either side of the bridegroom and the bride must be children whose parents are still alive.

since its possession gave promise of long life. (If either husband or wife had been trapped into marriage and at this moment wished, incongruously, to ensure the other's rapid death, the bride, if she secured the torch, should extinguish it and place it under the marriage bed, the bridegroom, if he secured it, should leave it to burn itself out on a tomb. So, in an extraordinary passage, the learned Festus informs us.[49])

The bride rubbed oil and fat—wolf's fat in olden days, when wolves were common—on the doorposts, and wreathed them with wool; and then she was carried over the threshold.[50] Once inside the house, she touched fire and water[51] (elements as fundamental in the private home as in the House of State which the Vestal Virgins occupied). In the hall of the house was a small marriage bed—not for the married pair themselves, but for their spirits, the bridegroom's *genius* and the bride's *juno*.[52] Then, while the *epithalamium* was sung, one of the boys escorted the bride to the bedchamber, where she was undressed by women who had been married only once. They retired; the bridegroom was admitted; and so to bed.[53]

Next morning the young wife, now a matron, took part for the first time in the religious cult of her new family.

In an ideal society, perhaps, no woman would be married more than once, and Tacitus thought that he had discovered in certain of the tribes of barbarian Germany, where men refused to marry a woman who was not a virgin, a society of such a kind,[54] a society in which a woman 'loved not her husband, but the married state'. In Rome women who had been married but once (*univirae*) had a *cachet*; such women alone could undress a bride on her wedding night.

In the case of a second or subsequent marriage, the snatching of the bride from her mother would have been a ludicrous absurdity; and, as has been seen, feast days, which were inappropriate for a first marriage, were not considered inappropriate at all in the case of a woman who had been married once already. When in 50 B.C. Cato remarried Marcia, his second wife whom he had previously divorced, the ceremony was naturally a very quiet affair. No guests were invited; and Cato's nephew M. Brutus acted as *auspex*, to pronounce the necessary formula.[55]

In the case of a widower or a *divorcé*, whose new bride was marrying for the first time, the same objection did not apply. The ceremony, indeed, may have been carried out in all its detail for the child-bride

who for a few long months was second wife of the sexagenarian
Marcus Cicero.*

There were also fictitious marriages, whose only object was to cheat
the law, when there was no intention on either side to live together as
husband and wife. What one or perhaps both of the parties sought was
to escape the penalties which Augustus' legislation had imposed on
those who were below a certain age and unmarried.

It is not to be supposed, however, that the whole of the complicated
wedding ceremonial was always observed even in the case of first
marriages, any more than it is to be supposed that in any modern country respect is paid always to the wealth of persistent superstition which
surrounds a wedding. What we know of ancient weddings we owe
in the main to the patient inquiry and wild speculation of the re-
searchers and anthropologists of antiquity. Wall-paintings help, of
course. But, though there survives in Catullus' *epithalamium*[56] an
infinitely charming and elegant account of the ceremonies, we have no
detailed account of an actual Roman wedding in our ancient sources.
The main features of the occasion were the flame-coloured bridal veil;
the signing of the marriage contract; the wedding formula of the
auspex; the sacrifice; the breakfast; the torch-lit procession; and the
nuts. And for references to these, even, we are largely dependent on
satirical accounts of the degradation of imperial Rome[57]—two occasions on which a youth (once, the Emperor Nero) was 'married' to
his male lover, and one in which an Empress (Messalina) was married
formally to a commoner, in the lifetime—some even said, in the
presence—of the Emperor, her husband.†

VI. Dowry[58]

A bride must have a *trousseau*, and she must also bring a dowry; for
when, on marrying Clodia, whose father Appius Claudius, consul of
79 B.C., had just died and left his family in desperate poverty, L.
Lucullus—who was well able to afford such a gesture—declined to
accept a dowry, his act was unusual.[59] Normally, it is to be assumed,
the size of the dowry was fixed after hard bargaining between the
father or guardian of the prospective bride and her future husband and
father-in-law. In the early Republic the sum had been small and there

---

* See page 219.
† See page 106.

is no evidence to suggest that its payment was ever an unreasonably harsh exaction on the bridegroom's part, as in modern India is sometimes the case; by the early Empire, if the family was rich, a million sesterces was the conventional sum.[60] It was due for payment after the marriage in three annual instalments. Polybius has a nice account of its payment in the first half of the second century B.C. for the two daughters of the great Scipio Africanus.[61]

'Before his death the elder Scipio had fixed the dowry of each of his two daughters as fifty talents,* and his widow paid half this amount over to the two sons-in-law at the time of their marriages, but she died leaving the other half unpaid. The discharge of the outstanding debt was, therefore, the responsibility of the younger Scipio, who was nephew of the two ladies in question.

'It is the practice at Rome to allow ten months for the full provision of a bride's *trousseau* and by law the dowry itself must be paid in three annual instalments. But Scipio without a moment's hesitation instructed his banker to pay the balance of twenty-five talents for each of his aunts within the ten months. At the end of this period the two husbands, Tiberius Gracchus and Scipio Nasica, went to the bank and asked if Scipio had given any instructions about payment. When they were told that they could have the entire balance of the dowry at once and a draft for twenty-five talents was being made out for each of them, they told the banker that there must be a mistake, since legally it was not the whole of the balance but only a third that they should be getting. When the banker replied that those were Scipio's instructions, they found this hard to believe and, on the assumption that there was a misunderstanding, they went to call on the young man.

'In this they acted reasonably enough because, so far from paying up a sum as large as twenty-five talents which is not due for three years, a Roman would never think of paying a single talent one day before it was due.'

The younger Scipio was rich enough to afford such a gesture. More than a century later Cicero was not rich enough to afford any gesture at all. His daughter Tullia's third marriage to Dolabella took place in 50 B.C., and the three instalments of her dowry were due for payment on July 1st, 49, 48 and 47. Each time he wrote desperately to his banker Atticus to ask where the money was to be found, and in 47 he wondered whether it would not be better to avoid payment by arranging a

---

* Roughly a million and a quarter sesterces: a lot of money. The dowry of the mother of the younger Scipio (wife of Aemilius Paullus) had been only half that sum.

divorce (for which there were grounds enough in all conscience), even if this meant that the two-thirds of the dowry already paid might have to be written off as a dead loss.[62]

When the audience in Plautus' *Mostellaria* was addressed from the stage as 'You husbands with a lot of old women for your wives, to whom you have sold yourselves for a dowry,' there were many no doubt in whose case the shaft found its mark.[63]

The dowry (whose payment was not, as in Greece, a necessary condition for the validity of a marriage) represented in origin the bride's contribution to the expense of running the new *ménage*. Under the old form of marriage, where a wife was in the absolute power of her husband, the dowry became the absolute property of the husband if his wife was independent at the time of her marriage; but if she was previously in the power of her father, the dowry was a settlement which, already in the third century B.C., allowed in certain cases for a claim for recovery; and under the free form of marriage, which later became normal, its recovery could always be claimed: at first when the husband died or was the guilty party in the event of divorce, later, after divorce, even where the wife was the guilty party. The legal problems involved in such actions were already by Cicero's time so complicated that the distinguished jurist Ser. Sulpicius Rufus was provoked to write a book on the subject.[64]

The claim to recovery on the part of the divorced wife or widow (*actio rei uxoriae*) had this practical foundation, that she needed the dowry for further use, if she was to marry again. The husband's claim to keep at least a part of the dowry, if his wife's misbehaviour had caused the divorce, rested on two foundations: first, the retention of part of the dowry was—as once the retention of the whole of the dowry in such cases had been adjudged to be[65]—punitive; secondly, since he retained the custody of the children, it was reasonable that he should retain part of the dowry for their upkeep. On the first ground the law allowed him to claim retention of one-sixth of the dowry if his wife was guilty of adultery, one-eighth if her offence was something less grave, on the second one-sixth for each child, up to a maximum of three children. As the retentions on the two grounds were cumulative, the wronged husband might retain as much as two-thirds of the whole. Claims could be made for further reduction of the sum to be repaid on various reasonable grounds; for instance, in the case of real property, on account of money which the husband had himself expended on its capital improvement. Where repayment was made in cash, this was effected (just as the dowry had originally been paid) in three annual instalments—unless the husband's adultery was the ground of the divorce; in that case the whole of the dowry had to be repaid at once.[66]

If, after Augustus, the divorced wife was prosecuted and condemned for adultery in the courts, in addition to banishment she was fined a sum equal to one-half of her dowry.*

* See page 219.

VIII

CHILDREN

As was stated explicitly in the Roman marriage contract, marriage exists for the procreation of children.[1] At Rome there were many no doubt who married for this and for no other reason; but there can have been few men who emulated the single-minded persistence of the consular Q. Hortensius in the last days of the Republic. When he was in his early sixties, a widower with grown-up children, his mind—evidently by this time long past its best—turned to schemes of eugenic enterprise. Wishing to mix his family's blood with that of Cato's, he asked the younger Cato for his daughter's hand. When Cato answered that his daughter was happily married already, Hortensius, undeterred, asked whether in that case he might marry Cato's wife Marcia and establish in the next generation an affinity between the families, even if it was not a blood relationship. She was Cato's second wife, and, by bringing three children into the world, had given an admirable start to his second family. 'Of course,' was Cato's surprising answer, 'if her father agrees.' We do not know if Marcia was consulted. Her father (L. Marcius Philippus, consul of 56 B.C.) raised no objection; Cato divorced Marcia—and then gave her away at the ceremony when Hortensius married her. But there were no children; Hortensius died, and the ending was a happy one only in as far as Marcia, who now remarried Cato, returned to his household a far wealthier woman than she had been when she left it. The story is partly repulsive, partly comic; and it was a serious mistake on Lucan's part to seek, in the *Pharsalia*, to invest it with tragedy.[2]

Most states—modern India is an exception—have thought it just, wise or necessary in the State's own interest to penalize the unmarried and to reward, among married couples, those who have raised a family of reasonable size. In ancient Sparta the unmarried man suffered a certain social stigma; and, among married men, the father of three children was excused military service and the father of four children was excused the payment of taxes.[3] In Rome the story was told that at a date as early as 403 B.C. elderly bachelors had not merely been reproved by the censors Camillus and Postumius for failing in their natural duties but had been forced to pay a heavy fine.[4]

The fact of a declining indigenous population cannot but be a matter of concern to responsible Authority; and in the ancient type of society a decline in the upper class was a matter of particular concern, for it was this class—which acquired new members, naturally, both from below and from outside—which provided the politicians, the top administrators and the army officers. In an empire like Rome's, which did not care to depend on mercenaries, it was of the utmost importance that there should be a continuous supply of good recruits for the ranks, and the Romans believed both that countrymen (*rustica proles*) made the best soldiers and also that, as a general rule, people who lived on the land produced the largest and healthiest families. Sparta was concerned on account of its falling Spartiate population in the fourth century B.C.; Greece generally on account of the extinction of upper class families in the second century; and in Rome, in particular as concerned recruits for the legions, the problem was seen by more than one statesman to be urgent in the same century, in the years which followed the extinction of Carthage. In 133 B.C. Tiberius Gracchus launched his idealistic, if forlorn, scheme for reviving small-scale agriculture and repopulating the Italian countryside with small owner-farmers who were Roman citizens. Two years later the censor Q. Metellus Macedonicus[5] made that public speech in favour of the married state, which Augustus quoted when in 18 B.C. he introduced legislation which in part emulated the laws of ancient Sparta and in some respects, in its heartless severity, went far beyond them.*

The censor Metellus did not seek to invest matrimony with romance and glamour; he simply spoke of it as an inescapable necessity of social existence. Already, therefore, young men were shying away from marriage. Their reluctance was not in any way due to homosexuality; because in antiquity the homosexual man never constituted the problem which he is generally thought to constitute today. The same men were attracted—sometimes grossly, sometimes not grossly at all—by youthful good looks, now in one sex, now in the other. As has been well said, men were bi-sexual.

The truth was that many young men who could afford to indulge

* See pages 76-9.

their tastes shunned the responsibilities of matrimony in favour of life with a mistress. A mistress, unlike a wife, was a man's own choice, not his father's. He might, indeed, be deeply in love with her. She might well be a woman of different social class whom convention—indeed, if she was a registered prostitute (*meretrix*), the law—prevented him from marrying. Inevitably she had charm and vitality which distinguished her from the normal chaste, dull wife, the sort of woman whom Propertius shunned.[6] In the late Republic and early Empire there were innumerable women of this sort, freedwomen for the most part, elegant and attractive. These are the women whom we have to thank for so much that is charming—and indeed for not a little that is obscene—in Roman poetry.

The Nemesis of Cornelius Gallus, the Lycoris of Tibullus, were such women; so were Propertius' Cynthia and Ovid's Corinna. Cynthia was Roman; her real name was Hostia, and she claimed descent from an epic poet of some distinction who wrote at the time of the Gracchi; she was a courtesan (*meretrix*) and so, since Propertius was a freeborn Roman, marriage was out of the question. Reference has already been made to the happy poem which he wrote in celebration of the fact that legislation which had threatened in 28 B.C. did not materialize,[7] legislation by which he might have been forced to abandon his Cynthia, to marry some respectable woman and become the father of soldier-sons.*

Such liaisons, whether or not they constituted concubinage in the technical sense,† could be discontinued very easily, once they had lost their glamour.

To what extent women of good social class deliberately avoided marriage, we cannot say. Even if the instinct which attracts some women to nunneries had existed in pagan antiquity, there was no opportunity for women to follow it. There may well have been women who could have made good marriages, but who preferred to live as a man's mistress rather than as his wife.

In this free association of unmarried men and women, the arrival of a child was naturally something of a disaster, to be avoided, if possible, by an abortion. That this operation often proved fatal, and that public opinion was unsympathetic in such cases, we know from two singularly tasteless poems by Ovid, written when Corinna found herself in such a plight.[8] The first of them was a prayer to Isis for her survival,

* See page 76.
† On which see page 231.

the second an elaboration of the self-evident truth that, if all pregnant women behaved in such a manner, the human race would scarcely survive. The Emperor Domitian was said by his enemies to have seduced his niece Julia, daughter of Titus, and then to have insisted on an abortion which proved fatal.[9] Juvenal, writing in the second century A.D., suggests that abortionists were highly skilled: 'so great is the skill, so powerful are the drugs, of the abortionist, paid to murder mankind within the womb'. It was not until the rule of Septimius Severus at the end of the second century A.D. that abortion became a criminal practice.[10]

The elder Pliny, who suggests that the smell of a lamp when it was being extinguished was often enough to procure a miscarriage, refers to abortion as if it was not an unusual practice, and states that there were two months of pregnancy, the fourth and the eighth, in which it was particularly dangerous.[11]

The illegitimate child (spurius) was easily put out of the way, by exposure on a convenient hillside; for this was the conventional way of disposing of unwanted babies in Rome as, for long centuries, in Greece. Some were allowed to live, and under Trajan's family-relief system two illegitimate children (a boy and a girl) are found side by side with 279 legitimate children as beneficiaries at Veleia in North Italy.[12] Children born from concubinage, though they were not Roman citizens, had a recognized status,[13] and were described by the later jurists as 'natural children'.

We do not know enough to generalize about the birth-rate in Rome and through the Empire; but there is sufficient evidence about well-to-do people, particularly of families which were prominent in Roman politics, to prompt a number of interesting questions.

From time to time there were very large families, and we can only regret that the size of families did not, as a subject, more greatly excite the elder Pliny's tedious curiosity. He mentions the twelve children of Cornelia and Sempronius Gracchus and the nine children of Germanicus and Agrippina only because of the unusual fact that in both cases the children were born in regular alternation of sex: boy, girl, boy, girl.[14] But he gives two examples of men who left an unusually large number of descendants: Q. Metellus Macedonicus, the censor of 131 B.C. who urged young men to marry, and a certain C. Crispinius Hilarus of Fiesole, who made a pilgrimage to Rome in 5 B.C. and sacrificed with the whole of his vast-family on the Capitol. Metellus at his death had four sons and two daughters and eleven grandchildren.[15] Hilarus had six sons, two daughters, twenty-seven grandsons, eight grand-daughters and eighteen great-grandsons. An epigram of Martial records a woman who in a single marriage bore, and was outlived by, five sons and five daughters.[16] And the younger Faustina, wife of Marcus Aurelius, had at least twelve children.[17]

There were men and women who were evidently extremely fertile. M. Antonius was the father of children by three different wives. Fulvia, his first wife, was the mother of children by Clodius and Curio as well as by him. And, most remarkable of all, Vistilia, mother of the general Corbulo and mother-in-law of the Emperor Gaius Caligula, bore children in succession to six different husbands.

On the other hand, as the elder Pliny himself observed, there were marriages which produced no children at all, and others which produced only one child; and the history of the late Republic and early Empire abounds with examples of this kind. The marriage of Tiberius Gracchus' sister to the great Scipio Aemilianus floundered because there were no children.[18] Though it is evident that Julius Caesar was very highly sexed, only one child, a daughter, was born from his first marriage, no children at all from his second and third marriages; nor is it certain at all (though gossip, ancient and modern has suggested it*) that he had children by any of his mistresses, even by Cleopatra.

When Augustus—then Octavian—took Livia into his household in 39 B.C., he already had a daughter by his first wife and Livia was pregnant with her second child. Both were still young and as anxious as any couple can ever have been to have children; yet together they produced no issue. Trajan and Plotina had no children; Hadrian and Sabina had no children either.† Of less exalted personages, in the second half of the first century B.C. 'Turia'—whose adventures will be described in the following chapter—a woman as modest as she was generous, assumed responsibility for the fact that she was childless, and begged her husband—in vain, because he loved her—to divorce her and to seek another wife.[20]

From the numerous inscriptions which show rich men and women bequeathing the whole of their property to their freedmen and freedwomen it is reasonably inferred that these are cases of men and women who left no children.

---

* That Caesar was father of Cleopatra's son Caesarion is more than doubtful.[19]
† On Hadrian, see page 199 below.

Small families, and disappearing families. How are the facts to be explained?

It has been suggested[21] that in the upper classes of a capitalist society the rich heiress commands a premium; that, on the ground of wealth, an only daughter is a more desirable match than one who has a number of sisters; that only daughters, therefore, make the best marriages and that the ability to produce one child and no more—a quality whose existence the elder Pliny noticed—is, like other physical qualities, transmitted by inheritance. There was, therefore, a natural law which worked in favour of the gradual disappearance of upper-class families.

But it is impossible to know how much is to be explained by the hypothesis of sterility or comparative sterility. The historical fact which so often confronts us is the tragic one of married couples without children; but there are other and more evident explanations, for the Roman world was a world without hospitals, without skilled obstetricians and without deep knowledge of the problems of infant welfare.[22]

First of all, miscarriages were distressingly frequent. Caesar's daughter Julia suffered a miscarriage four years after her marriage to Pompey and died in childbirth a year later. The Empress Poppaea died of the same cause in A.D. 65. There can be no other explanation of the fact that the expectation of the birth of an heir to Domitian in A.D. 90 simply evaporated.[23] And in respectable upper-class circles we are all too well informed of the misfortune of the third wife of the younger Pliny, frankly communicated in letters to her grandfather and to her aunt.[24] 'You will be sorry to hear that your grand-daughter has suffered a miscarriage. Silly girl, through failure to recognize that she was pregnant, she neglected to take certain precautions and did other things that she should have avoided. She has learned her lesson. Indeed, she might well have died.' Pliny's facile inference that, now that his wife's fertility had been established, he might confidently expect children in the future, was evidently not based on medical advice and was, in the event, proved false.

There were other factors which operated powerfully to limit the size of families. Death took a heavy toll of women and children in childbirth, and infant mortality was extremely heavy;[25] in all social classes the proportion of children who survived their infancy was frighteningly small. A disproportionate number of inscriptions record the deaths of young children, and it does not seem that, as concerned the survival of their children, the rich fared greatly better than the poor. Of the twelve children of Cornelia and the elder Gracchus, only three survived their childhood.[26] The child born to Julia after her inauspicious marriage to Tiberius in 11 B.C. died—enviably, perhaps— soon after it was born.[27] The birth of a daughter to Agricola (later to be the wife of the historian Tacitus) was doubly welcome for his only other child, a boy, had died.[28] Nero's daughter—his only child—died before she was four months old.[29] Domitian's only son died in infancy before, and was consecrated after, his father's accession, to survive, sadly, only as a coin-type, an engaging small boy sitting on top of the world.[30] Of Marcus Aurelius' huge family only five children (less than half) survived their father.

These were the objective causes which frustrated the natural desire of married couples to have children and to see their children grow up, well and healthy.

It is harder to know to what extent the birth and upbringing of children was frustrated by family planning.

Sometimes, no doubt, a delinquent wife who found herself pregnant by a man who was not her husband resorted to the abortionist—but not always, for Juvenal consoles a husband whose wife is sterile on the ground that at least he does not find himself the father of gladiators' sons.[31]

Of the nature and use of contraceptives by the Romans we know nothing at all;[32] and it is surprising that in the third book of Ovid's *Art of Love*, which is in effect a *vade mecum* for the attractive courtesan, nothing is written about the avoidance of pregnancy. We are told— by the satirists again—of married women who refused to bear children, and who sometimes acquired supposititious children instead.[33] For it was not until late in the fourth century that the law forbade the expo- sure of children at birth. Plautus referred to the exposure of children as a common enough happening, and Suetonius even quotes a source to the effect that in about 63 B.C., on account of a portent, the Senate passed, and all but enforced, a decree that all male children should be exposed.[34] Indeed, when Augustus' disgraced grand-daughter gave birth to a child several years after she had become a widow, he ordered that the child should not be brought up. In the middle of the first century A.D. it was evidently still a not uncommon practice, for, with that enlightenment which typified his thinking, Musonius Rufus protested against it.[35]

The commonest reason for which children were exposed was that their parents could not afford to bring them up; and it was the imaginative purpose of benefactors, both private men and Emperors, from the late first century onwards to strike at the root of this evil by the institution of children's allowances to poor parents. Such were the 'alimentary schemes' of which we know from Pliny's letters, from inscriptions and from reliefs on Trajan's magnificent arch at Benevento. Both the elder and the younger Faustina were commemorated by endowments for a similar purpose.[36] And Constantine issued an edict to Italy and to Africa, instructing magistrates to give immediate relief to parents who made a declaration that they could not afford to bring up their children.[37]

From the fact that in the family-allowances scheme at Veleia, the number of boys for whom relief was given was 246 and the number of girls only thirty-five it has been inferred that, among the poorer classes, baby girls were exposed at birth in greater number than boys.[38] This may indeed be true, but it cannot be inferred with certainty from the inscription; for the scheme was devised with an eye to recruiting for the army,[39] and in the selection of children to enjoy its benefits, a preference may well have been shown for boys.

In wealthier families there was a temptation to restrict the size of families on economic grounds; and the evidence of Polybius about Greece in the second century B.C. can certainly be applied to Rome. In Greece the most persistent cause of the disappearance of upper-class families was the fact that, wishing their children to enjoy the same standard of living as themselves, parents deliberately refrained from having—or at least from bringing up—more than one or two children.[40] When, through disease or war, those children died, the parents realized too late the folly of their thoughtful planning. Augustus, as has been seen, thought, like the earlier Spartans, that a family of three children or more was a family of the right size; and he endeavoured by legislation to win others to his way of thinking.

It would be natural to expect that in a society in which promiscuity was so widespread, more substantial evidence of illegitimacy than the jibes of the satirist should be common too. But the elder Pliny's instances of twins who reproduced the features of different fathers are neither of them Roman, and his only mention of an ancient equivalent of the modern blood-group test concerned the all-but extinct tribe of the Pselli in North Africa, where the legitimacy of newly born children was tested by exposure to snakes, who fled from them, repelled by their smell, if they were legitimate; otherwise they bit them.[41]

There is evidence of the birth of illegitimate children on papryri
from Egypt; and that there were illegitimate children even in the
highest ranks of Roman society is certain. There is a nice story told by
Macrobius of a Roman who came from the provinces, and whose
resemblance to Augustus was the talk of Rome.[42] When Augustus was
so offensive as to ask him if his mother had ever been in Rome, the
man answered smartly, 'No, but my father was.' And cases of sons
who, so far from bearing any resemblance to their fathers, reproduced
the features of a gladiator or of someone as discreditable, were
savoured by the satirists with sinister relish. There is an epigram in
which Martial mocks the father of seven children, every one of whom
was the split image of one member or other of his household staff.[43]

In Ovid's version—not in Vergil's—Dido was pregnant when
Aeneas abandoned her;[44] and after Caesar's death, Cleopatra, queen of
Egypt, boasted—probably with no truth at all—that Caesar was
father of her son Caesarion, and made no attempt to conceal the fact
that Antony was father of her subsequent children, unashamedly born
out of wedlock.[45]

If a married woman of good rank was pregnant with a child conceived in adultery, her husband, no doubt, sometimes condoned the
act and even boasted of his own paternity. There is a crude but amusing passage in Juvenal in which a client claims that, thanks to his
services, his impotent master can claim all the rights of a father of three
children.[46] Otherwise he divorced his wife and she returned to the
discipline of her own family who, if they did not encourage an abortion, might, like Augustus in the case of his grand-daughter's child,
insist that the baby should be exposed at birth.

Of that successful charlatan of the late second century A.D., Alexander of the Golden Thigh, of Abonuteichus in Paphlagonia, Lucian
records[47] that 'many women even boasted that they had had children
by him, and their husbands confirmed the truth of what they said'.

In royal, noble and ecclesiastical society from medieval times to the
eighteenth century illegitimacy was common and carried little stigma;
it is therefore at first sight surprising that the close aristocratic society
of the Roman republic and, indeed, of the early Empire should have
left next to no record of bastard children. Prosecutors in the courts
and scandalmongers in the streets enjoyed nothing more than to discredit
the origins of their opponents or their victims; but the accusation
which they commonly made was not of illegitimacy but of low-
class ancestry—of being descended from 'one great-grandfather who

was a freedman and a rope-maker from the country round Thurii and another of African extraction who first sold scent and later bread at Aricia': this was the story which Antony spread about Octavian, the future Emperor Augustus.[48]

At moments of revolution impostors appeared who claimed descent, however false, from men of distinction: L. Equitius, a 'son of Tiberius Gracchus', elected tribune and murdered in 100 B.C.; C. Amatius, who claimed to be a son of the younger Marius, and who was executed in 44 B.C. In the Empire we know of occasional claims on the part of an upstart or of a pretender: of Julius Sabienus of the Lingones in Gaul in the revolt of 69/70 to be descended à la main gauche through his Gallic great-grandmother from Julius Caesar; of the profligate Nymphidius Sabinus, praetorian prefect in Nero's last years, to be the son of Gaius Caligula.[49] And in the early third century A.D., as has been seen, illegitimacy was claimed, falsely perhaps but not without great pride, on their sons' behalf, by the mothers of Elagabalus and Alexander Severus; both were declared to be the illegitimate sons of Caracalla.[50]

Imaginative French scholarship[51] has devoted seventy-nine pages of a book to 'le bâtard d'Hadrien'. This was the L. Ceionius Commodus (Aelius Caesar) whom Hadrian so surprisingly adopted, who fortunately survived his adoption a mere two years and whose son L. Ceionius Commodus (L. Verus) was later associated in his rule by M. Aurelius from 161 until his death in 169. The ancients, for whom the problem of his adoption was as great as it is for us, could only suggest that he was good-looking and that Hadrian had a weakness for good-looking men. It would be out of character for them to miss a titbit of scandal, if it was staring them in the face, and it is unlikely in the extreme that for nearly two thousand years the secret should be kept that Hadrian, so far from being Aelius Caesar's lover, was in fact his father.

Claims to descent from a distinguished mother—as being far easier to discredit—were naturally rarer still. The man who claimed to be the son of the virtuous Octavia and who was sent to the galleys for his effrontery did not impute adultery to Octavia; he claimed that, because of his bodily weakness, he was farmed out in infancy and replaced—in the person of Marcellus, presumably—by a supposititious child.[52]

IX

HAPPY MARRIAGES

++

UNDER THE older form of marriage the young wife was from the start a dependant of her husband. But normally by the late Republic she was married by free marriage and she remained under the authority of her father;[1] she was *filiafamilias uxor*. Indeed, until the second century A.D. a capricious father could on his own initiative recall his daughter, divorcing her from her husband against her will. This, however, was, in general, no real threat to the married couple.

The young wife was *puella*—a young lady—still; and anyhow in Republican times was not called *mater familias* unless she was under the authority of her husband, married in the old-fashioned way. Catullus nicely imagines in the *Epithalamium* her chaste concern as to whether she would succeed in holding her husband in face of the allurement of the fascinating and unprincipled coquettes who could be suspected of having designs upon him.[2]

She was mistress of her new home from the moment when, on the morning following her wedding night, she officiated in the family cult. If she had a mother-in-law and the mother-in-law lived in the house, she had a formidable critic from the start and she needed to call on all her resources of patience and tact. In the case of Caesar's wife Pompeia, whom he divorced in 61 B.C. (after a man had broken into his house during the Bona Dea celebrations*) on the ground that 'the High Priest's wife must be above suspicion', it is hard not to believe that Caesar's mother Aurelia, who provided most of the evidence, was anything but dismayed by the opportunity of incriminating someone whom she regarded as an unsatisfactory daughter-in-law.

Whether technically a *mater familias* or not, the Roman wife acquired from the start responsibilities and social duties such as never belonged to a married woman in Greece. When Cornelius Nepos, like a good sociologist, criticized the parochial attitude of those Romans who made their own national habits the norm, and despised Greek conventions

* See page 245.

just because they were different, he wrote:[3] 'Much that in Rome we hold to be correct is thought shocking in Greece. No Roman thinks it an embarrassment to take his wife to a dinner party. At home the wife (*mater familias*) holds first place in the house and is the centre of its social life. Things are very different in Greece, where the wife is never present at dinner, unless it is a family party, and spends all her time in a remote part of the house called The Women's Quarter, which is never entered by a man unless he is a very close relation.'

If he had been married already and had children, a wife could at once either antagonize or delight her husband by the attitude which she adopted to her stepchildren.[4] Nothing in the life of Augustus' sister Octavia is more attractive than her concern for her stepchildren, despite the treatment which she received from their father.

The seal of success was placed on marriage by the birth of a child, in particular the birth of a boy.

Aulus Gellius tells a story of the philosopher Favorinus who, hearing in Rome in the early second century A.D. that the wife of one of his pupils, a man of senatorial family, had given birth to a son, insisted on calling at once to congratulate him.[5] 'We all escorted him and went to the house with him. Finding the father in the hall, he embraced him and congratulated him and, after he had sat down, asked how long and difficult the labour had been. On being told that the mother was tired out and had gone to sleep, he said, 'She will, of course, suckle the child herself?' The grandmother answered, 'We must have a little consideration for my daughter and use wet-nurses. She has gone through a very painful time and we must not impose on her further the difficult and exhausting task of feeding the child.' To this Favorinus answered, 'Dear lady, I beg you, let her be more than half a mother to her son.'

He proceeded at great length to deliver such a lecture as only a philosopher could give, on the duty of a mother to feed her baby. But what he said was firm conservative doctrine at Rome. It was regarded as one of the indications of increasing degeneracy at the end of the Republic that this function and, indeed, the whole upbringing of children in their early years was no longer performed by mothers, but was entrusted to slaves. We have, from Rome, the simple epitaph of a freedwoman:[6] 'To Graxia Alexandria, a woman of exemplary chastity who fed her sons at the breast; she lived 24 years, 3 months, 16 days.'

A girl was named on the eighth day, a boy on the ninth.[7] By Augustus' legislation (*lex Aelia Sentia* of A.D. 4, and *lex Papia Poppaea* of A.D. 9) the birth of a legitimate Roman child had to be registered within thirty days. In the second century A.D. the registration of illegitimate children was allowed. Parents could obtain a birth certificate.

In Rome, after the legislation of Augustus, the birth of a third child must have been greeted with particular rejoicing. Three children constituted the Augustan norm of a successful family; and parents who had done their duty so well received their material reward. There was no restriction henceforward on the legacies which either of them might receive. The mother, if she was not independent in law already, now acquired full legal independence; and, if he was in public life, the father, among other benefits, received accelerated promotion in his career. This in Rome itself; outside Rome it was only after the birth of a fourth child, and in the provinces only after the birth of a fifth that parents could claim these privileges. It was enough to make a foreigner laugh. 'People marrying and breeding,' Plutarch remarks, 'not in order to produce heirs, but in order to qualify for inheritances.'[8]

In the course of time, this regulation became a little ludicrous when worthy married couples failed through no fault of their own to have children, and bountiful Emperors—who as likely as not, had no children either—awarded them The Right of Three Children, *honoris causa*. Domitian gave it to Martial, who was not even married.[9]

Still the parents who produced three or more children were justified in their feeling of satisfaction. Martial rarely deviates in his epigrams from eroticism, sycophancy towards the great and castigation of unnatural vice or physical blemish[10] (false or dyed hair, for instance, or false teeth); yet even he was moved on occasions to send elegant congratulatory poems to his friends. Pudens received such a poem when he married; he received another when his wife produced her third child.[11] She was Claudia Rufina, who could have passed for a Roman or a Greek, though in fact her ancestors were Britons, stained with woad.

> *Di bene quod sancto peperit fecunda marito*
> *quod sperat generos quodque puella nurus.*
> *sic placeat superis ut coniuge gaudeat uno*
> *et semper natis gaudeat illa tribus.**

* May the gods bless her in that she, a fertile wife, has borne children to her constant spouse, in that she hopes, though youthful still, for sons—and daughters-in-law. So may it please the Gods above she should joy in one mate alone, and joy for ever in three sons. This is the translation of W. C. A. Ker in the Loeb Classical Library.

Children make for the happiness of the home; and Romans probably loved children as much as Italians do today, and perhaps spoiled them as badly. There is a famous passage in which Lucretius describes the happiness which in a moment death may destroy:[12] the successful young father, proudly conscious of his responsibilities, and the gay welcome which, on returning home, he receives from his splendid wife and his adored children, who rush out to embrace him. From scores of unimportant families there are the tragic surviving epitaphs, which speak truth, in which parents deplored the premature deaths of their children.

In general a mother's relationship was more intimate with her daughter than with her son. Their association was continuous, and as close as that of a mother and her daughter in Italy today. And when the time came for the daughter's marriage and for its preparation, there were innumerable intimacies which the two women shared.

Yet there were certainly cases in which mothers played a large part in the education of their sons; and it is a curious fact that under the Republic the three mothers who were particularly renowned on this account were women whose sons, from the orthodox conservative point of view, went so dangerously off the rails—Tiberius Gracchus, Gaius Gracchus, Sertorius and Julius Caesar.[13] Another woman— because her grand-daughter married a literary man—is remembered for her views on education. This was the mother of Agricola, who was to govern Britain for seven years and to lead the first Roman army into Scotland. In his student days she wisely persuaded him to restrict his study of philosophy in the University of Marseilles (Massilia) when she considered that his intemperate enthusiasm for the subject might well stand in the way of his prospective career in public service.[14]

It was believed that in the early centuries of the Republic young boys were taken by their fathers to the Senate, in order that they might be accustomed early to the atmosphere of a body in whose deliberations they might be expected themselves in the fullness of time to play an important part. They may not have enjoyed the privilege; but in one case at least a boy, a Papirius, if the story is to be believed, did not allow it to kill his sense of humour.[15] Since the story reflected on the insatiable curiosity and the gullibility of women as a sex, it naturally appealed to all that was ungallant in the elder Cato; thanks to the fact that Cato told it—to an audience of soldiers in 167 B.C.—the story has survived.

The senatorial debate which the young Papirius attended was

adjourned at night before a vote had been taken, and a resolution was passed that for the time being nobody outside the House should be told what was the important subject which was under debate.

When the young Papirius returned home, his importunate mother asked him what the Senate had discussed. His answer—that he had been told to keep his mouth shut—did not satisfy her. So, when she would not leave him alone, he thought up a pretty and amusing story to tell her. 'The question under debate,' he said, 'is this: which would be more in keeping with the public interest—that a man should have two wives, or that a woman should have two husbands?' Horrified by what she heard, the mother slipped out of the house and lost no time in communicating the news to other married women in Rome. As a result, when the senators approached the Senate House on the following morning, they found their way blocked by crowds of hysterical women shouting, 'It *must* be two husbands to one wife, not the other way round.' They wondered, naturally, if the women had gone mad—until they were inside the Chamber, and young Papirius told his story. They decided, reasonably enough, that the practice of allowing young boys to attend the Senate had better stop; but they were so delighted with the young man's wit that they gave him the name of Praetextatus.* And that, according to the story, was how the name came into a branch of the Papirius family.

Attention has already been drawn† to the increasing degree to which in the late Republic and early Empire the wives of men engaged in public life at Rome were enabled to share their husbands' interests. The sudden horror of the proscriptions at the end of 43 B.C. brought out the best in some, the worst in others, of those who were closely connected with the proscribed;[16] and many wives of rich and important men at Rome risked death in order to save their husbands' lives. 'The utmost loyalty was displayed by their wives, considerable loyalty by their freedmen, a little by their slaves and none at all by their sons.'[17] We know of the terrifying experience of an anonymous woman, whom conventionally we call Turia, though there is no reason to think that was her name.[18] We know about her because we can read the long address which, after her death, her husband made—not about but to her—in an inscription, which was put up, no doubt, beside her tomb. It is hard to believe that Rome ever produced a more

---

* Meaning that he was a very bright boy; for the *toga praetexta* was worn by boys (who at adolescence changed it for the *toga virilis*) and by magistrates.

† See pages 45, 59.

noble, more gentle—and at the same time a tougher—woman. Her father and mother were murdered, perhaps by their slaves, at their country house in 49 B.C., when her fiancé was overseas, at the war. She ensured that the murderers were brought to justice. Then, when an ingenious attempt was made to deprive her of her inheritance, she was clever enough to see that it was frustrated. After Pharsalus, her fiancé returned, and they were married. But he was a republican and, in 43, one of the proscribed. But for her courage, he could not have escaped from Rome alive. When after Philippi Octavian pardoned him, she had to go down on her knees at Rome and to endure the utmost ignominy, in her attempt to induce the bestial Lepidus, who was in control of the city, to honour his colleague's word. There followed, for husband and wife, the long happiness which both deserved, forty-one years in all of tranquil married life, happiness which save in one respect was flawless. They had no children. Assuming, as this generous woman would assume, that the fault was hers, she begged her husband to divorce her, to retain the whole of her evidently considerable property, to marry again and to allow her to live as a sister to him and a second mother to his children. 'I must admit,' he says, 'that at this I exploded; I went out of my mind; I was so horrified by your suggestion, that I could scarcely pull myself together. The very idea of your even imagining the possibility of ceasing to be my wife, when you had once clung so firmly to me when I was an exile, and as good as dead. How *could* having children matter to that degree?' After this it was almost bathos to record that she possessed all the copybook virtues of a modest Roman wife and, in addition, nice, imaginative qualities, such as a generous insistence (if her husband and brother-in-law had not prevented her) on providing the dowries whenever her young cousins and nieces married. Warde Fowler, most imaginative of English scholars, has surmised that, if her husband had died first (and his only sorrow was that he did not), she would have composed an inscription to him as deeply and ingenuously affectionate.[19] More than this, the inscription makes it clear that they were not only a happy family of two. Her sister and her sister's husband—whose name, C. Cluvius, we *do* know—were bound to them by the most intimate of family ties.

Business, or the administration of property, provided a field in which a wife could share her husband's interests or occupy her time fruitfully if she was a widow. Pompeia Celerina, mother of Pliny's second wife, may have leaned heavily on her son-in-law and did well to take his advice in financial matters, for he was a financier. At the same time she was evidently by no means devoid of practical sagacity; Pliny, indeed, suggested that if she was to pay a visit of inspection to his own estates, his staff might be stimulated to work harder.[20]

In the equestrian—the business—class, we meet such women and, in the families of freedmen we are introduced to Fortunata, the childless wife of Trimalchio, in the *Satyricon* of Petronius, written in the middle of the first century A.D. She displayed her jewels with great vulgarity, and she got drunk in the presence of guests; but she was a loyal wife in bad times as well as in good; she had even sold her jewels once, to help her husband, when he was alarmingly short of money.[21] And inscriptions record cases of women with good heads on their shoulders who, when their husbands died, took over the business and ran it successfully.

In more cultured reaches of society, Pliny's third wife Calpurnia so delighted her husband with her interest in his talents that he was inspired to catalogue her virtues in a letter to her aunt:[22] 'More than this, from sheer affection for me, she has acquired an interest in literature. She has copies of my pleadings, reads them over and over again, and even learns them by heart. She is a bundle of nerves when I am about to appear in court, and she is overcome with joy when the case is over. She employs special messengers to tell her what support and what applause I have received, and whether I have won the case or not. Whenever I give a recitation, she listens nearby from behind a curtain, her ears pricked up to catch approving comments. As for my poems, she sings them and sets them to music, a technique which she has learnt not from a music master but from Love, which is the best of teachers.'

An inscription, probably from the time of Augustus, records the virtues of a certain Murdia.[23] She had married twice, and had children by both marriages. When she died, she left money to her second husband, to show her appreciation of him and, in making legacies to her children, was careful to see that the son of her first marriage received from her the money which she had inherited from his father. It was this son who erected the inscription. After recording the facts which did such credit to his mother's integrity and good judgement, he stated that 'as the vicissitudes of a woman's life had so much less significance than the vicissitudes of a man's, it was difficult to find anything new to say in a woman's praise'. This commonplace is borne out by the thousands of surviving epitaphs erected by widowers to their wives.[24] One consisted of the blunt statement: 'I have no complaint to make of her'—'De qua nihil queror'. Women were praised in conventional terms for the same domestic virtues: for being old-fashioned (*antiqua vita*); content to stay at home (*domiseda*); chaste (*pudicitia*); dutifully obedient (*obsequium*); friendly and amusing (*comitas, sermone lepido*); careful over money (*frugi*); not over-dressed (*ornatus non conspiciendi*); religious without being fanatics (*religionis sine superstitione*).

Above all a wife was commended for her spinning and weaving[25] (*lanifica, lanam fecit*). This virtue was thought to justify mention even in 'Turia's' case and in Murdia's.

Banal, conventional epithets—supplied, if necessary, no doubt, by the monumental mason. But in their abundance in every quarter of the Roman Empire these inscriptions record the uneventful happy marriages of thousands and thousands of ordinary men and women. They supply the antidote to the light-hearted verse of the careless and unprincipled philanderer and to the sharp barbs of the vitriolic satirist; the women whose memory these inscriptions perpetuate were not Ovid's or Propertius' women, nor were they the women of Juvenal and Martial.

Not that surviving literary sources fail altogether to record marriages which were as successful as they were unspectacular. There are the letters which the younger Pliny wrote when he was away from his wife, showing that he missed her with every moment of the day.[26] And, also from the latter part of the first century A.D., there is a charming poem of Statius which takes us to the very heart of family life.[27] Claudia has been a splendid wife to him; she has never been attracted by the glamour of the theatre or the games; she has never shown interest in any man but her husband; she has shared the disappointments and triumphs of his literary career and has not complained when he has had to spend time away from her—yet, after all this, she will not leave Rome and go, as he wishes, to live on the Bay of Naples. The reason is that she is concerned—as he is concerned too—over the fact that her daughter—his step-daughter—is more than old enough for marriage, but no suitor has shown himself. But Statius will have nothing of this objection. Is she not just as likely to find a husband in Naples as in Rome?

Long, happy marriages—one, which an inscription records, of sixty years. 'Turia's' lasted forty-one years. The younger Pliny wrote of a widower, disconsolate at the loss of his wife after thirty-nine years of married life.[28] Augustus and Livia reached their golden wedding a year before Augustus died.

If husbands were desolate often when their wives died, widows were as often desolate when they lost their husbands. They too erected tombstones, composed inscriptions. Julius Classicianus, Financial Secretary (Procurator) in Britain, who was so disloyal to the Governor, Suetonius Paulinus, after the suppression of Boudicca's revolt, died in Britain, and in London we have the inscription which his wife, Julia Pacata erected in his memory.[29] '*Infelix uxor*', she called herself: 'his unhappy widow'.

One of the fragments of Seneca's lost essay on Marriage contains a list of such wives:[30]

'When Cato's younger daughter Marcia was in mourning for her husband and women asked her when her mourning would end, she said, "At the same time as my life." When a relative advised Annia to marry again, since she was still young and handsome, she said, "I never will. Suppose I find a good husband; I do not want to live in constant dread of losing him. If I pick a bad one, why, after the best of husbands, must I put up with the worst?" When somebody was praising a nice woman who had married for the second time, the younger Porcia said, "A woman who is really happy and chaste never marries more than once." When the elder Marcella was asked by her mother if she was glad that she had married, she answered, "Blissfully. That is why I should never marry again." Valeria, sister of the Messalae, when asked why she would not marry again after the death of her husband Servius, said, "As far as I am concerned, he is alive still, and always will be."'

These were women whom the Romans called *univirae*, and respected, because they were married only once.*

But, the realist must ask, what of the heartless regulations by which Augustus penalized childless widows who did not remarry?

If a widow possessed ample means, she did not have to bother about them; she could snap her fingers at the legacies which, through her failure to remarry once two years had passed, she was debarred from receiving. If she was over fifty, the law did not affect her.

* See page 185.

X

UNHAPPY MARRIAGES, AND DIVORCE

++

1. Unhappy Marriages

THE SUCCESS of a marriage may be destroyed from outside or from within, and in the smart social life in Rome of the late Republic and the Empire, when a wife was young and attractive, it was from outside, from the seductive and unprincipled philanderer, that danger first threatened. Cornelia, an innocent if one ever was, no sooner became Pompey's wife in 52 B.C. than she was pestered by a practised seducer, C. Memmius, the man whom Catullus was so right to hate. She handed his letters to her husband, and Memmius, conveniently prosecuted on a different count, was exiled and left Rome to cool his ardour in Athens.[1]

Though adultery may not represent either in itself or in its consequences one of the finer flowerings of civilized life, yet in literature (as on the English Restoration stage) a Don Juan attracts—how, if he did not, could he seduce?—and, whether old or young, contempt and amusement, rather than pity, is bestowed on the cuckold. For those who are light-heartedly and frankly immoral, stolen fruit is best. The younger the wife and the closer the guard which her husband sets on her, the greater the satisfaction of her unprincipled captor. Horace in his sensible way might ask whether the game was worth the candle.[2] Ovid and Propertius would answer, according to the smart convention of the libertine whom in certain moods they reflect, that it was.

The jealous husband kept his wife at home like a prisoner; she was a *clausa puella*, and the slaves of the house were her warders.[3] But slaves for a consideration might be persuaded to open doors and to carry love letters. '*Quis custodiet ipsos custodes*'; 'Who is to keep guard over the guards themselves?'

If a wife was innocent, her husband's jealousy could not but prove an irritant.

Far worse was the frustration which developed in husband and wife alike if time passed and there were no children. There were devices, of course, for the avoidance of such disaster; women stood in the streets of Rome, for instance, on the Lupercalia (February 15th), holding out their hands, so that the half-naked priests might strike them with thongs of goat skin. But even these and similar devices sometimes failed.[4]

It was an unusual wife who in this dilemma behaved like 'Turia',* and generously took the initiative in suggesting to her husband that their marriage should be dissolved, that he should divorce her and look for a wife who was likely to prove fertile.[5] Failure to have children, indeed, was the ground for what Roman tradition believed to be the first divorce in Roman history. Spurius Carvilius wanted children, and was convinced that it was his wife who was sterile not himself. Trimalchio patted himself on the back because he did not divorce Fortunata on account of her failure to bear children.[6]

A husband might, of course, want children but at the same time, like 'Turia's' husband, love his wife; and in such a case neither the future of his family nor the happiness of his home was automatically doomed. It was always possible to adopt a son; and while, in Roman society generally, boys were adopted only in special circumstances (by childless parents who were rich, or by an uncle whose nephew was left an orphan), the great families often resorted to adoption in order to save themselves from extinction. But for adoption, the families of the two great heroes of the second Punic war, Q. Fabius Maximus and P. Scipio Africanus, would have become extinct on the male side after a single generation. The grandson of Fabius Maximus and the son of Scipio were forced to resort to adoption; they adopted brothers, the sons of L. Aemilius Paullus by his first wife Papiria, whom he had so surprisingly divorced;† and a great tragedy, in the event, this proved, from Aemilius Paullus' point of view, to be; for the two sons of his second marriage, whom he retained and who might have seemed to constitute sufficient guarantee for the happy future of his own line, both died when they were still boys. From Julius Caesar and Augustus onwards, a whole succession of Roman emperors, failing to beget sons, adopted sons instead.

Childlessness was the first reason why the marriage of Tiberius Gracchus' sister Sempronia to Scipio Aemilianus broke down.[7] The second reason was that she lost her good looks—a misfortune common

* See pages 204 f.
† See pages 211 f.

enough and one which was not likely to escape Juvenal's cynical attention:[8]

> But yet Sertorius what I say disproves.
> For though his Bibula is poor, he loves.
> True! but examine him; and, on my life,
> You'll find he loves the beauty, not the wife.
> Let but a wrinkle on her forehead rise,
> And time obscure the lustre of her eyes;
> Let but the moisture leave her flaccid skin,
> And her teeth blacken, and her cheeks grow thin;
> And you shall hear the insulting freedman say,
> 'Pack up your trumpery, madam, and away.
> 'Nay, bustle, bustle; here you give offence,
> 'With snivelling night and day—take your nose hence.'

With the passing of time irritations inevitably develop in married life, and a strain is placed on the forbearance of husband and wife alike. This fundamental aspect of human existence was admitted by the censor Metellus Macedonicus in his famous speech in 131 B.C.* At the tail-end of the Republic in one of his Menippean satires Varro wrote, 'A husband must either put a stop to his wife's faults or else he must put up with them. In the first case he makes his wife a more attractive woman, in the second he makes himself a better man.'[9]

Plutarch, in his *Precepts of Wedlock*, tells this very moral story which he repeats in his Life of Aemilius Paullus, in connexion with Aemilius' baffling behaviour when he divorced his wife Papiria, mother of his two splendid sons.[10] 'Because she was sensible, rich and lovely, his friends criticized him for divorcing her. In reply he stretched out his leg and said, "This shoe of mine is nice and new—but it pinches, just where, none of you can tell. So it is a mistake for a woman to rely on her wealth, her breeding and her looks; she should think more of the qualities which affect her husband's life, of those traits of character which make for harmony in domestic relationship. Instead of being impassive or irritating in everyday life, she must be sympathetic, inoffensive and affectionate. Doctors will tell you that they are not nearly as much alarmed by a very high temperature whose cause is evident as they are by one which rises steadily and whose cause they cannot diagnose. In the same way it is a succession of small inconspicuous pin-pricks and irritations, occurring day after day between a man and

* See page 78.

his wife, which destroys their marriage and makes it impossible for them to go on living together".'

Always, be it noticed, in the ancient sources, it was the wife who was in danger of getting on her husband's nerves. You might think there were no irritating husbands.

Open quarrels offered better hope of reconciliation. On the Palatine at Rome there was a temple of Juno Viriplaca, 'the Appeaser of Husbands'. If a husband and wife visited this sanctuary and indulged in a violent quarrel, they returned home, we are told, happily reconciled.[11] So obligingly did the gods dispense in antiquity the services which the psychiatrist provides today.

The household of Cicero's brother Quintus was anything but happy. He was a hot-tempered man, incapable of patience or of gentleness; he married a hysterical woman who was older and a great deal richer than himself. This was Pomponia, sister of his brother's rich banker friend Atticus. It was a marriage of convenience—a marriage which suited the convenience of his brother, and was expected at the start to strengthen his brother's connexions with Atticus. There was an adhesive mother-in-law. But there was also a son—whom in due course each parent sought to prejudice against the other; yet somehow, despite recurrent threats of shipwreck, the marriage survived for over twenty years. There is a terrible picture in a letter of Cicero's to Atticus of their leave-taking in 51 B.C., when he and his brother were going out to Cilicia. They had travelled from Arpinum, their birthplace, to Quintus' villa at Arcae; and, without consulting his wife, Quintus had sent a freedman ahead to order the meal. Since it was the day of a *festa*, he suggested to his wife that she should entertain the women, while he entertained the men. She answered, 'But I'm just a guest here.' 'Day after day it is like this,' Quintus told his brother. When the guests took their places at dinner, their hostess did not appear. Quintus had dinner sent out to her, and she sent it back untouched. They slept in separate rooms that night, and when Quintus said good-bye to her next morning, she was in the same forbidding mood. In the end, when the marriage broke up in 45 B.C., Quintus contemplated a second marriage, but decided against it with the telling observation that life offered no happiness greater than a single bed.[12]

Juvenal naturally revelled in describing the rich variety of intolerable wives: the daughter of a distinguished family, who talked of little else; the wife who thought it smart to look and talk like anything but a Roman woman; the wife who disliked and antagonized her husband's oldest friends; the wife who was inseparable from her mother and corrupted by her; the bickering and nagging wife; the gossip; the blue-stocking; women who were gross in their behaviour, fanatically enthusiastic athletes or simply stage-struck or games-struck.[13]

And there was, of course, the wife who took to drink. Juvenal's hostess who kept her guests waiting an intolerable length of time before she arrived, sank—for *aperitif*—two pints of wine and, to the embarrassment of husband and guests alike, was immediately sick on the floor, was such a monstrosity as the Republic cannot have envisaged and the Empire cannot often have experienced. The deeply ingrained Roman dislike of a woman who drank was not due to apprehension of such social coarseness but to an association, in women, of drink with sexual aberration, as if the one was an inevitable result of the other. '*Quid enim Venus ebria curat?*' 'What cares Love, when Love is tipsy?'[14]

The elder Pliny gives terrible examples of early Roman severity in this matter.[15] 'It is recorded that Egnatius Maetennus beat his wife to death for drinking wine from the cask and was pronounced Not Guilty of murder by Romulus. In Fabius Pictor's *History* there is an account of a married woman, who because she opened the drawer in which the keys of the wine cellar were kept, was forced by her family to starve herself to death. Cato states that the reason why women are kissed by their relations is in order to discover if they smell of drink.* In the case of a wife who, without her husband's knowledge, was found to have drunk wine in excess of the bare requirement of health, Cn. Domitius gave judgement that she should be mulcted of her dowry.'

Alcoholism was thought to be an aggravation of the crime of Augustus' daughter, Julia, and when she was banished to the island of Pandateria, Augustus gave orders that she should be given no wine to drink.†

Religion has always offered a refuge from unhappiness, and the addiction of women to the novel oriental cults which in the late Republic and the Empire established themselves in Italy and the Western world, did not escape the satirist's contemptuous notice. The astrologer—believed by so many to be master of an exact science—was a particularly powerful magnet to the dissatisfied wife. When would her husband, when would her lover, die? The first event could not be too

---

* See page 21.
† See page 85.

near, or the second too far away.[16] More desperately she might
expedite her husband's end. Scandal even declared that Sempronia, the
unhappy wife of Scipio Aemilianus, killed her husband, and that her
mother helped her to do it.[17]

We cannot complain of lack of information about the weaknesses
and shortcomings of Roman wives. 'A perfect wife,' Juvenal says, 'is
as rare as a black swan.'[18]

What of a perfect husband? What of the boors, the lechers, the
misers and the spendthrifts to whom decent Roman women had the
misfortune to find themselves married? Such men are pilloried, of
course, by the satirists, but not as husbands, or from the women's
point of view. In the surviving literature of antiquity social criticism
is a male preserve.

Not that the men who wrote were in any way disingenuous. They
took for granted and frankly admitted that there was one standard of
moral behaviour for wives and another for husbands. The elder Cato
could state smugly,[19] 'If you should take your wife in adultery, you
may with impunity put her to death without trial. If you commit
adultery or indecency yourself, she dare not lay a finger on you, and
she has no legal right to do so.' It is one of the many marks of enlightenment in Musonius Rufus in the first century A.D. that, holding
the married state in the highest esteem, and believing in the equality of
the sexes, he protested against a moral convention which, while con-
demning a woman for infidelity with one of the house-slaves, considered her husband to be within his rights if he slept at will with any
of the slave-girls. This same view had, in fact, been expressed on the
stage more than two centuries earlier, and in Cato's lifetime, in
Plautus' *Mercator*, by an old slave-woman in the house, after the detection of her master by her mistress. 'Oh, I wish there was the same
rule for the husband as for the wife. . . . If husbands were taken to
task for wenching on the sly, the same way as wanton wives were
divorced, I warrant there'd be more lone men about than there now
are women.'[20]

This was wild paradox, and from a slave-woman's mouth: not
serious criticism, perhaps, but a fantasy to make the audience laugh.

When a wife's immorality was notorious, as was that of Sempronia,
wife of the consul of 77 B.C. and of Clodia (Lesbia), wife of the consul
of 60, it is difficult to believe that her husband alone can have been
ignorant of her behaviour. And there were cases, no doubt, where

husband and wife agreed to turn a blind eye, each to the other's infidelities. Indeed Juvenal suggests that, when a man married an extremely rich wife, he was allowed to enjoy her wealth only on condition that he allowed her the utmost freedom in her private life.[21] Ovid could even observe that a man concerned with his wife's adultery was a bore who simply did not know the social conventions of Rome.[22]

There were plenty of cases, of course, in which unfaithful wives sought to delude their husbands. The absence of large hotels and of hotel life must have made their life the harder; and this may be the reason why discovery in the act of adultery plays so prominent a part in Roman divorce law. The connivance of slaves, always dangerous and unreliable allies, was essential. And, however the truth came to light, both the wife and her lover after Augustus were subject to the extreme rigour of the law.

Unfaithfulness in a husband—as long as it took account both of the law and of convention—was, in general, a concern neither to his conscience nor to the law. That a man's virility might reasonably require greater outlet than his matronly wife could provide was a fact, men held, which should be realistically appreciated, by no one more than by the wife herself. Aemilia, wife of the great Scipio Africanus, turned a blind eye to her husband's lapses and, when he died, went so far as to free the slave-girl who was his favourite mistress and marry her off respectably to one of her freedmen.[23] When Augustus' wife Scribonia played the heavy moralist and refused to tolerate the airs of his mistress, this 'moral perversity of hers'—as he called it, if Antony is to be believed—was the ground on which he divorced her. Her successor, Livia,[24] knew better how to play the part of an understanding wife.*
Claudius' wives, to distract attention from their own scheming and infidelity, were thoughtful in supplying partners for their husband's bed. And when Narcissus sought to inform Claudius of his wife's infidelity, it was through his mistresses that he revealed the truth.[25]

As long as a husband amused himself with slave-girls and freedwomen, all was well (though it was asking too much of a wife to expect her to interest herself in the offspring of such unions).[26] When he conducted an intrigue with a married Roman woman, he endangered her but not, under the Republic, himself—unless he was so unfortunate as to be caught in the act. It was only after Augustus made adultery a public crime and, more than this, made adultery with a

* See page 68.

woman of the imperial family actionable at law as treason, that prominent men in Roman society paid heavily for their infidelities.*[27]

II. Divorce[28]

Though in the classical period thoughtful Romans were depressed by the low standards of the age in which they lived, they liked unctuously to idealize the high moral standards of Rome's past. It was even asserted that for the first five hundred years of Roman history there had not been a single case of divorce; for it was not until about 230 B.C., you would have been told, that Spurius Carvilius divorced his barren wife and started an ugly fashion. It was an idyllic picture; but it was not true.[29] The Twelve Tables of 451 B.C. already recognized the divorce formula ' Res tuas tibi habeto'—'Take your things and go'— and the wife's surrender of the household keys. And, indeed, Carvilius' divorce may well belong to the seventh or the sixth century B.C. and not to the third.[30]

When marriage had taken place in the old-fashioned form, a husband could divorce his wife (though the procedure was complicated), except, it seems, for the Flamen Dialis, married as he had to be by *confarreatio*. We know of only one Flamen Dialis who succeeded in divorcing his wife, and this only with the special permission of the Emperor Domitian.[31] The ceremony, we are told, 'involved numerous horrible, extraordinary and dismal rites'.† In no circumstances could a wife who was married by ancient form divorce her husband. Under the free marriage system, however, which had become normal by the late Republic, a wife—or her father acting on her behalf—could divorce her husband as easily as a husband could divorce his wife.

By the last century of the Republic the reasons for divorce were often trivial; often in the highest classes of society at Rome they were a matter of political manipulation and intrigue. Livia, sister of Livius Drusus, the gifted tribune of 91 B.C., was married at her brother's instigation to his friend Q. Servilius Caepio, and bore him a daughter

---

* Under Article 559 of the Italian penal code today adultery by a wife is a crime punishable by gaol, while the husband can be penalized only if he keeps a mistress in his own house or in a public and notorious way. A ruling of the Constitutional Court has established that this does not contradict Article 29 of the Constitution, which establishes the equality of all citizens before the law, or Article 3, in which the principle of non-discrimination between the sexes is inscribed (*Times* of November 29th, 1961).

† See page 180.

Servilia;* then, when the two men quarrelled—over a ring at an auction—the marriage broke up. She was divorced, or divorced her husband, and married M. Porcius Cato instead. The young Pompey, with an eye on his career, accepted Sulla's suggestion that he should divorce his first wife and marry a connexion of Sulla's; the young Julius Caesar, confronted by a similar proposition from Sulla, preferred marriage with his wife, who was Cinna's daughter, to the potential future for which Sulla made it a condition that he should divorce her.[32]

Under the Republic there were no divorce courts and, though she might repudiate the marriage (if she was married under the free system), a wife could not take any legal punitive action against an unfaithful husband, even if she discovered him in adultery.[33] Whatever the form of their marriage, if her husband caught her in the act, the law recognized his right to kill her and even to beat, mutilate or kill the lover.[34] If, without necessarily discovering her in circumstances so compromising, a husband found that his wife was unfaithful, he simply divorced her and retained a portion of her dowry; if the marriage was of the old-fashioned kind, he—or, if he was not independent, his father—summoned a family tribunal, which included his wife's blood relations, to sit in judgement on her; and in such an event she might well be condemned to death.[35]

When the Republic collapsed, the whole question of divorce invited the attention of the reformer; and Augustus was at hand to effect reform. His objects were to devise some satisfactory form of proof that divorce had in fact taken place; to make adultery and other gross immorality (*stuprum*) crimes actionable before a special court, and to prevent connivance in a wife's adultery on a husband's part by encouraging the public informer who, at Rome, doubled the part of public prosecutor.

On the first point Augustus' legislation introduced a formal procedure, recognizable in law, for the notification of divorce.[36] The act of divorce consisted of separation for a reasonable time of the two parties, restoration of dowry, remarriage or some act of indisputable significance, like the expulsion from her husband's house of a woman detected in adultery. The message of divorce was, as before, '*Res tuas tibi habeto*' or '*Condicione tua non utor*', but now the issue of this formal message of divorce had to be witnessed by seven adult male citizens; if it was in writing, it must carry their seven seals. Henceforward this, and this alone, was evidence of divorce, acceptable in law.

* On whom, see pages 51 f.

When, by the *Lex Julia de Adulteriis* of B.C. 18, adultery was made a public crime, a permanent court was established to hear cases against married women and, whether they were married or not, their paramours. And husbands themselves were made to walk more warily. By the new law a married man was liable to prosecution if he seduced another man's wife and she was prosecuted for adultery by her husband; if he connived at his own wife's misbehaviour; or if he practised unnatural vice (*stuprum*), an offence of which he might be guilty if he had a mistress who was not a registered prostitute; and when women with respectable origins, even married women, sought to make things easier by registering as prostitutes, the Senate closed this loophole to them.[37]

Yet the position of the husband was still in no way on a par with that of his wife, and it was not until Constantine that the law was altered and adultery was made actionable in the case of a husband as well as in the case of a wife. Already for centuries Stoicism had deplored the licensed privilege of a husband, and there were classes of people in the Empire—Jews, for instance, and Christians—whose religious code imposed upon men a far higher standard of moral conduct than the public law enforced. As Plutarch wrote, 'A husband who bars his wife from the pleasures in which he himself indulges is like a man who surrenders to the enemy and tells his wife to go on fighting.'[38]

As concerned the punishment of his guilty wife, at least, Augustus' new laws taught the husband his duty. When he detected his wife in the act of adultery, he—or, if he was dependent on his father, his father on his behalf—must divorce her; if he failed to do this, he could himself be prosecuted for condonement and, if condemned, was himself punished as an adulterer.[39] He was given sixty days from the divorce in which to bring an action for adultery against her and against her lover. Should he wish to forgive her and to try again to make a success of their married life (like the military tribune whose wife had taken a centurion for her lover, and whose reluctance to divorce her met with no sympathy from the Emperor Trajan and his counsellors),[40] or should he feel that divorce in itself was punishment enough, the common informer was at hand to frustrate such a show of weakness. After the sixty days were over, this detestable figure, to whom more than one of Augustus' laws were to provide so profitable a living, was allowed four months in which to prosecute.[41] No prosecution could be brought later than six months after the divorce or more than five years after the alleged offence. It was to Constantine's credit that he restricted the right of prosecution to a woman's husband or near relations.

If found guilty, the wife and her lover were banished to different islands. The wife lost a half of her dowry and a third of her own property besides, and it was a criminal offence after this for anyone to marry her; the lover was mulcted of half his property. After Constantine both parties were condemned to death.[42]

At least Augustus' legislation saw the end of the husband's right to kill his wife if he found her in adultery—though, if the discovery was made in his house, he might kill her lover, if he was an inferior person —a slave, for instance, or a family freedman.[43] If caught in such compromising circumstances, however, she might still be killed by her father, as long as he killed, or did his best to kill, the adulterer at the same time.[44] The law also put an end to those sinister family tribunals, except for rare occasions when the Senate or the Emperor decided that a wife's alleged offence should be investigated in private instead of by a public court.[45]

When divorce took place, the children remained in the custody of their father.

When it was suggested to the Emperor Marcus Aurelius that he should divorce his wife, the younger Faustina, he made a joke. He said, 'What—and return her dowry?' meaning by this the Empire, in which he had succeeded her father.[46]

For divorce has always had its crude financial aspect; and when a husband had no better ground of divorcing his wife than the fact that he found her company tedious, he was frequently restrained, no doubt, by the chill realization that he could not divorce her without repaying her dowry. Cicero was at his wits' end to find the necessary money when he divorced Terentia in late 47 or early 46 B.C., and it is probable that when he died four years later, the dowry was still not repaid. In the meanwhile, like the gambler that he was, he had hoped by marrying again to acquire a new dowry which could be used to repay Terentia's; but his second marriage lasted only for a few months, and so he was frustrated.[47]

A divorced wife—or her father or tutor acting on her behalf—had often to go to law[48] to recover the dowry.* In the early Republic the judge had complete discretion; he could even refuse in an arbitrary

* See, for further details, page 188.

way to sanction the return of any part of it,[49] like the judge in the case of the wife who had been divorced for drinking.* But by the end of the Republic, as has been seen,† there were fixed rules. If the wife— or her father—occasioned the divorce, the husband might retain a sixth of the dowry for each child of the marriage, up to a maximum of one-half of the dowry. If the wife was divorced for adultery, the husband was entitled to retain in addition one-sixth of the dowry; if she was divorced for drinking or some slightly less serious offence, he might on that ground retain an eighth.[50]

There is a story which does credit to the sagacity and wit of C. Marius; that he was called upon to adjudge an application by a certain C. Titinius of Minturnae to retain his divorced wife's dowry, on the ground of her immoral character. Marius realized that Titinius had known her character well before marriage, and that he had married her with the deliberate intention of divorcing her at the earliest oppor- tunity and retaining a part of her dowry. He advised Titinius to drop the case. When Titinius refused, Marius gave judgement. He fined the woman a trifling sum; he fined Titinius a sum equal to the value of the dowry. Late, in 88 B.C., the woman Fannia was able to repay Marius' kindness. It was she who extracted him from the marshes and hid him in her house when he was in flight from Sulla.[51]

Of the relations between husbands and their divorced wives we know little. When Pompey's divorced wife Mucia married M. Aemilius Scaurus and had a son by him, Scaurus took the view— though Pompey did not share it—that a close affinity existed between himself and Pompey.[52] Of Augustus' relations with Scribonia in the long interval between their divorce and her self-chosen exile with their daughter Julia, we know nothing at all. There is a curious story about a P. Quirinius at the end of Augustus' and the early years of Tiberius' principates. He married an Aemilia Lepida, who was grand enough to have been betrothed to Augustus' grandson L. Caesar. But L. Caesar died; so she married Quirinius, who was already well advanced in middle age, and, after no long interval, she was divorced by him and married the reprobate Aemilius Scaurus, the grandson of the man whom Mucia married. In A.D. 20, some fifteen years after her divorce, when Quirinius was in his seventies, she was brought into court by him on a variety of charges. One was that she had tried to poison him; another that she was falsely representing as his a daughter who by this

* See page 213.   † See page 188.

time must have been about fifteen years old. Quirinius was already an old man and, as he died in the following year, perhaps a sick one. Lepida, it seems, was waiting with the intention, when the time came, of producing the daughter as Quirinius' rightful heiress and securing, with her discreditable husband, the administration of a tidy property. But the case went against her; and she retired into banishment instead.[53]

III. Divorcées and Widows

Death ended marriage, and so did divorce. And there were other circumstances in which a wife could secure dissolution of her marriage: if her husband incurred certain types of criminal sentence, if he was a prisoner, if he deserted her or—probably by a regulation of Augustus, which survived until the third century A.D.—if he joined the army as a ranker.[54]

Though a widower, it was thought, might reasonably marry again directly his wife was dead, a widow was expected, out of decent respect for her late husband, to wait ten months, and in the Empire twelve. This regulation had the practical advantage of ensuring that she was not pregnant by her former husband at the time when she remarried; but it was not enforced for that purpose. For, had this been its sole object, a woman who gave birth to a child soon after her husband's death should have been free at once to marry again.

The ban was at first religious, but later a matter of secular law, and a widow who remarried within the forbidden period—together with her new husband—was penalized under the praetorian edict. She had to relinquish any inheritance which she had received from her former husband and she was debarred from intestate succession except to her nearest relatives.[55]

Augustus cared more for propagation than he did for sentiment. For him the romantic picture of the loyal widow sadly and faithfully devoted to the memory of her husband had no appeal. Children were what the State needed. So, by his earliest moral law a childless woman between the ages of twenty and fifty was penalized if she remained unmarried for longer than a year after the death of her husband or for longer than six months after divorce.* This outrageous regulation was so far relaxed by his later *lex Papia Poppaea* that the period within which a woman was not penalized for remaining unmarried

---

* A woman who, after divorce, was found guilty of adultery, of course, was banished and forbidden to remarry (see page 219).

was extended to two years in the case of a widow and eighteen months in the case of a woman who was divorced.[56]

Such regulations were abolished later by the Christian emperors, since Christianity regarded a second marriage as an impropriety. Already, in view of the high regard paid by Christianity to celibacy, Constantine had abolished the other regulations of Augustus by which celibacy was penalized.

If a wife was under the full authority (*manus* or *potestas*) of her husband, and had not been emancipated by him, he might by his will appoint a tutor for her, or give her the power of selecting a tutor for herself.[57] She succeeded to his estate on death; if he left children—whether by her or by an earlier marriage—the estate was divided between widow and children in equal parts.

If, as was normally the case, she had been married by a free marriage, she had no right of intestate succession to her husband's property, but he could make her a legacy as long as it was not larger than the amount which he left to his heir. There were circumstances, however, in which she might be left very badly off. While Augustus' extraordinary legislation was in operation, from the beginning of the Christian era until the fourth century A.D., she could inherit only a tenth of her husband's bequest, if she was over twenty and under fifty and he was between twenty-five and sixty at the time of his death, and there were no children of the marriage; so that a man might leave a quarter of his estate to his mistress and only a tenth of it to his wife.[58]

Even an unhappy marriage could have what a cynical materialism might consider a happy ending: to outlive your partner in marriage and to enjoy, in unfettered irresponsibility, a rich old age, as an 'orbus' or an 'orba.' Surrounded by parasites and legacy-hunters, wealthy Old Age battened on flattery, had no fear of solitude, amused the satirist and—because Old Age has not always lost its wits—often amused itself.

'Call no man happy until he is dead,' Solon had once told Croesus. Martial did better.[59] 'Call no man happy,' he suggests, 'until his wife is dead—particularly if she is rich.'

The rich widow attracted the attention of every sort of gigolo and confidence trickster. Either she knew her power, and enjoyed the tyranny that she exercised, or she was ridiculously gullible. Even the younger Pliny, whose outlook on life was anything but satirical, has entertaining stories to tell of M. Aquilius Regulus as a legacy-hunter—

of his forcing his way into the bedroom of the rich Verania, widow of the Piso whom Galba so tragically adopted, doing a quick calculation of her horoscope, assuring her that, grave though her illness was, she would recover, absenting himself for a moment from the room and returning with the news that a soothsayer outside had confirmed his diagnosis. The results were a quick codicil, and a curse called down on his head by Verania as she died. When Regulus found a woman called Aurelia making her will and begged her to add a codicil leaving him the clothes which she was then wearing, he was less successful. Aurelia did not die.[60]

XI

LESS REPUTABLE WOMEN

++

1. Prostitutes[1]

PROSTITUTES (*scorta, meretrices, lupae*) were to be encountered in
Rome and in all Italian cities and were no more difficult to recognize in
Roman antiquity than in the modern world. Many of them were
foreigners, women from Syria and Egypt.[2] Their faces were heavily
made up, they wore no bands in their hair and their clothes—a short
tunica and a toga (the stigma also of women who had been detected in
adultery), for naturally they did not wear the long gown, the *stola*, of
the respectable matron,[3]—were usually in outrageously bright colours.
They walked the streets, or else they sat or stood—'*prostare*'—outside
brothels. In Rome they were to be encountered particularly on the
Sacra Via, in the Subura, outside the walls in the Esquiline-Viminal
district, on the Caelian and in the Circus Maximus.[4] Prostitutes were
also attached to most of the temples of oriental divinities in Rome.[5]
They were registered with the police (the aediles) and in the Empire
from the principate of Gaius Caligula onwards the prostitute paid a
tax. This, based on Eastern practice, was the sum which in any day she
received from a single client.[6] Our knowledge about these women,
which is considerable, derives in part from Roman writers, particularly
Juvenal and Martial, and in part from archaeology, in particular from
the remains of Pompeii; for the ashes and mud from the eruption of
Vesuvius in A.D. 79 have preserved fresh for our inspection vestiges of
the daily life—and of the nightly life, for brothels were not allowed to
open before three o'clock in the afternoon—of the lowest as well as of
the highest stratum of society in that stricken town.

Sometimes the prostitute plied independently, paying a rent to the
owner of the brothel or inn where she had a room. Sometimes she was
an employee of the brothel proprietor (the *leno* or *lena*). Such women
were also in the employment of low-class hotels (*tabernae cauponiae*)
and sometimes of establishments run in close co-operation with the

public baths.[7] The practised client, of course, would go direct to one or other of these establishments in search of his pleasure.

There were in the later Empire as many as forty-five brothels in Rome, and they were under the official supervision of the aediles. In Pompeii there were at least seven (one run in connexion with a hair-dressing establishment). And we know of one at Puteoli.[8] None, it seems, have been discovered at Ostia.

Should any man be impelled by curiosity to set eyes on a Roman brothel (*lupanar*), he need only go to Pompeii and find his way to Insula 12, No. 18 (opposite the Albergo di Stittio). There—unless the building is under repair—a *custode* will unlock the door for him and, according to his character, either stand in shocked silence or give him a graphic, but not necessarily accurate, account of the happenings which, in its time, the building has witnessed. It was on two floors, the rooms upstairs, which had their own entrance from the street, being, probably, rather larger than those below. The interior of the upper storey has not survived. The ground floor survives intact, with its two doors on the street (exit and entrance), its *gabinetto* and its five rooms, which mea-sure each about eighteen feet by six, and whose stone beds (on which mattresses were laid) take up about a third of the space. There are eight pictures in fresco on the passage walls; and it would be difficult to imagine pictures more obscene.

When the eruption of Vesuvius closed the establishment down, the partners who owned it were called Africanus and Victor. We have the names of a number of the girls—Glycera and Phoebe were two—and also of several of their clients and of the clients of another brothel in the town who have left their signatures on the walls. Most of them were slaves, with names like Felix, Romulus, Mars and Scamander.

Even without the testimony of writers like Juvenal and Martial,[9] it would be obvious that such establishments were hot, smelly, sordid and filthy. They catered, in general, for men of the lowest class, par-ticularly for slaves. Charges at Pompeii varied from two asses to eighteen.[10]

Yet in Rome it was thought natural that youths, even of good family, should receive a part of their adolescent education in such places, and Cicero felt no embarrassment in saying this[11] in public in his defence of Caelius in 56 B.C. There was a nice story of the elder Cato,[12] that when he saw a young man emerging from a brothel, he said, 'Good.' When he saw him emerging from the same establishment a number of times, he observed, 'When I said, "Good", I did not mean that you should make this place your home.'

Slave-girls were bought and sold by brothel-keepers at auctions. Martial has an epigram about a slut whom the auctioneer kissed repeatedly, so as to persuade people that she was clean. His act had one result; the only bid which had so far been made for the girl was withdrawn.[13]

Where innocent young slave-girls were sold by auction to brothel-keepers, there was a white slave traffic on which belatedly Authority frowned. Hadrian forbad it; and his regulation was perpetuated by succeeding emperors.[14] The existence of brothels themselves was attacked in strong terms by Dio Chrysostom but not, in surviving literature, by any other writer in Roman antiquity.[15]

In Paris may be seen a relief found at Aesernia in Campania with an inscription in which some wit typified a certain sort of hotel bill:[16]

Erected in his lifetime by C. Calidus Eroticus to himself and Fannia Voluptas. Innkeeper, my bill, please. You have got down: a pint of wine, one as; bread, one as; food, two asses. Agreed. Girl, 8 asses. Agreed, Hay for mule, 2 asses. That mule is going to make me bankrupt.

It was long thought that the Romans were unaffected by the scourge of venereal disease; but, largely because of evidence in a most surprising source, a letter of the younger Pliny on the noble suicide of a husband and his wife, competent medical opinion now considers that there were cases of syphilis.[17] In view of the silence of the erotic poets, of Ovid, for instance, in his *Art of Love*, it is hard to believe that the disease was at all widespread.

II. Courtesans

A wide gap separated the coarse drabs of the brothel-world from the charming, elegant and expensive ladies of the town, the Delias, the Cynthias, the Lesbias and the Corinnas, by whom Tibullus, Propertius, Catullus and Ovid were at different times enchanted, tormented and enraged. It was as a handbook to success for such charmers that the third book of Ovid's *Art of Love* was written.

The young woman of this type lived with her mother (and perhaps her sisters), who encouraged her way of living and no doubt shared her profits, or she lived under the general care and protection of a respectable and presentable procuress (*lena*) of the 'old nurse' type. Or perhaps she was provided by her lover with an establishment of her own, where she lived elegantly with servants (a male doorkeeper and slave-girls) to look after her. If he tired of her, the staff would remain for her successor.[18]

It was expensive to keep an attractive mistress. The hero of Plautus' *Mostellaria* sold his father's property in order to free and set up the slave-girl whom he loved; and among the large number of those who were in debt to money-lenders at the end of the Republic, there were plenty of young men who had borrowed money to spend not on their political careers, but on their women.

The courtesan's tragedy, perhaps, was to fall in love with the man who kept her—but who might throw her out at any moment. Let him be deeply in love with her, and she as a coquette might enjoy all the opportunities which life offered to anyone who possessed her charm. Let him be tortured by jealousy, by the anxiety—whether justified or not—that she was unfaithful. In particular, let him fear that she would leave him for a richer man, for somebody who could afford luxuries which were beyond his means. These were the anxieties by which Propertius and Ovid were tormented.[19]

Courtesans of this sort were generally Roman, sometimes freed women, but often of respectable origins. One of the earliest to be encountered in Roman history, the *scortum nobile* Hispala Fecenia, who, more than anybody else, was responsible for the exposure of the Bacchanalian conspiracy in B.C. 186, was a slave-girl who had been freed.*

If they were Roman and if, being married, they were not to be liable to punishment for adultery and if—after the legislation of Augustus—the men who associated with them were not to be guilty of unnatural vice (*stuprum*) or of adultery, they must register, like common prostitutes, with the aediles.[20] When, in the principate of Tiberius, it was found that a respectable married woman, from a family in which there had even been praetors, had—and with her husband's cognizance—applied for such registration, the law was tightened up. The Senate decreed that no licence should be granted to a woman whose husband, father or grandfather was, or had been a Roman knight.[21] Nor, *a fortiori*, one is bound to believe, if he was, or had been, a senator.

The number of cases in which husbands connived at their wives' unfaithfulness can hardly have been large. It may well be that the woman of breeding who applied for registration under Tiberius had

* For her story see pages 37-43.

been divorced by her husband, but that he had failed to go further and to prosecute her for adultery.* Yet Horace, contrasting the degradation of contemporary life with the noble men and women who in an earlier age had made Rome great, depicted dancing and culture as the first stages of a young woman's downfall and adultery with the connivance of her husband as the last. With her husband's full knowledge, she would leave the table and go off with men. And what men at that: commercial travellers and Spanish ship-captains.[22]

It was not only their morals which distinguished these courtesans from the respectable married women—the *castae puellae*—whom Propertius kept at arm's length. They were *doctae puellae*—talented, cultured, lively conversationalists. They played the harp and the cithara. They sang. They were well-read in the classics (Greek literature) and, if they observed Ovid's instruction, they were familiar with modern literature, the poetry which he and his contemporaries were writing. Also they danced; adventuring far beyond the sober eurhythmics in which a respectable matron might indulge without attracting comment, they displayed their bodily charms in a positively unladylike manner.[23]

Though Ovid might emphasize when he wrote his *Art of Love*, and repeat afterwards, that it was no book for long-gowned female respectability,[24] respectable married women would have been very unfeminine indeed if they had not stolen copies of the book and studied with intense care the advice which Ovid gave to their attractive rivals, the ladies who had to make a living out of their charm. In the third book they found advice on the right colour to wear, on make-up and hair styles (even dyes and wigs). They were advised to brush their teeth, to wash their faces every morning, and to show consideration to their servants. They were told how to remedy such defects as halitosis and bad teeth; how to conceal the fact of being too short or too thin. They should hold themselves well, and talk and laugh quietly. They must cultivate their talents.[25] And at this point, perhaps, the *casta puella* should have put the book down. The rest was not for her.

The courtesan was advised to appear in public as much as decency allowed (for she could never tell when she might pick up a man) but to avoid men who were effeminate or crooks. She should never give extravagant expression to her feelings (whether of laughter or of sorrow); she should answer love-letters, but not too promptly; she should insist on receiving her proper price; she should make allowances for

* See page 218.

difference of age, between the ardent young, and the practised middle-aged, lover; she should tease and, within limits, tantalize her lover if she wished to keep his affection. She was taught how to escape from supervision, how to give her lover the slip in favour of another assignation; she was told what was the best invisible ink to use for love-letters; and given tips about plausible excuses, if her lover complained of calling and finding her away from home—'she had religious duties', or 'she had been visiting a sick friend'. She was even told how to dope a tiresome lover with sleeping powders. She must always convince her lover of her love for him; she should require good evidence before she believed in the existence of a serious rival. At parties she should arrive a little late, have nice table manners and drink—but never get so drunk that she saw double or went to sleep.[26]

For a Roman, after Augustus had passed his legislation, marriage with such a woman was out of the question. There was a large class of women whom Romans were forbidden to marry: a prostitute, an ex-prostitute, a procuress, a woman given her freedom by a procurer, a woman found guilty in a criminal court, a woman found in adultery, an actress or anyone who had ever been an actress.

So they were confronted, all of them with the spectre—if they survived the strain—of a lonely, unloved and, if they had played their cards badly, impoverished old age. We possess a nasty, vindictive and unfeeling poem written to such a woman at a time when her charm has vanished. Gentle Horace wrote it.[27]

Sulla had enjoyed the company of actors and actresses as of few other people;[28] Cicero could not conceal his admiration for the distinguished actor Asopus; emperors like Gaius and Nero were stage-struck; and in the society of the Empire women lost their hearts to actors with fanatical indiscretion. Yet the theatrical profession never appeared to Authority at Rome to belong anywhere but to the world of the unprivileged, even the criminal, classes.[29] No son of an actor or actress could be a town counsellor under the law which Julius Caesar drafted for municipal government in Italy. By Augustus' laws no member of a senatorial family might marry an actress. At the very highest, an actress ranked as high as a freedwoman; at the lowest she was classed with the prostitutes.[30]

III. Slave-women, Freedwomen, and Concubines

The elder Cato, a realist interested in getting full value out of his slaves, went so far towards recognizing that male slaves were human beings, that he established slave-brothels on his estates.[31] By the end of the Republic, with an even greater sense of the realities, large slave owners appreciated that among slaves, as among other men and women, married and family life was a source of happiness and, in consequence, of efficiency, and that children from such marriages might go some way to making good the fall in the supply of new slaves from overseas sources. So by the end of the Republic, in Varro's time, slaves were encouraged to marry;[32] by Columella's (mid-first century A.D.), slave-women might be rewarded like freedwomen if they succeeded in bringing children into the world.[33] Columella gave freedom to any of his slave-women who was the mother of more than three children.

Not that, among slaves, there could be 'marriage' in any legal sense. The relationship was described as *contubernium*, a sharing of the same roof. But the make-belief was complete. Slave families were families like any others, of husband and wife, parents and children, addressing one another in the normal language of family relationship.[34] There is a nice inscription from Carthage, erected in memory of a man and woman who lived and died as slaves, Victor who lived to the age of a hundred and two and Urbica who lived to the age of eighty; it was erected 'to his most devoted parents'—'*parentibus piissimis*'—by their son, who forged ahead in the world, was a freedman and held an important post in the imperial service.[35]

When a married slave was freed, his first act, naturally, was to purchase the freedom of his wife (to whom he could then be formally married) and of his children.

The slave-girl who attracted her master had little choice, if he was married, but to become his mistress, one perhaps of his many mistresses. This, evidently, was the experience of numerous slave-girls in the imperial household of Augustus and, with Messalina's full approval, in the imperial household of Claudius.* Even when she was sole favourite, a slave-girl's relationship with her master's wife was not always disagreeable; when Scipio Africanus died, his widow enfranchised his favourite slave (*paelex*) and even found a freedman to marry her.†

But her master might not be married and, particularly if he was

* See above, page 99.
† See above, page 215.

young, he might be so deeply in love with her that he wished to marry her. This he could do by freeing her—as long as he did not belong to a senatorial family.[36]

The occasions on which a member of a senatorial family wanted to marry a slave-girl may not have been frequent; and from the evidence of inscriptions it seems that the men who freed and married slave-girls were generally freedmen or demobilized soldiers.[37] In many cases, no doubt, they both wished to regularize—sometimes because the woman was going to have a baby—an association which was already established. By Augustus' legislation a freedwoman who was married to the man who had been her master when she was a slave, but afterwards left him, was not allowed to marry again without his consent.[38]

If a man of good family wanted to free and marry a slave-girl, he could not disregard the fact that, thanks to the snobbery which pervaded the whole of his social class, his wife's position in society was likely to be difficult; and he might prefer—and so might she—that they should not marry, but that she should become his concubine. 'It is more proper that a patron should make a freedwoman his concubine than wife and mistress of his household.'[39]

Concubinage—*concubinatus*—was a convenient social relationship which the Roman law recognized and which, indeed, Augustus' laws encouraged.[40] The man and woman lived together in all respects as husband and wife; nothing distinguished their condition from that of two married people save the absence of 'the married feelings' or 'intention'—the *adfectus maritalis*.[41] Since a psychological condition of this kind is anything but self-evident, it was by certain external circumstances (for instance, the fact that no dowry had been given) that a relationship, if challenged, was proved to be concubinage, not marriage. The children of a Roman and his concubine were not legitimate, and did not even become legitimate if their parents subsequently married; they were known after Constantine as natural children, *liberi naturales*.

Concubinage made marriage possible in all but name to those whom Augustus' laws forbad to marry. Legionary soldiers (before A.D. 197) could not be married, but there was nothing to prevent them from having concubines (whom later, on discharge, they were free to marry).[42] If he was unmarried, a senator's son, or even a senator, might have a freedwoman for his concubine.

As long as a man's concubine was a woman who, because of difference between his social position and hers, could not have expected

to marry him, the relationship might be a happy one. It was embarrassing only in cases where the impediment to marriage was the
inability of the girl's relations to produce a dowry. The haggling
which takes place over the fixing of a dowry in modern India is notorious; and much of middle- and lower-class life in ancient Rome, was,
no doubt, similarly disfigured. There were doubtless cases where a man
offered to make a girl his wife if the money was found and insisted, if it
was not, on her becoming his concubine. Young Lesbonicus in
Plautus' *Trinummus* was in the plight of not being able to find a dowry
for his sister:[43] 'I can't have people saying that, by giving my sister to
you without a dowry, I have committed her to you as your concubine
and not your wife. If I did that, people would think me the greatest
scoundrel in the world.'

It seems unlikely that a married man ever kept a concubine; nor is it
certain that in the early days of the Empire a man ever lived in concubinage with more than one woman at the same time.[44]

The status was not incompatible with the highest social position in
the land. When, after his wife's death, the elder Cato discovered the
irritation which was caused to his son and his daughter-in-law by the
fact that a slave-girl in the house was, quite openly, his mistress,[45] he
might have given respectability to their relationship by freeing her
and making her his concubine, and would perhaps have done this
(instead of breaking off relations with her and making a horrifying
mésalliance when he married again) if his son and daughter-in-law had
not objected so strongly to the girl herself. Vespasian, indeed, having
lost his wife, lived in concubinage during the whole time that he was
Emperor—until her death—with the freedwoman Antonia Caenis.[46]
She resided unobtrusively in the Palace, got in nobody's way, amassed
great wealth and enjoyed herself behind the scenes in the exercise of
tremendous patronage. Vespasian's example was followed extensively
by emperors in the second century. Both Antoninus Pius and Marcus
Aurelius took concubines and did not remarry after the deaths of their
wives, M. Aurelius because he did not wish his children to suffer from a
stepmother. At the same time he congratulated himself in his *Meditations* that he had not been too long in the hands of his grandfather's
concubine in the course of his upbringing;[47] so that a concubine's influence on the children of the house was evidently not always a good
one. At the end of the second century, though Commodus was young
and had no children when he rid himself of his wife, he none the less
did not marry again, but took as his concubine the admirable Marcia,

who served him well for a period and then served the world well when she put him out of the way.

This respectable concubinage has little in common with the promiscuity of Gordian ii in the third century, who with his twenty-two acknowledged concubines, each of whom bore him three or four children, provoked what is probably the best-known witticism in Gibbon's *Decline and Fall*.[48]

Gordian had declared bluntly that marriage was not for him. Vespasian and the second-century emperors had thought concubinage a preferable alternative to remarriage for a widower. Later we meet cases of young men who lived with concubines (because, presumably, of the social status of the women with whom they fell in love) and had children by them, but who for political or other reasons wished later, or were forced, to marry. The discarded concubine was well compensated, it is to be assumed, for she had to make a home for herself and for the children. The Emperor Constantius was perhaps the illegitimate son of the third-century Emperor Claudius by a concubine.[49] His own son Constantine was the son of his concubine Helena, whom he discarded when he had to marry Theodora.[50] Constantine himself lived with a concubine before he was married, and had a son, Crispus, by her before he was eighteen years old.[51] There was therefore, despite the fact of illegitimacy, no great stigma about being a concubine's son.

History tells us little of the attitude of a wife to her husband's discarded concubine. We have one inscription of a man who raised memorial stones side by side to his wife and to his concubine.[52] The concubine's son—if Constantine is typical—was devoted to his mother but jealous, naturally, of his half-brothers who were legitimate.

Relationship was not so easily established between a woman who was free and a man who was a slave.

It was not thought proper for a Roman woman to free a slave in order to marry him, unless she was herself a freedwoman, and they had both been slaves together, or unless the slave was left to her by will on the understanding that she should free and marry him. Septimius Severus forbad such marriages altogether.[53]

But there was still concubinage, and the number of free woman who lived in concubinage with slaves was, in Claudius' time, so large as to cause anxiety to one who might not have been expected, or indeed thought qualified, to set up as a censor in such matters. This was the imperial freedman Pallas; for, according to Claudius, it was Pallas who drafted the resolution which the Senate passed in A.D. 52, the famous 'senatusconsultum Claudianum'. A free woman henceforth was reduced to slavery if she lived in concubinage with a slave without his master's knowledge; if the master approved, she was debased to the rank of a freedwoman. This is Tacitus' account. Gaius, however, suggests that children of such unions were in either case to rank as slaves, until Hadrian modified the law. After which, if the mother remained free, her child was free also.[54]

HOLY WOMEN, RELIGIOUS WOMEN AND DIVINE WOMEN

✦✦

1. Holy Women

THE VESTAL VIRGINS exercise their powerful fascination still on historians and novelists alike. To invent a parallel, you would have to imagine that in the whole of modern Italy there was only one body of Nuns, and that there were a mere six members of that body. And you would have to imagine them as performing their holy duties under the careful watch of the government in Rome.[1]

At the south-east of the ancient Roman forum there were Precincts. There, in close contiguity, were the Regia, the Chapter-House of the Pontifex Maximus and the College of Pontiffs; the official residences (*domus publicae*) of the Pontifex Maximus and the Flamen Dialis; the Temple of Vesta (a partial restoration of which still stands), whose fire the Vestal Virgins tended; and the House of the Vestals, the Atrium Vestae, where today the tourist dawdles to watch the goldfish and where, in antiquity, the Vestal Virgins lived. The official residence of the Rex Sacrorum was a little distance away.[2]

The activities of all these functionaries represented, in commission, the religious functions of the primitive royal house. The Vestal Virgins either, in the person of the Chief Virgin, the Virgo Vestalis Maxima, represented, for religious purposes, the wife of the primitive King (himself now partly transmogrified into a Pontifex Maximus) or, as a College, they represented the daughters of the original royal house; the issue is one on which scholars disagree.[3] There is no disagreement, however, about their activities; they drew water, they had the heavy responsibility of ensuring that the sacred fire in the temple of Vesta never went out, and their presence was necessary at a number of the most deeply-rooted religious ceremonies of the State. 'In all the public duties performed by them a reference can be traced to one leading idea—that the food and nourishment of the State, of which the sacred fire was the symbol, depended for its maintenance on the accurate performance of their duties.'[4] It also depended, of course, on their remaining virgins without spot or blemish.

The election of a Vestal Virgin was not an everyday affair; it happened no more frequently on an average than once in every five years. Twenty candidates—girls between six and ten years old, both of whose parents must be living—were selected by the Pontifex Maximus, and from these one was chosen by lot. Under the Republic daughters of the noblest families alone were eligible, at first only patricians. There was no dearth of candidates in the early and middle republic; but times changed, and Augustus lowered the social qualification greatly when in A.D. 5 he was forced to admit the daughters of freedmen as candidates.[5]

At the dramatic moment when the lot had made its choice, the child was 'taken' by the Pontifex Maximus who addressed her as 'Amata' and pronounced the traditional formula for admission to the Order. Immediately she passed out of her father's control (*patria potestas*), and indeed right out of her family; after this she would not count as one of the next of kin if even her closest blood-relative died intestate; nor, if she herself died intestate, did her property pass to her blood-relations.[6] It went, instead, to the State. But she could make a will, for she acquired legal independence on becoming a Vestal Virgin; and, indeed, she became from the start a young woman of property.[7] For she was given money—the equivalent perhaps of a dowry—at the start. By the time of the early Empire this sum, voted by the Senate, might be as large as two million sesterces, twice the amount of a rich girl's normal dowry; and there was even a case where an unsuccessful candidate was given a million sesterces.[8] If candidates no longer came forward willingly, it was necessary to attract them by bribes. This is a not unfamiliar principle of public economy.

So, with little understanding of the trials and temptations which lay ahead, the child was committed to thirty years of virginity. When she was forty, or a year or two younger, she would be free to leave the Atrium and live a normal life—even, if she could find a husband, to marry. It is not surprising that, when the time came, many preferred to continue—as they were allowed, if they wished, to continue—their unnatural life, and perhaps win, for chill reward, a place in the history books; like Occia, who started as a novice in 38 B.C. and died, after fifty-seven years of service, in A.D. 19, or Junia Torquata who was a Vestal Virgin for sixty-four years.[9] Those who returned to the world rarely married; there was a superstition that such marriages were never happy.[10]

The child, aged six to ten, entered the diminutive feminine community; of her five colleagues, the senior might be in their late thirties, or, indeed, a great deal older than that. For thirty years, if her health remained good, the Atrium was to be her home, which she could leave only in the service of the State; and for at least eight hours out of every twenty-four she had, with one of her fellows, the terrifying responsibility of keeping the sacred fire alight.[11] Within the College the 'Three Seniors' had certain privileges, and the Senior Vestal Virgin of all, the Virgo Vestalis Maxima, enjoyed undisputed power and prestige.

They were all of them, in the last resort, under the control of the College of Pontiffs, whose president was the Pontifex Maximus. If one of the Virgins fell sick and had to be sent out of the Atrium for nursing, the Pontiffs met to approve the household—one under the presidency of a respectable matron—to which she should be sent. And if grave charges were brought against them, the Pontiffs, under the Pontifex Maximus, were their judges.[12]

There was, through the year, a succession of religious festivals which the Vestal Virgins attended officially,[13] and there were many vital religious functions, all concerned with the earth and the fundamentals of living, which they alone could perform. On May 14th or 15th they threw straw figures into the Tiber from the *pons sublicius*, the oldest bridge in Rome, and for the novices this must have been the best occasion of the year.[14] Their storehouse (*penus*) was, symbolically, the storehouse of the State, and was open to inspection from June 7th until June 14th.[15] From October 15th a jar in the penus contained the blood which flowed from the head of the slaughtered 'October horse';[16] on April 15th it acquired the ashes of the calves which were torn by attendants of the Chief Virgin from the corpses of the thirty-one cows slaughtered in calf on the festival of Fordicidia and then cremated. The ashes and blood were mixed, and poured on to burning straw, over which people jumped at the Parilia on April 21st.[17] Between May 7th and 14th the three seniors collected ears of spelt on alternate days, roasted them and, from their flour, salted cakes—*mola salsa*—were made for consumption at the Vestalia (on June 9th), on the ceremonies of September 13th and at the Lupercalia on February 15th.[18]

To compensate for these often, no doubt, monotonous operations,

the Vestal Virgins enjoyed dignified and pleasing privileges. There
were dinner parties, for one thing. We have an account of a banquet
at which on August 24th, 69 B.C., four Vestal Virgins were present—
the four seniors, it may be assumed, while the two juniors, like a pair of
Cinderellas, stayed at home to look after the fire. The dinner celebrated the installation by an augur of a new Flamen Martialis. The
pontiffs occupied two tables, the ladies (who included the wife of the
new Flamen and his mother-in-law) occupied a third. The menu is
preserved too; and by comparison the banquet of the most apolaustic
of City Companies would appear to be a frugal meal. Its thirty dishes
included asparagus, oysters (as many as anyone could eat) and delicious
pâtés of all kinds.[19]

Vestal Virgins travelled through the streets of Rome in carriages at
public festivals. They were attended in public by a lictor. When they
gave evidence in court, they were exempted, together with the Flamen
Dialis, from the necessity of taking an oath. They could annul the
death sentence of a prisoner whom they encountered, as long as it was
by accident, on his way to execution.[20] And under Augustus and his
successors they not only attended the theatre, but sat there in privileged
seats, where they were joined by the ladies of the imperial house.[21]
And when the greatest of these imperial ladies, the widow of Augustus,
was consecrated, they were made responsible for her cult.[22]

Their public importance, especially at moments of crisis, was
indisputable. It was through the senior Vestal Virgin that the Empress
Messalina in her last desperation sought to influence Claudius. And
when in A.D. 69 Vitellius hoped to arrest for a moment the march of
the victorious Flavian army on Rome, the Vestal Virgins carried his
letter to the Flavian commander. Their sacrosanctity gave the security
of a strong room; and so they guarded important documents, the wills
of leading statesmen, for instance, and even the wills of emperors, who
were themselves High Priests.[23]

What of their relation with men—who, as a sex, were allowed to
enter the Atrium by day, but never by night?

The purity of the Vestal Virgins was the token and guarantee of the
good health and salvation of Rome itself; how often, knowing this,
they must have prayed to Vesta that they might not succumb to temptation. There were many forms in which the temptation might come.
There were times when, with the highest standards of integrity pre-
vailing in the College, a girl, through no fault of her own, fell violently
in love. There were undoubtedly periods of persistent religious and

moral laxity when the whole College was corrupt, and from early days the novice was exhorted not to be a prig, but to follow the example of the rest; it was perfectly safe, she would be told. Safe, indeed, if there was not a national calamity or some political ferment in which politicians would expose the scandals of the Vestal Virgins if by this means they could win political kudos for themselves.

The disaster of Cannae in 216 B.C. was such a national calamity. Inevitably it was suggested that the battle was lost not on the field but in Rome; that there was a rottenness at the core. So, guilty or not, two Vestal Virgins were denounced and declared guilty.[24] Corruption of the whole College was alleged at the end of the second century B.C., and in 114 the Pontiffs held an inquiry and condemned one of the Vestal Virgins; in the following year, on the motion of the tribune Peducaeus, who accused the Pontiffs of partiality, a secular court was set up to hold a re-trial, and two of the Vestal Virgins who had been acquitted a year earlier were condemned.[25] Domitian, too, in his acts of A.D. 83 and 90 claimed that the College was a sink of corruption which his father and brother had neglected to reform.[26]

There were times when even innocence had cause for fear. Immorality was sometimes suspected for no better reason than that the sacred fire went out or that a Vestal Virgin's dress and manners were thought to be a little on the gay side;[27] at other times innocent Vestal Virgins might find themselves the victims of scheming politicians. The Roman history books contained splendid, if improbable, stories of charges which were made in the remote past and proved false. A certain Aemilia, whose morals were suspect because she let the fire go out, prayed to Vesta, and threw a piece of linen on the stone-cold embers. The sudden miraculous blaze which followed placed her innocence beyond the reach of doubt. And there was another, Tuccia, who, in a similar predicament, proved her innocence by carrying from the Tiber a sieveful of water from which not a drop leaked.[28]

In 73 B.C. Fabia, half-sister of Cicero's wife Terentia and a Vestal Virgin, was alleged to have been seduced by Catiline; and, worse still, Licinia by her cousin, the eminent Crassus. Both were acquitted. There is no reason to suspect guilt in the first case, and there was certainly none in the second. Crassus had spent some time in private with his cousin, admittedly; but he was only trying to make money, to buy some land from her at less than its proper price.[29]

When the Pontiffs accepted a charge, usually based on information provided by a slave, the suspected Vestal Virgin was suspended from

her duties and forbidden to part with any of her slaves—for 'incest',
the charge brought against her, and high treason, were the only cases in
which the evidence of slaves could be taken under torture against their
employers.[30] She was then tried before the Pontiffs.

Whereas if a Vestal Virgin was found to have let the sacred fire go
out, she suffered nothing worse than a thrashing by the Pontifex
Maximus, if she was found guilty of sexual immorality, the partner in
her guilt was flogged to death—like a slave, *sub furca*—in the Comi-
tium[31] and she was immured alive in an underground chamber under
the Campus Sceleratus by the Colline Gate. If, by contrast, a *bona fide*
secular virgin was doomed to death by strangulation—like the young
daughter of Sejanus, who was supposedly implicated in her father's
scheming in A.D. 31—she was debauched by her executioner when the
rope was already around her neck, because it was inauspicious to execute a virgin.[32]

Plutarch gives this grim description of the erring Vestal Virgin's
doom.[33]

'A small underground chamber is constructed with access from above
by a ladder. It contains a bed, a lighted lamp and small portions of the
bare necessities of existence—bread, water in a jar, milk and oil; so
that the Romans may feel easy in their consciences and nobody can say
that by starvation they have murdered a woman consecrated by the
most sacred ritual.

Inside a litter enclosed by curtains, bound and gagged so that her
voice may not be heard, they carry the victim through the Forum.
People make way without a word, and escort the procession in utter
silence and deep dejection. There is no spectacle in the world more
terrifying and in Rome no day of comparable horror.

When the cortège reaches the end of its journey, the attendants
undo the bonds and, after he has prayed in silence, stretching out his
hands to the gods to explain the necessity of his act, the Pontifex
Maximus takes her by the hand, a thick cloak hiding her face, and sets
her on the ladder. He and the rest of the Pontiffs turn away while she
descends the ladder. Then the ladder is pulled up and the entry to the
chamber closed and covered with deep earth level with the surrounding
ground.'

This was not, obviously, an everyday happening in Rome. Indeed,
there are less than ten occasions in the whole of Roman history when
this punishment is known to have been exacted.[34]

Its origin is variously explained by scholars. It has been suggested that the Vestal Virgin's unchastity was, in the Roman technical sense, a 'prodigy' (like the birth of a misshapen child), and so she had to be put out of the way. Others have thought that from the moment when she was 'taken' by the High Priest, she was symbolically his wife; and he punished her and punished her seducer as if it was a case of adultery. But no explanation is satisfactory. The answer lies in the remote field of Rome's earliest and unknown religious belief.[35]

That such gruesome punishment was exacted even in the last 150 years of the Republic is improbable. It was, therefore, an extraordinary practice to revive at the end of the first century of the Christian era. In A.D. 83 the Emperor Domitian, not unconscious of his own divinity and uninvolved as yet in the scandal which later smirched his reputation (the death through an abortion of his niece, whom he debauched), determined, with a profession of puritanism, to reform the public morals of the State.* Vespasian and Titus, he declared, had known, but had not concerned themselves with, the fact that the College of Vestal Virgins was corrupt. The Pontiffs met; one even died of a heart attack under the strain. Three of the Vestal Virgins— one half of the College—were invited to commit suicide, and their seducers were banished. But this was not the end. Seven years later the Pontiffs were summoned irregularly, not to the Regia but to Domitian's Alban villa, and the Chief Virgin Cornelia, absolved at the earlier examination, was condemned, unheard and absent, to living entombment, and her supposed seducer was beaten to death. Domitian delegated the distasteful operation to his colleagues in the Pontifical College.[36]

'The Pontiffs were at once dismissed to see to the death and burial. Cornelia stretched out her hands to Vesta and to the other gods and, among other protestations, cried out more than once, "How can Caesar think me corrupt when my sacred ministration brought him victory and triumphs?" Whether she said this in hope of mercy or in mockery, from confidence in her own integrity or from contempt of the Emperor, who can say? Whether innocent or not, she certainly gave the impression of innocence, as she was conducted to her doom. When she was descending the ladder to the tomb and her dress was caught up, she turned and freed it. The executioner offered her his

* Domitian might, of course, have been moved by genuine superstition.

hand, but she turned away and shrank back as if, by a final display of her integrity, she was guarding her pure, chaste body from contact with something foul.'

This is the younger Pliny's account of her end, written in a letter describing the misfortune of an ex-praetor who had concealed one of Cornelia's freedwomen and who prudently retired into a self-imposed banishment. He was to be found later in Sicily, giving elocution lessons for a living.[37]

The College of Vestal Virgins survived. In A.D. 215 the Emperor Caracalla satisfied his evil humour by seducing a Vestal Virgin and then ensuring that she and two others were buried alive. A few years later, in A.D. 220/1, from religiosity or from simple depravity, the Emperor Elagabalus married a Vestal Virgin, Aquilia Severa.* He divorced his first wife for the purpose, and granted Aquilia dispensation from her vows. They were, it seems, divorced and remarried more than once. There was no offspring of the marriage; a pity, for he had assured the Senate that, as he was High Priest himself and his wife had been a Priestess, their children would be no ordinary mortals.[38]

Just as the halls of women's Colleges in Oxford and in Cambridge have, hanging on their walls, the portraits of former Principals, so round the Atrium Vestae stood portrait statues of Senior Vestal Virgins on inscribed pedestals, many of which survive in Rome today.[39]

While the Pontifex Maximus was free, within the normal rules of social decorum, to marry whomever he wished and however he wished (a fact which shows that, in remote antiquity, he was something of an upstart), the Priests of Juppiter, Mars and Quirinus must have for their wives women whose parents had been married by the elaborate formality of confarreatio, and must have married in accordance with the same formalities.[40] Even so, the wives of the Flamen Quirinalis and of the Flamen Martialis themselves exercised no priestly functions.

The wife of the Rex Sacrorum (the Regina Sacrorum) and the wife of the Flamen Dialis (the Flaminica), on the other hand, were priestesses—the latter Priestess of Juno—and, as such, had to observe rigorous formalities in their dress and were subject to a number of engaging tabus. The Flaminica Dialis might not climb more than three rungs of a ladder, unless it was a 'Greek ladder' (whatever that was); she might not bathe in May or comb her hair in the first half of June or on those

* See page 159.

days in March when the Priests of Mars (Salii) were dancing; she might not cut her nails in the first half of June either. So vital was she to her husband's exercise of his office that, to hold the priesthood, he had to be a married man; he was not allowed to divorce his wife; and he was compelled to resign his priesthood if his wife died.

Under the Empire the spread of emperor-worship brought into existence a number of priestesses in the provinces, charged with the cult of the women of the imperial family who had been consecrated.

In Rome itself, in Republic and Empire alike, there were times when the incidence of public calamity or reported prodigies of quite abnormal horror drove the government to inquire from the appropriate priests what propitiatory offerings should be made. When the priests in their wisdom discovered that Juno in particular was the goddess who required propitiation, a call was made sometimes on 'thrice nine' unmarried girls ('virgines'), sometimes on married women ('matronae'). In 207 B.C. twenty-seven virgins, clad in long gowns, sang in Juno's honour a song which to later taste seemed barbarously uncouth, beating out the time with their feet. Twenty-seven girls were pressed into service for a similar purpose seven years later. After the great fire in Rome in A.D. 64 married women were required to perform a number of propitiatory acts.[41]

II. Religious Women

There were forms of religious ritual from which women were excluded—the public sacrifice to Hercules on the *ara maxima* for instance and, in the farming world, the regular sacrifices for the well-being of the herds.[42] Equally there were religious ceremonies in which men might play no part, like the cult of the Bona Dea.

There were two occasions in the year when women, and women alone, did honour to this goddess. The first was on May Day, in her temple on the Aventine. The second was on a night early in December, selected each year on some principle unknown to us.[43]

This celebration, which lasted all night, took place in Rome in the house of a senior curule magistrate.[44] He, together with all the other male members of the household, spent the night elsewhere; representations of male persons and animals, in statues, paintings and mosaics, which could not be removed so easily, were decently veiled. The magistrate's wife, normally, was hostess; her fellow celebrants were society ladies, and the Vestal Virgins, of course, were present in an official capacity (having, presumably, to leave the house at intervals to go to the Temple of Vesta and look after the fire). There was music and drinking, with the observance of strict tabus. The wine was called milk, and the wine-jug was called a honey-pot. The central point of the evening's celebration was the sacrifice of a sow. Houses in the centre of Rome not being large, it was, one would guess, a crowded, stuffy and smelly occasion. Of what took place, naturally, men knew no more than women chose to tell them. Plutarch thought the occasion as decorous as one of Mrs. Proudie's *conversazioni*, Juvenal pictured it as an orgy.[45]

In 63 B.C. it was celebrated (only a day or two before the arrest of the Catilinarian conspirators) in the house of the consul Cicero. In 62 it was held in the Precincts, in the official house of the Pontifex Maximus, Julius Caesar—not because he was High Priest, but because he held the praetorship in that year. Where and with whom he dined, we do not know. At his home Aurelia, his mother, appears to have been in control, with her daughter Julia. C. Octavius, the future Emperor Augustus, having been born a year earlier, Aurelia was a great-grandmother, and Julia a grandmother; both overshadowed Caesar's barren wife Pompeia, who was, presumably, the nominal hostess.

At some time during the night a slave-girl called Habra came to Aurelia with the shocking news that a man was wandering about the house disguised as a female harp-player.[46] Aurelia went to him, and ordered him to leave the house at once; which he did. Whether any other women saw him is uncertain; but they were told what had happened and, as soon as they got home, the married women told their husbands all about it. The Vestal Virgins, whether in the house or in their own Atrium, then performed over again certain of the vital ceremonies, for it was their evident duty to ensure that Rome and her great empire took no harm from the intruder's peccadillo.[47]

We do not know how dark it was, and we know nothing about the goodness or badness of Aurelia's eyesight. She declared firmly that she had recognized the intruder as one of the prominent young men of Rome, quaestor-elect and member, though already a somewhat discredited member, of one of the smartest families in Rome. She had recognized him as P. Clodius. The story was soon round Rome, whether or not it was Aurelia who started it, that he had entered the house with the intention of debauching Caesar's wife while the celebrations were in full swing.

Political respectability—with its own political axe to grind—

clamoured for a public trial, and was not deterred by the fact that the alleged crime was one which no existing law appeared to prohibit.[48] The intriguers worked overtime, and Cicero was unwisely persuaded to side with those who pressed for a trial. The Pontiffs and the Vestal Virgins were asked for their official views, both bodies, of course, having the Pontifex Maximus, Caesar himself, for their chairman; and, in view of their answers, it seemed possible to bring Clodius to trial. Caesar divorced his wife with the very proper remark that 'the High Priest's wife must be above suspicion'—distorted, in the telling, into 'Caesar's wife must be above suspicion'—but made it clear by his continuing friendship with Clodius that he did not take the affair too seriously. The sympathy of the public was all on Clodius' side.

Clodius' simple defence was that of 'alibi'; he claimed—and produced evidence—that he was at Interamna on the night when the Bona Dea rites were celebrated, ninety miles away from Rome.[49] Three witnesses were produced to break this alibi, Caesar's venerable mother and the slave-girl, who said that they had caught him in the house, and Cicero, who said that, since Clodius had made a public call on him on the morning before the celebration, he could not have reached Interamna that night.[50] The jury found Clodius not guilty. Obviously its members had been bribed; of this Cicero and his friends had no doubt at all. Historians, following like tame spaniels at Cicero's heels, have reversed the decision of the jury. Unanimously they find Clodius guilty.

One would like to know something of the celebrations of the following year. In whose house were they held? Were guards posted at every entrance? Was Aurelia invited? And by contrast with the excitement of a year earlier, did it all seem very tame?

The story of 'Clodius among the ladies', better than that of Achilles on Scyros, was never forgotten, and tempted Juvenal to a wonderful pastiche.[51] The celebration of the Bona Dea rites becomes an orgy in which the women work themselves into a drunken frenzy, open the doors and cry out for men; 'the buckmouse, conscious of its virility, scuttles away'. It is a disgustingly funny picture; to use it as historical evidence, and to claim on the strength of it that the Bona Dea ceremony degenerated under the Empire into an acknowledged debauch, would be to exhibit a lack of humour and of sound judgement by which nobody would be more shocked than Juvenal himself.

So much for rites which were celebrated by women only. In the common religious cult both of the household and of the state, women, no doubt, continued to observe the formalities as much as men, and at the same time they must have shared the religious cynicism which prevailed, especially among the educated, in the last century of the Republic. Still, married women of the upper classes attended, and took their children to, official religious ceremonies and they did this, no doubt, the more ostentatiously under Augustus, when the attempt was made to bring the traditional religion back into fashion. So they are to be seen, with their children, on the reliefs of the 'Ara Pacis'.

Little in the event was gained by Augustus' attempts to buttress up a dead religion whose foundations were already undermined. The Roman world at the end of the civil wars was a different world from the Rome which Sulla had mastered fifty years earlier. As a result of contacts with oriental princelings, of the movements of troops to and fro to the East and of the great increase of commerce by sea in the Mediterranean, there was a new cosmopolitanism; and from the East Rome imported something more important by far than luxury goods. It imported oriental religions: particularly the cults of the Syrian goddess, of Isis and of Mithras. The number of Jews increased; and, in due course, Christianity reached Rome.

Though linguistically Rome condemned such cults as *superstitiones*, Roman religion being the one and only true *religio*, their attraction was immediate and inescapable. They were living religions, by contrast with a religion which was dead. They had the attraction of mysticism and of hope; they had a personal and spiritual significance which was new, and there was an exaltation in their concepts of purification and of atonement. The new deities were intimately concerned with the personal life of the individual, unlike the Roman gods, who were like powerful absentee landlords, from whom the best that you could hope was that they would leave you alone if you paid your rent correctly and at the proper time.

That women, as a sex, are more gullible than men, may be true; and it was easy for Juvenal to mock women for the fact that they were taken in by the charlatans and impostors who were among the practitioners of the new cults. More important is the fact that women, as a sex, are more religious than men; they could not fail to be attracted by what in the new cults was attractive.

It was to the *demi-monde*, to the middle and lower classes, that the appeal was greatest; and here, for women, the cult of Isis was the most attractive of all, this being the cult of which, in Rome, Authority was most reluctant to approve. Antony's influence in the triumvirate gave it a short-lived respectablity; but it was not until Gaius Caligula that there was a temple of Isis within the city walls themselves, though there were temples outside.[52]

Notoriously the cult of Isis—like that of Ceres—prescribed complete abstinence from the pleasures of the flesh at certain periods and, since courtesans appear, almost as a profession, to have been her devotees, the erotic poets monotonously complained of the hardships which the goddess imposed upon them.[53] Less creditably, a wife would play on her husband's credulity, announcing that she was about to visit the temple of Isis, when in fact she had an assignation with her lover.[54] The greatest scandal of all occurred in A.D. 19. The victim was a certain Paulina. That she was young, handsome, wealthy, virtuous and blue-blooded, as Josephus states, may well be true, but hardly that she was sagacious.[55] An equestrian, Decius Mundus, to whom she refused her favours, bribed the priest of Isis to tell her that Anubis wished to pass the night with her in the temple. She told her friends, secured the permission of her complaisant husband and all would have been well if, after it was all over, her lover had not bragged of his achievement. The unhappy woman told her husband, who informed the Emperor. Tiberius held an inquiry. The priests of Isis were crucified and Isis-worshippers were among the four thousand persons whom Tiberius deported to Sardinia 'to put down brigands and, if the climate killed them, they would not be missed'—*vile damnum*. Mundus, surprisingly, escaped with the sentence of exile, though Tiberius' motive for leniency is hardly likely to have been what Josephus imagines: 'that, if he had done wrong, it was love which led him astray'.

The remainder of the four thousand to be banished were Jews, for there had been a Jewish scandal too. A dishonest Jew, exiled from Judaea, with three accomplices, had taken money from a well-born woman called Flavia, nominally as alms to be sent to Jerusalem, really as profit for themselves.[56]

There was, it is true, a large community of Jews in Trastevere, but as Judaism did not canvass proselytes as extensively as Christianity sought them later, the Roman government suspected it less in Rome than it suspected other oriental cults. It was a religion in which a number of women of good class took much interest; indeed, the Empress Poppaea—who, anyhow, supported a positive retinue of astrologers—was no stranger to the Jewish religion and has even been thought by some, though wrongly, to have been a proselyte.[57] Public opinion was too strong to allow Titus to marry Berenice and give the Romans a Jewess for Empress.[58]

Christianity's earliest converts in Rome, men and women alike, were drawn from the lower social classes; but it has been suggested that in the first century of our era at least two women of distinction were converts not to Judaism, as pagan sources might suggest, but to Christianity. The first was Pomponia Graecina, wife of Aulus Plautius, commander of the force which invaded Britain in A.D. 43 and after that first governor of Britain. She was a woman of importance, an *insignis femina*, a woman whom Tacitus may well have met. From the year of her husband's conquest of Britain, which was also the year in which a woman to whom she was devoted—Julia, grand-daughter of the Emperor Tiberius—died, she lived for forty years in mourning so deep and unremitting as to appear unnatural. In 57, the third year of Nero's principate, she was prosecuted, charged with addiction to a foreign cult and, in accordance with the traditional decencies, handed over to her husband. He, again, observing the traditional decencies, summoned the rest of the family to pronounce judgement. They declared her innocent, and for twenty-six more years she lived in continuance of her sad practices.

By what foreign cult was she seduced? By Judaism or Isis-worship—neither of which, in fact, was criminal? Was it a disease that she had picked up from her husband's residence in Britain, and was she in fact a crypto-Druid? Was she a Christian? Or, in view of the judgement of her relatives, was the source of her melancholy not religious at all?[59]

Christianity has claimed for its second woman-martyr Flavia Domitilla, niece of the Emperor Domitian, married to her second cousin, Flavius Clemens, first cousin of the Emperor. In the year A.D. 95 her abnormally indolent husband was first raised to the consulship by Domitian, then executed. He had been accused, with his wife, of religious unorthodoxy ($\dot{\alpha}\theta\epsilon\dot{\sigma}\tau\eta\varsigma$). Domitilla was sent to banishment in Pandateria (Ventotene). A cemetry outside Rome on the via Ardeatina at Tor Marancio, where there are Christian catacombs, was in an estate which once belonged to a Domitilla. So Christian tradition, with the respectable support of Eusebius, has claimed her as a martyr, variously believing that she was forced to death soon after her husband, that she endured a protracted martyrdom, or that she was not the wife of Clemens at all but—in the highest category of martyrs—a virgin.

It must be admitted, however, that Eusebius, writing in the fourth century, is our earliest source for the suggestion that she was a Christian. There is some reason for thinking that the Christian catacomb is not earlier than the second century A.D.; and it has even been suggested that Judaism, not Christianity, was the unroman 'superstition' to which she was converted.[60]

In the second and third centuries the Court could not remain unaffected by the rapid spread of Christianity. As has been seen above, Marcia, the concubine of Commodus, was a good friend to Christians and, when the time came for the official recognition of Christianity early in the fourth century, the womenfolk both of Diocletian and of Constantine were deeply sympathetic; Helena herself embraced Christianity not with her heart only, but with her head; she had her own very definite opinions on matters of doctrine.

III. Divine Women

In 90 B.C. when the Italian allies were in revolt from Rome, the highly born Caecilia Metella dreamt that, since women had taken to using her temple as if it was a public lavatory and a bitch had even whelped in a basket placed at the foot of her statue, the goddess Juno Sospita had decided—understandably enough—to abandon the place and to leave Rome, for which she evidently prophesied a series of disasters, which in the event came true.[61] In answer to Caecilia's entreaties, however, she consented to remain. This was the dream. Caecilia thereupon cleaned out the temple and restored it to its original splendour. To this supernatural experience of Caecilia the superstitious Romans ascribed their subsequent victory in the war. 'Miracles of liberation remain engraved in the hearts of peoples. The miracle achieved by Caecilia in a war of secession crowned her for ever with a mysterious halo which distinguished her from all the rest of womankind.' So much, in the way of history, can a little evidence and a strong French imagination achieve.[62]

Of the women who, after their death achieved consecration in Rome, few had titles as good.

Egypt of the Pharaohs believed in the divinity of the reigning king and of his consort, and in the Hellenistic kingdoms of the eastern Mediterranean which grew out of Alexander's conquests, rulers were consecrated after death (by a practice which owed something to the hero cult of the Greeks) and, in some cases, from the second and third generation onwards, in their lifetime. They were the objects of cult, with temples and priests, the queens with priestesses. As these Hellen-istic kingdoms fell before the advance of Roman power, strong dissuasion was necessary to prevent their sycophantic people from paying similar polite compliments to the proconsuls who came out from Rome; and when, in Greece and the eastern Mediterranean, Antony disported himself in the costume of Dionysus, it was only the Romans, victims of Octavian's propaganda, who were profoundly shocked.

Already, however, at Rome Julius Caesar had followed in the distant steps of Romulus. When Romulus died, he became the god Quirinus; Julius Caesar was murdered in 44 B.C. and two years later by decree of the Senate he became a god, Divus Julius. A temple of Divus Julius was built. Augustus died in A.D. 14 and, by vote of the Senate again, became Divine Augustus, with temple and priesthood (the Sodales Augustales).

Two gods; but no goddess as yet.

When Julia Augusta, Augustus' widow, died in A.D. 29, there were whispered suggestions of consecration, no doubt. But by now she shared much of the unpopularity of her son Tiberius; and Tiberius himself had already left the Senate in no doubt that the consecration of rulers was something of which he disapproved—Augustus, of course, excepted.

In the event it was the twenty-one-year-old Drusilla, sister of the capricious Emperor Gaius Caligula, who was the first Roman woman to become a goddess.* She died on June 10th, A.D. 38, and was decreed a goddess on September 23rd. The Romans had already decided that, if consecration of human beings was not in its origins a Roman practice, it should at least be performed in a traditionally Roman manner; that evidence of some prodigious happening should be required before a formal vote of consecration was passed. After the miraculous appearance of a comet at the games in honour of the dead Julius in July, 44 B.C., there was no more need of evidence in his case. After Augustus' death there were more prodigies than one; an eagle flew out of the funeral pyre, and a senator testified on oath that he had witnessed his ascent to heaven. Testimony of this latter kind was easily obtained, and gave satisfaction. So now a senator of some seniority, an ex-praetor, announced that he had seen Drusilla going up to heaven, even consorting with other gods; and he swore by the gods (Drusilla tactfully included) that he spoke the truth. His evidence was

* See page 96.

accepted and, as an observant man, he received a reward of a million sesterces.[63]

No temple was built at Rome to Divine Drusilla, and even the shrine which was voted seems never to have been constructed. And, when Gaius was killed a little more than two years later, the goddess Drusilla and her cult were generally forgotten, though two inscriptions survive to show that in the neighbourhood of Turin the cult survived the accession of Claudius. Claudius himself was statesman enough to feel that there was an outstanding injustice which needed correction; however belatedly, his grandmother Augusta should join her consort among the gods. So, with what formalities we do not know, she was voted a goddess; her statue was placed in the temple of Divine Augustus, and the Vestal Virgins were made responsible for her cult.[64]

For the rest, the consecration of females in the first century A.D., though it may have reflected the deep sorrow of bereavement or the contrition of a killer, indicated little more than the growing servility of the Senate, too ready always to please, and suggested a belief in the embryonic divinity of anyone born or married into the imperial house which intelligent opinion at Rome certainly did not accept. There were a number of new goddesses, some of them children, all ephemeral to a degree—Claudia Augusta,[65] the daughter of Nero and Poppaea, who died at the age of four months in A.D. 63, and Flavia Domitilla, the daughter of Vespasian, who had died before his accession.[66] Others were consecrated, whose conduct in their lifetime had shown them to be anything but divine—Nero's wife Poppaea who died as a result of a kick from her husband,[67] and Titus' daughter Flavia Julia, Domitian's niece, who died in circumstances more distressing still.[68] Not the least commendable of Paetus Thrasea's acts, and one which brought his own death nearer, was his refusal to attend the meeting of the Senate which voted Poppaea a goddess.[69]

In the second century some sense of proportion was restored.[70] The women who were consecrated when they died were all outstanding persons: Trajan's wife Plotina, his sister Marciana and his niece Matidia (under Hadrian), Hadrian's wife Sabina, and—whatever, in their lifetimes, their morals may have been—the elder and the younger Faustina, wives of Antoninus Pius and of Marcus Aurelius.

WOMAN'S DAILY LIFE

++

1. Dress

A WOMAN's underclothing consisted of a light sleeveless under-tunic, a shift (*intusium*) and a *fascia* or *strophium*, her brassières. The garments which she showed the world were a *tunica* (which, from the first century B.C., came to be called *stola*), and a *palla*. Though girls once wore the toga, the habit had ceased by the time of the early Empire, and respectable women used it in no circumstances at all. This garment which in boys and men marked the exclusive dignity of the Roman citizen and, with its variations, even revealed his social rank, was, in the case of women, the dress of prostitutes—and of those who had been tried and found guilty of adultery.[1]

In early Republican Rome a woman, when out of doors, revealed no more of her body than does a nun today; and it was, reputedly, on the simple ground that she had appeared in public with her head uncovered that, at some early date, C. Sulpicius Gallus divorced his wife.[2]

A woman's *stola* extended to the ground; her *palla* might cover her head, but by Augustus' time, as the sculptures of the 'Ara Pacis' show, it was a matter of indifference whether women pulled the *palla* up over their heads or not. This *palla* was nearer to a very large rectangular shawl than to any other piece of modern clothing; its lower edge extended as far as the knees. It survived without change until the third century A.D., and then its size was reduced. A different, and smaller, mantle was the *ricinium* which, whatever its origin, had by the late Republic become a mourning veil. Yet another form of head-covering was the *rica*, a sort of kerchief worn, particularly, it seems, by priestesses.[3]

The modern descendant of the *tunica* or *stola* is a one-piece dress with kimono sleeves; 'it was made of two lengths of cloth of equal length, which constituted the back and the front of the garment, and were sewed together along their edges about three-fifths of their entire length, from the bottom. The unjoined portions were then folded over, back and front, forming a cuff or apron. The top of the garment, back and front, was then gathered or laid in folds on the shoulder'—the gathered portions being sewed firmly together—'and the groups of folds were joined together on the shoulders, either by brooches or by seam, leaving a neck opening and arm holes. A girdle was tied just below the bust'. A Roman matron, then, was *stolata*; and great emphasis was laid by writers on one particular feature of the *stola*, the *instita*. This was its lowest portion and, with great decorum, covered the lady's feet. This has been thought of sometimes as a flounce, but there is no indication of a flounce in any sculptured representation of a woman's dress. It must, therefore, simply have been a border and, as it is not marked in sculpture, it was presumably a band sewed on the lower edge of the dress, and was probably often distinguished by being in a colour different from that of the dress itself.[4]

In a world of change, nothing in modern times changes faster than fashion in women's clothing. It is a startling fact, therefore, that Roman women seem, from representation in sculpture, to have dressed in almost the same—rather dull—way in the second century A.D. as they had done three hundred years earlier. The only passage in Roman literature in which there is a suggestion of variety in women's costume is in Plautus' *Epidicus*, produced very early in the second century B.C. (which, like all Plautus passages, may, of course, have greater application to Hellenistic Greece than to contemporary Rome). In vigorous translation, the passage is as follows: 'What are they at, sir, these women that invent new names for garments every year? The Loose-knit tunic, the Closeknit tunic, the Linenblue, the Interior, the Goldedge, the Marigold or Crocus tunic, the Shift—or Shiftless—the Mantilla, the Royal or the Exotic, the Wavy or the Downy, the Nutty or the Waxy—and not a kernel of sense in all of it.'[5]

This passage, in fact, reveals the truth. It is self-evident that women cannot have lived for centuries without novelty in their clothes. Fashion changed, without doubt, from season to season, but change was made not so much in the cut and shape of the *stola*, as in the texture of the material, and its colour.

Though silk was mentioned by Aristotle in the fourth century B.C., the culture of silkworms was not introduced to Europe until the sixth century A.D. Silk was imported, therefore, from China, and was exceedingly expensive, a pound of silk being worth a pound of gold in the third century A.D. Not only was the price prohibitive, but because of its thinness and transparency it was thought to be an unroman and indelicate fabric. It was not without significance that Elagabalus wore silk regularly and his virtuous successor Alexander Severus hardly at all.[6]

The texture and weight of woollen cloth varied greatly; it was thick for winter use and thin for summer.

But colour, above all, gave women's clothes their attraction, and 'purple', with gold, was traditionally the epitome of extravagance in dress, as the debate on the repeal of the Oppian law well indicates.* This word was applied to a wide range of colours, from blue and red to purple itself. Among the fancied colours were dark rose (*nigrantis rosae color*), hard and brilliant scarlet (*nimiae eius nigritiae austeritas illa nitorque*), amethyst and 'the colour of congealed blood, blackish at first glance, but gleaming when held up to the light'. These were, in the main, shell-fish dyes from the *murex*, the remarkable nature of whose secretions was first discovered and put to commercial use in the eastern Mediterranean at Tyre. The elder Pliny describes the process with his accustomed thoroughness.[7]

The Romans also used vegetable and mineral dyes, and these produced a wide variety of colours: sea-green (*cumatile*), saffron, Paphian myrtle, amethyst, pale rose, Thracian crane, acorn, almond, according to Ovid's list. Sober colours, too, have his recommendation: white for women with dark complexions, black for those who are fair.

Certain colours were thought to be too startling for a lady to wear. They were worn by prostitutes, who having the further advantage over staid matrons that their feet were exposed, could wear jewelled anklets.[8]

The vanity of rich clothing was for Tertullian and the Christian teachers part of the common vanity of earthly pleasure. Suppose Eve had enjoyed the luxury of silk and of Tyrian dyes; what enjoyment would they have brought her when she was expelled from paradise and dead? Had the omnipotent Creator approved of such colour, is it likely that at the Creation he would have neglected to fill the countryside with purple and with scarlet sheep? How strong these arguments appeared to those to whom they were directed, we cannot tell.[9]

* See pages 33-7.

II. Coiffure

The arranging of her hair naturally occupied a large part of a woman's time and thought. The operation was performed by a female hair dresser (*tonstrix*, *ornatrix*) or by one or more of her slaves, who were particularly trained for the purpose. We should not be deluded by Martial and Juvenal into imagining, as an everyday scene, a hysterical mistress frenzied by a mistake which had been made, attacking the girl's face with her nails, seizing her arms and scratching them with her very sharp-pointed hair-pins (*acus*), tearing her hair, or thrashing her with a mirror. Wall-paintings from Pompeii give a placid and, one hopes, more usual picture; the lady examines herself in a mirror, and is evidently delighted by what she sees. In Juvenal's unhappy scene at least three slaves were engaged in the operation; on a stone relief in the museum at Trier three slaves were employed too, one doing her mistress's hair, one holding a mirror for her mistress to watch the operation; and in this there are no strained looks.[10]

As for hair-style, it was in the Empire the ladies of the Court who set the fashion; from the continuous series of their coin-portraits, which are always identifiable, and from their sculpted portrait-heads, which can often be identified with certainty, it is easy to follow the changes—often very startling changes—of fashion. At the same time even at Court not everyone followed the same fashion slavishly at any time, and in the middle and lower ranks of society there must always have been great divergences of hair-style. A coiffure which is becoming to one face or one shape of head is highly unbecoming to another, as Ovid pointed out.[11]

In the Republic younger women dressed their hair in simple style, drawing it to the back of the head to form a simple knot, which was thrust through with a pin. Women sometimes wore a thinly woven net (*reticulum*) over their hair which, to judge by the one which survives ornamented with small golden flies, in the museum at Aquileia, could be very lovely. Trimalchio's Fortunata boasted that hers was woven of pure gold. There was an old-fashioned method of hair-dressing, which the Vestal Virgins perpetuated, in which coils of hair, bound in fillets (*vittae*) were massed at the top of the head, so that their hair was in the general shape of a cone (*tutulus*).[12]

The fillets (*vittae*) and pin (*acus*) never altogether disappeared. 'The simple strips of rough wool, emblem of chastity and symbol of the honour due to a married woman, which originally enclosed the mass of the *tutulus*, changed to linen or silk ribbons in bright colours. In a variety of shapes and sizes, they were placed in the hair, in differing styles. When they were of precious materials, fringed with gold, held firm by pins or little gold buckles embroidered with pearls or other precious stones, they lost all utilitarian character, and passed into the category of jewels.' Of these, diadems were the most splendid and expensive.[13]

Though, to judge by coins and busts, there were continuous changes in coiffure in the Julio–Claudian period, there were broadly two styles, according as there were two parallel partings or the hair was simply parted in the centre. In the two-parting system, generally called 'the Octavia style' because it was worn by Augustus' sister, the central portion was combed forward, and rolled to form a toupet over the centre of the forehead, before it was drawn back to join the other two sections in a knot at the back.[14]

It is hard to believe that this style was as becoming as the simpler one which replaced it; by this the hair was parted in the centre and the parted hair was drawn across the temples in close waves, part to fall in long curls over the ears on to the neck, the rest knotted at the back over the nape of the neck.

That Julia, the daughter of Titus—whose life was so cruelly wrecked by her uncle Domitian—was attractive, there can be no doubt. It was she, it seems, who started a period of sheer fantasy in feminine coiffure which even eighteenth-century extravagance could hardly out-match. This was the time when, one must assume, hours upon end were devoted to the curling-tongs, and tempers, according to Juvenal, were badly frayed. Curl climbs on top of curl and over the forehead there arose something which at its best looked like the *chef d' œuvre* of a gifted pastrycook and, at its worst, like a dry sponge. At the back the hair was plaited, and the braids were arranged in a coil which looks like basketwork. The towering splendour was to be viewed from one direction only, the front, and women must have manœuvred at social gatherings, to keep out of view the ridiculous anti-climax which the backs of their heads constituted. 'Story on story are built up on her lofty head. See her from in front; she is Andromache. From behind she looks half the size—a different woman, you would think.' So Juvenal mocked.[15]

This was what Martial called 'a globe of hair' and Statius, 'the glory of woman's lofty front, her storied hair'; and this was the time when Juvenal's poor slave-girl was chastized, because one of the innumerable curls was out of place. A resplendent diadem (*stephané*) sometimes divided the edifice, and sometimes constituted its crown and climax, To what extent a framework was employed, and what calls were made on false hair to complete the splendour, we do not know. Were these masterpieces destroyed each night, and recreated every morning? How often were they simply taken off at night, placed on the dressing-table and put on again the following day? For in some portrait busts the line between the brow and the hair is so sharply marked as to suggest that all this splendour was in fact a wig.

Plotina seems to have had her own way of doing her hair. 'The hair was drawn loosely from the forehead, then caught together and tied over the scalp. This long hair is rolled, and the roll allowed to fall across the front of the head to just above the ears in a diadem effect.'[16] It was Sabina who decided to have done with half a century of extravagance. Her hair was worn in a simple manner, parted at the centre and drawn down on either side of the head in rippling masses. The elder Faustina's style, with a coil of plaits at the top of her head, like a sleeping snake, was simple and dignified, and her daughter, favouring all the time a less and less ornate coiffure, started with a style by which the hair was elaborately ribbed and knotted in a chignon at the back and ended by waving her hair from the top to a low chignon a little above the neck. The simple style of the late second century gave way to a heavy artificially-waved structure which sat, like a close-fitting Balaclava helmet, on the head of Julia Domna. After this, the hair was sometimes gathered at the back in the form of a flat and unattractive bun and was, by the time of Helena, attractively massed at the back, and the whole ornamented, in Tudor manner, with strings of precious stones.

Young girls do not dress their hair like elderly women and, while mothers may have aped the hair-style of the Court, their daughters often went their own way. So from all periods of the Empire there are portraits of girls with hair parted in the centre, charmingly waved, and with curls hanging at the sides or at the back, or with their hair segmented in a style which was in origin Greek, to which German scholars have given the apt if inelegant title of *Melonen-frisur*.

Writing in Africa two centuries later than Ovid wrote in Rome, the Christian Tertullian is his perfect foil. Ovid glorified and sought the refinement of every pleasure which the flesh affords; Tertullian would have the rest of humanity as ascetic as himself. Women must be reformed like everybody else; among other things, they must stop devoting so much time and thought to the arrangement of their hair.

'All this wasted pains on arranging your hair—what contribution can this make to your salvation? Why can you not give your hair a rest? One minute you are building it up, the next you are letting it down—raising it one moment, stretching it the next. Some women devote all their energy to forcing their hair to curl, others to making it hang loose and wavy, in a style which may seem natural, but is not natural at all. You perpetrate unbelievable extravagances to make a kind of tapestry of your hair, sometimes to be a sort of sheath to your head and a lid to the top of you, like a helmet, sometimes to be an elevated platform, built up on the back of your neck.'[17]

'There is nothing graceful about becoming bald. Snatched by age, our hairs fall like autumn leaves torn by a chill wind from the trees. When woman's hair turns white, she dyes it with German herbs,* and seeks by artificial means a colour which is better than any which is natural. She has a mass of hair—all bought. She puts the money down, and some other woman's hair is hers. She buys it without a blush.' . . . 'If there is anything the matter with a woman's hair, she should post a watchman at the gate or arrange her coiffure in the temple of the Bona Dea.† There was a lady once to whom my arrival was announced unexpectedly. She was in such a fluster that she put on her wig back to front.' So Ovid wrote in his *Art of Love*.[18]

False hair was worn by women whose hair was thin; wigs were worn by those whose hair was inadequate (destroyed often by unskilful dyeing and excessive use of the hot tongs), sometimes by women whose hair was adequate, but they disliked its colour and, rather than resort to dyes, they preferred to wear a wig. There must have been innumerable German blondes whose fate it was, on being taken captive, to have their hair cut off, for sale to the wig-makers in Rome.[19]

The women of ancient, as of modern, Italy were, in general, dark-haired; and fair hair evidently had the same fascination for the ancient Roman that it has for so many Italians today. There were evidently many colours between red and flaxen; Poppaea's hair, for instance, was fair, and Nero in a poem called it 'amber-coloured'. In some cases such colours were natural; often they were not.[20]

Even in early times when women led a cloistered life, it was thought legitimate for them 'to redden their hair with ashes', to give pleasure to their husbands. To dye their hair to a fair colour, Roman women

* *Femina canitiem Germanis inficit herbis.*
† Access to which was forbidden to men.

used a substance which had been discovered in use in the Rhine district, called 'spuma Batava'—'Batavian foam'—or 'Wiesbaden soap-tablets'—'pilae Mattiacae'—and this corresponded, no doubt, to Ovid's 'German herbs'.

The elder Pliny gives the components of a soap invented in Gaul 'for reddening hair'—'rutilandis capillis'—'which was available both in solid and liquid form, and which was used in Germany, more by men than by women'. It was a mixture of fat, preferably goat-fat, and ashes, preferably of beechwood.[21]

It is natural to assume that this concoction of Pliny (described in modern dictionaries—with wild inaccuracy, as it seems—as 'letharge of silver') is the dye to which Ovid and Martial refer. Experiment, however, shows that, while it makes a tremendous lather and is an admirable shampoo, it is not a dye at all.[22]

That German men dyed their hair is in itself unlikely, and is not mentioned by Tacitus in his treatise on Germany. That they washed their hair with a good shampoo is not improbable at all; and, if their hair was generally dirty when they washed it and its natural colour was reddish, a foreigner might well be mistaken in thinking the shampoo to be a dye. If that was the case, the concoctions described by Ovid and by Martial, though they came from Germany, must have been different; or else there was some further ingredient in Pliny's shampoo which—understandably enough, if there was a big foreign market for the stuff in Rome—was not revealed by the manufacturers.

But this is not the end of the story. There remains Plutarch's embroidery to an account which, in its outlines, reaches us also from a number of other sources, of the remarkable life lived under Vespasian by the Gaul Julius Sabinus of the Lingones (who boasted descent à la main gauche, through his Gallic great-grandmother, from Julius Caesar), who took part in Civilis' revolt on the Rhine in A.D. 70 and who, if the revolt had succeeded, would have been a forlorn candidate for the purple. When the failure of the revolt was assured, he retired to his house and burnt it down over his head. Instead of perishing in the fire, as was generally assumed, he survived in a cellar, and in this cellar, to the knowledge of only a few friends and of his wife Epponina, who paid him surreptitious visits, he survived for the next nine years. In the course of this period she bore him two sons who, once delivered, were presumably brought up in the cellar by their father. After nine years of this extraordinary life (in the course of which, with her husband in disguise, she went to Rome in the vain hope of securing a pardon for him), she was brought a second time to Rome and, with her husband, executed in circumstances of peculiar horror. The sons, however, survived and grew to manhood, and Plutarch met one of them when he paid a visit to Delphi. Plutarch's account, therefore, is likely to derive from a good source.[23]

Its extraordinary feature—which appears in none of the other versions of the story—is its insistence that, since her husband was generally believed to be dead, Epponina was forced on both occasions to conceal the fact of her pregnancy from the other women in the neighbourhood, and this despite the fact that she was in the habit of bathing naked with them. 'There is an ointment which women rub on their hair to make it gold or red; it contains grease which fills or puffs out the flesh and produces a sort of dilation or swelling. She spread this ointment in profusion on all other parts of her body except the abdomen and thus concealed its size as it swelled and filled out.' So Plutarch declares. But, in its details, his story cannot be true. Epponina cannot have pretended to have been dyeing her hair every time she bathed. Presumably she was using the shampoo which Pliny describes; and its value to her must have lain in the concealment which its greasy lather afforded, not in its power to produce a dropsical inflation of her chest.[24]

Men did not approve always of women's enterprise in changing the colour of their hair, and we possess a poem in which Propertius takes Cynthia severely to task on this account.[25] If a woman dyed her hair blue—which, after all, was the colour with which Britons were known to stain their bodies—she would not be admired; why, Propertius asks, was it any wiser to think 'the Belgian colour' an improvement on the natural tint of Cynthia's hair?

III. Make-up and Jewels (Cultus)

'If you saw women getting out of bed in the morning, you would find them more repulsive than monkeys. That is why they shut themselves up and refuse to be seen by a man; old hags and a troupe of servant-maids as ugly as their mistress surround her, plastering her unhappy face with a variety of medicaments. For a woman does not just wash away her sleepiness with cold water, and proceed to a serious day's work. No, innumerable concoctions in the way of salves are used to brighten her unpleasing complexion. As in a public procession, each of the servants has some different object in her hand; a silver basin, a jug, a mirror, a multitude of boxes, enough to stock a chemist's shop, jars full of mischief, tooth powders or stuff for blackening the eyelids.'

This ungallant account of a woman's toilet was, naturally, written by a man;[26] so, indeed, were most of our accounts of the operations of the Roman beauty-parlour. In Hellenistic comedy—and so in Plautus—advice to the young woman on her make-up, her coiffure and her dress was given by the experienced courtesan or by the procuress or by a male character speaking from an experience of women which he possessed, or at least claimed to possess. In elegiac writing—Greek, then Roman—the poet himself is the instructor; and the third book of Ovid's *Art of Love* is a manual of instruction, just as some of Propertius' poems contain instructions, to young women on how to make the best of themselves. On the other hand we have the venomous critics of women, whom it is a mistake to call misogynists: Juvenal, Martial and, in the passage quoted above, the second-century humourist Lucian. All men.

Cultus was the word. It included make-up and scents (*mundus*) and the external embellishment of jewellery (*ornatus*). And, reasonably enough, this constituted the centre of interest in the lives of a very great number of women, in particular of Ovid's own clients, the expensive courtesans. In pagan Rome only the Vestal Virgin was forced to suppress a sigh, knowing that such vanity was not for her. Her fate was decided as early as 420 B.C., when 'Postumia, a Vestal Virgin, was tried for incest, a crime of which she was not guilty, but suspicion had been raised by the fact that she was always got up prettily (*cultus*), and she had a wit which was a little too loose for a Virgin. After an adjournment she was found Not Guilty. Delivering judgement on behalf of the College of Pontiffs, the High Priest told her to stop making jokes and, in her dress and appearance, to aim at looking holy rather than at looking smart'.[27]

Later on, Christian women received similar instruction from their teachers. Tertullian abhorred make-up as much as he abhorred elaborate coiffure; it was an attempt to improve on the handiwork of God.[28]

In museums all over the world which was once Rome's, show-cases are full of mirrors, the empty pomade jars, the combs, the tweezers, the hairpins and all the other instruments of the Roman woman's dressing-table. The poets take us farther, and fill the empty jars.

As a foundation for make-up, a disagreeable substance derived from the sweat of sheep's wool was used. And Juvenal, in his mischievous way, suggests that it was the husband who suffered at night from the highly scented cream with which his wife anointed her face, and from the bread-pack which she placed over her cheeks. These were a preparation for the make-up with which on the following day she would seduce her lover.[29]

In the hundred surviving lines of Ovid's poem *On making up a woman's face* (*Medicamina faciei femineae*) there are several prescriptions for the manufacture of unguents. For one, you mixed a concoction of barley-meal, ground pulse, eggs, ground antlers, narcissus bulbs, gum, honey and wheat-flour from Tuscany; for another, grilled pale lupins, cooked beans, white lead, froth of red nitre, Illyrian iris. To whiten her face, a woman used white-lead (*cerussa*), chalk or Melian-white (*melinum*); naturally she also needed rouge (*purpurissum*). And a black substance was used for the eyelids and to lengthen the line of the eyes. That she coloured her lips, is to be assumed.[30]

'*Cura dabit faciem*,' Ovid wrote.[31] 'If you take pains over your face, you can be sure to look nice.'

Purchased scents came either from the East, or, in Italy, from Capua. Seplasia, the perfume market of Capua, was famous, and Seplasium has been described as the *eau-de-Cologne* of the Roman world. Poppaea, who gave an outstanding lead to feminine fashion at Rome in her short three years as Empress, introduced what was evidently a rather strong scent, whose popularity survived her, and which went by her name. Few of her female admirers, however, can have been able to afford to emulate the means by which she preserved the softness of her skin; five hundred she-asses were milked daily for her bath.[32]

Prostitutes, who are to be encountered so frequently in the poems of Martial, no doubt used too much scent; and this mistake might be made, it seems, even by a woman as cultured as Cynthia.[33]

Rich Roman women under the Empire possessed a tremendous wealth of gold and precious stones.[34]

When the *lex Oppia* was debated in 195 B.C., gold was the only precious metal whose use by women was discussed. The amount of gold on the market is said to have increased greatly after Sulla's return from the East early in the first century B.C., and the import of precious stones and of jewels from the East to have begun[35] with Pompey's triumph in 61 B.C. In the Empire rich women possessed precious stones of every kind—opals, sapphires, emeralds, beryl, jasper, sardonyx, carbuncles, topaz, onyx, diamonds (which came chiefly from India and which, since they could not be cut, were used largely on rings)[36] and, above all, pearls. Jewels were worn in ear-rings (*inaures*), necklaces, bracelets, rings, brooches, diadems in the hair and—though not, of course, by respectable matrons—in anklets.

Our knowledge of the jewellery of Roman women comes from a variety of sources. Two inscriptions of imperial date found in Spain list the jewellery which adorned two statues,[37] one of them a statue erected to a woman on her own instruction by the terms of her will. A *cache* of jewellery was discovered at Lyons in 1841 and can be seen today at Lyons in the Musée des Beaux Arts; while the Museo Nazionale at Naples contains the remarkable jewels discovered in the House of Menander and in the Villa Boscoreale at Pompeii. And other great museums, like the British Museum, have remarkable pieces on display.[38] In addition, the elder Pliny and other writers—Seneca, for instance, and the satirists—have much to tell us about the jewels which women wore. They wrote not as connoisseurs, but as moralists, emphasizing the vulgarity and extravagance of women who overloaded themselves with jewellery; the degeneracy of such ornament, when contrasted with the unadorned simplicity of the Roman matron of legendary antiquity; the cost of Roman extravagance in terms of human life to the pearl-divers in the hazards of the Indian Ocean, off the Arabian coast and in the Persian Gulf; and, economically the alarming drain of currency from the Empire to foreign countries in the East, estimated by the elder Pliny as being a hundred million sesterces a year. 'That is what luxury and women cost us.'[39]

From the north came little of value, except amber (from the Baltic). British pearls were a sad disappointment—undersized and of very poor colour.[40]

According to Pliny women spent more money on their ears, in the purchase of pearl ear-rings, than on any other part of their person. Seneca said scathingly that some women wore on a single ear the value of two or three estates. Ear-rings were often very heavy and, through wearing them, women sometimes badly distorted the shape of their ears.[41]

'The highest praise given to the colour of pearls,' Pliny wrote,[42] 'is for them to be called alum-coloured. The longer ones also have a charm of their own. Those that end in a wider circle, tapering lengthwise in the shape of perfume-baskets, are termed 'probes' (*elenchi*).

Women glory in hanging these on their fingers and using two or three for a single ear-ring . . . which they call 'castanets' (*crotalia*), as if they enjoyed even the sound and the mere rattling together of the pearls; and nowadays even poor people covet them—it is a common saying that a pearl is as good as a lackey for a lady when she walks abroad.'

At the end of the Republic the debauched Caecilia Metella, whose husband, the son of Cicero's reputable friend, the consul of 57, had to divorce her because of her misbehaviour with Cicero's disreputable son-in-law Dolabella, and who ended by marrying the wealthy and unstable son of the actor Aesopus, is said to have dissolved a pearl worth a million sesterces in vinegar. Cleopatra had done even better. Wearing in each ear a pearl worth ten million sesterces, she consumed the sum at a gulp, when she dissolved one of the pearls in vinegar and drank it.* And Pliny saw Lollia Paulina at an ordinary betrothal party, wearing on her hair, ears, neck and fingers, jewels which were valued at forty million sesterces. This at a time when she was not yet married to the Emperor Gaius Caligula, so that the jewels were her own, and not the imperial jewels. In a very different level of society, Scintilla, friend of Trimalchio's wife Fortunata and united to her by a common bond of vulgarity, carried a splendid pair of gold ear-rings in a locket which she wore round her neck; she boasted, when she exhibited them, that, thanks to her husband's generosity, no woman alive had better ear-rings than she. Her husband's ungracious retort was that, if he had a daughter, he would cut her ears off, to put a stop to such nonsense. In one of the two surviving marriage contracts (from Egypt, in about A.D. 100) the bride's jewellery, which is listed, included 'one very long ear-ring'.[43]

Rich wives of poor husbands are represented as the women who spent money most extravagantly on jewels. If taxed with their extravagance, they would perhaps have retorted that jewels, like gold, retained their value, and that they constituted, therefore, a safe investment for their money. The investment might be a matter of quiet good taste and refinement; among vulgarians, naturally, it was not a matter of refinement at all. One has only to join Trimalchio and his friends after dinner:[44]

---

* So Pliny records (ix, 121). But, as vinegar does not dissolve pearls now, it is improbable that it dissolved pearls then. And, if it did, so powerful a dissolvent would, presumably, have caused some little disorder to the drinker. In his note on the passage in the Loeb Classical Library, H. Rackham solves the dilemma.

'The next thing I knew Fortunata was undoing the bracelets on her grotesquely fat arms and showing them off for Scintilla to admire. Then she undid her anklets, and finally her hair-net, which she kept insisting was woven of pure gold. Trimalchio, who was observing this by-play with interest, ordered all her jewellery to be brought to him. "Gentlemen," he said, "I want you to see the chains and fetters our women load themselves with; this is how we poor bastards are bankrupted. By god, she must be wearing six and a half pound of solid gold. Still, I must admit I've got a bracelet that weighs a good ten pounds on its own."'

iv. Baths

People probably washed too little in early Republican Rome; in the days of the Empire they may well have washed too much. Baths, public and private alike, increased in elegance all the time; in particular, from being dark and gloomy (and, probably, smelling very dank) they came to be well lighted, with large windows. The members of well-to-do Roman families sometimes took their baths at home and sometimes went out to the public baths. In country villas from the second century B.C. onwards there were normally baths in the house. Tourists at Liternum in the early Empire could inspect the villa in which the elder Scipio lived in his retirement at the beginning of the second century B.C. and (if they were not moralists, like Seneca) shudder at the idea of anybody using baths which were so small and in particular, so dark. There were private baths in a number of the largest houses in Pompeii, and in the Villa of the Mysteries outside it. There were baths in Cicero's villa at Tusculum, and the last letter that Cicero wrote to Terentia before their divorce in 47 was an instruction about the cold-water basin (the *labrum*) in the hot chamber (*caldarium*). There were baths in Pliny's Laurentine villa, but the neighbouring village had as many as three public baths, 'which is a great convenience if you arrive unexpectedly, or if you are staying such a very short time that you do not feel inclined to have the fires in your own bath lit'.[45]

The private bath in the house, originally known as *lavatrina*, was, in fact, earlier than the public bath (*balneum* or *balneae*), which was something which the Romans borrowed from the Greeks.

In the second century B.C. in Plautus' *Truculentus* it was inside the house that the courtesan Phronesium took such an interminable time over her bath that her lover Diniarchus was driven to say, 'I believe fish, whose life is one long bath, take less time over it than Phronesium. If women would let you love them for as long a time as they take over their baths, their lovers would turn bath-attendants to a man'. In the *Mostellaria* it was a cold bath—and this, in a Mediterranean summer, is more than understandable—that the courtesan Philematium enjoyed so much. These passages, in plays of the early second century B.C. may, of course, reflect the life of the Hellenistic world, the environment in which the original plays from which Plautus translated were performed. But at the same time they were statements which did not sound absurd to the Roman audience; a hundred years later, when bathing was a universal practice on the part anyhow of well-to-do people, they made better sense still. Augustus' mother used to attend the public baths until, on account of a physical blemish, she was too embarrassed to bathe in public.[46]

Though intemperate bathers might take more than one bath a day, it was the general habit of Roman men, both in and out of Rome, to go to the baths after the midday meal (if they ate at midday) and the siesta—at the eighth or ninth hour (two or three o'clock in the afternoon), and a client thought it tiresome if his patron, whom he had to attend to the baths if he was to receive his dole, bathed as late as the tenth hour. That—or later—was the time when, in a household as irregular as Trimalchio's, host and (male) guests together made for the bath in the desperate hope of sobering down. For a hostess such as Juvenal describes to go to the baths at an hour later than this, indeed at night, when her guests were already assembled and waiting to go in to dinner, was, presumably, a solecism and, in any case, an act of insufferable rudeness. In the case of a public bath at Rome, such behaviour would not have been possible under the Republic, for then the baths shut at dark; though outside Rome, as is shown by the large discovery of lamps in the oldest baths at Pompeii, they were kept open after nightfall, and by the early Empire Rome had fallen into line with this practice.[47]

A passage in Varro, whose text unfortunately is not certain, suggests that the earliest public baths were constructed in two sections, one for men, and one for women. This was evidently not the case at Teanum Sidicinum, as the famous story of the consul's wife makes clear*; but the earliest—second-century—baths at Pompeii were of this kind. Such baths reproduced in two separate but adjoining buildings a similar series of chambers. By the fact that they adjoined (though they had

* See page 44.

separate entrances) a great economy was effected, because the same heating system was used for both sets of baths.[48] As a general rule, the chambers in the women's baths were smaller in size and less expensively and ornately decorated than the men's. The design can be followed, thanks to the archaeologist, at a large number of places as far apart as Vezelay and Cyrene and, in particular, at Pompeii and Herculaneum.

There was, generally, in each part, a waiting-room, which led to the changing-room (*apodyterium*), where—and also in the warm-room (*tepidarium*)—there were shelves with compartments for clothes and towels. From the *tepidarium* the bather moved into the hot-chamber (*caldarium*), the temperature in both rooms being controlled by hot-air flues under the floors and in the walls. In the *caldarium* there was a tank of water for the hot bath and a fountain (*labrum*) for washing the hands and face. The bather returned to the *tepidarium*, and went from there to the cold plunge (the *frigidarium*). This—duplicated for men and for women—is the plan of the Stabian *Thermae*, first built in the second century B.C., and of the Forum baths, which were of late Republican date, at Pompeii, and also of the Thermae in the centre of Herculaneum, which were erected in the early years of the principate of Augustus. In the women's section of these baths at Herculaneum the rooms are vaulted, the waiting-room has a simple red dado, and there is a small chamber for keeping linen between it and the *tepidarium*, which has a mosaic pavement of a Triton surrounded by dolphins and fishes. In the *caldarium* there are elegant marble benches, where women sat to rest between the sweating (*sudatio*) and the hot bath, and where today, paradoxically, the tourist sits on a hot day relishing the delicious joy of being cool.

It is an interesting fact, established by the heating control of the Stabian baths at Pompeii, that the women's hot-chamber was kept at a lower temperature than the men's, and that there was nothing corresponding to the dry-heat chamber (*laconicum*), which existed for the men.[49]

While women's baths of this kind seem never to have had the spacious palaestra, in which men could exercise or lie in the open air, once their bathing was over, they often had beauty-parlours and similar amenities. And there were cafés in close proximity, for them as for the men.

Women might be attended in the baths by male slaves, and male slaves were employed to massage them afterwards.[50]

Men's baths were for men only, and women were excluded from them. A notice of the third century A.D. survives from Trastevere in Rome: MEN'S BATHS. NO WOMAN ADMITTED. BY ORDER. At Praeneste, however, an inscription suggests that on April 1st, when cult was done to Fortuna Virilis, women of the lower class sacrificed at, perhaps even bathed in, the men's baths.[51]

Women wore a 'two-piece' (*subligar*) in the baths; or they might wear a more extensive costume (*balnearis vestis*). Men wore leather trunks (*aluta*), though, bathing by themselves in the men's baths, they often bathed naked.[52]

A man paid a quarter of an as (*quadrans*) for admission, but a woman paid twice as much.

In places which had only one set of baths, recourse was had to staggered hours, in order to meet the needs of both the sexes. Details of such an arrangement in the early Empire are known to us from Lusitania (Portugal) from an inscription, the *lex metalli Vipascensis*, which lays down rules for the running of the mineral baths connected with the copper mine. The contractor of the baths was bound to open them to women in the morning, from daybreak until the seventh hour (about one o'clock), and to men from the eighth hour (about two o'clock) until nine o'clock at night (the second hour). As far as men were concerned, Roman hours were evidently observed. In the morning, when the baths were reserved for women, it is to be assumed that most of the men were at work in the mine. As was the common custom, these baths were more expensive for women than for men, costing an as instead of half an as.[53]

It is anything but easy to know how many baths there were in which men and women bathed together at the same time. The practice of mixed bathing is first mentioned by the elder Pliny as something which would shock the republican hero Fabricius, if he was restored to life. Quintilian, who was no fool, said that it was a sign of loose character in a woman if she bathed with men; and a succession of second- and third-century emperors (Hadrian, Marcus Aurelius and Alexander Severus) prohibited the practice. Finally the Council of Laodicea in A.D. 320 forbad men who were members of the Christian Church to bathe with women.[54]

On the other hand, the latest of the baths at Pompeii, the Central Thermae, consisted of a single, not a double, set of chambers, and the extensive excavations at Ostia have revealed no double set of baths; indeed, no certain women's baths at all. From this evidence, and from a number of passages where Martial refers to men and women bathing together, the inference has been drawn that, though authority disapproved of mixed baths, the popular taste embraced them, and that from the early Empire onwards—except for periods in which imperial prohibition was effective—mixed bathing was the common practice.[55]

There are strong arguments against such a view. First of all, if the practice had been all but universal, we should have heard far more of it from ancient writers, from Juvenal in particular, and from the moralists. Secondly, the women whose presence in the baths with men provoked Martial's epigrams were evidently women of the lowest character, prostitutes in fact. There is the further argument that, if mixed bathing had replaced the separate bathing of the sexes, this profound change must have been reflected in the lay-out of the baths themselves; and that is not the case.[56]

The truth is surely this. All baths were not of the same standard. Side by side with the palatial imperial baths in Rome there were a number of inferior bathing establishments, and similarly there were two categories of public baths in large towns like Ostia.[57] As new public baths for men were built, it is possible that the baths which they superseded were turned over to women; indeed the Flavian redecoration of the Stabian baths at Pompeii shows that, even after two new baths had been built, this, the earliest public bath of all, was still in use. This might have been the case at Ostia too.

At the same time there were a vast number of other baths, to some of which the poor, to others of which the vicious, resorted. There were 170 free warm-bathing establishments in Rome at the beginning of the principate, and the number had increased by the elder Pliny's time.[58] And there were also, no doubt, among the lower bathing establishments those which were run as profitable private enterprise by men who might otherwise have been in charge of more questionable establishments still. These catered for people of both sexes whose ideas were enlightened, or whose morals were debauched. In them men often bathed naked and so sometimes, did women. It was the coarse behaviour encouraged by this type of establishment that Martial described. These were the baths which Quintilian so reasonably condemned, and which a number of enlightened emperors tried—with little success—to close down.

If it is asked where at Ostia, for example, respectable women bathed, the answer can only be that some of the excavated baths which appear to be men's baths, and which may, indeed, have been men's baths at the start, were in fact used exclusively by women, or else a number of men's baths must have been reserved, like those baths in Portugal, at certain hours of the day, for use by women.

v. Woman at Home

The Romans being for the first centuries of their existence an agricultural people, their houses, large or small, were country houses, and while the husband took care of the land, his wife took care of the household. She held the keys of the store-cupboard, she brought up the children. The larger the establishment, the greater the number of slaves, both in the house and on the land.

In poorer families daughters went to school, like their brothers, and were taught by schoolmasters; in richer families they were generally educated at home. A part of their upbringing, spinning and weaving, they learnt working with the slave-girls under the supervision of their mother. This domestic manufacture of home-spun, which never died out in poorer households, survived even in the houses of the great down to the early Empire. At the end of the Republic, in 52 B.C., in the town house of M. Aemilius Lepidus (the later triumvir) a loom on which cloth was being woven stood in the hall (*atrium*); and when a mob of ruffians broke in, they destroyed this as well as the couch on which, presumably, Lepidus' wife—that 'lady whose integrity was a byword' —reclined, to supervise the work. And, as has been seen, Augustus wore home-made cloth inside the house, and insisted that in his family the tradition of weaving should be observed.*

There is evidence of a considerable staff of clothing specialists in the inscriptions of the *columbarium* in which the ashes of Livia's slaves and freedmen were placed; her household staff included five patchers, two supervisors, six women in charge of clothing, one cloak-maker, one tailor and two fullers. In similar fashion the vault of another family, the Statilii Tauri, contained the ashes of eight spinners, one supervisor of the wool, four patchers, four weavers, two dyers and four fullers.[59]

Writing in the middle of the first century A.D., Columella states that this style of living survived to his young days, but that a general change had taken place, anyhow in richer families, during his lifetime. In country houses the bailiff's wife had come to exercise what had

* See page 71.

once been the mistress's housekeeping responsibilities. It was no longer smart to wear homespun; instead clothes were bought, far more expensively, from shops.[60]

While in the modern world, the furnishing and decorating of a house is either a wife's responsibility and interest, or a responsibility and interest which she shares with her husband, there is no evidence to show that furniture was a matter of great interest to Roman women. Rooms in Roman houses were small and, by modern standards, very sparsely furnished. Cicero's letters give evidence of the purchase of busts for his library (a transaction in which it is unlikely that Terentia was consulted) and Pliny tells us that Cicero once spent half a million sesterces on a table. Tables, indeed, particularly of citrus wood (sometimes with ivory legs) and sofas inlaid with tortoise-shell or ornamented with precious metal, were an extravagance of rich men. Women sometimes bought objects for the household; 'one *materfamilias*, and not a particularly rich one' paid 150,000 sesterces for a wine-ladle. But, in general, if money was to be spent, a woman preferred to see it spent on jewels. Furniture was a male extravagance; and Pliny [60a] tells us that when husbands protested against the sums which their wives spent on pearls, the wives were often able to retort, 'What about you and your tables?'

What of the wall-paintings and the mosaics? When there was a question of artist, of subject, of design, of colour, how often had a wife the deciding vote? We have no means of knowing.

How much of a woman's day was taken up in household duties and in supervision of her slaves is, again, something which we do not know. From Aelius Aristeides' remark in his Roman Oration at the middle of the second century A.D. that 'it is a pauper's household in which the same person has to do the cooking and the dusting and to make the beds', it is evident that you had to sink to a very low level indeed in society to find a *materfamilias* who was faced with what today are the ordinary housewife's chores.[61]

Down to the second century B.C. the mistress of the house had taken an active part in the housekeeping; indeed before 164 B.C. she is said to have baked the bread. After this, bakeries were started; large kitchen staffs were engaged by rich households, and 'a chef became as expensive as a horse'.

The mistress continued, presumably, to order and to supervise the ordinary family meals. Whether (apart from official banquets*) she

* Such as that described on page 238.

was also responsible for, or even attended, the gargantuan dinners which in the late Republic and early Empire were given from time to time in rich households, and which so deeply shocked men whose morals were as high and whose appetites were as poor as Seneca's, we cannot say. Seneca does not mention them; and it is extremely improbable that, in any but the most debauched households, respectable women and young children sampled the kind of after-dinner coarseness and indelicacy into which such parties sometimes degenerated.

In a household like Trimalchio's the mistress performed all the functions of an active housekeeper. Fortunata dashed in and out of the dining-room with the slaves during a dinner party, and when at the end of the meal the monumental mason Habinnas called and asked for her, Trimalchio told him that she never joined the guests until she had seen the silver locked up and given the slaves their supper.[61a]

We must not be misled by the satirists and the moralists into thinking of banquets (whether or not they became debauches) as being, except in degenerate imperial society, anything but rare occasions. Dinner even in a rich household, whether or not there were guests, was in general a polite and restrained occasion, and at Rome the women of the family were present, as they had always been present, at the meal. Until the time of Augustus they sat (as in Etruscan funerary sculpture the wife sits, while her husband reclines); but after Augustus they reclined like the men—graciously in gracious circles, less graciously in the households of Trimalchio and his like.

There was a similar distinction in the matter of drinking. While Trimalchio's wife got drunk, the women of better-class families observed by instinct and upbringing the rules which Ovid laid down for his less impeccable young ladies; if they drank at all, they drank sparingly. No civilized society has ever liked the notion of an intoxicated woman; in the Roman tradition, dislike was an obsession.

That many women played an important part in conversation on social occasions, is certain. A woman's conversation—*sermo*—was often singled out for praise. Maecenas' wife Terentia talked amusingly. Debauched as Sempronia was, by Sallust's account, he admits that she was a good conversationalist. Macrobius remarks on the fact that Augustus' disappointing daughter Julia talked well. Juvenal describes the women who talked too much and talked too loudly; their existence implies as a corollary women who talked quietly and talked well. Here again Ovid's instructions are significant: not only to talk quietly and with restraint, but also to be well informed on the subjects about which men of culture liked to talk.*

In the third book of his *Art of Love* Ovid advised his clients to read the classics (Greek poetry) and, more than this, to interest themselves in current literature. His limp defence that, if married women had read his poem, they had disobeyed his explicit instruction to them to leave it unread, is evidence enough of what could in any case be safely assumed, that even in respectable households educated women liked to keep abreast of what was being written and published. More than this, there were, even in such households, women, whether gifted or not, who found amusement or sought relief in writing and in other forms of original composition. These were *doctae puellae*, women gifted with that literary talent which, Ovid declared, was the ambition of many but the achievement of few. The younger Pliny's wife, as has been seen, set her husband's poems to music. The younger Agrippina wrote a family history. And Balbilla, who toured Egypt with Hadrian and Sabina, was not the only Roman woman who wrote poems. A gifted poetess of the time of Augustus has left, in the fourth book of Tibullus' poetry, six moving elegies which have kept alive through the centuries her passionate love for 'Cerinthus'. She was Sulpicia, the niece and perhaps the ward of M. Valerius Messalla Corvinus, a member of his literary circle (which included Tibullus) and something of an anxiety and a responsibility, it seems, both to her mother and her uncle.[62] Her namesake, another Sulpicia, may, one suspects, have caused at least a trifling embarrassment to her husband Calenus. They were married at the time of Domitian, for fifteen blissful years; and exhilarated by the natural and irreproachable enjoyments of the marriage bed, she committed her ecstasy to verse. We have two epigrams from Martial, a fervent admirer of her writing. 'Let all young wives read Sulpicia, who wish to please their lords alone; let all husbands read Sulpicia, who wish to please their brides alone . . . She describes pure and honest love, toyings, endearments and raillery. He who shall weigh well her poems will say no maid was so roguish, will say no maid was so modest . . . With her as your school-mate, or with her as your teacher, you would have been more learned, Sappho, and you would have been chaste.' A manuscript discovered in Bobbio in 1493 has been thought by a few to perpetuate seventy lines of her verse.

This is no jewel of chaste eroticism; it is a dialogue—in anything but

* See, also, page 228.

faultless hexameters—between Sulpicia and the Muse, purporting to be written under Domitian and deploring the sad state of the times. It was not written by the lady but, without doubt, by a well-read but not particularly gifted poet some centuries after Martial's Sulpicia was dead.[63]

Dancing in Rome was not ballroom dancing. Apart from the respectable eurhythmics of choruses on certain religious occasions, it was a matter of miming or of ballet, often of the kind of *pas seul* which attracts clients to the least reputable of modern night-clubs. Panto-mime dancing, both in the subjects represented and in the manner of their representation, was often exceedingly obscene—the 'adultery mime' was a standing favourite—and, as the fourth century A.D. mosaics from Piazza Armerina in Sicily show, dancing-girls,* dressed only in bikini, left little of their attractive bodies unexposed. Danc-ing of this kind in the ancient, as in the modern, world was the business of professionals (girls from Cadiz, for instance) and since Roman opinion, as exemplified often in its law, classified actresses with prosti-tutes, and presumably did so not without reason, dancing was not a relaxation which a Roman gentleman wished to see practised by his daughter or, for that matter, by his son. Of singing he held the same poor opinion.[64]

The Roman attitude to dancing and singing was markedly different from that of the Greeks, and in the early days of Augustus Cornelius Nepos drew attention to this difference in outlook when, in his *Life of the Theban Epaminondas*, he anticipated the surprise of his Roman readers on finding that he recorded the names both of Epaminondas' music-master and of his dancing-master.[65] 'Readers should not judge foreign customs by their own, or assume that other peoples have neces-sarily shared their own views on what is despicable.† We do not need to be told that, by Roman convention, music is unbecoming to a person of prominence, and dancing is thought to be positively vicious. In Greece, on the other hand, these are held to be agreeable and laudable diversions.'

This, the established Roman point of view, however, was one which for more than a century before Nepos wrote young people had refused to accept; for in 129 B.C., the last year of his life, Scipio Aemilianus, a

---

* Not women-athletes, despite their prominence in the Exhibition of Sport at the Olympic Games in Rome in 1960.

† See also pages 200 f.

stalwart of the Old Guard, told the Roman world from a platform of his rueful experience. When he refused to believe reports that boys and girls of good families were to be seen, musical instruments in hand, consorting with the practitioners of these arts, men of notorious immorality, he was taken to a dancing-class, and there found five hundred boys and girls, including one young boy who was dancing with the castanet a dance 'which it would be a disgrace to a slave with no morals at all to perform'. Yet this was a boy whose father was a candidate for public office.[66]

In the course of the last century of the Republic, a compromise was effected. Dancing was countenanced as long as it was not at a public performance, and as long as it was kept within the bounds of decency. The infamous Sempronia was condemned by Sallust not because she sang and danced, but because she sang and danced like a professional, not like a lady. In the third book of the *Art of Love* Ovid recommended his young ladies to sing and to play musical instruments; and late in the first century A.D. Statius evidently regarded her dancing as one of his stepdaughter's charms. Dancing was legitimate if it was done in the house, and done with restraint. It was done for the benefit of the family and their guests; often, no doubt, at the guests' invitation. Trimalchio evidently resented the fact that none of his guests had asked his wife to dance, and she herself was anything but unwilling to give a performance; but it is not to be imagined that in such a house her dancing was marked either by delicacy or by restraint.[67]

The 'Ionic movements' which, to Horace's dismay, grown girls were learning to execute were, presumably, more lascivious than the dancing which by that time was thought permissible; Horace presented such 'movements' as the first step on the downward path; dancing today, adultery tomorrow. Yet when Terentia, wife of his patron Maecenas, danced, this brought her no discredit—but she was not executing a *pas seul*, or even a *pas de deux*; she was dancing in chorus, and in a religious chorus at that.[68] How could this be more disreputable than it was for children of both sexes to sing in public, as long as it was Horace's *carmen saeculare* that they were singing?

Apart from the Vestal Virgins, the only Roman women who enjoyed absolute independence in the management of personal property were those who, after Augustus, had presented their husbands with three—in Italy (or in Rome, if they were freedwomen) four; outside Italy, five—children, or who, with their husbands, had been given the honorary status of productive parenthood. Women married under one or other of the primitive marriage ceremonies were dependents of their husbands (*in manu*) and, when married, held no possessions of their own. A woman married under the system of free marriage (unless, after Augustus, she was independent on account of the number of her children) was not independent of her father; she was *in patria potestate*. When her father died, she had a guardian ('tutor') who was a man appointed under her father's will; or, if her father had not appointed a guardian for her, a man who was either next of kin or a nominee of the magistrate in response to an application which she herself had made. A woman who had been *in manu* when married likewise had a 'tutor' if she became a widow, a man appointed by her husband or, with his agreement, chosen by herself. A woman could not be appointed guardian even to her own children.[69]

Such in strict law was the position of a woman in the late Republic and in the Empire. But in fact she was all but independent, for her guardian took his duties very lightly; if he was tiresome, a woman had only to apply to the praetor, and he was replaced by someone more accommodating. If, on the other hand, she required substantial help in a difficult matter, she applied for the appointment of an administrator, a 'curator'.

A wife who owned property in her own right might either hand over its administration to her husband, who was accountable to her for the income, or she could administer it herself through her own agents and slaves. Such independence on a woman's part was naturally something of which the elder Cato disapproved. A woman's property of this sort, bequeathed in the main to her second husband, was the subject at issue in the case in which Cicero defended Caecina in 69 B.C. And we have from the end of the first century A.D. an epigram of Martial warning a husband against a 'curled spark' who was his wife's agent and, Martial suggested, her lover too. This, indeed, was one weakness of the smart young agent; dishonesty was another.[70]

The property of the wealthy ladies of the imperial family must have been very large indeed. We can gauge the size of Livia's personal staff from the number of inscriptions of her freedmen and slaves which have been recovered from the *columbarium* built to house their ashes on the Appian way. Burrus, who ended his life as Prefect of the Guard, had once been employed as her agent.[71]

Many women, without doubt, were engaged in business. Often they were widows who took over the control of their husbands' affairs. There were enough freedwomen or women living in Italy outside Rome with shipbuilding interests for Claudius to offer them special rewards if they co-operated in his shipbuilding programme. And inscriptions bear witness to a number of women—freedwomen, perhaps, in the main—who were lady doctors.

Apart from serious and commendable activities, there were, of course, innumerable foibles on which rich women, like rich men, could squander their wealth. Ummidia Quadratilla kept a private company of ballet-dancers, who performed in public and also privately in her house. When she died, just over eighty years old, in A.D. 107, they were inherited, with two-thirds of her property, by her prig of a grandson, who had lived in her house (since the age of twenty-four, with his wife), and who had ostentatiously refused ever to see them perform. After her death, they gave one public performance, and then he got rid of them. A shocking old lady: Pliny, too, was at his most priggish, sharing her grandson's opinion of her.[72]

VI. Woman Abroad

Women went out of the house in order to shop, to go to the baths, to pay social calls, to worship at temples or to attend some public spectacle. The wives of clients were sometimes dragged round by their husbands when they called upon their patrons, in order that they might claim a larger dole. With greater decorum, wives went with their husbands to dinner parties. Of the eighty senators who dined once with the Emperor Otho, many were accompanied by their wives.[73]

In Rome they might not drive about the city, the privilege of travel in a *carpentum*, a small covered wagon drawn by two horses, being reserved for Vestal Virgins and for priestesses of the State. The right was granted exceptionally to two Roman empresses, Messalina and the younger Agrippina.[74]

A woman travelled normally in a Sedan chair (*sella*) or in a litter (*lectica*). For a short distance a chair was more convenient and, if hired, no doubt far cheaper. For a long journey the litter would commend itself, preferably carried, as was the smartest fashion, by eight Bithynian bearers. The litter was something a great deal grander and more comfortable than a stretcher. It was covered over and curtained, and might have windows.[75]

A variety of legal restrictions were placed on the use of litters in the city. Julius Caesar allowed them only at certain hours, and then only to ladies over a certain age. Domitian forbad their use by courtesans and prostitutes. And, generally, it seems that to travel in litters women had to be of a certain rank.[76] Cassius Dio speaks of 'a covered litter, such as is used by the wives of senators'.

By the third century there were evidently as many varieties of litter in Rome as there are of cars today and, as has been seen,* Elagabalus' Senate of Women was given the task of drafting a code of regulations defining the social standing of those qualified to use one kind of litter or another.

Women's journeys from the house for religious purposes were regarded by the elegists and the satirists with grave suspicion. They went usually to centres of female cult, like the temple of Isis or of the Bona Dea, where men could not follow them, and chiefly they went, the satirist declared, because they had assignations with other men. 'What is the good of setting a guard on a woman,' Ovid asks, 'when there are so many theatres in Rome, when she enjoys chariot-racing, when she attends the festival of Isis, when she goes to ceremonies which are for women only, because the Bona Dea forbids the presence of men (unless, of course, they have come at her personal invitation), when there are the Baths, when there is always a sick friend to visit— the kind of sick friend who will accommodatingly place a bed at her disposal.' Ovid, of course, is writing of the jealously kept mistress, not of the wife; but the opportunities open to the one were open, naturally, to the other.[77]

It would be absurd, however, to believe that the whole female population of Rome was composed of the persons whom Juvenal caricatures, Martial mocks and Ovid so callously describes. The majority of women no doubt emerged from their houses in order to shop and to call upon their friends; their objects were tedious, trivial and innocent. If they read Ovid or Juvenal, they were shocked to learn of the existence of women whose life was so unlike their own.

The theatre and the circus constituted for women as for men one of the great attractions of life in the capital. The more surprising was it, therefore, since Statius' wife enjoyed neither, that she was so reluctant to live out of Rome[78]

'When women go off to the show, it is to show themselves off that they go,' Ovid wrote. Naturally; they would not have been women, if they did not think of the effect which their appearance would create.

* See also page 160.

The satirist, of course, had eyes only for those who were vulgarly over-loaded with jewels. But there were, no doubt, as many who were charmingly dressed. An empress, of course, could not afford to go unnoticed; the younger Agrippina must have been a startling sight as she sat at Claudius' naval games in a cloak wholly woven of gold thread.[79]

The sexes sat indiscrimately at games in the circus. Augustus thought it wrong that women should watch athletics (including boxing), and issued an edict that they should not appear before the fifth hour (about 11 o'clock), by which time the athletic events were over. There was no ban on women watching the chariot-racing, which they enjoyed with the same frenzied excitement as the men.

Men and women sat indiscriminately at the amphitheatre also in Republican times. It was, indeed, thanks to this fact that, at the age of sixty in 79 B.C., Sulla acquired the young, well-bred coquette Valeria as his sixth wife. As she passed behind him on her way to her seat, she plucked a thread from his cloak and, when he turned round, excused herself on the ground that she wished to be infected with his good luck. Sulla inquired who she was. 'After that, they kept on catching each other's eyes, turning round to look and exchanging smiles—and in the end they came to an agreement and arranged to marry.'[80]

Under the Empire seating arrangements at the theatre and amphi-theatre were different. The Vestal Virgins had special seats, where they might be joined by ladies of the imperial family, and other women sat by themselves in a reserved block of seats, and it was only during the promenade in the portico that assignments with men could be made. Inside the theatre they could draw attention to themselves, as the case of Aemilia Lepida showed, who made a great demonstration in the theatre at the time of Tiberius, to advertise her wrongs. How coarse and immoral were the farces, since none survive, we can only guess. The pantomimes, usually with mythological subjects, were extremely obscene. Tertullian is, of course, not an impartial witness.[81] 'You preserve your unmarried daughter,' he writes, 'from hearing a single foul word—and then you take her to the theatre to listen to the actors and watch their gesticulations.'

Nobody can doubt the existence of a singularly cruel and vicious streak in the Roman character—derived in part from the Etruscans, and something which distinguished the Romans sharply from the Greeks—in virtue of which men and women alike not only admired the skill of the gladiators and the men who fought wild beasts, but positively

enjoyed the sight of death. Tertullian was entirely justified in inveigh-
ing against these spectacles as he did, and many pagan Romans—
Seneca, for instance—had felt about the games exactly what Tertullian felt. The only pity is that he should have spoilt his admirable
case by promising to Christians who kept away from the games the
ultimate reward of a spectacle which in startling and triumphant
horror would eclipse anything that they could hope to witness in the
amphitheatre—the agonizing torture of sinners in the hour of their
condemnation on the Day of Judgement.

If men like Cicero and Seneca avoided the amphitheatre, as they did,
we can be certain that a very great number of women avoided it too.
Statius' wife was not a solitary paragon of her sex.

That women of the highest class became infatuated by pantomime
actors, dancers such as Mnester at the time of Claudius, Paris and
Bathyllus* at the time of Domitian, by charioteers and by gladiators is
attested by the record of history as well as by the invective of the
satirists.[82] Mnester and Paris enjoyed the favours of Empresses.
Shocking as such behaviour may have been, it is easily comprehensible
to the psychologist. The elopement of a senator's wife with a gladiator
would be headline-news today. Here is Juvenal's splendidly shocked
account of the event:[83]

> Hippia, who shared a rich patrician's bed,
> To Egypt, with a gladiator, fled,
> While rank Canopus eyed, with strong disgust,
> This ranker specimen of Roman lust.
> Without one pang, the profligate resign'd
> Her husband, sister, sire; gave to the wind
> Her children's tears; yea, tore herself away
> (To strike you more)—from PARIS and the PLAY.
> And though, in affluence born, her infant head
> Had pressed the down of an embroidered bed,
> She braved the deep, (she long had braved her fame;
> But this is little—to the courtly dame),
> And, with undaunted breast, the changes bore
> Of many a sea, the swelling and the roar.
>
> Have they an honest call such ills to bear?
> Cold shiverings seize them, and they shrink with fear;

---

* The more famous dancer Bathyllus lived earlier, at the time of Augustus.

But set illicit pleasure in their eye,
Onwards they rush, and every toil defy.

Summon'd by duty to attend her lord,
How, cries the lady, can I get on board?
How bear the dizzy motion? how the smell?
But, when the adulterer calls her, all is well.
She roams the deck, with pleasure ever new,
Tugs at the rope, and messes with the crew;
But with her husband—O how chang'd the case!
Sick! Sick! she cries, and vomits in his face.

But by what youthful charms, what shape, what air,
Was Hippia won, the opprobrious name to bear
Of FENCER'S TRULL? The wanton might well doat!
For the sweet Sergius long had scrap'd his throat,
Long look'd for leave to quit the public stage,
Maim'd in his limbs, and verging now to age.
Add, that his face was batter'd and decay'd;
The helmet of his brow huge galls had made,
A wen deformed his nose, of monstrous size,
And sharp rheum trickl'd from his bloodshot eyes;
But then he was a SWORDSMAN! That alone
Made every charm and every grace his own;
That made him dearer than her nuptial vows,
Dearer than country, sister, children, spouse—
'TIS BLOOD THEY LOVE: Let Sergius quit the sword,
And he'll appear at once—so like her lord.

XIV

EPILOGUE

++

COMPLETE EQUALITY of the sexes was never achieved in ancient
Rome because of the survival, long after it was out of date, of a deep-
rooted tradition that the exclusive sphere of a woman's activity was
inside the house, the exclusive sphere of a man's outside it.[1] In the
field of domestic economy, woman's power and *expertise* were unchallenged. She looked after the food, the clothes, the servants and the
upbringing of the children in their infancy.

But for active participation in public affairs woman was considered,
from the circumstances of her daily life, to lack the knowledge and
experience which were needed. So women were never given the vote;
and it was unthinkable that they should compete for public office. In
the Empire, though nobody could doubt the political sagacity of such
imperial women as Livia, Plotina or Julia Maesa, they were barred
from official participation in government. The suggestion that a
woman should be chosen to rule as Empress was never even mooted.

Similarly, in civil procedure women could not sit on juries; far less
could they plead in court. They were not allowed, before Justinian, to
be appointed legal guardians to their own children. They were not
even allowed—unless, after Augustus, they produced the requisite
number of children or were given the honorary status of a fruitful
mother—the independent administration of their own affairs.

It suited a barrister often to refer to women as the weaker sex, and
to suggest that they lacked the necessary toughness to compete in the
rough and tumble of public life. '*Infirmitas consilii*' was a moving
expression in a good orator's mouth.[2] But while the Romans were
hypocritical enough to pretend that inexperience was an insuperable
barrier to women's participation in public life, they were not so
hypocritical as to pretend with any seriousness that woman's intelligence was of a lower order than man's.[3]

Not that women are known ever to have sought to enter the world
of politics, administration or law. Indeed we have no knowledge of

their even seeking an alteration in the law, so that they might have a legal claim for maintenance by their husbands.

It was only in the substitution, quite early in the Republic, of the free form of marriage for the older forms, by which a wife was all but indissolubly bound to her husband (*in manu*), that a very substantial advance was made. Of this Fritz Schulz has written admirably :[4] 'The classical law of marriage is an imposing, perhaps the most imposing, achievement of the Roman legal genius. For the first time in the history of civilization there appeared a purely humanistic law of marriage, viz. a law founded on a purely humanistic idea of marriage, as being a free and freely dissoluble union of two equal partners for life.'

Once women had achieved this equality in marriage, it was ridiculous that they should not acquire such independence as men possessed in the administration of their own property. Had Augustus' ideas on the position of women been progressive instead of reactionary and had he not been obsessed with the importance of women bearing a number of children, the reform might well have come. Certain changes in the law were made, it is true, in women's interest. The restrictions imposed by the *lex Voconia* on a woman's inheriting property, for instance, were abolished after the time of Augustus, and the humanistic spirit of the lawyers of the Empire was shown in their administration of the law as it stood. Though in most cases a woman still needed a 'tutor', this requirement was treated as little more than a formality.

In marriage, despite the curb which Augustus' legislation placed on a husband's licensed immorality, a husband was never required to live the chaste life which was expected of his wife. In this matter, the conversion of the Roman world to Christianity was to bring a great change in woman's status. Reform, which Stoicism had long advocated, was introduced, and infidelity was punished with the same rigour in a husband as in a wife. And with Christianity the chaste unmarried woman, whom Augustus had punished, became an object of respect, even of veneration.

It may not be improper to repeat at the end of this book something which was written at the beginning.

One has only to reflect on the tremendous contribution to the understanding of social history which has been made from the eighteenth century onwards by the writings of women, to realize that the

historian of women in the ancient world lacks the evidence which most
of all he needs. Cicero's wife and daughter were the only women to
whom, from his vast surviving correspondence, he is known to have
written; and we possess no letters which they wrote to him. And there
are only seven women among the correspondents to whom the younger
Pliny wrote, and only ten letters in all that he wrote to them, six of
those ten to his wife, his wife's aunt and his mother-in-law. The other
four letters show little more than that the four women to whom they
were sent could reasonably say of him that he was a very generous
friend of the family.[5]

It was, indeed, as well that no woman who was contemporary with
Ovid, Martial, Tacitus or Juvenal could know that posterity would
feast its eyes on his distorting mirror and think that what it saw there
was a true image of herself.

GENEALOGICAL TABLES

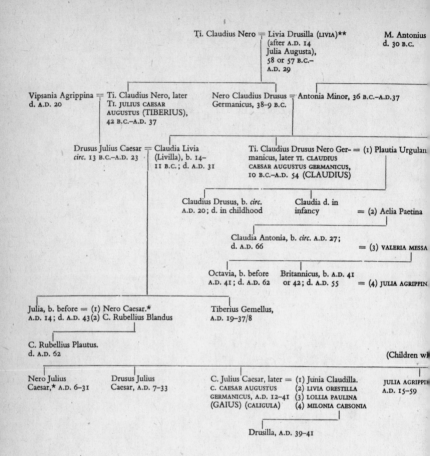

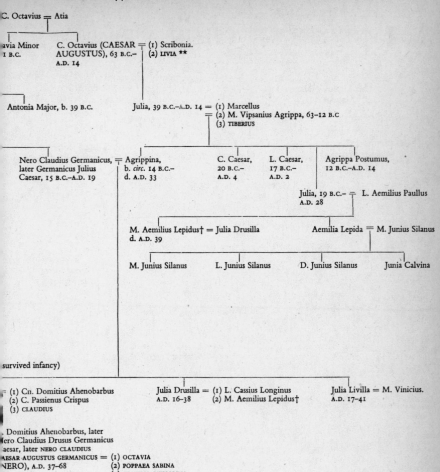

C. Octavius = Atia

...avia Minor
...I B.C.

C. Octavius (CAESAR = (1) Scribonia.
AUGUSTUS), 63 B.C.– | (2) LIVIA ★★
A.D. 14

Antonia Major, b. 39 B.C.

Julia, 39 B.C.–A.D. 14 = (1) Marcellus
= (2) M. Vipsanius Agrippa, 63–12 B.C
(3) TIBERIUS

Nero Claudius Germanicus, = Agrippina,
later Germanicus Julius   b. *circ.* 14 B.C.–
Caesar, 15 B.C.–A.D. 19   d. A.D. 33

C. Caesar,
20 B.C.–
A.D. 4

L. Caesar,
17 B.C.–
A.D. 2

Agrippa Postumus,
12 B.C.–A.D. 14

Julia, 19 B.C.– = L. Aemilius Paullus
A.D. 28

M. Aemilius Lepidus† = Julia Drusilla
d. A.D. 39

Aemilia Lepida = M. Junius Silanus

M. Junius Silanus

L. Junius Silanus

D. Junius Silanus

Junia Calvina

(survived infancy)

= (1) Cn. Domitius Ahenobarbus
(2) C. Passienus Crispus
(3) CLAUDIUS

Julia Drusilla = (1) L. Cassius Longinus
A.D. 16–38   (2) M. Aemilius Lepidus†

Julia Livilla = M. Vinicius.
A.D. 17–41

. Domitius Ahenobarbus, later
...ero Claudius Drusus Germanicus
...aesar, later NERO CLAUDIUS
...AESAR AUGUSTUS GERMANICUS = (1) OCTAVIA
...NERO), A.D. 37–68   (2) POPPAEA SABINA
(3) STATILIA MESSALINA

THE WOMENFOLK OF TRAJAN AND HADRIAN

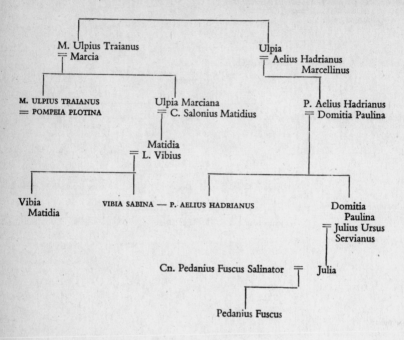

THE WOMENFOLK OF THE ANTONINES

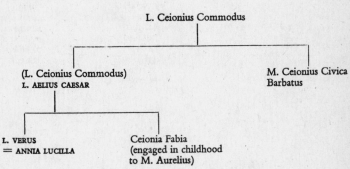

THE WOMENFOLK OF SEPTIMIUS SEVERUS, ELAGABALUS AND SEVERUS ALEXANDER

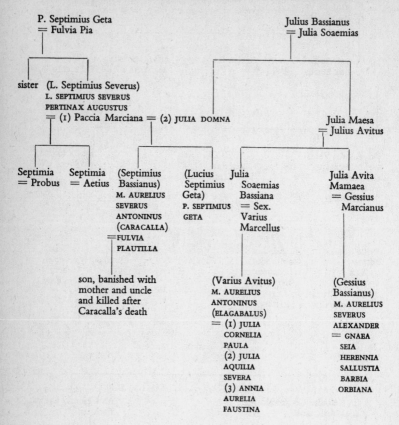

P. Septimius Geta
= Fulvia Pia

Julius Bassianus
= Julia Soaemias

sister   (L. Septimius Severus)
L. SEPTIMIUS SEVERUS
PERTINAX AUGUSTUS
= (1) Paccia Marciana = (2) JULIA DOMNA

Julia Maesa
= Julius Avitus

Septimia
= Probus

Septimia
= Aetius

(Septimius
Bassianus)
M. AURELIUS
SEVERUS
ANTONINUS
(CARACALLA)
= FULVIA
PLAUTILLA

(Lucius
Septimius
Geta)
P. SEPTIMIUS
GETA

Julia
Soaemias
Bassiana
= Sex.
Varius
Marcellus

Julia Avita
Mamaea
= Gessius
Marcianus

son, banished with
mother and uncle
and killed after
Caracalla's death

(Varius Avitus)
M. AURELIUS
ANTONINUS
(ELAGABALUS)
= (1) JULIA
CORNELIA
PAULA
(2) JULIA
AQUILIA
SEVERA
(3) ANNIA
AURELIA
FAUSTINA

(Gessius
Bassianus)
M. AURELIUS
SEVERUS
ALEXANDER
= GNAEA
SEIA
HERENNIA
SALLUSTIA
BARBIA
ORBIANA

Introduction

1. TA 4, 53, 3.
2. TA 14, 30, 1.
3. T., *Germ.* 19; CD 77, 14, 2.
4. Virg., *Aen.* 4; Ovid, *Heroid.* 7.
5. L. 30, 12–15.
6. On whom, H. Volkmann, *Cleopatra: A Study in Politics and Propaganda* (tr. T. J. Cadoux), London, 1958 and *RE* xi, 750–81, Kleopatra no. 20. For a Roman appreciation, Hor., *Odes* 1, 37 ('Nunc est bibendum'), on which, E. Fraenkel, *Horace* (Oxford, 1957), 158–61.
7. TA 14, 31–37; CD 62, 2–12 describe this revolt.

Chapter I

1. On the historicity of early Roman history, P. Fraccaro, *Opuscula* i (Pavia, 1956), 1–23; A Momigliano, *JRS* 1957, 104–14. Burning the boats: Aristotle, fr. 609 Rose; Plut., *Mor.* 243 E–244 A; DH 1, 72, 2. Kissing: Plut., *Mor.* 244 A, 265 Bff. (QR 6), 268 Df. (QR 20); Serv. ad *Aen.* 1, 737.
2. L. 1, 4; DH 1, 76–79; Platner–Ashby, s.v. 'Ficus Ruminalis' and 'Lupercal'; G. Lugli, *Roma Antica* (Rome, 1946), 420–3.
3. L. 10, 23, 12; E. Strong, *Sulle tracce della lupa romana* (Rome, 1937).
4. Plut. *Mor* 272F–273B (QR 35); AG 7, 7, 5–8 (cf. 7, 7, 1–4 on Gaia Taracia); *RE* i, 131–4, 'Acca Larentia'; vii, 480–3; Th. Mommsen, 'Die echte und die falsche Acca Larentia,' *Röm. Forschungen* ii (Berlin, 1879), 1–22.
5. Diod. 7, 5.
6. *RE* iA, 341–5, 'Rea Silvia'.
7. DH 1, 79.
8. *Confarreatio*, DH 2, 25; Sabine women, 2, 30.
9. L. 1, 11–13; DH 2, 38–46; Tarpeia, DH 2, 38–40.

10. Plut. Mor. 284F (QR 85). H. J. Rose, *The Roman Questions of Plutarch* (Oxford 1924), p. 173, 'Food prepared by a woman would be ceremonially impure for a man's use'.

11. See G. De Sanctis, *Storia dei Romani* I² (Florence, 1956), 365 f., who thinks the legends date from not later than the fourth century B.C.; also references in note 1 above.

12. L. 1, 24–6; DH 3, 13–22; VM 6, 3, 6; A. Momigliano, *JRS* 1957, 112, 'The ancients themselves found it difficult to decide which were the enemies and which the champions of Rome'.

13. L. 1, 46–8; see U. Coli, *Regnum* (Rome, 1951), 50–52, for the view that there never was such a man as Servius Tullius.

14. L. 1, 57–60; DH 4, 64–85.

15. L. 1, 59, 13.

16. L. 3, 44–58; Diod. 12, 24; DH 11, 28–49. On the traditional account of Appius Claudius, see Th. Mommsen, *Röm. Forsch.* 1, 298; *RE* iii. 2698–2702 (F. Münzer). Münzer thinks the whole story to be folklore, the characters having acquired names (which in Diodorus' account they did not possess) from the late second century, Appius Claudius from the father-in-law of Tiberius Gracchus.

17. DH 11, 35, 4 (tr. E. Cary, LCL).

18. DH 11, 39, 6 (tr. E. Cary, LCL).

19. L. 3, 58, 2.

20. L. 3, 58, 11.

21. G. Wissowa, *RK²* 257 f.; *RE* vii, 20 ff., s.v. 'Fortuna'.

22. L. 2, 33–35, 37–40; DH (whom Plutarch followed in his Life of Coriolanus) 6, 92–94; 7, 19, 21–67.

23. L. 2, 40, 11.

24. So Schur in *RE* Suppl. v, 653–60, s.v. 'Marcius', no. 51; but F. Münzer did not wholly agree (*RE* xiv, 1536, s.v. 'Marcius'); Th. Mommsen, 'Die Erzählung von Cn. Marcius Coriolanus', *Hermes* 1870, 1–26 and *Röm. Forschungen* ii, 113–52.

25. L. 8, 18.

26. L. 40, 37; cf. L. *Per.* 48; VM 6, 3, 8.

27. L. 10, 31, 9; Serv. ad *Aen.* i, 720; G. Wissowa, *RK²* 289.

28. Serv. ad *Aen.* 1, 720; Platner-Ashby, s.v.; but see *RE* iii, 1408, s.v. 'Calva' (G. Wissowa).

29. Diod. 14, 116, 9.

30. Oddly, the passing of the law in 215 is not mentioned by Livy; only the repeal of it in 195.

31. *NH* 7, 120.

32. L. 29, 14; Ovid, *Fast.* 4, 291–344. On the introduction of the cult to Rome, see H. Graillot, *Le culte de Cybèle* (Paris, 1912), 25–69.

33. Claudia Quinta: Suet., *Tib.* 2, 3; Graillot (see note 32), 60–66. Miraculous preservation: VM 1, 8, 11; T*A* 4, 64, 4; Frazer, *Ovid's Fasti*, vol. iii, p. 241.

34. Plut., *Cato mai.* 8, 4.

35. L. 34, 2–4. The case against its genuineness rests on the belief that stylistically it is unlike Cato's surviving speeches, and the fact that no quotation from it is found in any author but Livy. See H. H. Scullard, *Roman Politics, 220–150 B.C.* (Oxford, 1951), 257; H. Malcovati, *ORF*², 14; P. Fraccaro, *Opuscula* (see note 1 above) 1, 178–81. There are still some scholars, however, who reject the argument from style, and believe the speech genuine, e.g. D. Kienast, *Cato der Zensor* (Heidelberg, 1954), 21 f. L. Valerius' speech, L. 34, 5–7.

36. VM 9, 1, 3.

37. Reading 'cultus', or even 'comptus', for the *MSS* 'coetus'.

38. Most probably a paste of naphtha (bitumen or petroleum), quick-lime and sulphur. See *History of Technology* (ed. C. Singer, Oxford, 1957) ii, 374 ff., esp. 376 and note 1. I am indebted to my colleague Dr. R. F. Barrow for this information.

39. H. H. Scullard (see note 35 above), 147 f., 154 f.; cf. G. Wissowa, *RK*², 63 f.

40. Cult of Cybele in Rome: DH 2, 19, 4 f., Instruction to magistrates curtailing Bacchic worship, L. 39, 14.

41. L. 39, 17, 6 (cr. *ORF*², p. 31 for 'coniuratio'.)

42. L. 39, 18, 7 f.

43. Bruns⁷ 36; *FIRA* 30.

44. L. 39, 19. 4 ff.

45. E. Fraenkel, 'Senatus consultum de Bacchanalibus', *Hermes* 1932, 369–96, esp. 388, n. 2.

46. As does Mommsen, *Röm. Strafrecht* 348, n. 2. See M. Gelzer, 'Die Unterdrückung der Bacchanalien bei Livius', *Hermes* 1936, 275–89, with references to all other literature on the inscription. A. H. Macdonald discusses the matter with admirable good sense in *JRS* 1944, 26–31.

47. Sall., *Cat.* 23, 3; 28, 2 (cf. L. 39, 9, 5). According to Diod. 40, 5, she went to Cicero's wife.

48. L. 39, 18, 4; cf. Sall, *Cat.* 16, 1–3.

49. P. 31, 26; Papiria: *RE* xviii, 1075, no. 78.

50. AG 10, 6, 1; Suet, *Tib.* 2, 3 says she was tried for treason.

51. Cic., *Pro Caelio* 34; for her father's career, *RE* iii, 2848, no. 295.

52. AG 10, 3, 3.

Chapter II

1. Letters: *Ad Fam.* 14, 1–24; on Terentia, *RE* vA, 710–16, no. 95 (S. Weinstock).

2. *Ad Att.* 11, 24, 3.

3. *Ad Att.*, 5, 1, 3 f.; see W. H. Johnson, 'The sister-in-law of Cicero', *CJ* 1913, 160–5; W. Wiemar, *Q. Tullius Cicero* (Halle, 1930), 19 ff.

4. 6, 53–55.

5. Cic., *De Orat.* 2, 44. Livy's statement that a resolution was passed in B.C. 390 that the married women who had given their gold to pay the ransom to the Gauls should be similarly honoured, is unlikely to be true.

6. Suet., *DJ* 6, 1.

7. *RE* ii, 2543, no. 248. On her part in the Bona Dea affair, see page 244.

8. *Cat.* 24, 3–25, 5

9. F. Münzer, *Römische Adelsparteien* (Stuttgart, 1920), 272 f.; R. Syme, *PAPA* 1960, 327.

10. T*A* 13, 45.

11. Sall., *Cat.* 23, 3 f.; 26, 3; 28, 2; *RE* vii, 280 f., no. 112.

12. VM 9, 1, 8.

13. V. Gardthausen, *Augustus und seine Zeit* (Leipzig, 1891), 92; *RE* vii, 284; O. Vessberg, *Studien zur Kunstgeschichte der römischen*

Republik (Leipzig, 1941), 248 and plate xiii, 7 and 8; *BMC Rep.* i. 570, 575 and plate lvi, 1 and 10. There is an element of doubt, as all these writers make clear.

14. Cic., *Phil.* 3, 4; 5, 22; 13, 18; CD 45, 13, 2; 45, 35, 3.

15. App. *BC* 4, 136 f.

16. *CIL* xi, 6721, 3–5 and 14; Martial 11, 20, 3–8.

17. *RE* vii, 281–4, no. 113 (F. Münzer); *Antony and Cleopatra*, i, 2; ii, 1.

18. Porcia, *RE* xxii, 216–8, no. 28; Servilia, *RE* iiA, 1817–21, no. 101 (F. Münzer).

19. *Ad Att.* 15, 11, 1 f.

20. *Ad Brutum* 20 (1, 12), 1 f.; 21 (1, 13); 23 (1, 15), 13; 36 (1, 18), 1 and 6.

21. Julia; *RE* x. 892 f., no. 543 (F. Münzer); Mucia: *RE* xvi, 448–50, no. 27; Plut., *Ant.* 32, 1; CD 48, 15, 2; 16, 2; 27, 4; 51, 2, 5; App., *BC* 5, 267, 270 f.

22. Plut., *Lucullus* 6, 2 f.; Cic. *Ad Fam.* 9, 26; *RE* ix A, 883.

23. Born about B.C. 94, F. Münzer, *Adelsp.* 273; on her identity, *RE* iv, 105–7, no. 66 (F. Münzer); C. J. Fordyce, *Catullus* (Oxford, 1961), xiv-xviii, who thinks the identification of Clodia and Lesbia 'not unlikely'.

24. Cat. 77; see R. G. Austin, *Cicero, Pro Caelio*[3] (Oxford, 1960), 148–50.

25. Cic., *Pro Caelio* 35.

26. Cic., *Pro Caelio* 55–57.

27. AG 17, 18, quoting Varro; Macrob., *Sat.* 2, 2, 9 (her brother's view of her); cf. *RE* iv, 1599 f.; iA 1916 f.; viii A, 2165.

28. *RE* iii, 1235 f., no. 137.

29. Porphyrio on Hor., *Sat.* 2, 3, 239.

30. Plut., *Pomp.* 55, 2.

31. Prop. 1, 2, 26–32; 1, 7, 11; 2, 3, 19–22; 2, 11, 6.

32. *RE* viii, 2481 f., no. 16.

33. VM 8, 3, 3; App. *BC* 4, 136–46; Quint. 1, 1, 6.

34. 6, 398–412; 434–456.

35. TA 15, 63 f.

36. Pliny, *Epp.* 3, 16, 2; 9, 13, 3–5.

37. CD 60, 16, 5 f.

38. Pliny, *Epp.* 3, 16; Mart. 1, 13.

39. TA 16, 10 f.; cf. 6, 29 for two similar cases in A.D. 34, and Pliny, *Epp.* 6, 24.

40. TA 16, 34; Pliny, *Epp.* 3, 11, 3; 7, 19: Fannia: *RE* vi, 1995, no. 22.

41. See above, page 44.

42. *Ad Att.* 6, 3, 8.

43. Plut., *Lucullus* 38, 1.

44. *Ad Att.* 1, 12, 3; Suet., *DJ* 50, 1; CD 37, 49, 3.

45. Prop. 3, 12, 'Postume, plorantem potuisti linquere Gallam?'

46. Caecilia Metella with Sulla in Greece in B.C. 86 was exceptional (Plut., *Sulla* 13, 1; 22, 2); Livia in Greece, CD 54, 7, 1 f.; military *legati* of Augustus only allowed to be with their wives in winter quarters, Suet., *DA* 24, 1; Agrippina and Plancina, TA 2, 55, 5; 3, 33, 3; cf. Plut., *Otho* 6, 6.

47. TA 4, 20, 6.

Chapter IV

1. Suet., *DA* 99, 1, 'Livia, nostri coniugii memor vive, ac vale'.

2. Suet., *DA* 62, 2.

3. Date of the marriage, *Année Épigraphique* 1937, no. 5; J. Carcopino, *Passion et Politique chez les Césars* (Paris, 1958), 65-82.

4. CD 54, 19, 3; Suet., *DA* 71, 1; CD 58, 2, 5.

5. It is curious that later ages thought 'to be happier than Augustus' the acme of human happiness: Eutrop. 8, 2, 'felicior Augusto, melior Traiano'. Suet., *DA* 65, 1, 'Fortuna destituit', is truer.

6. By, e.g., A. Stahr, *Röm. Kaiserfrauen* (Berlin, 1865).

7. Her beauty, Plut., *Ant.* 31, 4; 57, 5; head in the Louvre, *CAH*, plates iv, 166a.

8. The story of CD 48, 31, 4, that Octavia was pregnant at the time is patently false; see M. Hammond, *RE* xvii, 1860.

9. Born in 40 B.C., *RE* xi, 760.

10. *BMC, Rep.* ii, 499 (the Berlin *aureus*); 502 f.; 515; plates 114, 1-4; 14; 115, 1-2; 4-9; V. Kahrstedt, *Klio* 1910, 291.

11. CD 50, 3, 2.

12. Suet., *DA* 73, 1; 64, 2.

13. Suet., *Tib.* 42, 1; CD 53, 26, 1.

14. See R. Syme, *The Roman Revolution* 344 f. for the view (which I do not share) that this marriage of Tiberius was a brilliant piece of scheming on Livia's part.

15. Sen., *Cons. ad Marciam*, 2, 3; VP 2, 93, 1 f., both perhaps deriving from Augustus' *laudatio* of Marcellus.

16. CD 53, 30, 3 f.

17. CD 53, 31, 1–34, 1.

18. 3, 18; on which see H. E. Butler and E A. Barber, *The Elegies of Propertius* (Oxford, 1933).

19. *Aen.* 6, 860–86.

20. *Odes* 1, 12, 45–48.

21. *Cons. ad Marciam*, 2; cf. Plut., *Marcellus* 30, 10 f.; Suet. *De gramm.* 21; *CIL* vi, 2347–9.

22. CD 53, 33, 4.

23. Suet., *DA* 63, 1.

24. TA 4, 40, 8 f.; *RE* xxiii, 72–74 (R. Hanslik); R. Syme, *The Roman Revolution* 358, is rightly sceptical.

25. On the marriage, *RE* ix, 2385 f.

26. TH 5, 9, 3; Suet., *D.Cl.* 28; *RE* i. 2618; v, 1741, no. 2.

27. Suet., *DA* 64.

28. Para 9. On this and, the date at which Livy wrote it, (soon after 27 B.C.), see H. Dessau, 'Die Vorrede des Livius', *Festschrift zu Otto Hirschfelds sechzigstem Geburtstage* (Berlin, 1903), 461–6.

29. Prop. 2, 7, 13, 'Gavisa es certe sublatam, Cynthia, legem.' Cf. Hor., *Odes* 3, 6; 3, 24 (of circ. 28 B.C.).

30. *Pro Marcello*, 23, 'Comprimendae libidines, propaganda suboles.'

31. Hor., *Car. Saec.* 56, 'Pudorque priscus . . . neglecta Virtus'; cf. *Odes* 4, 5; 4, 15.

32. Cicero had prohibited celibacy in his ideal state, *De legg.* 3, 3, 7; For details of Augustus' legislation, see *CAH* 10, 441–56; P. Jörs, *Die Ehegesetze des Augustus* (Marburg, 1894).

33. CD 54, 16, 2; Ulp. 13, 1; Cic., *Pro Sest.* 110.

34. Gaius 1, 145; 2, 111 and 286; Ulp. 14.

35. Tiberius still thought this on occasion the right tribunal, TA 2, 50, 4 (A.D. 17).

36. *CAH* 10, 444–447; *Dig.* 48, 5, 2, 2, (Ulpian).

37. Pliny, *Epp.* 6, 31, 4–6.

38. *CAH* 10, 447 (Hugh Last); cf. Plautus, *Captivi* 889, 'Liberorum quaerundorum causa ei, credo, uxor data est'; Livy, *Per.* 59 (the censor Metellus in 131 B.C.).

39. T*A* 3, 25, on the ineffectiveness and bad results of this legislation.

40. Livy, *Per.* 59; Suet., *DA* 89, 2; AG 1, 6.

41. CD 54, 16, 4 f.

42. W. Warde Fowler, *Roman Essays and Interpretations* (Oxford, 1920), 111–26; in criticism, E. Fraenkel, *Horace*, 364–82.

43. E. Fraenkel, *Horace*, esp. 373 f.

44. W. Warde Fowler, *Roman Essays and Interpretations*, 115.

45. T. E. Page, *Horace, Odes* (London, 1901), 458.

46. 'Municipalis adulter,' T*A* 4, 3, 4.

47. T*A* 2, 82, repeats the story; Suet., *D.Cl.* 1, 4 f., rejects it as nonsense.

48. *Consolatio ad Liviam*, PLM 1, 97–121 (no. 5).

49. Suet., *DA* 63, says Augustus first considered a number of other possible men, even equestrians.

50. CD 55, 10, 13 suggests something of the kind.

51. T*A* 1, 53, 2.

52. T*A* 1, 53, 5; 6, 51, 3.

53. T*A* 6, 51; Suet., *Tib.* 10–13; CD 55, 9, 5–7.

54. Pliny, *NH* 21, 9; Sen., *De benef.* 6, 32; CD 55, 10, 12.

55. *RE* v, 1431; xiv, 184.

56. Macrob., *Sat.* 2, 5.

57. Cf. W. Speyer, *Rhein. Mus.* 1956, 278.

58. Suet., *Tib.* 11, 4.

59. Pliny, *NH* 7, 149; 21, 9; Sen., *De benef.* 6, 32; Suet., *DA* 65, 2.

60. Suet., *DA* 65, 1; 101, 3; CD 55, 10, 12–16.

61. Suet., *DA* 101, 3; CD 56, 32, 4.

62. Sen., *De benef.* 6, 32.

63. Suet., *DA* 65, 2; CD 55, 10, 16.

64. Suet., *Tib.* 11, 4.

65. VP 2, 100, 5; CD 55, 10–14

66. Sen., *Epp.* 70, 10.

67. Varro, *RR* 1, 8, 5.

68. Suet., *DA* 65, 3.

69. CD 55, 13, 1; cf. p. 40 above, for similar behaviour by Bacchanals.

70. TA 3, 24, critically.

71. VP 2, 100; CD 55, 10, 15.

72. This is the implication of R. Syme, *The Roman Revolution*, 425 ff.

73. For the view that the denunciation of Julia was a deliberate act of malice on Livia's part, V. Gardthausen, *Augustus und seine Zeit* (Leipzig, 1896), 1, 2, 1028; 1, 3, 1101.

74. *NH* 7, 149; cf. Sen., *De brev. vit.* 4, 6.

75. E. Groag, 'Der Sturz der Julia, ' *Wien. Stud.* 1919, 74–88.

76. J. Carcopino, *Passion et Politique chez les Césars*, 83–142, esp. 129 ff.; the evidence is given in *RE* x, 901–3.

77. CD 55, 13, 1a (Zon. 10, 36).

78. Suet., *DA* 19, 1; Schol. Juv. 6, 158; R. Syme, *The Roman Revolution*, 432, n. 4.

79. TA 4, 71, 6 f.; Suet., *DA* 65, 4.

80. TA 3, 24.

81. Schol. Juv. 6, 158; TA 1, 3, 4; 1, 4, 3; Suet., *DA* 65, 1 and 4.

82. Suet., *DA* 65, 4.

83. 3, 40.

84. *Tristia* 2, 207 ff.

85. Schanz-Hosius, *Geschichte der römischen Literatur* (Munich, 1935), ii, 206 ff. and, on the *Ars Amatoria*, ii, 226–8; A. L. Wheeler, 'Erotic Teaching in Roman Elegy and the Greek Sources', *CP* 1910, 440–50; 1911. 56–77.

86. *Tristia* 2, 247 f., tr. A. L. Wheeler (LCL); *AA* 1, 31 ff.

87. *CAH* 10, 452–6.

88. Ulp. fr. 14.

89. TA 1, 3, 3; 1, 5, 1; 1, 10, 4; 3, 17, 2 f.; 4, 71, 7. M. P. Charlesworth, 'Livia and Tanaquil,' *CR* 1927, 55–57. For the suggestion that Tacitus was not forgetful of Plotina when he wrote of Livia's part in securing the principate for Tiberius, see R. Syme, *Tacitus* (Oxford, 1958), 481–4.

90. E.g. 4, 57, 5. On the emphasis on Livia at the opening of the *Annals*, see E. Koestermann, 'Der Eingang der Annalen des Tacitus', *Historia* 1961, 330–5.

91. VM 6, 1, 1; VP 2, 75, 3; 2, 130; Sen., *Cons. ad Marciam*, 6, 3 f., *De clem.* 1, 9, 6.

92. CD 58, 2. 4 f.; Suet., *DA* 99, 1.

93. Suet., *DA* 71, 1; CD 54, 19, 3; 58, 2, 5; Hor., *Odes* 2, 12.

94. Suet., *DA* 81.

95. Suet., *DA* 84, 2.

96. *De clem.* 1, 9, 6; CD 55, 14–22.

97. See W. Speyer, *Rhein. Mus.* 1956, 277–84, in favour of the truth of the story; j. Béranger, *Hommages à Max Niedermann* (Collection Latomus, vol. xxiii, Brussels, 1956), 52–70.

98. T*A* 5, 1, 5, 'Sanctitate domus priscum ad modum, comis ultra quam antiquis feminis probatum'; CD 54, 16, 5; Macrob, *Sat.* 2, 5, 6.

99. *Ex Ponto* 3, 1, 117.

100. Suet., *D.Cl* 41, 2; the evidence of the letters (*DCl.* 4) tells against *D.Cl* 3, 2, 'pro despectissimo semper habuit'.

101. VM 4, 3, 3.

102. T*A* 4, 71, 7; cf. VP 2, 130, 5; CD 58, 2, 4.

103. T*A* 3, 15, 3 (Plancina); 2, 34 (Urgulania).

104. Sen., *Cons. ad Marciam* 4, 2.

105. H. Marucchi, *Le Forum romain et le Palatin*[3] (Rome, 1933), 347–54; G. Lugli, *Roma antica* (Rome, 1946), 458–68, pointing out that it was probably the house not of Livia, but of Augustus. Anyhow, she lived there.

106. *CIL* xv, 7264; though this may be Julia, the daughter of Titus (see G. Lugli, note 105 above).

107. CD 48, 52, 3 f.; Pliny, *NH* 15, 136 f.; Suet., *Galba* 1.

108. Ovid, *Ex Ponto* 3, 1, 141 f.; Pliny, *NH* 34, 3; H. Willrich, *Livia* 71 ff.; CD 55, 2, 5; 56, 10.

109. Suet., *Galba* 5, 2; *C. Cal* 16, 3.

110. T*A* 1, 8, 2.

111. CD 56, 46, 1; Tacitus (*Ann.* 1, 14, 3) states that Tiberius refused to sanction this honour.

112. TA 1, 14, 1–3 ; Suet., *Tib.* 50, 2 f. ; CD 57, 12, 4 ; Th. Mommsen, *Röm. Staatsrecht* II, ii³, 821 ff. Adulatory titles, refused at Rome, appeared occasionally in the provinces, e.g. 'Julia Augusta genetrix orbis' of Julia Augusta on a coin of Romula in Spain, *BMC Emp.* I, cxxxvi.

113. CD 57, 12, 2.

114. *Act. Arv.* of A.D. 27, Henzen xxxiii f.

115. V. Ehrenberg, A. H. M. Jones, *Documents illustrating the reigns of Augustus and Tiberius²* (Oxford, 1955), 102.

116. TA 3, 64, 1.

117. Cf. Suet., *Tib.* 50, 2.

118. TA 4, 47, 4 f. ; CD 57, 12, 6 ; Suet., *Tib.* 51.

119. TA 3, 64, 1.

120. TA 4, 57, 4 ; CD 57, 12, 6.

121. TA 4, 52, 6 ; Suet., *Tib.* 53, 1.

122. TA 4, 53.

123. Suet., *C. Cal.* 23, 2.

124. TA 5, 1, 5, 'Cum artibus mariti, simulatione fili bene composita'.

125. Jos., *AJ* 18, 181 f.

126. Or was executed, CD 58, 11, 7.

127. TA 6, 25.

128. TA 5, 3, 1 ; 6, 51, 6.

129. See J. P. V. D. Balsdon, *The Emperor Gaius (Caligula)* (Oxford, 1934), 33.

Chapter V

1. Valeria Messalina : *RE* viiiA, 246–58, no. 403. On her father's side, her grandmother was Claudia Marcella, daughter of Octavia's first marriage ; on her mother's side, her grandmother was the elder Antonia, daughter of Octavia's second marriage.

2. Cameo of sardonyx in the Cabinet de Médailles, R. West, *Portrat-Plastik* (Munich, 1933), 1, 216 and pl. lix, 257 ; *CAH* plates iv, 158c.

3. *PIR*, 'P' 629 ; TA 13, 45, 2, 'Aetatis suae feminas pulchritudine supergressa'.

4. Juv. 6, 115–32, and Schol.; Pliny, *NH* 10, 172; CD 60, 31, 1. T*A* 11, 26, 1, 'Facilitate adulteriorum ad incognitas libidines profluebat', does not suggest that Tacitus had described such fantastic excesses in the lost books.

5. T*A* 11, 12, reading 'opperiri'. Silius was related to—conceivably brother of—the Silia who was intimately connected with T. Petronius Arbiter, author of the *Satyricon*, *RE* 111A, 96, no. 29.

6. With P. Silius Nerva, consul in 20 B.C.; Juv. 10, 332; Stemma, *RE* iiiA, 69 f.

7. R. Syme, *Tacitus* 67.

8. Suet., *D.Cl.* 29, 3.

9. CD 60, 31, 2.

10. Juv. 2, 117–26; 8, 199–210; *RE* iiA, 1374 f., Sempronius no. 44.

11. T*A* 15, 37, 8 f.; Suet., *Nero* 28, 1.

12. T*A* 11, 2, 5.

13. Suet., *D.Cl.* 26, 2.

14. T*A* 12, 1; Suet., *D.Cl.* 26, 3.

15. T*A* 12, 5–7.

16. Suet., *D.Cl.* 26, 3.

17. See R. Syme, *Tacitus* 376 f. and 744 for doubts about this part of the story; also G. B. Townend, *Hermes* 1961, 244–7.

18. Henzen, *Act. Arv.* lxxiv and 77 f.

19. Henzen, lxiv, lxx.

20. Henzen, lxxiv f, and 77 f.

21. *Nero*, 34, 4.

22. T*A* 14, 62.

23. T*A* 12, 27, 1.

24. Suet., *Nero* 5, 1.

25. Suet., *Nero* 6, 1; CD 61, 2, 3.

26. CD 59, 22, 8 f.; Suet., *C.Cal.* 39, 1.

27. Schol. Juv. 1, 155; CD 59, 23, 9.

28. Suet., *Galba* 5, 1.

29. T*A* 12, 26, 1; Momms., *Staatsr.* II, ii³, 821.

30. T*A* 12, 65–69.

31. Text and translation in LCL; annotated edition by W. B.

Sedgwick (Oxford, 1925); Juv. 6, 622 f. evidently refers to this work.

32. The doctor, who was Claudius' own doctor, was called Xenophon: T*A* 12, 61, 2; 67, 2.

33. Much interest was taken by the Italian newspapers in September 1961 in the case of a man who, on his deathbed, declared himself to have been poisoned. The charge was sufficiently plausible for the doctors to insist on a post-mortem. He was found to have died a natural death.

34. T*A* 14, 12, 7; Suet., *Nero* 34, 5; CD 61, 17, 1.

35. T*A* 4, 53, 3; Pliny, *NH* 7, 46.

36. Henzen, 57.

37. Henzen, lxix, lxxiv, lxxvi; Quint. 8, 5, 15.

38. Suet., *D.Cl.* 26 f. They were married in about A.D. 10. See J. Heurgon, *CR Acad. Inscr.* 1953, 92-97, on the 'Etruscan nationalism' of the family, the explanation of Claudius' own research into Etruscan history. Urgulanilla had few morals; her brother, M. Plautius Silvanus (whom Augustus recommended as a tutor for Claudius, Suet., *D.Cl.* 4) got rid of his wife by throwing her out of a window (T*A* 4, 22).

39. On him, see *RE* xiii, 340 f; *PIR*, 'P' 477; R. Syme, *The Roman Revolution*, Table 5; *ILS* 955.

40. *RE* iv, 1522, Cornelius no. 391.

41. Suet., *C.Cal.* 35, 1; *D.Cl.* 27, 2; CD 60, 5, 8 f.

42. Suet., *D.Cl.* 26, 2; for the descent, see *RE* iv, s.v. 'Cornelius', nos. 377, 378, 390, 391.

43. T*A* 13, 23; 13, 47; 14, 57 and 59, 5 f.

44. Date of birth: the figure in T*A* 14, 64, 1 cannot be right. Name: the explanation in the text is more probable than the suggestion that she was adopted into the Octavii so as to avoid the imputation of incest when she became engaged to her stepbrother Nero.

45. T*A* 13, 13, 2-6; 13, 18, 3-5.

46. Marriage: T*A* 13, 45, 4. Her mother's downfall: T*A* 11, 1-4.

47. So T*A* 13, 45, correcting the earlier account in T*H* 1, 13. On the variant accounts of CD 61, 11, 2 f. and Plut., *Galba* 19, see G. B. Townend, *Hermes* 1961, 242-8.

48. T*A* 13, 45, tr. M. Grant (Penguin Classics).

49. *Cat.*, 25.

50. Pliny, *NH* 37, 50.

51. Pliny, *NH* 11, 238; 28, 183; Juv. 6, 462.

52. TH 1, 22. That it was she who made a singer out of Nero (*RE* xxii, 86) is a guess which no evidence supports.

53. Jos., *Vita* 16. It is notable that Josephus does not hesitate to mention her favourably after her death; B. W. Henderson, *The Emperor Nero* (London, 1903), 467. The suggestion of her anti-Christian activity in A.D. 64 comes from J. Beaujeu, *L'incendie de Rome en 64 et les chrétiens* (Collection Latomus xlix, Brussels, 1960), 40.

54. TA 13, 46; 14, 1.

55. See 'Seneca', *Octavia* 181-8; 591 f. For a different explanation of the—in Tacitus' account—delayed marriage, see G. B. Townend, *Hermes* 1961, 247.

56. TA 14, 60.

57. Suet., *Nero* 35.

58. TA 14, 61.

59. TA 14, 62.

60. TA 14, 62-64.

61. TA 14, 64, 4 f.

62. *Act. Arv.* Henzen lxxviii; TA 15, 23, 1-3.

63. TA 15, 23, 4.

64. TA 16, 6; Suet., *Nero* 35, 3.

65 Suet., *Nero* 35, 4; TA 15, 53, 4 f.

66. Suet., *Nero* 28, 1 f.; *RE* iiiA, 1886 f.

67. TA 15, 68 f; Suet., *Nero* 35, 1.

68. *ILS* 8794. This is she, not Valeria Messalina; *RE* iiiA 2209 f.

69. Suet., *Otho* 10, 2.

70. *CIL* vi, 15176, 10549; B. W. Henderson, *The Emperor Nero*, 459 f.

71. TH 1, 78.

72. C. J. Herington, 'Octavia Praetexta: a Survey', *CQ* 1961, 18-30; see also P. J. Enk, 'De Octavia Praetexta', *Mnemosyne* 1926, 390-415.

73. TA 12, 4; Sen., *Apocolocyntosis* 8, 2.

74. T*A* 12, 4, 2.

75. *ILS* 6239.

76. Suet., *D. Vesp.* 23, 4. I am grateful to F. A. Lepper and G. B. Townend for interesting me in Junia Calvina.

Chapter VI

1. Suet., *D. Vesp.* 3.

2. Suet., *D. Vesp.* 3; 21; *Domit.* 12, 3.

3. Domitia Augusta after his accession (*Act. Arv.* of 81, Henzen cxi); CD 66, 3, 4; *RE* v, 1513–16, no. 103 (A. Stein). Josephus was indebted to her, *Vita* 429.

4. Mart. 6, 3.

5. *ILS* 272; 23 April A.D. 140.

6. Juv., *Sat.* 6, 156–60; *PIR*, 'I' 431; *RE* iii, 287–9, no. 15.

7. *Acts* 25 f.

8. T*H* 2, 2; 2, 81.

9. T*H* 5, 1. Agrippa was there; so she was certainly there too.

10. Suet., *Tit.* 7, 1; CD 66, 15, 4 f. and 18, 1; *Epit. Caes.* 10, 4–7; J. A. Crook, 'Titus and Berenice', *AJP* 1951, 162–75.

11. *PIR*², 'F', 426.

12. Suet., *Domit.* 22, with G. W. Mooney's notes; on her coiffure, see page 256.

13. Juv. 2, 29–33; Pliny, *Epp.* 4, 11, 6; title 'Augusta' under Titus, *BMC*, *Emp.* II, 247, pl. 47, 14–17.

14. *RE* xxi, 2293–8, Pompeia no. 131 (R. Hanslik); Marciana, *PIR*, 'U' 584; Matidia, *RE* xiv, 2199–2202 (G. Herzog-Hauser).

15. 'Antiqui moris', T*H* 2, 64.

16. Pliny, *Pan.* 83; cf. *Epp.* 9, 28, 1; CD 68, 5, 5.

17. CD 69, 1, 3.

18. R. Syme, *Tacitus* 604 f.; her statement, CD 68, 5, 5.

19. CD 69, 1, 2.

20. *H A, Hadr.* 2, 10.

21. See H. Mattingly, *BMC*, *Emp.* III, lxxxiii, 108 and pl. 18, 17 for a coin issue of Marciana, which might suggest that Hadrian's adoption was foreshadowed from A.D. 112 onwards.

22. *Pan.* 84.

23. *BMC.*, *Emp.* III, xxiii, cvii.

24. E.g. at Lyttos in Crete and at Lindos in Rhodes, *RE* xxi, 2295.

25. Cf. F. A. Lepper, *Trajan's Parthian War* (Oxford, 1948), 198–204.

26. *Epit Caes.* 42, 21, on her contribution to Trajan's reputation.

27. *ILS* 1792.

28. CD 69, 1, 3 (N.B. contradiction with 68, 5, 5).

29. So H. Dessau, 'Die Vorgänge bei der Thronbesteigung Hadrian's', *Festschrift für H. Kiepert* (Berlin, 1898), 85–91, esp. 89 ff.

30. CD 69, 1, 4.

31. *CIL* xiv, 3579; Th. Mommsen, *Ges. Schr.* i (Berlin, 1905), 422 ·8.

32. *Epit. Caes.* 42, 21.

33. *P. Oxy.* x. 1242, 26–32.

34. *ILS* 7784; *SIG*³, 834.

35. CD 69, 10, 3a.

36. On the date of Marciana's consecration, J. H. Oliver, *Harvard Theological Review*, 1949, 35–40.

37. Basilica at Nîmes, *HA, Hadr.* 12, 2. From the fact that there was no issue of coins in honour of the deified Plotina, R. Syme, *Tacitus* 246, assumes (somewhat gratuitously, against H. Mattingly, *BMC, Emp.* III, cxxxiii) that Plotina by this time had become something of an embarrassment to Hadrian.

38. For the suggestion that L. Ceionius was his illegitimate son, see p. 199.

39. *PIR*², 'D' 186.

40. Whom *RE* has so far failed to record.

41. *HA, Hadr.* 2, 6.

42. CD 69, 2, 6; 17, 1; *HA, Hadr.* 23, 1–8.

43. *Epit. Caes.* 14, 8.

44. *HA, Hadr.* 11, 3, 'morosam et asperam'.

45. *HA, Hadr.* 11, 3.

46. *RE* x, 923–5, no. 559.

47. *CIG* iii, 4725–30; G. Kaibel, *Epigr. Graec.* 988–92.

48. Seneca, *NQ* 4a, 2, 13 f.

49. That Antinous' death should have taken place three weeks *before* Hadrian was at Thebes (B. W. Henderson, *The Emperor Hadrian*,

131) is inconceivable. The authority for October 30th as the date of Antinous' death is *Chronicon Paschale*, which (for A.D. 122) gives that as the date for the foundation of Antinoopolis.

50. *HA, Ael,* 6, 9; *MA* 4, 5.

51. *HA, MA* 6, 2 and 6; 16, 17.

52. *HA, AP* 5, 2; on Faustina i, see *RE* i, 2312 f., no. 120.

53. *ILS* 349; *HA, AP* 6, 7; 13, 3 f.; *CIL* vi, 1005, 2001; Platner-Ashby, s.v. 'Antoninus et Faustina, templum.'

54. *BMC, Emp.* IV, xlii f.; lviii–lxiii.

55. *HA, AP* 8, 1; *BMC, Emp.* IV, 48 and pl. 8, 3 f.

56. *HA, AP* 10, 2. On Faustina ii, see *RE* i, 2313 f., no. 121.

57. This issue starts in 157; *BMC, Emp.* IV, cxii.

58. *BMC, Emp.* IV, 398; pl. 55, 5.

59. 1, 16; 6, 30.

60. CD 71, 10, 5; *HA, MA* 26, 8; *CIL* xiv, 40.

61. *HA, MA* 26, 5–7; CD 71, 31, 1 f.

62. Fronto, *Ad A.P.* 2, 2; Th. Mommsen, *Hermes* 1874, 204, thinks the reference is to the younger Faustina.

63. *HA, AP* 4, 8.

64. 1, 17, 8.

65. *HA, MA* 29, 10.

66. *CIL* vi, 8972; *HA. AP* 8, 9; *MA* 29, 10.

67. *Rev. Arch.* 39 (1901), 121; cf. Galen 14, 661 ff., Kühn.

68. *HA, AP* 3, 7.

69. H. Mattingly, *BMC, Emp.* IV, li f.

70. If Faustina really believed such action to be in the interest of Commodus himself (W. Weber, *CAH* 11, 361), she had learnt nothing of the lessons of Roman imperial history. CD 71, 22, 3 made no such silly suggestion.

71. CD 71, 29, 1.

72. *HA, MA* 19; 23, 7; *Verus* 10, 1.

73. *HA, MA* 19, 1–7.

74. *HA, MA* 19, 8 f.

75. See Norman Baynes, *Historia Augusta* (Oxford, 1926), esp. 80–82, and, for an admirable analysis of the problem of date, A. Momigliano, *Journal of the Warburg Institute*, 1954, 22–46.

76. 71, 34, 3 f.

77. *HA, MA,* 9, 4–6.

78. CD 72, 4, 4 f.; Herodian 1, 8, 3 f.; *HA, MA* 20, 6 f.; *Carac.* 3, 8; *PIR*[2], 'C' 973.

79. Herodian 1, 8, 3 f.

80. Quintianus, *PIR*[2], 'C' 975. The attempt at murder: Herodian 1, 8, 5 f.; *HA, Com.* 4, 1–4. CD 72, 4, 6 dates Crispina's death in 182, but her brother was consul in 187.

81. Herodian 1, 16 4; *RE* xiv, 1064 f., no. 118.

82. *PIR*[2], 'A' 358. For the murder of Commodus, see Herodian 1, 17.

83. *HA, Com.* 17, 12 ('incest with them', 5, 8).

84. CD 72, 4, 7.

85. *HA, SS* 15, 7.

86. CD 74, 3, 1–3; Herodian 2, 9, 3–6.

87. *HA, SS* 3, 2; *ILS* 440.

88. An inference from *HA, SS* 3, 6 (text corrupt); 9,4; *RE* xii, 1562.

89. A mere matter of turning the Semite name Martha into Domna, and calling that a horoscope? A. von Domaszewski, *Rhein. Mus.* 1903, 222, n. 4.

90. So *RE* x, 930; but he may have been born in 188. The evidence for this, and for the fact that he was Julia's child, not Marciana's, is given with admirable clarity by M. Platnauer; *The Life and Reign of the Emperor Lucius Septimius Severus* (Oxford, 1918), 48–53.

91. List of those known in 1902 in M. G. Williams (see note 112). Add the inscriptions in J. M. Reynolds and J. B. Ward Perkins, *The Inscriptions from Roman Tripolitania* (British School at Rome 1952).

92. M. G. Williams (see note 112), 285.

93. *ILS* 426.

94. CD 75, 15, 7; *PIR*[2], 'F' 554; *RE* vii, 270–8, no. 101.

95. CD 75, 15, 6; *HA, SS* 18, 8.

96. CD 75, 14, 5 (Plautilla's abnormally spoilt upbringing); Herodian 3, 10, 5 and 7.

97. CD 78, 24, 1.

98. Philostr., *Vit. Apoll. Tyan.* 1, 3.

99. M. Platnauer (note 90), 146.

100. *Vita Soph.* 30.

101. M. Platnauer (note 90), 143 f.

102. With Vestal Virgins and 110 matrons, M. G. Williams (note 112), 273.

103. For an admirable account of his fall, see M. Platnauer (note 90), 129-33.

104. CD 76, 4, 4, tr. E. Cary (LCL)

105. *BMC, Emp.* V, cxxxv, cxxxix, cxlviii, clii f., clxxi f., cxci.

106. 4, 3, 5; but this may be Herodian's invention.

107. CD 77, 2, 5.

108. CD 77, 16, 6a; Herodian 4, 6, 3.

109. CD 77, 16, 1.

110. *Act. Arv.* Henzen cxcvii; *ILS* 451.

111. CD 77, 18, 2.

112. Bibliography on Julia Domna: *RE* x, 926-35, no. 566 (Gertrud Herzog); Mary G. Williams, 'Studies in the Lives of Roman Empresses, i, Julia Domna', *AJA* 1902, 259-305; O. Schulz, *Beiträge zur Kritik unserer litterarischen Überlieferung für die Zeit von Commodus Sturze bis auf den Tod des M. Aurelius Antoninus (Caracalla)*, Leipzig, 1903.

113. CD 77, 16, 5.

114. Julia Maesa, *RE* x, 940-4, no. 579; Mamaea, x, 916-23, no. 558; Soaemias, x, 948-51, no. 596 (all by Gertrud Herzog) Mary G. Williams, 'Studies in the Lives of Roman Empresses; Julia Mamaea', *Univ. of Michigan Studies* i, 1904, 67-100; Orma Filch Butler, 'Studies in the Life of Heliogabalus', *Univ. of Michigan Studies* iv, 1910; J. Stuart Hay, *The Amazing Emperor Heliogabalus* (London, 1911); R. V. Nind Hopkins, *The Life of Alexander Severus* (Cambridge, 1907).

115. Herodian 5, 3, 2; *HA, Macrinus* 9, 1.

116. Herodian 5, 5, 1; cf. 5, 7, 1.

117. Elagabalus, *RE* viiiA, 391-404 (s.v. Varius Avitus).

118. CD 78, 31, 4.

119. CD 78, 38, 1; 79, 2, 2.

120. Gannys, *RE* vii, 708; CD 79, 6, 1.

121. *RE* vii A, 2412 f., no. 134.

122. Herodian 5, 5, 3–5.

123. CD 79, 6, 2, tr. E. Cary (LCL).

124. Herodian 5, 5, 6 f.

125. CD 79, 11, 1 f.

126. Herodian 5, 6, 3–5; CD 79, 12, 1.

127. Herodian 5, 6, 1f.

128. CD 79, 9, 3 f.

129. Herodian 5, 5, 6–10.

130. *HA, Elag.* 4, 1 f.

131. *CIL* viii, 2564; Herodian 5, 8, 8.

132. *HA, Elag.* 4, 4, tr. David Magie (LCL).

133. *HA, Aur.* 49, 6.

134. CD 79, 13.

135. CD 79, 14, 4–15, 4.

136. Herodian 5, 7, 1 and 5; CD 79, 19, 4.

137. Herodian 5, 7, 1–4; CD 79, 17, 2.

138. Herodian 5, 8; CD 79, 20, 1 f.

139. For her titles on inscriptions, see R. V. Nind Hopkins (note 114), 274 f.

140. Herodian 6, 1, 1.

141. Herodian 6, 1, 4.

142. Herodian 6, 1, 6.

143. *RE* iiA, 1128–30, no. 22; her father is to be found in *RE* iA, 1910–2, Sallustius no. 4.

144. Herodian 6, 1, 9 f.

145. Herodian 6, 7, 8–10; 6, 8, 9; *HA, AS* 63, 5 f.

146. Zon. 12, 15; Euseb., *HE* 6, 21, 3 f.

147. *HA, AS* 29, 1–3; cf. 22, 4.

148. Oros., *Adv. Pagan.* 7, 18, 7.

149. *HA.*, 30 *Tyr.*, 15 and 30; *Aur.* 22–30; J. G. Février, *Essai sur l'histoire politique et économique de Palmyre* (Paris, 1931), 103–41.

150. E. Gibbon, *Decline and Fall of the Roman Empire*, I, xiv.

151. *Pan. Lat.* 7 (6), 4, 'Liberavit ille Britannias servitute, tu etiam nobiles illic oriendo fecisti'. But 'oriendo' probably means 'by starting your rule'. See A. C. McGiffert, *The Church History of*

Eusebius (Oxford–New York, 1890), 441 f. Helena: *RE* vii, 2820–2, no. 2.

152. *ILS* 708.

153. Lact., *MP* 15, 1; Euseb., *HE* 8, 1, 3; Valeria: *RE* vii A, 2282 f., no. 7.

154. *Epit. Caes.* 39, 6.

155. *Pan. Lat.* 7(6). Fausta: *RE* vi, 2084–6, no. 2.

156. *Pan. Lat.* 7(6), 6.

157. Lact., *MP* 39–41.

158. Lact., *MP* 50 f.

159. Theodora: *RE* vA, 1773 f., no. 2.

160. Euseb., *Vita. Const.* 3, 44–46.

161. *CIL* vi, 1134 (*ILS* 709); 1135 f. A. M. Calini, *Atti della pont. accad. rom. d. archeologia*, serie iii, memorie vol. vii (1944), 418.

162. *RE* iv, 958, no. 13.

163. *RE* vii, 2822.

164. Euseb., *Vit. Const.* 3, 43.

165. *Epit. Caes*, 41, 11 f.

166. *Epit. Caes.* 41, 12.

167. *RE* iv, 958 f., no. 14.

Part II

Chapter VII

1. Juv. 6, 229 f., 'titulo res digna sepulcri'. On the choice of a husband, see P. E. Corbett, *The Roman Law of Marriage* (Oxford, 1930), 1–23.

2. For evidence about the age at which women married, see L. Friendlander, *Roman Life and Manners under the early Empire* (E. T., A. B. Gough, London, 1913), iv, appendix xviii, pp. 123–31.

3. AG 2, 7, 18–20.

4. L. 38, 57, 7. For a truer account, see Polyb. 31, 27.

5. Plut., *Ti.Gr.* 4, 3 ff.

6. Plut., *Pomp.* 44, 2–4; *Cato mi.* 30, 3–10.

7. *Epp.* 1, 14, 8.

8. 3, 160; cf. Mart. 5, 81; 6, 8.

9. Marriage of first cousins legitimized between 241 B.C. and 219, Livy, 20 fr., *Hermes*, 1870, 371–6; Plut, *QR* 6; L. 42, 34, 3 (marriage of first cousins in 171 B.C.); Cic., *Pro Cluent.* 11; T*A* 12, 6, 5; 12, 7, 1–3. C.D 68 2, 4 says that Claudius' innovation was rescinded by Nerva; but cf. Gaius 1, 62, who states that it was legitimate for a man to marry his brother's daughter, but not his sister's. Prohibition by Constantine: J. Marquardt, *Das Privatleben der Römer*[2] (Leipzig, 1886), 31.

10. P. E. Corbett (note 1), 30 ff. The children of Tettius Julianus (cos. A.D. 83), if any, will have been first cousins to the freedman's son, Claudius Etruscus (Stat., *Silv.* 3, 3; *RE* iii, 2670–2; v*A*, 1108–10).

11. *FIRA* iii, 19 (second century A.D.); P. Meyer, *Konkubinat.* 104; *Dig.* 23, 2, 65 (Paulus); 24, 1, 3, 1 (Ulpian); 34, 9, 2, 1 (Marcian). Alteration of the law about marrying rankers by Septimius Severus, Herodian 3, 8, 5 (severely critical). The whole matter is admirably discussed by H. Nesselhauf, *CIL* xvi, 154 f.

12. Grants on discharge: *ILS* 1986 ff.; 9052 ff. Volubilis: M.P. Charlesworth, *Documents illustrating the reigns of Claudius and Nero* (Cambridge, 1939), 36 f.

13. Gaius 1, 28 (Lex Aelia Sentia and Latini Juniani); 30; 80.

14. On this paragraph, see P. E. Corbett (note 1), 53–67.

15. E.g. Cat. 61, 71–13; Prop. 2, 7, 13 f.

16. *Dig.* 23, 1, 14; cf. A*G* 1, 12, 7.

17. CD 54, 16, 7.

18. CD 60, 5, 7. Earlier than Augustus' legislation, Atticus' granddaughter Vipsania Agrippina was scarcely a year old when she was betrothed in 33/2 B.C. to Tiberius, then aged 9; CN, *Att.* 19, 4.

19. Action for breach of promise before 90 B.C. in Latium, A*G* 4, 4. Engagement: *Dig.* 24, 2, 2, 2, (Gaius).

20. Cic., *Pro Cluent.* 28, 'nuptialia dona'; Juv. 6, 20 f.; *HA, Maximini* 27, 7, 'arrae regiae'; F. Schulz, *Classical Roman Law* (Oxford, 1951), 120, sect. 205; *FIRA* iii, no. 18 (*P. Lond.* 5, 1711, of late 6th century A.D.)

21. Schulz (note 20), 120 f., sect. 206.

22. See further, for the identity of Servilius Caepio, page 47 n.

23. The alternative, and less probable, account is that they were married from 43 to 41, but the marriage was not consummated (Suet., *DA* 62, 1).

24. The ring: Pliny, *NH* 33, 12 and 28; A. Rossbach, *Röm. Hochzeits- und Ehedenkmaler* (Leipzig, 1871), 27 f.; *RE* iA, 840.

25. *AG* 10, 10.

26. Suet., *DA* 53, 3; Pliny, *NH* 9, 117.

27. *Ad Att.* 1, 3, 3; *RE* vii A, 1329.

28. *Ad Q.f.* 2, 4, 2; 2, 6 (5), 2.

29. Ad Att. 6, 6, 1. On this marriage, J. H. Collins, 'Tullia's engagement and marriage to Dolabella', *CJ* 1952, 164–8.

30. See, on this subject, P. E. Corbett (note 1), chap. 3; *RE* xiv, 2259-86, s.v. 'matrimonium'.

31. *Coemptio*: Gaius 1, 113 and 119. *Usus*: Gaius 1, 111; Servius on Virg., *Georg.* 1, 31; *AG* 3, 2, 12 f.

32. Gaius 1, 112; Serv. on Virg., *Aen.* 4, 374.

33. G. Wissowa, *RK*², 506; *AG* 10, 15, 22; *TA* 4, 16.

34. List of inauspicious days, J. Marquardt, (note 9), 43; Ovid, *Fasti* (with J. G. Frazer's notes) 2, 557–62 (Parentalia); 5, 485–90 (May: 'Mense malum Maio nubere vulgus ait'); 6, 219–34 (early June); 3, 393–6 (March). On avoiding festivals, Plut., *QR* 105; Macrob. 1, 15, 21; Kalends, Nones and Ides, Macrob. 1, 15, 21; Frazer, *Ovid, Fasti* vol. ii, p. 79; iv, p. 53. *Mundus*: Festus, s.v., p. 144 L.

35. Cat. 61, 11.

36. In describing the wedding, I follow H. J. Rose, in his edition of Plutarch's *Roman Questions* (Oxford, 1924)—questions 1, 2, 7, 8, 29–31, 86 f., 105 are relevant—and W. Warde Fowler, *Social Life at Rome in the time of Cicero* (London, 1908), chap. 5.

37. Quint. 5, 11, 32; *Codex Just.* 5, 4, 22; *Dig.* 35, 1, 15 (Ulpian), 'Nuptias non concubitus sed consensus facit'; Schulz (note 20), 110, sect. 186.

38. In a not wholly convincing article, 'The Villa Item and a Bride's Ordeal', *JRS* 1929, 67–88, Jocelyn Toynbee interprets the frescoes of the Villa of the Mysteries outside Pompeii as evidence that the bride suffered a ritual flagellation on the eve of the wedding.

39. Festus, s.v. 'caelibari hasta', p. 55 L.; Plut., QR 87 (with H. J. Rose's notes); Ovid, Fasti 2, 560 (with J. G. Frazer's notes, vol. ii, pp. 441–5); A. Rossbach, *Untersuchungen über die röm. Ehe* (Stuttgart, 1853), 286–92.

40. Auspices: Cic., *De Div.* 1, 28; Pliny, *NH* 10, 21; Garland and veil: Cat. 61, 6–10; TA 15, 37, 9; Juv. 10, 334 (with J. E. B. Mayor's notes). Colour of the veil: Pliny, *NH* 21, 46. On her dress: L. M. Wilson, *The Clothing of the ancient Romans* (Baltimore, 1938), 138–45; A. Rossbach (note 39), 275–86.

41. *Officium*: Juv. 2, 132–5; A. Rossbach (note 39), 29, n. 920 for references. Bride's declaration: Plut, QR 30; Th. Mommsen, *Röm. Forschungen* (Berlin, 1864), 11 ff (Gaius-viz. Gavius-once a *nomen*, not a *praenomen*, and this dated from the time when all wives were 'in manu'); J. Marquardt (note 9), 49.

42. Juv. 10, 335 f.; TA 11, 27; 11, 30, 4; *RE* ivA, 1949–55, s.v. 'tabulae nuptiales'; *FIRA* iii, 17 (circ. A.D. 100); H. A. Sanders, 'A Latin Marriage Contract', *TAPA* 1938, 104–16; cf. *PSI* 730.

43. Juv. 2, 117–20; TA 11, 27. Expense of the breakfast, AG 2, 24, 7 and 14; Juv. 6, 202 f.

44. Cat. 61, 57–60; Festus, s.v. 'rapi', p. 364, 26 ff. L.

45. Plut., QR 31; Cat. 61, 119 ff. (126 ff.)

46. Virg., *Ecl.* 8, 30, 'Sparge, marite, nuces'; Cat. 61, 121 ff (128 ff.)

47. *Dig.* 23, 2, 5.

48. See J. G. Frazer, *Ovid, Fasti*, vol. ii, pp. 438–41; H. J. Rose (note 36), 103.

49. Serv. on Virg., *Ecl.* 8, 29 (about both torch and nuts); Festus, s.v. 'rapi', 364, 29 ff. L.

50. Pliny, *HN* 28, 142; Serv. on *Aen.* 4, 458.

51. Plut., QR 1; Ovid, *AA* 2, 598.

52. 'Genialis torus', H. J. Rose (note 36), 102; TA 15, 37, 9; Cat. 61, 164 f. (172 f.), with C. J. Fordyce's note; J. E. B. Mayor on Juv. 10, 334.

53. Cat. 61, 174 ff. (181 ff.); QR 65; cf. Juv. 6, 204.

54. *Germ.* 19.

55. Lucan, *Phars.* 2, 350–71, an occasion which is over-romanticized by J. Carcopino in his *Daily Life in Ancient Rome* (E. T. London, 1941), 83.

56. Cat. 61.

57. TA 11, 27; 15, 37, 8 f.; Juv. 2, 117–26.

58. On this, see P. E. Corbett (note 1), 147–204.

59. Varro, *RR* 3, 16, 2.

60. VM 4, 4, 10; TA 2, 86, 2; Juv. 6, 137; Mart. 11, 23, 3 f.

61. Polyb. 31, 27.

62. *Ad Att.* 11, 2, 2 (48 B.C., second instalment); 11, 23, 3 (third instalment). Had Cicero taken the initiative earlier, and had Tullia divorced Dolabella, the money would not have been lost. But the opportunity had been missed, and it was now Dolabella who was taking the initiative in divorce.

63. *Most.* 280 f.

64. AG 4, 3, 2.

65. AG 10, 23, 4.

66. On the 'retentions', F. Schulz (note 20), 128, sect. 219; P. E. Corbett (note 1), 133.

Chapter VIII

1. H. A. Sanders, 'A Roman Marriage Contract', *TAPA* 1938, 104–16 (esp. 110, l. 3; cf. *PSI* 730, l. 3).

2. *Phars.* 2, 326–71.

3. Plut., *Lycurgus* 15, 1–3 (penalty); Aristotle, *Pol.* 1270b.

4. VM 2, 9, 1.

5. 2nd. century Greece, Polyb. 36, 17; Metellus' speech in 131, *ORF*[2], 107 f.; Livy, *Per.* 59; AG 1, 6; Suet., *DA* 89, 2.

6. Prop. 1, 1, 5, 'Castas odisse puellas.'

7. Ovid, *AA* 3, 333 f.; Apuleius, *Apol.* 10; Prop. 2, 7, 1–4. On Cynthia, H. E. Butler, E. A. Barber, *The Elegies of Propertius* (Oxford, 1933), xx f.

8. *Amor.* 2, 13; 2, 14, esp. 37–40.

9. Juv. 2, 29–33; Pliny, *Epp.* 4, 11, 6; Suet., *Domit.* 22.

10. Juv. 6, 595 f.; *Dig.* 47, 11, 4.

11. *NH* 7, 40, 43.

12. *ILS* 6675.

13. *RE* iv, 837 f.; cf. P. Meyer, *Der röm. Konkubinat* (Leipzig, 1895), 34–39; 110–14.

14. Plut., *Ti.Gr.* 1, 5; Pliny, *NH* 7, 57.

15. *NH* 7, 59 f.

16. 10, 63.

17. *RE* 1, 2287 lists 13.

18. Vistilia, Pliny, *NH* 7, 39; Sempronia, wife of Scipio Aemilianus, App, *BC* 1, 83.

19. See J. P. V. D. Balsdon, *CR* 1960, 68-71.

20. *ILS* 8393, 41-60.

21. H. M. Last, *JRS* 1947, 152-6.

22. F. Münzer, *Röm. Adelsparteien*, 424 f., on the dilemma of the great families, on finding themselves without issue.

23. Mart. 6, 3.

24. Pliny, *Epp.* 8, 10 f.

25. E.g. Aemilia, whom Pompey married on Sulla's orders when she was already pregnant, Plut., *Sulla* 33, 4; *Pompey* 9, 4.

26. Plut., *Ti.Gr.* 1, 7.

27. Suet., *Tib.* 7, 3.

28. Tac., *Agric.* 6, 3.

29. *TA* 15, 23, 4.

30. H. Mattingly and E. A. Sydenham, *The Roman Imperial Coinage* ii (London, 1926), pl. v, 86; K. Scott, *The Imperial Cult under the Flavians* (Stuttgart-Berlin, 1936), 73-5.

31. Juv. 6, 368; 592-601; cf. 76-81.

32. Hor, *Odes* 1, 2, 24, 'Vitio parentum rara iuventus', could refer to birth-control, but more probably it alludes to the heavy casualties of the Civil Wars.

33. Juv. 6, 592-609.

34. Suet., *DA* 94, 3.

35. Musonius Rufus, *Reliquiae*, ed. O. Hense, 80 f.

36. The 'puellae Faustinianae'; See p. 142.

37. See *RE* 1, 1484-9, s.v. 'alimenta'; Constantine, *Cod.Theod.* 11, 27.

38. *ILS* 6675.

39. Pliny, *Pan.* 26, 3.

40. Polyb., 36, 17.

41. Pliny, *NH* 7, 14.

42. Egypt, *FIRA* iii, 4, (A.D. 145). Augustus' double, Macrob., *Sat.* 2, 4, 19 f; how did Pliny miss this story in his list of fortuitous' 'doubles', *NH* 7, 52–6?

43. Juv., 6, 78–81, 598–601; Mart. 6, 39.

44. *Heroid.* 7, 133.

45. On Caesarion, see note 19 above.

46. Juv. 9, 70–91.

47. Lucian, *Alexander* 42.

48. Suet., *DA* 2, 3; 4, 2.

49. VM 9, 7, 1; App., *BC* 3, 3; TH 4, 55; TA 15, 72, 4.

50. See pages 157, 161.

51. J. Carcopino, 'Le bâtard d'Hadrien et l'hérédité dynastique chez les Antonins,' *Passion et Politique chez les Césars* (Paris 1958), chap. 5, 143–222 (= *REA* 1949, 288–97).

52. VM 9, 15, 2.

Chapter IX

1. P. E. Corbett (chap 7, n. 1), 122–5.

2. Cat. 61, 82–86 (86–90), 97–105 (101–9), 144–6 (151–3); cf. Hor., *Odes* 2, 8, 21–24.

3. CN, *praef.* 6 f.

4. Juv. 6, 133 f., 627 f.

5. AG 12, 1.

6. *ILS* 8451.

7. Plut., *QR* 102. Registration of births, F. Schulz (chap. 7, n. 20), 75, sect. 126; *FIRA* iii, 1–5. The Romans did not register deaths.

8. On the benefits, Pliny, *Epp.* 10, 2 (with E. G. Hardy's notes); AG 1, 12, 8; *Dig.* 27, 1, 18; *Cod. Just.* 5, 66; Plut., *Mor.* 493E (*De amore prolis*).

9. E.g. Pliny, *Epp.* 10, 94 f. (grant, at Pliny's request, to Suetonius); Mart. 2, 91, 5 f.

10. E.g. 1, 72; 3, 43; 5, 43; 6, 12; 6, 74; 9, 37; 12, 23.

11. 4, 13; 11, 53.

12. Lucr. 3, 894–9.

13. Cornelia (Plut., *Ti.Gr.* 1, 6); Rhea (Plut., *Sert.* 2, 1); Aurelia (Tac., *Dial.* 28, 6.) Atia, mother of Augustus, was similarly renowned. (Tac. *Dial.* 28, 6).

14. Tac., *Agr.* 4, 4 f.

15. The story (in AG 1, 23) derives from a speech of the elder Cato (H. Malcovati, *ORF*², 67-69); but C. Cichorius plausibly suggested (*Röm. Stud.*, 91-96) that Aulus Gellius quoted wrongly, and that the boy's name, as given by Cato, was Sulpicius; for 'Praetextatus' is an attested *cognomen* of a branch of the Sulpicii, but not of any branch of the Papirii.

16. App., *BC* 4, 163-70; 189-92.

17. VP 2, 67, 2.

18. *ILS* 8393. Mommsen thought her the Turia of VM 6, 7, 2; App., *BC* 4, 189-92; but Dessau (*ILS* 8393, following Hirschfeld) shows that she was not.

19. *Social Life at Rome in the Age of Cicero* (London, 1922), 158-67.

20. Pliny, *Epp.* 3, 19, 8 f.; 1, 4.

21. *Sat.* 37, 67, 76.

22. Pliny, *Epp.* 4, 19, 2-4.

23. *ILS* 8394; cf. *CIL* xiv, 3579 (Hadrian's *laudatio* of his mother-in-law, Matidia).

24. *ILS* 8393-8; 8402 f., 8448, 8437.

25. *ILS* 8393 f., 8402 f.

26. Pliny, *Epp.* 6, 7; 7, 5.

27. *Silv.* 3, 5.

28. Pliny, *Epp.* 8, 5.

29. M. P. Charlesworth, *Documents illustrating the reigns of Claudius and Nero* (Cambridge, 1939), p. 42.

30. Seneca, *De Matrimonio* 72-7, ed. F. Haase, p. 432.

Chapter X

1. Suet., *De Gramm.* 14; R. Herzog, *Hist. Zeitschr.* 125 (1922), 193 f.

2. *Sat.* 1, 2, 28-134.

3. Ovid, *Am.* 3, 4; Prop. 3, 3, 47-50; cf. Plut., *Marius* 16, 7; Mart. 1, 73.

4. Corruption of guards, Juv. 3, 45 f.; 6, 234 f.; 275–8, O31–34. Lupercalia; Plut., *Romulus* 21, 7; *Caesar* 61, 3; Ovid, *Fast.* 2, 425–52.

5. See pages 204 f.

6 Plut., *QR* 14; AG 4, 3, 2; Petr., *Sat.* 74.

7. App., *BC* 1, 83. There is little evidence from papyri of adoption: only P. Lips. 28 and P. Oxy, 9, 1206, both of the fourth century A.D.

8. Juv. 6, 142–7, tr. W. Gifford (1802).

9. AG 1, 17, 4.

10. *Mor.* 141A f.; *Aem. Paul.* 5, 2 ff.

11. VM 2, 1, 6.

12. *Ad Att.* 5, 1, 3 f.; 14, 13, 5. See W. H. Johnson, 'The Sister-in-law of Cicero', *CJ* 1913, 160–5; W. Wiemar, Q. *Tullius Cicero* (Halle, 1930), 19 ff.

13. Juv. 6, 82–113 (the senator's wife who ran off with a gladiator); 166–71 (wife of breeding); 185–99 (plus grecque que les Grecs); 206–30 (the domineering wife); 231–41 (under the corrupting thumb of her mother); 246–67 (the athletic wife); 268–85 (the unfaithful wife); 379–97 (the musical wife); 398–412 (the woman of affairs); 412–33 (the grossly masculine wife). Mart. 2, 90, 9, 'Sit non doctissima coniunx'.

14. Juv. 6, 300.

15. *NH* 14, 89 f.; Polyb. 6, 11a, 4; Plut., *QR* 6.

16. Juv. 6, 562–68.

17. App., *BC* 1, 83.

18. 6, 165.

19. AG 10, 23, 5.

20. Musonius Rufus, *Reliquiae* ed. O. Hense, 68; Plaut., *Mercator* 823–9, tr. P. Nixon (LCL).

21. Juv. 6, 136–41, 'Vidua est, locuples quae nupsit avaro.'

22. *Am* 3, 4, 37–40; cf. 1, 4; 1, 9, 25 f.; 3, 8.

23. VM 6, 7, 1.

24. Suet, *DA* 62, 2; 69, 1; 71, 1; CD 58, 2, 5.

25. *TA* 11, 29, 3–30, 1.

26. Juv. 6, 627, 'Oderunt natos de paelice.'

27. T*A* 2, 50, 1.

28. On this, see P. E. Corbett (chap, 7, n. 1), chapters 5 and 9.

29. The past idealized: T*A* 3, 26. Carvilius: DH 2, 25, 7; AG 4, 3, 1 f; 17, 21, 44. Date circ. 600: VM 2, 1, 4.

30. Twelve tables: Cic., *Phil* 2, 69. Divorce formula, Plaut., *Amphitryon* 928; *Dig.* 24, 2, 2, 1 (Gaius). Plut, *QR* 14 lists early divorces.

31. Plut., *QR* 50.

32. Livia, *RE* xiii, 900, no. 35; Pompey, Plut., *Pomp.* 9; Caesar, Suet, *DJ* 1.

33. AG 10, 23, 5 (Cato). On divorce of a husband by his wife under the Republic, see P. E. Corbett (chap. 7, n. 1), 222. A case is mentioned by Cicero, *Ad fam* 8, 7, 2.

34. AG 10, 23, 5; VM 6, 1, 13.

35. DH 2, 25, 6; Plut., *Rom.* 22, 3.

36. P. E. Corbett (chap. 7, n. 1) 228–34 argues this convincingly.

37. T*A* 2, 85, 1.

38. *RE* i, 432–5, s.v. 'Adulterium'; Musonius Rufus, *Reliquiae*, ed. O. Hense, 12, p. 66; F. J. Dölger, *Antike und Christentum*, 1932, 132–48; Plut., *Mor.* 145 A.

39. *Dig.* 48, 5, 30 pr.

40. Pliny, *Epp.* 6, 31, 4–6.

41. P. E. Corbett (chap. 7, n. 1), 142–5.

42. Paul. *Sent.Recept.* 2, 26, 14; *Dig.* 48, 5, 30; F. J. Dölger (note 38), 143 f.

43. Paul. *Sent.Recept.* 2, 26 4; *Dig.* 48, 5, 25 pr.

44. If she was in his 'potestas', *Dig.* 48, 5, 21 (Papinian); 58, 5, 22 (Ulpian) and 24, 1.

45. T*A* 2, 50, 4; cf. 13, 32, 4; Suet., *Tib.* 35, 1.

46. *HA, MA* 19, 8 f.

47. *Ad Att.* 16, 15, 5; CD 46, 18, 3. For Quintus in the same dilemma, see *Ad Att.* 14, 13, 5 ('torquetur'.)

48. 'Actio rei uxoriae', Cic., *De Offic.* 3, 61.

49. Pliny, *NH* 14, 90.

50. Ulpian, *Reg.* 6, 12; P. E. Corbett (chap. 7, n. 1), 193.

51. VM 8, 2, 3.

52. Asconius, *In Scaur.* 19 C.

53. T*A* 3, 22 f.; Suet. *Tib.* 49, 1. I am grateful to Mr. G. B. Townend for attracting my interest to this case.

54. P. E. Corbett (chap. 7, n. 1), 211–17.

55. F. Schulz (chap. 7, n. 20), 136; P. E. Corbett (chap. 7, n. 1), 249–51.

56. See page 90.

57. P. E. Corbett (chap. 7, n. 1), chap. 4.

58. P. E. Corbett (chap, 7, n. 1), 119; Quint. 8, 5, 19.

59. Mart. 1, 10; 2, 26; 2, 65; 5, 37, 20 ff.; 10, 8; 10, 43, On the power of 'orbae', Hor., *Epist.* 1, 1, 77 f.; Juv. 3, 126–30; T*H* 1, 73 Mart, 1, 49, 34, 'Imperia viduarum'; 2, 32, 6.

60. Pliny, *Epp.* 2, 20.

Chapter XI

1. See *RE* xv, 1018–27, s.v. 'Meretrix' (K. Schneider), a mine of information, which gives the evidence for most of the statements which follow.

2. Prop. 2, 23, 21.

3. Hor., *Sat.* 1, 2 62 f. ('Ancilla togata'); Ovid, *Fast.* 4, 134; *AA*, 1, 31 f.; *Ex Ponto* 3, 3, 49–52.

4. 'Summoenianae uxores', Mart. 3, 82, 2; Subura, Mart. 11, 61, 3 etc.; Via Sacra, Prop. 2, 23, 15; Mart. 2, 63; Circus Maximus, Juv. 3, 65.

5. Juv. 9, 24, 'Nam quo non prostat femina templo?'

6. Suet., *C. Cal.* 40; *RE* xv, 1022.

7. Cat. 37, 1; Hor., *Epist.* 1, 14, 21; Petron., *Sat.* 7, 2; *Dig.* 23, 2, 43 pr. and 9.

8. Aediles: Mommsen, *Staatsr.* II, i³, 510 f. Brothels: *RE* xii, 1942 f., s.v. 'Lenocinium'; xv, 1023–5, with the numbers; Petron., *Sat.* 7, 2 (Puteoli).

9. Hor., *Sat.* 1, 2, 30; Juv. 6, 131 f.; 11, 172; Mart 12, 61, 8.

10. Inscriptions and graffiti in *CIL* iv; for references, see *RE* xv, 1025.

11. *Pro Caelio*, 48–50.

12. Porphyrio and ps-Acro on Hor., *Sat.* 1, 2, 31 f.

13. Mart 6, 66.

14. *HA, Hadr.* 18, 8.

15. *Or.* 7, 133 ff.

16. *ILS* 7478.

17. Pliny, *Epp.* 6, 24; cf. *Epit. Caes.* 40, 4 (Galerius Maximianus); *RE* xv, 1026.

18. Prop. 4, 7.

19. Prop. 1, 8 A; 2, 16; 2, 26, 21–28; Mart 11, 49 (50) (excessive demands of the courtesan).

20. See note 8 above.

21. *TA* 2, 85, 1; cf. Suet., *Tib.* 35, 2.

22. *Odes* 3, 6, 17–32.

23. Hor., *Odes* 3, 9, 10; 4, 13, 7; Prop. 1, 2, 26–30; Ovid, *AA* 3, 319 f., 329 f., 349 f.

24. *AA* 1, 31 f.,; 2, 599 f.

25. *AA* 3, 169 ff. (dress); 197 f. (washing and teeth); 199 ff. (make-up); 239 (behaviour to servants); 261 ff. (concealing physical blemishes); 281 ff. (social deportment), 311 ff. (music); 329 ff. (literary culture).

26. *AA* 387 ff. (public appearances); 433 f. (men to avoid); 469 ff. (love letters); 525 ff. (proper remuneration); 553 ff. (on making allowance for age); 577 ff. (on tantalizing lovers); 611 (on deceit); 747 ff. (party manners).

27. *Odes* 4, 13.

28. Plut., *Sulla* 2; 36, 1 f.

29. RE viii, 2126 f., s.v. 'Histrio'.

30. Bruns[7], 18, 123; 23, 1.

31. Plut., *Cato mai.* 21, 3.

32. Varro, *RR* 1, 17, 5; 2, 1, 26.

33. Colum. 1, 8, 19.

34. E.g. *ILS* 7432 C.

35. *ILS* 1680.

36. Gaius 1, 19; *Dig.* 40, 2, 19.

37. *ILS* 1519, 2049, 7063 etc.

38. *Dig.* 38, 11, 1, 1; F. Schulz (chap. 7, n. 20), 134, sect. 225.

39. *Dig.* 25, 7, 1 pr.

40. See P. Meyer, *Der röm. Konkubinat* (Leipzig, 1895); RE, iv, 835–8 (R. Leonhard); F. Schulze (chap. 7, n. 20), 137–41.

41. P. E. Corbett (chap. 7, n. 1), 95 f.

42. Regulation of A.D. 197; Herodian 3, 8, 5; H. M. D. Parker, *The Roman Legions* (Oxford, 1928), 237 f.

43. *Trinummus* 375; 689–91.

44. Paul. *Sent.* 2, 20, 1; *Cod. Just.* 7, 15, 3, 2 (A.D. 531). But see Pliny, *Epp.* 3, 14, 3 and F. Schulz (chap. 7, n. 20), 138 f., sects. 235–8. Constantine forbad a married man to keep a concubine.

45. Plut., *Cato mai.* 24, 2–7.

46. See page 131.

47. See page 145.

48. *HA, Gord.* 19, 3.

49. *RE* iv, 1040.

50. Zosimus 2, 8, 2.

51. *Epit. Caes.* 41, 4.

52. *CIL* v, 1918; cf. *ILS* 2423. For inscriptions recording concubines, see *ILS* iii, p. 932.

53. A. M. Duff, *Freedmen in the early Roman Empire* (Oxford, 1928), 33; 61 f.; *Dig.* 40, 2, 14, 1; *Cod. Just.* 5, 4, 3.

54. *TA* 12, 53, 1; Gaius 1, 84.

Chapter XII

1. On the Vestal Virgins, see H. Jordan, *Der Tempel der Vesta und das Haus der Vestalinnen* (Berlin, 1886); *RE* viii A, 1717–1776, esp. 1732–76, s.v. 'Vesta' (C. Koch); F. Münzer, 'Die röm. Vestalinnen bis zur Kaiserzeit, '*Philologus* 1937, 47–67; 199–222.

2. Platner-Ashby, s.v.; G. Lugli, *Roma Antica* (Rome, 1946), 202–12; G. Wissowa, *RK²*, 502 f., n. 7.

3. *RE* viii A, 1742; *RK²*, 509 f. Mommsen thought 'wife' (*Strafrecht*, 18); H. J. Rose thought 'daughters' ('De Virginibus Vestalibus', *Mnemosyne* 1926, 440–8).

4. W.Warde Fowler, *The Roman Festivals* (London, 1899), 114 f.

5. On details of admission and service, AG 1, 12. Cf. DH 2, 67, 2; Plut., *Numa* 10. Admission of freedmen's daughters, CD 55, 22, 5 (A.D. 5).

6. AG 1, 12, 9; 7, 7, 2; Gaius 1, 130.

7. L. 1, 20, 3.

8. TA 4, 16, 6 (AD. 24); cf. 2, 86; J. E. B. Mayor on Juv. 10, 335.

9. TA 2, 86, 1; 3, 69, 9; ILS 4923.

10. Plut., Numa 10, 4.

11. H. Jordan (note 1), 56 ff.

12. Pliny, Epp. 7, 19, 1 f.

13. See Ovid, Fasti; W. Warde Fowler (note 4) passim.

14. Ovid, Fast. 5, 603–62 (14th.); DH 1, 38 (15th.); W. Warde Fowler (note 4), 112–21; J. G. Frazer, The Fasti of Ovid, vol. iv, pp. 74–119.

15. G. Wissowa, RK², 159 f.

16. RE viiiA, 1738.

17. W. Warde Fowler (note 4), 83.

18. Servius on Virg., Ecl. 8, 82; W. Warde Fowler (n. 4), 110 f., 149, n. 3; J. G. Frazer, The Fasti of Ovid, vol. iii, p. 332.

19. Macrob., Sat. 3, 13, 11; L. R. Taylor, AJP 1942, 385–412.

20. Plut., Numa 10, 4 (including the lictor, whom CD 47, 19, 4 is probably wrong in dating as late as 42 B.C.); AG 10, 15, 31; RK², 508.

21. Suet., DA 44, 3; TA 4, 16, 6; CD 59, 3, 4; 60, 22, 2.

22. CD 60, 5, 2.

23. TA 11, 32, 5; TH 3, 81. State document, CD 48, 37, 1. Wills: Suet., DJ 83, 1; Plut., Ant. 58, 4–6 (on the genuineness or otherwise of this will of Antony's, which they produced, T. Rice Homes, The Architect of the Roman Empire (Oxford, 1928) i, 246 f.); TA 1, 8, 1.

24. L. 22, 57, 2.

25. Sources in A. H. J. Greenidge and A. M. Clay, Sources for Roman History, 133–70 B.C.² (Oxford, 1960), pp. 58–60.

26. Suet., Domit. 8, 3 f.; Pliny, Epp. 4, 11; cf. Juv. 4, 8–10, with J. E. B. Mayor's notes.

27. L. 4, 44, 11 f.; DH 2, 67, 5.

28. DH 2, 68 f. On Tuccia, RE viiA, 768–70, no. 12 (F. Münzer) For a scholarly account of the true and the false in recorded trials of Vestal Virgins under the Republic, see F. Münzer, n. 1 above.

29. Cic., *In Cat.* 3, 9; Fabia, Ascon., *In Tog. Cand.* 91; Licinia, Plut, *Crassus* 1, 4 f., *Mor.* 89 E.

30. L. 8, 15, 7; VM 6, 8, 1; Schol. Bob. 91 Stangl.

31. L. 22, 57, 3; Th. Mommsen, *Strafrecht* 919, n. 1.

32. TA 5, 9, 3.

33. *Numa* 10; cf. QR 96; DH 2, 67, 4 f.

34. See F. Münzer, note 1 above.

35. See *RE* viiiA, 1747–52.

36. Suet., *Domit.* 8, 3 f.; CD 67, 3, 4.

37. Pliny, *Epp.* 4, 11.

38. CD 77, 16, 1–3 (Caracalla); 79, 9 (Elagabalus); Zon. 12, 14; Herodian 5, 6, 2.

39. *CIL* vi, 32409–28; A. D. Nock, 'A diis electa: a chapter in the religious history of the third century', *Harv. Theol. Rev.*, 1930, 251–74 (list of honorands, 270–4); E. B. van Deman, 'The Value of the Vestal Statues as Originals', *AJA* 1908, 324–32.

40. Gaius 1, 112. Rule relaxed slightly for Flamen Dialis in A.D. 23, TA 4, 16, 5.

41. Flaminica Dialis, Plut., QR 86; Ovid, *Fast.* 3, 397 f.; 6, 227–30; AG 10, 15, 22 f.; G. May, 'Le Flamen Dialis et la Virgo Vestalis', *REA* 1905, 4–16; *RK*² 506. Priestesses of the imperial cult, Dessau, *ILS*, vol. iii, p. 574 for references. Choirs of women: L. 27, 37; 31, 12, 9; TA 15, 44, 1.

42. Plut., QR 60, with H.J. Rose's notes; AG 11, 6; Cato, *De agric.* 83.

43. Ovid, *Fasti* 5, 148, with J. G. Frazer's notes (vol. iv, pp. 16–18).

44. *RK*² 217, with references.

45. Plut, *Caesar* 9, 4–8; Juv. 6, 314–41.

46. 63 celebration, Plut., *Cic.* 19, 4 f. 62 celebration, Plut., *Caesar* 10; *Cicero* 28.

47. *Ad Att.* 1, 13, 3.

48. The main sources are Cicero's letters, *Ad Att.* 1, 12–16.

49. Schol. Bob. 85, 30 f. Stangl; Ascon. 49C.

50. *Ad Att.* 1, 16, 2; Schol. Bob. (n. 49 above.)

51. 6, 314–41.

52. *RK*² 351–9 on Isis-cult in Rome.

53. Prop. 2, 33A; 4, 5, 34; Ovid, *Am.* 1, 8, 74; 3, 9, 34 f.; Juv. 6, 535 f.

54. Ovid, *Am.* 2, 2, 25.

55. Jos., *AJ* 18, 65–80; T*A* 2, 85, 5; Suet., *Tib.* 36.

56. Jos., *AJ* 18, 81–84.

57. Expulsion of Jews in 139 B.C. for proselytizing, VM 1, 3, 3. On Poppaea, see page 126.

58. On Berenice, see pages 132 f.

59. 'Externa superstitio', T*A* 12, 32; *RE* xxi, 2351 f., no. 83; B. W. Henderson, *The Life and Principate of the Emperor Nero* (London, 1903), 344 f.

60. Euseb., *HE* 3, 18, 4; CD 67, 14, 1–3; Philostr., *Vit. Apoll. Tyan.* 8, 25; E. M. Smallwood, 'Domitian's attitude towards the Jews and Judaism', *CP* 1956, 1–11.

61. Cic., *De Div.* 1, 99; Obseq. 55.

62. J. Carcopino, *Sylla* (Paris, 1931), 185.

63. CD 59, 11; Seneca, *Apocolocyntosis* 1.

64. Inscriptions of Diva Drusilla, *CIL* v, 7345; *AE* 1952, 151. Consecration of Julia Augusta, CD 60, 5, 2; Suet., *D. Cl.*11, 2.

65. T*A* 15, 23, 4; 16, 6, 3; *Act. Arv.*, Henzen lxxxiv.

66. Stat., *Silv.* 1, 1, 97 and coins, Mattingly-Sydenham (chap. 8, n. 30), ii, p. 124.

67. T*A* 16, 6, 1; 21, 2; *Act. Arv.*, Henzen lxxxiii f.

68. See *PIR²*, 'F' 426, for the evidence.

69. T*A* 16, 21, 2.

70. See *RE* suppl. iv, 806–53, s.v. 'Kaiserkult' (G. Herzog-Hauser), esp. 838–52, for the period from Trajan to Constantine.

Chapter XIII

1. On all questions of women's dress, see L. M. Wilson, *The Clothing of the ancient Romans*, Baltimore, 1938. Toga worn only by prostitutes, Hor., *Sat.* 1, 2, 63; Mart. 2, 39.

2. VM 6, 3, 10.

3. Cic., *De Legg.* 2, 59; Nonius M542 (Lindsay, p. 869).

4. Quotation from L. M. Wilson (note 1 above), 134 f. The 'instita', Hor., *Sat.* 1, 1, 29; Ovid, *AA* 1, 31 f.; *Trist.* 2, 247 f; L. M. Wilson, 157 f.

5. *Epidicus*, tr. P. Nixon (LCL), discussed by L. M. Wilson (note 1), 153–5.

6. *HA*, *Elag*. 26, 1; *AS* 33, 3. Silk an extravagance, CD 43, 24, 2. Men forbidden to wear silk by Tiberius, CD 57, 15, 1.

7. Prop. 3, 13, 6–8; Pliny, *NH* 9, 125–41. The coloured frontispiece of L. M. Wilson's book (note 1) gives samples of different shades of 'purple', an astonishing range of colours.

8. Ovid, *AA* 3, 169–92. White as a favourite colour for 'matrons', Porphyrio on Hor, *Sat*, 1, 2, 35. 'Colores meretricii', Sen., *QN* 7, 31, 2.

9. *De cultu fem.*, 1, 1; 2, 10. The prodigy of a lamb with a purple fleece was, in fact, once reported: *HA*, *Geta* 3, 5.

10. Plaut., *Truc.* 405; Ovid, *AA* 3, 239–42; *Am.* 1, 14, 16–18; Mart. 2, 66; Juv. 6, 486–507; *Germania Romana*[2] (Bamberg, 1924), pl. xxxviii, no. 2.

11. *AA* 3, 137–40. On coiffure, see R. Steininger, *Die weiblichen Haartrachten* (Munich, 1909).

12. Ovid, *Met.* 8, 319; Petr., *Sat.* 67; Varro, *LL* 7, 44.

13. C. Barini, *Ornatus Muliebris* (Turin, 1958), 27 f. *Dig.* 34, 2, 25, 2 (Ulpian): 'Vittae margaritarum item fibulae ornamentorum magis quam vestis sunt.'

14. Ovid, *AA* 3, 139 f.

15. Hot tongs, Ovid, *Am.* 1, 14, 25 f.; Lucian, *Amores*, 40. Juv. 6, 502–4; cf. Mart. 2, 66, 1.

16. E. F. Leon, *Art and Archaeology* 24, 173.

17. *De cultu fem.* 2, 7.

18. 3, 161–7; 243–6.

19. Ovid, *Am.* 1, 14 ('Nunc tibi captivos mittet Germania crines'); Mart. 6, 12; 9, 37, 12, 23.

20. Mart, 5, 68; Lucian, *Amores* 40; Tertullian, *De cultu fem.* 2, 6; Poppaea's hair, Pliny, *NH* 37, 50.

21. Early times, VM 2, 1, 5; Batavian (or Chattan) dye, Mart. 8, 33, 20 ('Et mutat Latias spuma Batava comas'); 14, 26 ('Chattica spuma'); Pliny, *NH* 28, 191.

22. I am deeply grateful to my colleague Dr. R. F. Barrow and to my friend Mr. John Ashworth of the Biochemistry Department of the University of Leicester, who have gone to great pains to

establish the fact. They have drawn my attention to this statement in the *Encyclopedia of Technical Chemistry* (New York, 1954) xiv, 184: 'Native minerals such as rock alum, quicklime, crude soda and wood ash, occasionally combined with old wine, served as favourite blond washes. These preparations were left on the hair overnight or for several days, and gave reddish-gold shades.'

23. Plut., *Mor.* 770D–771C, esp. 771B; TH 4, 67; CD 66, 3, 1 f.; 16, 1 f. The following headline in the *Messagero* of October 10th 1961 might have been a description of Epponina: 'Si sospetta che la moglie della "vittima" sapesse che egli era vivo e che lo abbia aiutato nella sua assurda impresa.'

24. Plut., *Mor.* 771B, tr. W. C. Helmbold (LCL).

25. 2, 18C ('Turpis Romano Belgicus ore color', l. 26).

26. Lucian, *Amores* 39.

27. *Cultus*: Tertullian, *De cultu fem.* 1, 4; *Dig.* 34, 2, 25, 10. Postumia L. 4, 44, 11 f.

28. Tertullian, *De cultu fem.* 2, 5.

29. Ovid, *Remed.Am.* 347–56; Juv. 6, 461–74.

30. Ovid, *Medic fac. fem.* 53–68; 69 ff. Powder; Plaut., *Truc.* 294; Ovid, *AA* 3, 199. Rouge: Plaut, *Truc.* 294; *Most.* 258; Ovid, *AA* 3, 200. Black for eyes, Ovid, *AA* 3, 203; Tertullian, *De cultu fem.* 1, 2; 2, 5.

31. *AA* 3, 105.

32. Seplasium: M. W. Frederiksen, *Papers of the British School at Rome* 1959, 110; Juv. 6, 462; CD 62, 28, 1.

33. Mart. 3, 55; 4, 4; Prop. 1, 2.

34. Ovid, *Remed.Am.* 343–46; Prop. 3, 13, 11 f.; Tertullian, *De cultu fem.* 1, 5 f.; 2, 10.

35. Pliny, *NH* 37, 12.

36. Pliny, *NH* 37, 55–58.

37. *ILS* 4422; 5496.

38. For publications, see bibliography at end of book.

39. Pliny, *NH* 9, 106; 12, 84 (cf. TA 3, 53, 5).

40. Tac., *Agr.* 12, 6 f.; Pliny, *NH* 9, 116.

41. Sen., *De Benefic.* 7, 9, 4.

42. Pliny, *NH* 9, 113 f., tr. H. Rackham (LCL).

43. Hor., *Sat.* 2, 3, 239–42 (Metella); Pliny, *NH* 9, 121 (Cleopatra); 9, 117 (Lollia Paulina); Petr., *Sat.* 67 (Scintilla); H. A. Sanders, 'A Latin Marriage Contract', *TAPA* 1938, 104–16.

44. Petr., *Sat.* 67, tr. William Arrowsmith, Univ. of Michigan Press, 1959.

45. Sen., *Epp.* 86, 8–10; Cic., *Ad Fam.* 14, 20; Pliny, *Epp.* 2, 17, 11 and 26.

46. Plaut., *Truc.* 322–5; *Most.* 157; Suet., *DA* 94, 4.

47. Pliny, *Epp.* 3, 1, 8 (baths at 3 o'c in winter, 2 o'c in summer); Petr., *Sat.* 73; bathing at the 10th hour, Mart. 3, 36, 5; 10, 70, 13; Juv. 6, 419, 'Balneum nocte subit'.

48. Varro, *LL* 9, 68.

49. For this interesting information I am indebted to Mr. Barri Jones, Scholar of the British School at Rome.

50. Mart. 7, 35; 11, 75; Juv. 6, 422 f.

51. No women admitted: *CIL* vi. 579. Praeneste: *CIL* I. i², p. 235, with Mommsen's note at p. 314.

52. Mart. 3, 87; *HA, AS* 42, 1; Mart. 7, 35; 11, 75.

53. *ILS* 6891, 19–30.

54. Pliny, *NH* 33, 153; Quint. 5, 9. 14; *HA, Hadr.* 18, 10; *MA*, 23, 8; *AS* 24, 2; J. Marquardt, *Das Privatleben*² 279–97, esp. 282.

55. Mart. 3, 51, 3; 3, 72; 7, 35, 5; 7, 76, 4; 11, 75; R. Meiggs, *Ostia* (Oxford, 1960), 406.

56. D. Krencker, *Die Trierer Kaiserthermen* (Augsburg, 1929), 336, n. 5.

57. R. Meiggs (note 55), 407 ff.

58. *NH* 36, 121.

59. Asc., *In Milon.* 43C (for the identity of Lepidus' wife, *RE* i, 560 f.); Suet., *DA* 73, 1 (cf. *Vit.* 8, 1, 'vestis domestica'); *CIL* vi, 3926–4326; 6213–640; Tenney Frank, *Econ. Survey of Ancient Rome* v (Baltimore, 1940), 201, n. 43.

60. Columella, *praef.* 1–3, 7–9.

60a. Pliny, *NH* 37, 29; 13, 91.

61. 71b.

61a. Pliny, *NH* 18, 107; 9, 67; Petr., *Sat.* 37; 67; L. Friedlander, *Roman Life and Manners under the early Empire* ii, 146–85.

62. 'Doctae puellae': Ovid, *AA* 2, 281; *Am.* 2, 4, 17; Sulpicia, Schanz-Hosius, *Geschichte d. röm. Lit*⁴ ii, 189 f.; *RE* ivA, 879 f., no. 14.

63. Mart. 10, 35 (tr. W. C. A. Ker, LCL); 10, 38; *RE* ivA, 880–2, no. 15; Schanz-Hosius (note 62) ii⁴, 560 f. The Bobbio hexameters, PLM v, p. 93 ff.

64. Dancing girls from Cadiz, Pliny, *Epp.* 1, 15; Mart. 1, 41, 12.

65. CN, *Epam.* 1 f.

66. Macrob., *Sat.* 3, 14; *ORF*², p. 133.

67. Sall., *Cat.* 25, 2 (Sempronia); *AA* 3, 311–20; 349 f; Stat., *Silv.* 3, 5, 66 f.; Petr., *Sat.* 52.

68. *Odes* 3, 6, 21; 2, 12, 17.

69. See F. Schulz (chap. 7, n. 20), chap. 5, 'Guardianship'.

70. Cic., *Pro Caec.* 13–17; Mart. 5, 61, 'Crispulus ille'. Cf. 'Procurator calamistratus' of Seneca, *De matrim.*, ed. Haase, p. 429, para. 51.

71. *CIL* vi, 2926–4326; *ILS* 1321.

72. Shipbuilding: Suet., *D.Cl.* 18, 2 and 19. Lady Doctors: *ILS*, 7802–6. Ummidia Quadratilla, Pliny, *Epp.* 7, 24.

73. Juv. 1, 121–6; Plut., *Otho* 3 and 6.

74. Bruns⁷ 18, 56–65; Suet., *D.Cl.* 17, 3; TA 12, 42, 3; CD 60, 22, 2; 33, 2.

75. Cat. 10, 14 ff; Juv. 4, 21.

76. Suet., *DJ* 43, 1; *Dom.*, 8, 3; CD 57, 15, 4.

77. *AA* 3, 634–42.

78. *Silv.* 3, 5, 15 f.

79. Ovid, *AA* 1, 99; Plin., *NH* 33, 63.

80. Suet., *DA* 44, 3; Plut., *Sulla* 35, 5–11.

81. Suet., *DA* 44, 2 f.; Juv. 6, 60 f.; Tertullian, *De Spect.* 21.

82. Sen., *Epp.* 7; Juv. 6, 60 ff.; Petr., *Sat.* 126.

83. Juv. 6, 82–113, tr. William Gifford, 1802.

Chapter XIV

1. See F. Schulz, *Classical Roman Law* (Oxford, 1951), part 2, chap. 3, 'Husband and Wife' (pp. 103–41).

2. Cic., *Pro Murena* 27, 'Mulieres omnes propter infirmitatem consili maiores in tutorum potestate esse voluerunt'.

3. Gaius 1, 190 is honest about this.

4. F. Schulz (note 1), 103, sect. 180.

5. Cic., *Ad Fam.* 14; Pliny, *Epp.* 1, 4; 2, 4; 3, 3; 3, 10; 4, 19; 6, 4; 6, 7; 7, 5; 7, 14; 8, 11.

ABBREVIATIONS USED IN THE NOTES

AA	*See* Ovid.
Ad Att, Ad Fam., *Ad Q. f.*	Cicero's Letters to Atticus, to his Friends, to his brother Quintus.
AG	Aulus Gellius, *Noctes Atticae*.
AJP	*American Journal of Philology*.
Am.	*See* Ovid.
BC	Appian, *Bellum Civile*.
BMC, Emp.	Coins of the Roman Empire in the British Museum, by H. A. Grueber.
BMC, Rep.	Coins of the Roman Republic in the British Museum, by H. Mattingly.
Bruns[7]	C. G. Bruns, *Fontes Iuris Romani*, 7th edition, 1909.
CAH	Cambridge Ancient History.
Cat.	Catullus.
CD	Cassius Dio.
CIL	Corpus Inscriptionum Latinarum.
CJ	Classical Journal.
CN	Cornelius Nepos.
Cod. Just.	*Codex Justinianus*.
CQ, CR	*Classical Quarterly, Classical Review*.
DH	Dionysius of Halicarnassus, *Roman Antiquities*.
Dig.	*Digest*.
Epit. Caes.	(Incerti Auctoris) *Epitome de Caesaribus*.
FIRA	*Fontes Iuris Romani Anteiustiniani*, ed. S. Riccobono, etc.
HA, Hadr., AP, *MA, etc.*	Scriptores Historiae Augustae, *Lives of Hadrian, Antoninus Pius, Marcus Aurelius, etc.*
ILS	*Inscriptiones Latinae Selectae*, ed. H. Dessau.
JRS	*Journal of Roman Studies*.
Juv.	Juvenal, *Satires*.
L.	Livy.
LCL	Loeb Classical Library.
LL	*See* Varro.

MP	Lactantius, *De Mortibus Persecutorum*.
NH	Pliny, *Natural History*.
*ORF*²	*Oratorum Romanorum Fragmenta*, ed. H. Malcovati, 2nd edition, 1955.
Ovid, *AA, Am.*	Ovid, *Ars Amatoria, Amores*.
P.	Polybius.
PAPA	*Proceedings of the American Philological Association*.
PIR	*Prosopographia Imperii Romani*.
*PIR*²	,, ,, ,, 2nd edition, 1933–58, 'A' to 'H'.
Platner-Ashby	*A Topographical Dictionary of Rome*, ed. S. B. Platner, revised by Thomas Ashby (Oxford 1929).
Plaut.	Plautus.
Plut.	Plutarch's *Lives*.
Plut., *Mor*	Plutarch, *Moralia*.
PLM	Poetae Latini Minores.
QR	The *Roman Questions* of Plutarch.
Quint.	Quintilian, *Institutio Oratoria*.
RE	Pauly-Wissowa, *Real-Encyclopaedie der classischen Altertumswissenschaft*.
*RK*²	G. Wissowa, *Religion und Kultus der Römer*, 2nd edition, 1912.
RR	See Varro.
Sall, *BJ, Cat.*	Sallust, *Bellum Jugurthinum, Catilinae Coniuratio*.
Suet., *DJ, DA, Tib., D.Cl., etc.*	Suetonius' *Lives of Divine Julius, Divine Augustus, Tiberius, Divine Claudius, etc.*
TA, TH	Tacitus, *Annals, Histories*.
TAPA	*Transactions of the American Philological Association*.
Varro, *LL, RR*	Varro, *De Lingua Latina, De Re Rustica*.
VM	Valerius Maximus.
VP	Velleius Paterculus.

BIBLIOGRAPHY

GENERAL

R. H. Barrow, *Slavery in the Roman Empire*, London, 1928.

C. Daremberg and E. Saglio, *Dictionnaire des antiquités grecques et romaines*, 1877–1919.

S. Dill, *Roman Society from Nero to Marcus Aurelius*, London, 1904.

A. M. Duff, *Freedmen in the early Roman Empire*, Oxford, 1928.

L. Friedländer, *Roman Life and Manners under the early Empire* (tr. by J. H. Freese and A. Magnus from 7th edition of *Sittengeschichte Roms*), London, 1908-13, especially vol. 1, chap. 5, 'The Position of Women'.

H. F. Jolowicz, *Historical Introduction to the Study of Roman Law*, Cambridge, 2nd edition, 1952.

    Roman Foundations of Modern Law, Oxford, 1957.

J. Marquardt, *Das Privatleben der Römer*, Leipzig, 2nd edition, 1886.

Pauly-Wissowa, *Realencyclopädie der classischen Altertumswissenschaft*, Stuttgart, 1894– (articles on individuals and on subjects, e.g. 'matrimonium', 'nuptiae').

F. Schulz, *Principles of Roman Law* (tr. M. Wolff), Oxford, 1936.

    Classical Roman Law, Oxford, 1951.

W. Warde Fowler, *Social Life at Rome in the age of Cicero*, London, 1922.

BOOKS PARTICULARLY ON WOMEN,
OR ON PARTICULAR WOMEN

J. R. de Serviez (tr. Hon Bysse Molesworth), *The Roman Empresses*, London, 1752.

M. della Corte, *Loves and Lovers in ancient Pompeii*, 1960.

Guglielmo Ferrero, *The Women of the Caesars*, London, 1911 (viz. Livia; Daughters of Agrippa; Agrippina; Caligula's Wife; Wedding of Messalina; Mother of Nero).

B. Förtsch, *Die politische Rolle der Frau in der römischen Republik*, Stuttgart, 1935.

V. Kahrstedt, 'Frauen auf antiken Münzen,' *Klio* 1910, 291–314.

E. Kornemann, *Grosse Frauen des Altertums*, Leipzig, 1942 (includes Livia, Agrippina i, Julia Domna, Julia Maesa, Julia Mamaea, Zenobia).

Johannes Leipoldt, *Die Frau in der antiken Welt und im Urchristentum*, Leipzig, 1954.

H. Malcovati, E. Paratore, G. Giannelli, A. G. Amatucci, A. Calderini, G. Corradi, *Donne di Roma antica*, in *Quaderni di Studi Romani*, Rome, 1945/6 (viz. Clodia, Fulvia, Marcia, Terentia, Plotina, Sabina, Faustina i and ii, Julia, Servilia, Domitilla, Helena, Le donne dei Severi, Donne inspiratrici di poeti nell' antica Roma).

A. Stahr, *Römische Kaiserfrauen*, Berlin, 1865.

F. Sandels, *Die Stellung der kaiserlichen Frauen aus dem Julisch-Claudischen Hause*, Diss. Giessen, 1912.

PORTRAITURE

A. de Franciscis, *Il ritratto romano a Pompeii*, Naples, 1951.

A. Hekler, *Greek and Roman Portraits*, London, 1912.

B. M. F. Maj, *Iconografia romana imperiale di Severo Alessandro a M. Aurelio Carino*, Rome, 1958.

R. Paribeni, *Il ritratto nell' arte antica*, Milan, 1934.

O. Vessberg, *Studien zur Kunstgeschichte der römischen Republik*, Leipzig, 1941.

M. Wegner, *Hadrian, Plotina, Marciana Matidia, Sabina (Das römische Herrscherbild*, II, 3), Berlin, 1956.
   Die Herrscherbildnisse in antoninischer Zeit (Das römische Herrscherbild, II, 4), Berlin, 1939.

R. West, *Römische Porträt-Plastik*, 2 vols, Munich, 1933–41.

MARRIAGE

P E. Corbett, *The Roman Law of Marriage*, Oxford, 1930.

H. J. Rose, edition of Plutarch, *Roman Questions*, Oxford, 1924, esp. pp. 101–8.

A. Rossbach, *Untersuchungen über die römische Ehe*, Stuttgart, 1853.
   Römische Hochzeits—und Ehedenkmäler, Leipzig, 1871.

CONCUBINAGE

Paul Meyer, *Der römische Konkubinat nach den Rechtsquellen und den Inschriften*, Leipzig, 1895.

DRESS

L. M. Wilson, *The Clothing of the ancient Romans*, Baltimore, 1938.

JEWELLERY, ETC.

C. Barini, *Ornatus muliebris*, Turin, 1958.

G. Becatti, *Oreficerie antiche dalle minoiche alle barbariche*, Rome, 1955.

L. Breglia, *Catalogo delle oreficerie del Museo nazionale di Napoli*, Rome, 1954.

Étienne Coche de la Ferté, *Les bijoux antiques*, Paris, 1956.

R. A. Higgins, *Greek and Roman Jewellery*, London, 1961.

A. Maiuri, *La casa del Menandro e il suo tesoro di argenteria*, Rome, 1933.

F. H. Marshall, *Catalogue of the Jewellery, Greek, Etruscan and Roman in the Department of Antiquities, British Museum*, London, 1911.

R. Siviero, *Gli ori e le ambre del Museo nazionale di Napoli*, Florence, 1954.

INDEX